KATE
IN FACT
&
FICTION

The Life and Legend of
Sarah Catherine "Kate" (King)
Quantrill-Evans-Batson-Head
a.k.a. Kate Clarke

85th Anniversary Commemorative Biography

Virgil Hoftiezer

Virgil D. Hoftiezer, Ph.D.
and Vicki P. Beck

Copyright © 2014 by Virgil D. Hoftiezer and Vicki P. Beck.

All rights reserved. Without permission in writing from the publisher, no part of this book may be reproduced or transmitted in any form or by any means, electronic or mechanical, including photocopying, recording, or by any information storage and retrieval system.

Hoftiezer, Virgil D., Ph.D. (1941-) and Vicki P. Beck (1955-)
   Kate, In Fact and Fiction: The Life and Legend of
   Sarah Catherine "Kate" (King) Quantrill-Evans-Batson-
   Head, a.k.a. Kate Clarke
362 p.   cm.
   Includes bibliographical references, illustrations, and index.

ISBN-13:   978-0692307908 (Orderly Pack Rat, The)
ISBN: 0692307907

First Edition.

85th Anniversary Commemorative Biography

1. Missouri–Biography. 2. Missouri--Jackson County--Genealogy. 3. Jackson County (Mo)--History--Civil War, 1861-1865. 4. King, Sarah Catherine (1848-1930). 5. Quantrill, William Clarke (1837-1865). I. Hoftiezer, Virgil D., Ph.D. (1941-). II. Vicki P. Beck (1955-). III. Title.

Published in the United States of America by:
The Orderly Pack Rat
david.jackson@orderlypackrat.com
orderlypackrat.com

DEDICATION

This work is dedicated to

Donald R. "Don" Hale
(1930-2008)

Don was a friend and mentor to Vicki P. Beck. Don shared his love for local Missouri history and his passion for William Clarke Quantrill through his life's work, numerous publications and willingness to share with others having similar interests. He carried in his wallet the Proverbs 22:28 Bible verse: *"Remove not the ancient landmarks, which thy fathers have set."* Don has left his mark on this biography, both directly and indirectly, from its inception, and he would be proud. He is greatly missed.

and to

Sarah Catherine "Kate" (King) Quantrill-Evans-Batson-Head
aka. Kate Clarke
(1848-1930)

Kate, a relative of Virgil D. Hoftiezer, lived life as she found it. Her life and legend—long exaggerated and misconstrued—continues to raise more questions with each factual discovery, even 85 years after her death. May she rest in peace . . . while others clamor to better understand her truth.

Contents

Introduction	Kate, the Legend	7
Chapter 1	Kate's Timeline: Sequence of Events in the Life of Sarah Catherine "Kate" (King) Quantrill-Evans-Batson-Head	15
Chapter 2	What's in a Name?	33
Chapter 3	Kate's Family: Blood Is Thicker than Water	41
Chapter 4	Kate's Life with Quantrill: The Emergence of Kate Clarke	73
Chapter 5	That 'Other Woman' — Naughty Nancy	105
Chapter 6	Kate's St. Louis Years: Social Evil and the Great Experiment	119
Chapter 7	Kate and Bertha: Motherhood and Beyond	147
Chapter 8	Kate's Fate: The End, and Her Final Resting Place	175
Endnotes		199
Appendices		247
A	General Order No. 2 issued 13 March 1862	247
B	General Order No. 10 issued 18 August 1863	249
C	General Order No. 11 issued 25 August 1863	251
D	*St. Louis Democrat*, 17 August 1873	253
E	*St. Louis Daily Globe,* 22 February 1874	255
F	Final Settlement, Anson M. King Estate, Sept. 1921	259
G	Heirs Identified in Anson M. King's Estate	263
H	*Kansas City Star,* 23 May 1926	269
I	Letters from Fred A. Ford	279
J	Notes Regarding Persons Named in the Ford Letters	293
Illustrations		311
Bibliography		321
Authors		347
Index		349

INTRODUCTION

Kate, the Legend

> *"It was the best of times, it was the worst of times,*
> *it was the age of wisdom, it was the age of foolishness,*
> *it was the epoch of belief, it was the epoch of incredulity,*
> *it was the season of Light, it was the season of Darkness,*
> *it was the spring of hope, it was the winter of despair,*
> *we had everything before us, we had nothing before us,*
> *we were . . . "*
> Charles Dickens (*A Tale of Two Cities*)

Like the famous opening lines of Charles Dickens' 1859 classic, *A Tale of Two Cities,* the story of Kate is also a tale about the times, about conflicts, about hope, despair, love, and even hate. Kate's story is an enigma buried in the cloak of history, a mystery with a sad ending, a story waiting to be told.

The legend of Kate began in 1861 when she, Sarah Catherine King, a lively, attractive, teenage girl, was riding her equally high-spirited horse across the Missouri countryside and impressing the handsome young man riding with her. Sarah was "a buxom girl, of sturdy build and well developed for her years" with dark hair and dark eyes.[1] She had grown up around horses and had learned to ride as a very young child because her father was known for the fine horses he raised.[2] She enjoyed the concern the young man expressed when she recklessly forced her horse to jump fences and creek beds. The romance with her admirer ended, but the legend continued for 65 years until 1926 when an old and more wise Sarah Head responded to a reporter's questions while quietly sitting at the Poor Farm in Jackson County, Missouri. The tale ended in 1930 when Sarah Head was buried in a then unmarked grave. But her legend survives to this day.

KATE IN FACT AND FICTION

**Sarah Catherine King, as a young woman,
before she assumed the alias, Kate Clarke**

Perhaps this is the picture of "Aunt Kate" that "Uncle Walter used to have," as noted by Halys Morris Wyrick Boman (Kate's great-niece referring to Kate's nephew, Walter Robert King, of Independence, Missouri). In this photograph, Kate bears a striking resemblance to a great-grandniece born 100 years and three generations later.

Introduction

Her life's story is nebulous, but intriguing. That romantic and idyllic opening scene was followed by a life filled with turmoil, danger, and revenge which lead to hardship, the need for assuming different aliases and identities, and brushes with the authorities and appearances in court rooms.

Kate is a story of the survival of a young woman, who, at the age of seventeen, found herself alone in war-torn Missouri, alienated from her family after having been involved with the notorious guerrilla leader, William Clarke Quantrill.

Kate Clarke was just one of the several pseudonyms that Sarah Catherine King used throughout her life time. But her complex life has been relegated or marginalized simply as the young consort of William Clarke Quantrill by historians and scholars of the border conflict between Missouri and Kansas. Authors writing about Quantrill and the guerrilla warfare in Missouri and Kansas identified her as either Quantrill's spouse or his mistress depending upon their particular point of view about guerrillas and/or geopolitics of the border conflict. There was obviously much more to this woman than being merely the shadowy companion of Quantrill. She was barely seventeen years old when Quantrill died, and she lived six and a half decades beyond that short phase of her life.

There is no doubt that the three and half years that Kate spent with Quantrill drastically affected the rest of her life. But, as more details about her life were uncovered, both before and especially after her time with Quantrill, there emerged a complex, multifaceted individual who lived life as she found it. This work examines the context of the circumstances, concerns and events that influenced her existence.

After being abandoned in St. Louis when Quantrill was killed in 1865, young Sarah turned to prostitution, and became the madam known as Kate Clarke. She operated one of the two foremost establishments of its kind in St. Louis.

She appeared in St. Louis City Court as defendant and plaintiff, as well as a witness in the trial of an accused 'boat burner.'

KATE IN FACT AND FICTION

Perhaps Kate, as a madam, already living outside the perimeters of legitimate society, was even involved with the "Confederate underground" then existing in St. Louis.[3]

Kate Clarke, as a madam in St. Louis, Missouri

Kate was definitely in the middle of the controversial great social experiment in St. Louis when the city attempted to regulate prostitution by implementing the Social Evil Ordinance.[4] Reverend William Greenleaf Eliot, the Unitarian minister who founded Washington University, brought a case against Kate in St. Louis City Court to challenge the legality of the Social Evil Ordinance. After losing that lawsuit in the St. Louis City Court, she adamantly continued her fight for what she

This photograph was taken by Cramer, Gross & Co. of St. Louis. Gustuv Cramer (1834-1914), photographer and developer of photographic dry plates, was in partnership with Julius Gross. They were recognized as the 'Best Photographers' at the 1867 St. Louis World's Fair. They had the first photographic studio on a ground floor at 1001 South Fifth Street from 1872 to 1878. In 1878, the photographic partnership dissolved, and Herman Norden joined Cramer to manufacture dry plates.

Thus it is presumed that a leading madam of St. Louis walked over from Sixth Street and had her photograph taken by the best photographers in the world, sometime between 1872 and 1878 . . . perhaps in 1874, after the Missouri Supreme Court ruled in her favor.

Introduction

believed was her rights...and won. The Supreme Court of the State Missouri in 1874 reversed the lower court ruling against her.

Another veil lifted revealed that Kate was also a mother and a grandmother. Given her early profession in St. Louis, it is ironic that her grandson, Pliny R. Castanien, became such a well known police reporter that a television character was based on him. Pliny went on to become the historian for the San Diego Police Department and wrote a book about the department.[5] It was incongruous that the grandson of a former notorious madam should write a book about a police department. This was not the only paradox surrounding Kate's life.

During periods of family strife and hardship, Kate never abandoned her family. Instead, she left St. Louis and returned to Jackson County, Missouri. She paid for the rebuilding of her parent's home after it was burned during the Civil War when martial law was vigorously enforced under an edict called, "General Order No. 11." She later lived in the same household with her daughter and family in Oklahoma. She reportedly kept house for her brother after his wife died. Yet, Kate ended up becoming an indigent inmate at the Jackson County Home (former the County Poor Farm) at Little Blue, Jackson County, Missouri. One might wonder what happened to all the money she made while operating the Clarke Bawdy House in St. Louis. In the final settlement of the probate of the King estate in 1921, she received only $123.08 as her share in the land her father had originally purchased seven decades earlier.[6]

After her death at the Jackson County Home in 1930, Kate's body was not buried for over a month because the funeral home supposedly could not locate her relatives. Her daughter was still living in Oklahoma and many nieces and nephews were living in Jackson County, Missouri, at this time. It is unfathomable that it took the funeral home over a month to locate her relatives.

KATE IN FACT AND FICTION

Two separate monuments in two different cemeteries in two different states were erected by two different parties at two different times in the memory of Kate King. A memorial monument was placed by two admirers at Slaughter Cemetery in Jackson County, Missouri, near the graves of Kate's parents, Robert L. and Malinda (Stringer) King. A headstone was placed on her actual grave—Grave 6, Lot No. 63—in Maple Hill Cemetery in Kansas City, Wyandotte County, Kansas. Donald R. Hale ascertained Kate's burial site in 1976, and he and Virgil Hoftiezer shared the cost of placing this headstone in 1997.

This paradigm illustrated the importance of re-examination and re-interpretation of Kate's story.

Many aspects of Kate's life were difficult to verify because little information came directly from her. She left no autobiography, memoir, diary, journal or letters. There were isolated pieces of her story divulged previously. Some are well-known and have been noted and discussed by many people; but, only in disassociated solitary fragments.

Only recently has an attempt been made to assemble separate and disparate portions of her life into a coherent unit. Professor LeeAnn Whites extracted three segments of Kate's story to address the experience of women and the significance of gender relations in the guerrilla war.[7] Until now, Kate has been slighted, and either misunderstood or misrepresented in history. A retrospective examination of Kate's life, with a contemporary perspective, was long overdue.

In his opening words Charles Dickens set the stage for *A Tale of Two Cities*, describing a time when peasants suffered under the dominance of an uncaring aristocracy which lead to radical social and political upheaval during a time of a brutal reign of terror and total war. Total war is defined as a war which does not differentiate between combatants and civilians. It is one of several parallels between the French Revolution and the Missouri and Kansas Border and Civil War. This conflict was the stage and background in the first act of Kate's story.

This work—20 years in the making—is made available through the thoughtful contributions of many individuals, as the extensive bibliography reveals.

Introduction

We wish to express gratitude to our immediate and extended families, as well as to our friends and acquaintances, who have been subjected to obsessive discussions regarding Kate for the past two decades.

Special thanks is extended to Lester 'Terry' Palmer (friend and relative of Virgil Hoftiezer) for reading the original manuscript not once, but twice. Librarians, genealogy volunteers and county clerks across the country, over two decades, deserve special recognition for their unending patience, professionalism, and expertise . . . in particular Felicia Barrett; Jeanne Reed (Mid-Continent Public Library System, Excelsior Springs, Mo.); and, Annette W. Curtis and the Midwest Genealogy Center (Independence, Mo.).

The authors also thank and acknowledge Jackson County, Missouri, historian and archivist, David W. Jackson, for his assistance in transforming our manuscript into the product you hold in your hands. Jackson, as The Orderly Pack Rat, provided additional historical research and materials; editing services; image discovery and procurement; and, designing and publishing services for this biography.

To Virgil's wife, Jan, who has 'vacationed' in libraries, court houses and cemeteries with him, he extends his sincere gratitude for her willingness to have lived with, "that other woman," Kate, in my life.

Kate's life is presented here in chronological order, based on known facts with newly discovered information to reveal as complete and comprehensive account of Kate as possible . . . and to debunk myths that have been perpetuated for far too long.

Every effort was made to separate fact from fiction, truth from fantasy, and reality from assumption, without apology or judgment of who Kate was, and what she did.

Hopefully this study will stimulate expanded interest and increased scrutiny of all aspects of this most intriguing character, Sarah Catherine King, a.k.a. Kate Clarke.

Virgil D. Hoftiezer, Ph.D.
Vicki P. Beck

KATE IN FACT AND FICTION

CHAPTER 1

Kate's Timeline

Sequence of Events in the Life of Sarah Catherine "Kate" (King) Quantrill-Evans-Batson-Head

"Not everyone's life is what they make it.
Some people's life is what other people make it."
Alice Walker, *You Can't Keep a Good Woman Down* (1981)

(Events directly involving Kate are in ***bold italicized*** font.)

1848 (ca.)	***Kate born "Sarah Catherine King" to Robert L. King and Malinda Rebecca (Stringer) King, in Polk County, Missouri***
1848	James K. Polk was President of the U.S. and the Mexican-American War just ended; junior officers in this war became the military leaders on both sides in the Civil War
1849 Mar 4	Zachary Taylor inaugurated President of U.S.
1850 July 9	Millard Fillmore inaugurated President of U.S.
1850 Oct 15	***Kate in the Federal Census with her parents in District 71, Polk County, Missouri (name enumerated as Rebecca, age 2). The family moved to Jackson County, Missouri, shortly thereafter*** [8]

KATE IN FACT AND FICTION

1852 Oct 19	Brother, Samuel Robert King, born in Lake City, Jackson County, Missouri (last child of Robert L. and Malinda, and their only child born in Jackson County)
1853 Mar 4	Franklin Pierce inaugurated President of U.S.
1855 Apr 9	Father, Robert L. King, purchased 40 acres in Section 18 in the NE ¼ of NE ¼ Township 49, Range 30, Jackson County, Missouri
1857	U.S. Supreme Court ruled against Dred Scott's petition for freedom
1857 Mar 4	James Buchanan inaugurated President of U.S.
1857 Apr 1	Father, Robert L. King, purchased 40 acres in Section 7 in the SW ¼ SE ¼ Township 49, Range 30, Jackson County, Missouri
1857 May 1	Father, Robert L. King, purchased 80 acres in Section 7 in the E ½ SE ¼, Township 49, Range 30, Jackson County, Missouri, which became the King family farm
1858 June 1	Father, Robert L. King, purchased 40 more acres in Section 7 in the NW ¼ SE ¼, Township 49, Range 30, Jackson County, Missouri
before 1860	Sister, Nancy A. King, died in either Polk or Jackson County, Missouri, after October 1850; but, before the 1860 census
1860 July 19	***Kate in the Federal Census with her parents in Sni-a-Bar Township, Jackson County, Missouri (enumerated as Sarah, age 12)***
1860 after July 19	Sister, Martha Jane King, married John Oath Ragland [location unknown, no marriage record found in Missouri]
1860 Aug 6	Claiborne Jackson elected Governor of Missouri
1860 Nov 6	Abraham Lincoln elected president of the United States. Stephen A. Douglas carried Missouri; Lincoln carried only Gasconade and St. Louis Counties in the state.
1860 Dec 10	Raid at neighboring Walker farm; first appearance of Quantrill in Jackson County, Missouri

Kate's Timeline

1861 Jan 11	First Federal troops arrived in St. Louis
1861 Feb 9	Jefferson Davis elected president of the Confederate States of America
1861 Mar 4	Abraham Lincoln inaugurated as 16th President of the United States of America
1861 May 10	Camp Jackson in St. Louis captured by Union forces commanded by Capt. N. Lyon
1861 Summer	*Kate first met Quantrill on her parent's porch when Kate came home from school*
1861 July 31	Missouri State Convention appointed Hamilton R. Gamble as Governor, after declaring all state offices vacant the day before (Following the inauguration of all the new appointees the next day, Missouri had duplicate state officers)
1861 Aug 7	Seven ironclad gunboats ordered from James B. Eads of St. Louis
1861 Aug 14	Martial law declared in St. Louis
1861 Aug 30	Martial law declared throughout Missouri
1861 Oct 8	First steamer burner in St. Louis by Confederate 'boat burners'
1861 Nov 28	Missouri admitted to the Confederacy (this action not recognized by the Union)
1861 Dec 22	First prisoners arrived at Gratiot Street Prison in St. Louis
1862 Mar 7-8	Battle of Pea Ridge, Arkansas
1862 Mar 13	General Order No. 2 issued (guerrillas declared as outlaws to be executed when captured, not taken as prisoners of war)
1862 Apr 6-7	Battle of Shiloh, Tennessee (casualties sent to Jefferson Barracks in St. Louis)

KATE IN FACT AND FICTION

1862 Apr	Confederate Congress enacted the Partisan Ranger Act, which conveyed the same status to guerrillas as regular Confederate military (Union did not recognize this)
1862 Jul 16	Quantrill and 93 members of his 'gang' appeared on a muster roll in Springfield, Cole County, Missouri[9]
1862 Aug 11	Quantrill in the Battle of Independence (First battle); they were *not* involved in the bloody, hand-to-hand combat of the Battle of Lone Jack four days later
1862 Sep 7	Quantrill and his men attacked Olathe, Kansas
1862 Oct 17	Quantrill and his men attacked Shawnee, Kansas
1863 Apr 25	Mary Louden, wife of Robert Louden (Confederate spy, saboteur and courier), arrested in St. Louis
1863 May 13	Large number of female southern sympathizers banished from St. Louis
1863 July	Female relatives of the guerrillas living in Jackson County, Missouri, were arrested and jailed in Kansas City, Missouri
1863 Aug 4	Steamer *Ruth* burned near Cairo, Illinois, carrying $2.6 million payroll for Union troops; Robert Louden later convicted for this crime
1863 Aug 13	Collapse of the jail building in Kansas City, Missouri, holding the female relatives of the guerrillas; four were killed and several others were seriously injured[10]
1863 Aug 15	***Unclaimed letter at St. Louis Post Office addressed to Kate Clark[11]***
1863 Aug 18	General Order No. 10 issued (authorized arrest and banishment of civilians who supported and aided the guerrillas)
1863 Aug 21	Raid on Lawrence, Kansas, by Quantrill and his band of guerrillas in retaliation for the jail collapse, Order No. 10, etc.

Kate's Timeline

1863 Aug 25	General Order No. 11 issued (banished all non-loyal inhabitants of designated Missouri counties bordering Kansas, including Jackson County, effective within two weeks)
1863 Sept 3	Robert Louden arrested in St. Louis; tried in December, convicted of spying, mail carrying and boat burning, and sentenced to death
1863 Summer	*Kate said to have married William Clarke Quantrill. Some reports claim in Jackson County (not recorded); Fred Ford said they were married in Howard County, Missouri, as 'Mr. and Mrs. William Clarke']*[12]
1863 Sept	*Kate lived in a cabin with Quantrill near Blue Springs, Jackson County, Missouri*[13]
1863 Sept 10	*Quantrill left Missouri to go to Texas [Kate probably did not go; her location during this time is not documented; but, she was probably in St. Louis.]*
1863 Sept 13-Oct 4	Seven steamers and a barge burned on the Mississippi River in St. Louis
1863 Oct 6	Battle of Baxter Springs, Kansas (Quantrill's group massacred the escort train and band of General James G. Blunt, killing 89 men) [Lawrence and Baxter Springs were the only major Confederate military victories in Kansas in 1863.][14]
1863 Oct 13	*'Kate Clark' made statement before Provost Marshal in St. Louis regarding Robert Louden (Confederate spy, saboteur and courier)*
1863 Nov 7	Absalom Grimes (Confederate mail runner) arrested in Memphis, TN; brought to St. Louis for trial in December; tried, convicted and sentenced to death
1863/4 Winter	Quantrill was in Texas [Quantrill was replaced as leader of the guerrillas]
1864 Jan 31	Governor Gamble died of pneumonia in St. Louis
1864 Mar 28	Quantrill arrested by Confederate forces and charged with plotting the murder of a Confederate officer; Quantrill escaped to Indian Territory

KATE IN FACT AND FICTION

1864 May 6	Louden's execution postponed by Presidential Order only hours before scheduled
1864 July 15	Four steamers burned on River in St. Louis
1864 Aug 25	Brother, William Jasper King, married America Jane Snodgrass, in Lafayette County, Missouri
1864 Sept 16	Confederate Army, under command of General Sterling Price, invaded Missouri
1864 Sept 27	Centralia Massacre (Bloody Bill Anderson's guerrilla group defeated Union troops)
1864 Oct 3	Robert Louden escaped during transfer of prisoners from St. Louis to Alton, Illinois (prisoners transferred due to threat of General Price's invasion of Missouri)
1864 Summer	***Kate supposedly lived with Quantrill in a tent camp in Howard County, Missouri[15]***
1864 Oct 15	Quantrill robbed bank ($21,000) in Glasgow, Howard County, Missouri (This may be the source of the money he left to Kate while on his death bed)
1864 Oct 21	George Todd, one of Quantrill's men who was reported to be a friend of Kate, killed in Independence, Jackson County, Missouri
1864 Oct 23	General Price defeated at the Battle of Westport which marked the end of Confederate military action in Missouri
1864 Oct 26	Bloody Bill Anderson, another former Quantrill guerrilla, killed near Albany, Ray County, Missouri
1864 Nov 5	Quantrill and 93 members of his 'gang' appeared on a muster roll for an unidentified county in Missouri[16]
1864 Nov 8	Abraham Lincoln re-elected President of the United States
1864 Nov 13	***Kate taken/sent to St. Louis, St. Louis County, Missouri, when/before Quantrill left for Virginia[17]***
1864 Nov 15	Brother, Francis Marion King, married Eveline Lynch in Lafayette County, Missouri

Kate's Timeline

1864 Dec 9	Absalom Grimes pardoned by Presidential order and released from prison
1865 Spring	Quantrill, now leading only a few dozen men, staged several raids in western Kentucky
1865 Mar 7	Martial law in St. Louis ended
1865 Apr 9	General Robert E. Lee surrendered Confederate Army to General Ulysses S. Grant at Appomattox, Virginia
1865 Apr 14	President Lincoln assassinated in Washington, D.C.; Andrew Johnson sworn in as 17th President of U.S. the next day
1865 Apr 27	Steamer *Sultana* burned; (about 2,000 Union POW killed while returning north)
1865 May 10	Quantrill badly wounded near Taylorsville, Spencer County, Kentucky
1865 June 6	*William Clarke Quantrill died in prison infirmary in Louisville, Jefferson County, Kentucky, after Father Michael Power performed last rites [Kate, age 17, is reported to have been at Quantrill's bedside and was most likely at his graveside]*
1865 Nov	St. Luke's Hospital in St. Louis formed by Episcopalians
1866 Feb 14	Liberty Bank Robbery (first day-light, peace-time, bank robbery in the U.S. by former Quantrill guerrillas)
1866 Apr	St. Luke's Hospital received first patient at Ohio and Summer Streets in St. Louis
1866	Cholera epidemic in St. Louis
1867 Sept 13	Robert Louden died of Yellow Fever in New Orleans (he left St. Louis after admitting to sabotaging the *Sultana*)
1869	*Kate returned home presumably under the alias Mrs. J. R. Claiborne; she paid to have her parent's homestead rebuilt*

KATE IN FACT AND FICTION

1869 Sept 29	General Sterling Price died in St. Louis (he returned from exile in Mexico on 11 January 1867; never asked for nor received a pardon); largest funeral procession in St. Louis history
1869 Mar 4	Ulysses S. Grant inaugurated President of U.S.
1870 Mar 1	Parents, Robert L. and Malinda King, sold 40 acres of land in Sec. 18 to their son, William J. King (Kate's brother), for $500
1870 Mar 14	Missouri Governor signed the bill enabling the city of St. Louis to begin the Social Evil Experiment
1870 Mar	St. Luke's Hospital moved to Sixth and Elm Streets, St. Louis
1870 June 30	*Kate in the Federal Census in St. Louis, Missouri (listed as 'Kate Clark,' whore, age 22)*
1870 July 5	St. Louis passed an ordinance, known as the 'Social Evil Law,' to regulate prostitution within the city
1870 Aug 4	Federal Census of Kate's parents and three siblings: Martha J., Francis M., and Samuel R., near Auburn, Placer County, California [brother, William Jasper King, not located]
1871 Nov 15	Nancy Walker Slaughter Vaughn married David D. Wood [Nancy's marriage was confused for Kate; Kate never married a man named Wood]
1871	*Kate listed in the St. Louis city directory as "Miss Kate Clark," residing at 24 S. 8th Street*
1873 Mar 14	*Kate lived at 112 S. 8th Street, St. Louis, St. Louis County, Missouri (requested a permit to move her bawdy house to larger quarters)*
1873 Apr 1	*Kate signed a two year lease for rental of a building on the northeast corner of 6th and Elm Streets, St. Louis, St. Louis County, Missouri, for $2,000 per year; it had been previously leased to St. Luke's Hospital*
1873 June	St. Luke's Hospital moved to Pine Street between 9th and 10th Streets, St. Louis

Kate's Timeline

1873 July 21	First train robbery by James-Younger gang brought national notoriety to these former guerrillas
1873 Aug 6	*Rev. William Greenleaf Eliot filed a complaint against Kate and Lizzie Saville, the madam of the other fine bawdy house across the street from Kate's establishment, to challenge the legality of the Social Evil Law*
1873 Aug 10	*Kate interviewed by a newspaper reporter and showed a copy of the lease agreement for the building ($2000 rental annually for 23 months with option to renew at $2500/year for three years)*
1873 Aug 16	*Kate testified in court regarding Eliot's case against her and Lizzie Saville*
1873 Aug 17	*Kate lived at 112 6th Street, St. Louis, St. Louis County, Missouri (newspaper article regarding the lawsuit filed by Eliot against her and Lizzie)*
1873 Aug 23	*Kate found guilty, along with Lizzie Saville, of operating bawdy houses in St. Louis City Court; each fined $100*
1873 Nov 22	John Newman Edwards published "A Terrible Quintette," a 20-page newspaper supplement which expanded the myth of the Western outlaw as hero, especially in the case of Jesse James
1873 Dec 1	*Missouri State Supreme Court overruled the St. Louis City Court judgments against Kate and Lizzie Saville*
1874 Feb 21	*Kate lived at 6th and Elm Streets, St. Louis, St. Louis County, Missouri (newspaper interview regarding the court case)*
1874 Mar 18	Missouri Legislature repealed the bill which allowed St. Louis to enact the Social Evil Law
1874 April	St. Louis repealed the Social Evil Law and prostitution was no longer regulated or tolerated in the city
1875 Feb 4	*Sale of furniture and contents of Kate's Mansion at Sixth and Elm in St. Louis; plus the announcement of Kate's impeding 'business' marriage "with a gentleman of New York" (Kate may have suspected she was pregnant)*

1875 Oct 6	*Kate's daughter, Bertha E. Evans, born in St. Louis, St. Louis County, Missouri (Bertha's birth registration and death certificate designate 1875, even though multiple sources during Bertha's lifetime point to 1877)*
1876 Sept 7	James and Younger brothers attempt to rob a bank in Northfield, Minnesota (all three Younger brothers: Cole, Jim and Bob, wounded and captured)
1877 Jan 25	*Kate to be called as witness in Logan D. Dameron case against St. Luke's Hospital board (the building was then rented by Lizzie Saville and by a boarding house)*
1877 Mar 4	Rutherford B. Hayes inaugurated President of U.S.
1877	John Newman Edwards published his book *Noted Guerrillas*, which presented Quantrill positively
1878	Gratiot Street Prison in St. Louis demolished
1879 Jan 7	Rev. Michael Power, the priest who administered the last rites to Quantrill, died in Kentucky at age 52. He was buried January 9 in St. Louis
1879 June 25	James Robert Claiborne, Kate's lawyer, married Fannie Moore in Boonesville, Cooper County, Missouri [Kate never married a man named Claiborne]
1879	Grandmother, 'Betsey' Elizabeth (Scott) Stringer Rigney, died in Greene County, Illinois.
1879 Sept 7	Brother, Samuel Robert King, married Elizabeth L. Davenport in Jackson County, Missouri
1880 Jan 18	Mother, Malinda Rebecca (Stringer) King, died at age 71 in Jackson County, Missouri
1880 Mar 5	Father, Robert L. King, sold the 80 acre King farm to his son, Francis Marion King (Kate's brother), for $600
1880 June 19	Father, Robert King, in Federal Census, Blue Springs, Jackson County, Missouri, listed as age 58 [should be about age 70]

Kate's Timeline

1880 Nov 11   *Kate in the Federal Census at 717 Walnut, St. Louis, St. Louis County, Missouri (as 'Kate Clark,' age 38 [actually 32], widowed; daughter, Bertha, not enumerated in the household)*

1881 Mar 4   James Garfield inaugurated President of U.S.

1881 Aug 24   Aunt, Nancy King Chism, died in Jackson County, Missouri

1881 Sept 19   Chester A. Arthur sworn in as President of U.S.

1881   *Kate listed in city directory at 717 Walnut, St. Louis, St. Louis County, Missouri (as 'Kate Clark'); last known listing for her in St. Louis; information may have been collected and published shortly before her departure*

1881 April 23   *W. W. Scott's letter to "Miss Kate Clark," or "Mrs. Kate Quantrill," in St. Louis was returned to sender*

1882 Apr 3   Jesse James killed by Bob Ford

1882 Oct 5   Frank James surrendered to Governor of Missouri; acquitted in trial for robbery and murder (Some consider this the end of the Civil War in Missouri)

1884 Spring   W. W. Scott visited Louisville, Kentucky, and determined the location of Quantrill's grave in St. John's Cemetery

1884 Apr 3   Uncle William M. Stringer died in Greene County, Illinois

1885 Mar 4   Grover Cleveland inaugurated President of U.S. (first Democrat since Civil War)

1885 May 19   Patrick Shelly died in Louisville, Kentucky, at age 48; Shelly was Sexton of St. John's cemetery in Louisville, Kentucky, where W.C. Quantrill was originally buried

1887 Dec 7   Mrs. Caroline C. Quantrill, mother of William Clarke Quantrill, convinced sexton, Bridget Shelly, that her lost son's remains should to be moved to Dover, Ohio

1887 Dec 8   W. W. Scott had Quantrill's grave opened and the remains (bones and hair) removed; not all the bones, including Quantrill's skull, were re-buried until 1992

KATE IN FACT AND FICTION

1888 May 11	Mrs. Quantrill visited Blue Springs, Jackson County, Missouri[18]
1889 Mar 4	Benjamin Harrison inaugurated President of U.S.
1891 Feb 2	Father, Robert L. King, died, at age 81, in Jackson County, Missouri
1892 Oct 7	Nephew, 'Vady' Guy Ragland, died in Jackson County
1893 Mar 4	Grover Cleveland inaugurated President of U.S. (only president to serve two non-consecutive terms)
1894	Nancy Walker Slaughter Vaughn Wood died in Texas
1894 Mar 7	John C. King, undertaker at Quantrill's death, died at age 75 in Louisville, Kentucky
1896 Apr 25-Aug 12	Spanish-American War
1896 Dec 25	***Kate had a sterling silver spoon engraved with the letter "B" and "Xmas 96" indicating she was likely using the Batson surname at that time***
1897 Mar 4	William McKinley inaugurated President of U.S.
1897 Feb 5	Niece, Annie Georgeanna R. Ragland, married 'Babe' William Napoleon Hudspeth; 'Babe' rode with Quantrill
1899 Aug 21	Daughter, Bertha E. Evans, married Pliny Castanien in Oklahoma City, Oklahoma County, Oklahoma; Bertha was a resident of Harrah, Oklahoma County, Oklahoma
1900	***Neither Kate, nor Bertha and Pliny, have been located on the Federal Census. Kate would be 52; what name she used at this time is also unknown***
1901 Sept 14	Theodore Roosevelt sworn in as President of U.S.
1901	Winston Churchill published, *The Crisis*, a fictional account of the Civil War in St. Louis
1902 June 20	Nephew, William Robert Ragland, died in Jackson County, Missouri

Kate's Timeline

1902 Nov 6	William W. Scott died without completing his planned biography of Quantrill; Scott's widow sold his files to William E. Connelley, who was then an officer of the Kansas State Historical Society
1902 Dec	Grandson, 'Marley' Pliny Mannon Castanien, Jr., born in Oklahoma
1903 June 24	Grandson, 'Marley' Pliny Mannon Castanien, Jr., died at seven-months-of-age, in Sapulpa, Creek County, Oklahoma
1903 Nov 23	Mrs. Caroline Cornelia (Clarke) Quantrill, age 84, died at the Odd Fellows' Home, Springfield, Ohio[19]
1905 Feb 12	Brother-in-law, John Oath Ragland, died in Kansas City, Jackson County, Missouri
1907 Nov 16	Oklahoma admitted to statehood
1908 Aug 9	Grandson 'Cass' Pliny Raymond Castanien born in Braggs, Muskogee County, Oklahoma[20]
1908 Oct 30	Sister-in-law, America Jane Snodgrass King, died in Jackson County, Missouri
1909 Mar 4	William Howard Taft inaugurated President of U.S.
1909	Galusha Anderson published *The Story of a Border City During the War*, a decidedly pro-Union first-hand account by a minister who lived in St. Louis during the Civil War
1910	William Elsey Connelley published his book *Quantrill and the Border Wars*, which presented an extremely negative perspective of Quantrill and the guerrillas[21]
1910 Mar 18	***Kate (and Mrs. East) relinquished charge of the Northern Hotel to Mrs. Bonham, in Braggs, Oklahoma***
1910 Apr 15	Daughter, Bertha, and her husband, Pliny, in the Federal census in Braggs, Muskogee County, Oklahoma
1910 Apr 21	***Kate in the Federal Census in Vian, Vian Township, Sequoyah County, Oklahoma (listed as Sarah C. Batson, age 61, with 1 living child)***

KATE IN FACT AND FICTION

1910 June 24	*Daughter, Bertha, "formerly of Braggs," visited her mother in Vian. After a week, Pliny joined her, then he and Bertha left to, "take up their residence," in Sapulpa*
1911	*Kate listed in city directory at 233 S. Main in Sapulpa, Creek County, Oklahoma (as Sarah C. Batson)*
1911 Feb 21	Niece, Lucy A. King Young, died in Cass County, Missouri
1911 Mar 27	Absalom Grimes died
about 1912	Nephew, Earl R. King, moved to South Dakota
1912 July 20	Sister-in-law, Eveline Lynch King, died in Jackson County, Missouri
1913 Feb 27	*Kate, "an old time hotel lady," also described as, "a former hotel lady of this place," and, "one of the best public cateress' in the state," opened the Monticello Hotel in Braggs, Oklahoma*
1913 Mar 4	Woodrow Wilson inaugurated President of U.S.
1914 July 28	Great War (World War I) began in Europe
1915 May 7	British liner *Lusitania* sank by German U-boat
1916	*Kate listed in city directory with son-in-law Pliny Castanien in Sapulpa, Creek County, Oklahoma (listed as Sarah Batson)*
1916 May 5	Brother, Francis Marion King, transferred the 80 acre King farm to his son Anson Marion King for $1 and affection
1916 May 7	Brother, Francis Marion King, died at age 70, in Sni-a-Bar Township, Jackson County, Missouri [his obituary named his siblings but did not list their places of residence]
1917 Apr 6	United States declared war on Germany and entered World War I

Kate's Timeline

1918 May 14	Sister, Martha Jane King Ragland, died at age 75, at 1003 Prospect, Kansas City, Jackson County, Missouri [her obituary did not name any siblings]
1918 Nov 11	Armistice Day; World War I ended
1919 Mar 26	Brother, William Jasper King, died at age 78, near Grain Valley, Sni-a-Bar Township, Jackson County, Missouri
1919 March	***Kate lived in Sapulpa, Creek County, Oklahoma***
1920 Jan 8	***Kate in Federal Census in Sapulpa, Creek County, Oklahoma, with daughter, Bertha, and son-in-law, Pliny M. Castanien (as Sarah Batson, age 72, widowed)***
1920 May 29	Nephew, Anson Marion King, died intestate, at age 52, in Jackson County, Missouri
1920 June 11	Cousin, Malinda Chism, died at Jackson County Home, Jackson County, Missouri
1920 July 1	***Kate named as Aunt Sarah C. Batson in probate record of Anson M. King in Blue Springs, Jackson County, Missouri***
1920 July 23	***Kate reportedly attended auction and estate sale at King family farm along present-day Argo Road and Owens School Road, near Blue Springs, Jackson County, Missouri[22]***
1921 Mar 4	Warren G. Harding inaugurated President of U.S.
1921 Apr 15	***Kate's application to the Jackson County Court approved for admittance to the Jackson County Home (former Poor Farm at Little Blue, Missouri)***
1921 June 8	Brother, Samuel Robert King died, at age 68, in Independence Hospital, Jackson County, Missouri
1921 June	***Kate at Jackson County Home, Lee's Summit, Jackson County, Missouri (as Kate Barsen, per brother Samuel's obituary)***

1921 July 11	*Kate signed authorization for $100 payment to John W. Clements from the Anson King estate; signed as "Mrs. S. C. Batson," at Independence, Jackson County, Missouri*
1921 Sept 20	*Kate received $123.08 as final settlement of Anson King's estate; signature of "Mrs. Sarah C. Batson," was witnessed by Oscar King*
1921 Dec 1	Cousin, Eliza Chism, died at St. Joseph, Buchanan County, Missouri; Eliza Chism's internment in Slaughter Cemetery was the last burial there for 50 years
about 1922	**Kate and Walter Head ran away from the Jackson County Home and were reportedly married** [not in **Jackson County**]
1923 Aug 2	Calvin Coolidge sworn in as President of U.S.
1926	M. M. Quaife, Grime's biographer, published, *Absalom Grimes: Confederate Mail Runner*
1926 May 23	*The Kansas City Star published the article, "The Strange Romance of Quantrill's Bride: Kate King, Ending Her Days in an Alms House, Recalls Her Life With the Famous Guerilla Leader;" the reporter that supposedly interviewed Kate has never been identified.*
1927 Nov 10	Nephew, Rufus Hudspeth Ragland, died in Kansas City, Jackson County, Missouri
1929 Feb 11	Niece, 'Annie' Georgeanna R. Ragland Hudspeth, died in Kansas City, Jackson County, Missouri
1929 Mar 4	Herbert Hoover inaugurated President of U.S.
1929 Aug 12	*Kate listed as inmate of the Jackson County Home, Little Blue, Jackson County, Missouri (as Sarah Head, with guardian Jack Ragland)*
1930 Jan 9	*Kate died at the Jackson County Home, Prairie Township, Jackson County, Missouri, at age 82, from myocarditis*
1930 Feb 6	*Kate buried in Maple Hill Cemetery (Grave 6, Lot 63, Block 5) Kansas City, Wyandotte County, Kansas*

Kate's Timeline

1933 Mar 4	Franklin D. Roosevelt inaugurated President of U.S.
1934 May 6	Walter Head died at age 71 in Jackson County Home, Jackson County, Missouri, and is buried in Maple Hill Cemetery, Wyandotte County, Kansas
1965	Arthur D. Dealy and his family began the work of restoring Slaughter Cemetery
1971	*Kate's memorial marker erected in Slaughter Cemetery by Fred A. Ford and Arthur D. Dealy*
1973 Feb	Arthur D. Dealy died while working in Slaughter Cemetery
1976 Sept 21	Fred A. Ford died
1992	Quantrill's remaining bones were repatriated and re-buried. The long bones were interred in the Confederate Cemetery in Higginsville, Missouri, on 24 October; and, Quantrill's skull was buried a week later in the Quantrill family plot in Dover, Ohio, on 30 October
1997	*Kate's grave in Maple Hill Cemetery, Kansas City, Kansas, marked with a headstone placed by Donald R. Hale and Virgil Hoftiezer*
2008 Feb 24	Donald R. Hale died
2014	**Kate's first-ever biography published in advance recognition of the 85th year of her 1930 death**

KATE IN FACT AND FICTION

CHAPTER 2

What's in a Name?

"What's in a name? That which we call a rose
By any other name would smell as sweet"
William Shakespeare (Romeo and Juliet)

As William Shakespeare wrote in *Romeo and Juliet* the name does not matter so much as the way things are. However there was a young lady from Jackson County, Missouri, who assumed a different name with each new situation she encountered. When things changed, she acquired a new name and modified herself accordingly. Whether she was hiding out with her guerrilla lover, William C. Quantrill; trying to make a living on her own; or, raising a daughter as a single parent, Sarah Catherine King, commonly known as Kate, accumulated a variety of surnames and given names throughout her lifetime. Some of the epithets Kate adapted, as well as the reasons she chose to use those names, were obvious and widely known. Her other monikers were far less familiar.

Kate's exact given name remains nebulous. No birth certificate exists for those early days. No baptismal record or family Bible has been located. Three different given names have been associated with Kate:

1)   Rebecca in the earliest documented record of her existence when she was listed on the 1850 Federal census with her parents;

2)   Sarah C. in several Federal census records for her, and on assorted legal documents; and,

3) Kate, which is believed to be her childhood nickname, as well as an alias she used for two decades.

The only documented reference to her as Rebecca was on 15 October 1850 in Polk County, Missouri, where she was listed on the Federal census with her parents, as a two-year-old child. Rebecca is also believed to be her mother's middle name, suggesting she may have been named after her mother. Young children were often identified in the census by differing names, sometimes with a pet, or nickname, or even a middle name. Also note that census takers wrote what they heard, and sometimes the information may have been provided by a non-family member in the household, or even by a neighbor. No other record ever references 'Rebecca.'

Sarah C. was most likely her birth name, and she reclaimed it for at least the last two decades of her life. Sarah was also the given name that appeared on her death certificate.

Whether her middle name was Catherine (with a "C") or, Katherine (with a "K") is a minor point. Cate, as a diminutive of Catherine, and Kate, as a diminutive of Katherine, both have the same pronunciation. Although the obituary of her brother in 1916 identified her as 'Sarah Katherine,' she routinely used 'Sarah C.' as her name in later life. Her own signature is more reliable authentication than a third person obituary. Therefore, her middle initial 'C' indicates Catherine was her middle name.

Kate was the name she used as an alias for at least two decades. The earliest written references to her, as well as those made by later writers, always identified her as Kate.

This 'rose,' called 'Kate' by the authors of this biography, is a complex and often overlooked character in an important chapter in American history.

During her liaison and association with William Clarke Quantrill, Kate assumed the alias 'Kate Clarke' to protect her own identity and safety, as well as her family's personal well-being and reputation. This alias conjoins her childhood nickname and Quantrill's middle name 'Clarke' as her surname. The name 'Clarke' was also his mother's maiden name. The alias Kate Clarke continued to be used during her years in St. Louis when and where she operated one of the two most notorious houses of prostitution in the city. Many of the newspaper accounts and other written media often misspelled Kate's assumed last name by dropping the 'e' and spelled it as 'Clark.' When such sources were quoted directly, the name was repeated as printed. 'Kate Clark' and 'Kate Clarke' were one and the same person.

Kate employed a variety of surnames throughout her life. Of course she used her family name 'King' before she used the alias 'Clarke' for at least a decade and during her life in St. Louis. Since her daughter Bertha used the surname 'Evans,' it could be hypothesized that Kate used 'Evans' at some period in her life, while—or if—she was married to Bertha's father. Without a marriage record, it may be that Kate had an illegitimate child and either provided an assumed surname for the child; or, assigned Bertha's biological father's actual surname. In the written account of her life published in the *Kansas City Star* in 1926, Kate divulged her marriage to Evans; but, there was no mention of a child from that marriage. There is no evidence that Kate ever used the surname Evans as a married name.

It is well-documented that she used 'Sarah C. Batson' as her name for at least two decades. The search for a marriage record of Kate to a Mr. Batson continues; but, early vital records of Oklahoma are sparse.

Only during a handful of her last years was Kate known as 'Sarah Head.'

No marriage records for Kate have been found.

She may have married four times; but, definitely not six times, as some writers have alleged. The men identified as Kate's spouses include: Quantrill, Evans, Wood(s), Batson, Claiborne, and Head. Kate may have married some of these men; but, she never married David D. Wood or James R. Claiborne.

Whether Kate really married William Clarke Quantrill or if she was only his mistress is still debated. There were several reports that she and Quantrill were married by an unnamed and unknown country preacher when she was a young teenager. Paul Petersen, who has written several books about William Clarke Quantrill, has suggested that Kate and Quantrill were married by Rev. Hiram Bowman, a Baptist minister in Jackson County, Missouri. If Kate and Quantrill were married, she was widowed by the time she was 17-years-old.

It is possible that Kate was married to her daughter's father; but, the first name of this man, Evans, has not yet been found in any written record; neither the death certificate of his daughter, nor a family history from his grandson listed a given name for this person. At most, he was identified as the brother of Martin Evans, whose father, Robert Evans, was from England. Their daughter Bertha's marriage record listed her surname as Evans. No marriage record of her parent's has yet been found to certify the existence of a Mr. Evans. A news article in 1926 reported Kate had married a man by the name of Evans. A short sentence in the sixth paragraph from the end of the lengthy article reads:

> "Later Kate King married men by the name of Evans and Woods."

The time frame for "later' in this reference was stated in the next sentence:

> "Four years after the war, when things had quieted down along the border, she returned to visit her family as Mrs. J. R. Claiborne."[23]

There was no mention of offspring from these unions; and, the two marriages reported in these fleeting sentences never actually occurred.

The erroneous, but often repeated report of her marriage to a man named Wood(s) has proven to be an interpretive error first cited by Connelley. When William E. Connelley was writing his book about Quantrill, he misunderstood a sentence in a letter from Fletcher Taylor, one of Quantrill's men. Taylor used the pronoun 'she' while discussing both Kate and another woman named Anna Walker in the same sentence. It was Anna Walker, not Kate, who married David D. Wood.

What's in a Name?

Kate's alleged marriage to J. R. Claiborne is also unfounded.[24] James Robert Claiborne was a prominent lawyer in St. Louis, and he represented Kate in St. Louis City Court in 1873. But, they were never married. Three years after the court case in St. Louis, James Robert Claiborne was elected a Missouri State Senator. If he had been married to Kate, this marriage would certainly have been brought forth and discussed during the election campaign. There is no record of a Kate or a Sarah marrying Claiborne. However, there is a record of James R. Claiborne marrying Miss Fannie Moore in 1879 in Cooper County, Missouri. Thus, the question of where the reporter found the name Claiborne remains. It seems doubtful Kate gave that name to the reporter in 1926. He may have come across the Claiborne name while researching background newspaper stories about her. It is presumed that any subsequent references to a marriage between Claiborne and Kate came from this original, erroneous report which has no basis in fact.

It is also not known when, where, or even if, Kate married a man named 'Batson.' She may have assumed the surname Batson as just another alias. However, she may have married Batson as early as 1896 when she acquired a Towle "Old Colonial" sterling dessert place spoon with the monogram 'B' engraved on it. She later gave this spoon to her niece, Miranda Jane (King) Morris, as a gift.

Kate definitely used Sarah C. Batson as her name from at least 1910 on the census in Oklahoma through 1921 as her legal signature in Missouri. She was also identified as Sarah Batson (although misspelled) in her brothers' obituaries. Kate's marriage record to Batson has not been located.

Kate apparently did marry Walter Head after they ran away from the nursing home where they were both residing. This would have been around 1922, soon after she was admitted to the Jackson County Home for the Aged and Infirm (formerly, Jackson County's Poor Farm). Kate and Walter were found and returned to the County Home; but, were not allowed to live together as husband and wife. Their time together as man and wife was brief. Kate continued to use his name until she died in 1930, and she was buried with the surname Head. When Walter died four years later, he was buried near Kate.

KATE IN FACT AND FICTION

Thus, Kate, *i.e.*, Sarah Catherine (King) Quantrill-Evans-Batson-Head, aka. Kate Clarke, was married no more than four times. And, perhaps she never married. She obviously knew many men in her life time; but, she claimed late in her life that the only man she really loved was William Clarke Quantrill.[25]

Regardless of the multiple names Kate used to hide her identity, time and effort has revealed some of the many facets of her extraordinary life.

And, as Shakespeare asked, would things be the same if she had used only her name given at birth? Perhaps not. But it certainly would have been much easier to re-trace Kate's footsteps through history.

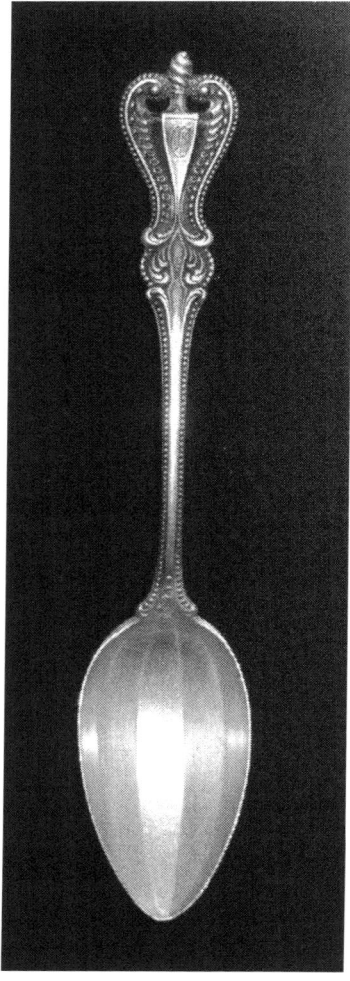
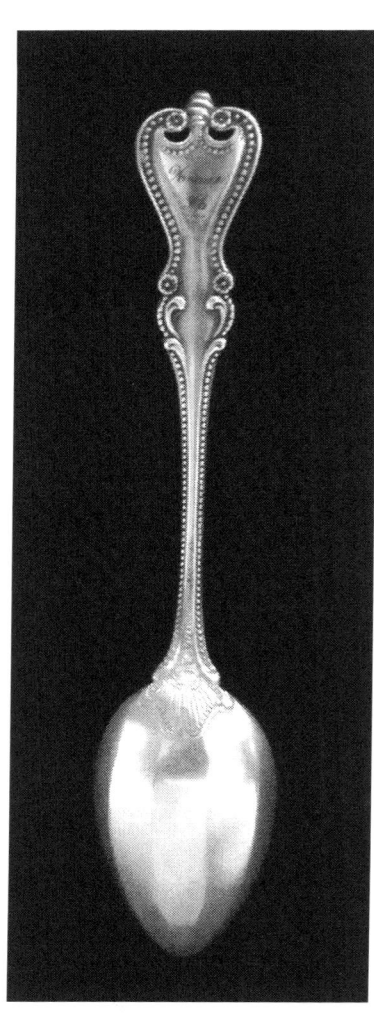

What's in a Name?

Towle "Old Colonial" sterling dessert place spoon

Kate may have married Batson as early as 1896 when she acquired a Towle "Old Colonial" sterling dessert place spoon with the monogram 'B' engraved on it.

She later gave this spoon to her niece, Miranda Jane (King) Morris, as a gift.

Miranda's daughter, Halys Morris Wyrick Boman, mailed the spoon to Virgil Hoftiezer in 1996, noting that it had been given as a gift to her mother by, 'Aunt Kate.'

The spoon has stamped on the back of the handle near the bowl two maker's marks, the word 'STERLING' and 'PAT 1895.'

There is a "B" monogram on the front of the handle, and on the back it is engraved, "Xmas 96."

At Christmas of 1896, Miranda would have been eleven, going on twelve, years old. In 1896, Kate's whereabouts are unknown. The monogrammed letter "B" indicates that Kate was using Batson as her surname at that time.

There was no indication of when this spoon was given to Miranda. It was likely many years later after the 1896 date. Perhaps Kate gave away various items when she broke up her own household between 1912 and 1916.

The dessert place spoon is seven and a quarter inches long which is intermediate in size between the standard teaspoon (five and five-eighth inches) and the standard tablespoon (eight and half inches).

"Old Colonial" is still (2014) an active pattern of Towle Silversmiths.

The major significance of this spoon is that it provides tangible evidence that Kate did maintain family ties with her nieces and nephews, as reported, and that each family had some heirloom or memento from Kate, even though they would not speak of her.

KATE IN FACT AND FICTION

CHAPTER 3

Kate's Family: Blood is Thicker than Water

> *"Weel, blude's thicker than water;*
> *she's welcome to the cheeses*
> *and the hams just the same."*
> Sir Walter Scott (Guy Mannering)

As first cited in English (from an old German proverb) by Sir Walter Scott in *Guy Mannering* in 1815, 'blood is thicker than water' and although we do not choose our family we are judged by our relatives as much as by the friends we choose or the company we keep. Just as immediate family influences each individual, the actions of an individual produces consequences that affect other members of their family. Thus, Kate's family was as affected by her actions and choices as much as, if not more than, she was initially influenced by them. Not surprisingly, her relatives and their actions impacted Kate throughout her entire life.

Research of siblings and other relatives help to piece together missing segments of a person's life. Detailed records regarding Kate's childhood were totally lacking so information about her siblings was examined closely to gleam some indication of at least the location and time periods of various events in her life. Relatives of her sisters-in-law and their families had roles in events that lead to major repercussions that both directly and indirectly influenced Kate's life. Mark W. Geiger determined that the extensive interfamilial connections of people with roots in east coast states explained the amplified guerrilla activity in Kate's part of Missouri as compared to other border regions.[26]

Sarah Catherine King was the fifth child and youngest daughter of six known children born to Robert L. King and Malinda Rebecca Stringer. The earliest documented record of her is in the 1850 Federal Census where she is listed as

Rebecca with her parents and four siblings in Polk County, Missouri. The family had moved to Polk County from Greene County, Illinois sometime between late 1840 and early 1843. An older brother was born in Greene County, Illinois in July 1840 where Robert and Malinda were married in 1837. An older sister was born in Polk County, Missouri in June 1843.

Although details are lacking, the paternal line of Kate's mother, Malinda Rebecca Stringer King, can be traced back through Kentucky to Virginia, and reportedly to Ireland.[27] Malinda's maternal ancestors, the Scott family, originated in Scotland.[28] Malinda was born about 1809 in Kentucky to Limeledge Stringer and his second wife, 'Betsy' Elizabeth Scott (married 18 June 1800 in Lincoln County, Kentucky).[29] Limeledge Stringer and 'Betsy' Elizabeth Scott had six children born in Kentucky:

1) Rachel Stringer (10 May 1800-1850);[30]
2) Levi Stringer (about 1803-before 1850);[31]
3) Sarah A. Stringer (1805-??);[32]
4) William M. Stringer (6 April 1807-3 April 1884);[33]
5) Malinda Rebecca Stringer (about 1809-18 Jan 1880) [Kate's mother]; and,
6) Ann Stringer (15 May 1811-23 Nov 1893).[34]

Malinda was orphaned very young —at about age three — when her father died in 1812, leaving her mother, Betsy (Scott) Stringer, widowed with six small children to support. Limeledge also left other surviving children from his first marriage to Anny Bly. To provide for her children and stepchildren, Betsy married again (one of few options available for widows with young dependent children) to Jesse Rigney, as his second wife, in Casey County, Kentucky, on 22 October 1816. Misfortune continued to stalk the family as Malinda's stepfather, Jesse Rigney, died in 1823. Betsy and most of her dependent children then migrated to Illinois with her son, William M. Stringer.[35] Malinda apparently came with her mother and brother during the moves to and within Illinois. Thus, Malinda [Kate's mother] was in Greene County, Illinois

Kate's Family

in 1837, when and where she married Robert L. King [Kate's father] on 20 April.

Kate's father, Robert L. King, was born about 23 January 1810 in Kentucky.[36] The definitive parentage of Robert L. King has not been proven, but William James King of Pickering, England, has been proposed as a possible father.[37] Although William James King did not name Robert as a son in his Will while he did name the sons from his marriage to Mary Anne Caldwell, perhaps Robert received the equivalent of his inheritance much earlier when he reached his majority.[38]

Robert [Kate's father] was believed to have a younger sister Nancy,[39] also born in Kentucky in about 1806, who married Alexander Chism in Greene County, Illinois on 28 November 1834, three years before Robert L. King married Malinda Stringer in the same county. Alexander died young leaving the widowed Nancy with four children: William (1836-), Gabriel (1837-), Eliza (1841-1921), and Malinda (1842-1920).[40]

Prior to his marriage in Greene County, Illinois, Robert L. King purchased an original land grant of 80 acres in 1836.[41] After his marriage, Robert signed a Mortgage Bond for this land to Luther Tunnel for $200 on 6 February 1837.[42] Robert L. King and Malinda Rebecca Stringer King continued to live in Greene County, Illinois, presumably on the original land grant property, until at least 1840. They had a son born there in July of 1840 and were in Carrollton Precinct, Greene County, Illinois on the 1840 census. Why and exactly when Robert and Malinda moved their family from Illinois to Missouri is not known. Were there economic incentives (either positive in Missouri or negative in Illinois), family strife situations, political issues or just plain wonder lust that propelled the family to move?

Whatever the driving force or forces, the family moved to Missouri sometime around 1841. Robert and Malinda had children born in Polk County, Missouri in June 1842 and September 1845.

Kate was born in Polk County, Missouri in 1848. The King family was still located in Polk County, Missouri, for the Federal census on 15 October 1850.

KATE IN FACT AND FICTION

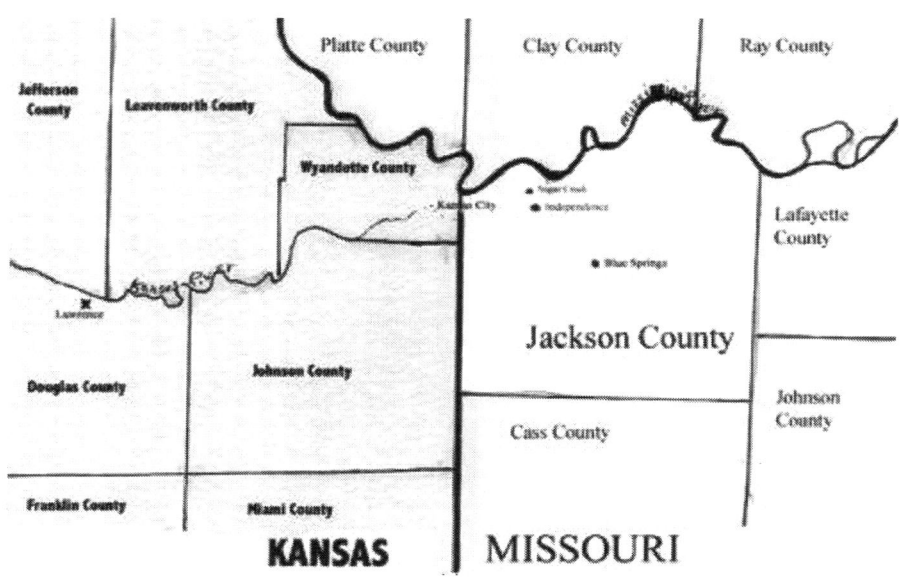

Above: Missouri and surrounding states (selected counties shaded)
Below: Western Missouri / Eastern Kansas

In 1855 and 1857, Robert purchased several tracts of land in Sections 7 and 18 in Jackson County, Missouri.[43]

The family had moved from Polk County to Jackson County before these land purchases as they were living in Jackson County in October 1853 when Robert and Malinda's last child Samuel Robert King [Kate's younger brother] was born. On 1 May 1857, a patent was issued for 80 acres of land in Section 7 which became the King family farm where Robert and Malinda raised their family.[44]

The three smaller forty-acre parcels of land adjoining the King family farm were sold before 1877. The 1877 *Jackson County Atlas* shows the neighbors of Robert L. King as Pat Powers ('Pat' Patrick Powers),[45] T. Torpee (Thomas Henry Torpey),[46] and son W. J. King.[47] The Powers and Torpey families both lived as next-door neighbors on the west side of the King family farm for many years. Whether the familial relationship, which developed later between the Powers and King families by marriage, was a factor in land transaction or vise versa is pure speculation. To date no familial relationships have been identified between the Torpey and King families.

Robert and Malinda, with their five children, were enumerated on the 1860 Federal census in Sni-a-Bar Township, Jackson County, Missouri, on 19 July. The upheaval and conflict along the Missouri and Kansas border, and certainly the horrendous General Order No. 11, issued 25 August 1863, dislodged this family forcing them to relocate.

On 4 August 1870, Robert and Malinda with two of their sons—Francis Marion (married with a son) and Samuel Robert (single and working away from home)—were in Township 3, near the town of Auburn, Placer County, California.[48] Robert and Malinda's daughter, Martha Jane (King) Ragland, with her husband, John O. Ragland, and their children were enumerated just a bit earlier on 27 July in the same place.[49] Robert and Malinda's son-in-law, Robert O. Ragland, [Kate's brother-in-law] was a registered voter in Auburn, Placer County, California, beginning 7 August 1866, through 7 August 1873.[50]

The entire family, except Kate, was back in Jackson County, Missouri, before the summer of 1880 when the Federal census was taken. They all probably returned to Jackson County, Missouri, before 7 September 1879, when Samuel Robert King married Elizabeth L. Davenport in Independence, Jackson County, Missouri. Robert and Malinda were definitely back in Sni-a-Bar Township in Jackson County, Missouri, before 18 January 1880, when Malinda died there. She was buried about two miles from her home in Slaughter Cemetery, in Section 16, in Sni-a-Bar Township, Jackson County, Missouri.

Robert was listed in the Federal census in Blue Springs, Jackson County, Missouri, on 19 June 1880.[51] Robert L. King died on 2 February 1891, at the age of 80 years, 11 months, and 21 days. He was buried beside his wife Malinda Rebecca (Stringer) King in Slaughter Cemetery in Jackson County, Missouri.

Nothing has been recorded about Kate's brief childhood which was cut short by events occurring in Jackson County, Missouri, before the Civil War. However brief, childhood sets the stage on which the rest of life plays. Family relationships established during this pivotal period persist throughout a lifetime. Therefore, all of Kate's siblings were chronicled to ascertain family relationships, including those of her nieces and nephews, as well as her sisters-in-law and brother-in-law.

The complex relationships and intermarriages of Kate's family clearly illustrated the intricate and convoluted interconnections of kinship as discussed by Geiger:

> "These families intermarried to a degree that most modern Americans would find unfamiliar. Three or four intermarriages between the same two families were common, sometimes in the same generation. Family connections were often generations old, surviving multiple migrations and going back to the pre-Revolutionary southern Tidewater region."[52]

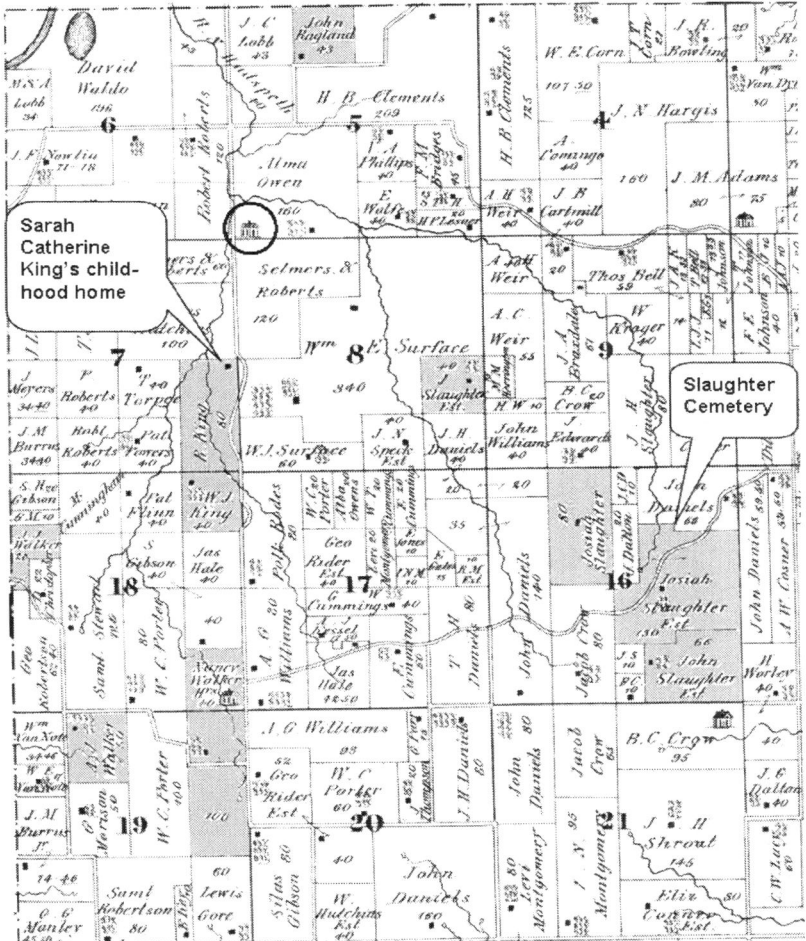

Jackson County, Missouri's Sni-a-Bar Township, 1877

Robert L. King's family farm is in Section 7 (each section is one mile square). The east-west section line dividing Robert L. King's property and that of W. J. [William Jasper] King to the south is present-day Argo Road in Blue Springs, Missouri. The north-south section line on the west side of their property is today (2015) Owen School Road. Other important nearby locations are: Slaughter Cemetery (Sec. 16); Walker family property (Sec.18 & 19); Pat Powers and T. Torpee (Sec. 7); John Ragland (Sec. 5); and, Surface family properties (Sec.8). Owen School, circled in the southwest corner of Section 5, is where Kate probably attended school; it was ½ mile from home [rather than the school located in the southeast corner of Section 18 (then adjacent to the Walker family property), which was 1.5 miles from the King home].

KATE IN FACT AND FICTION

Through such elaborate multiplex relationships Kate was related to two of the women killed in the collapse of the Union jail in Kansas City in 1863. Kate was related to Armenia Crawford Selvey and Susan Jane (Crawford) Whitsett Vandever by more than one intermarriage (not direct line blood relatives; but, relatives nonetheless).[53] Thus, Kate certainly was aware of this tragedy which so profoundly affected the subsequent events in the military conflict including her family along with the entire population of the border counties in both Missouri and Kansas. Additional family relationships also complicated Kate's life again almost six decades later in 1920 when the amount of her inheritance from the King estate was reduced from one-half to two-fifteenths by the claims of the heirs of her sister-in-law.[54] There may be other familial ties to Kate, not yet determined, that affected her as well.[55]

Robert L. King and Malinda Rebecca (Stringer) King were the parents of six children born within a span of about a dozen years:

1. Nancy A. King   (about 1839-)
2. William Jasper King   (1840-1919)
3. Martha Jane King   (1842-1918)
4. Francis Marion King   (1845-1916)
5. Sarah Catherine King   (1848-1930)
6. Samuel Robert King   (1852-1921)

Nancy A. King

Kate's oldest sister, Nancy King, was born about 1839 (about a decade before Kate's birth) in Illinois, probably in Greene County. Nancy was listed with her parents Robert L. King and Malinda Rebecca (Stringer) King at age 10 in the 1850 census. It was assumed she was the female, whose age was less than four years, with her parents in the 1840 census. Since no further record of her has been located—she is not on the 1860 census, and no marriage record for her in Missouri has been found—it is presumed she died young. It would be possible that she married, and that a marriage record has yet to found; but, certainly no heirs of Nancy were named in the 1920 probate of the King estate, which listed all known heirs of Robert L. and Malinda Stringer King (all known heirs included their children or the children of their children if the parent of the latter was deceased).

A female child, between five and nine years of age, listed on the 1840 census with Robert and Malinda, appeared to be too old to be their daughter. Her age indicated she was born before their marriage. This may have been a daughter whose age was listed incorrectly and then died before the next census. Or it could have been an unrelated female, perhaps a servant, with the family in this census. A possible identity of this female child could also be a young relative of either Malinda or Robert. Neither had a sister this young, but it could have been a niece or a more distant relative of either of them.

William Jasper King

Kate's oldest brother, William Jasper King, was born in Greene County, Illinois, on 8 July 1840 (about eight years before Kate's birth). However, he spent most of his childhood in Missouri, reaching adulthood just before the Civil War broke out. He was with his parents in Polk County, Missouri, listed as eight-year-old William J. King, on 15 October 1850. The Missouri/Kansas border conflict certainly affected him when he was displaced by General Order No. 11. He married in Lafayette County, Missouri, after everyone had been banished from their homes in rural Jackson County, Missouri. On 25 August 1864 William Jasper married America Jane Snodgrass, daughter of Bartley Snodgrass (24 September 1797-18 June 1881) and Lucy Ann Baker (1 December 1813-13 November 1890), in Lafayette County, Missouri. Their marriage was performed by A. A. Moore, a Presbyterian minister.

America Jane Snodgrass [Kate's sister-in-law] was born in Jackson County, Missouri, on 12 August 1847. Her parents moved to Jackson County, Missouri, from Botetourt County, Virginia, in about 1843. Bartley and Lucy Ann had a total of 12 children, five[56] born in Botetourt County, Virginia, and seven[57] born in Jackson County, Missouri.

**William Jasper King and America Jane (Snodgrass) King
Kate's brother and sister-in-law**

These photos were provided by their grand-daughter Halys Morris Wyrick Boman. Halys' mother, Miranda Jane King Morris, knew Kate well enough to write a personal history about her . . . although that history has never been seen by anyone except Fred Ford.

William Jasper and America Jane were the parents of ten surviving children who were some of Kate's nieces and nephews; eight of these children lived and died in Jackson County, Missouri. All ten of them knew Kate, and were known by Kate.

Where William Jasper and America Jane lived immediately following their marriage was not documented. They were obviously in Lafayette County in 1864 when they married and still there in 1865 at the birth of their first child. Letters written from Lexington, Missouri, in Lafayette County, between July 1864 and July 1867 by William A. Snodgrass, a brother of America Jane Snodgrass King, included several references to other members of the Snodgrass family living in Lafayette County during this time of banishment. William and America were not located on the 1870 census, but William

Jasper had purchased land from his parents on 1 March 1870 and it was presumed they were there, but 'missed' in the 1870 census.[58] They were not found in California with William's parents or his siblings; nor were they found in Jackson County, Missouri, with America's parents or siblings. However, William and America were listed on the 1880 census on 1 June in Sni-a-Bar Township, Jackson County, Missouri. They were still living there on 15 June 1900.

America Jane died in Jackson County, Missouri, at 61 years, 2 months, 18 days, on 30 October 1908. She was buried in Perdee Chapel Cemetery in Sni-a-Bar Township in Jackson County, Missouri. After her death William reportedly either lived alone or with his children. However he was not located in the 1910 census. He died in bed at the home of his brother-in-law Parmer Snodgrass near Grain Valley in Sni-a-Bar Township in Jackson Country on 26 March 1919 at 78 years, 8 months, 18 days of age. His obituary appeared in *The Jackson Examiner*:

W. J. KING DEAD
Was 79 Years Old -- Father of 13 Children -- Funeral Thursday

William Jasper King, one of the oldest residents of eastern Jackson County, died at the home of his brother-in-law, Palmer Snodgrass, near Grain Valley, early Wednesday morning, March 26, of heart failure.

Funeral services were conducted in the Grain Valley Baptist Church at 11 o'clock Thursday morning by the Rev. T. D. Payne of Blue Springs and burial was made in Perdee's Cemetery, south of town.

Jasper King was born in Greene County, Illinois, July 8, 1840. At an early age he came to Jackson County where he spent the remainder of his life. On August 25, 1864, he married Miss America Snodgrass, whose death preceded her husband's by several years. He was formerly a farmer, but after the death of his wife he lived with first one and then another of his children.

Mr. King was the father of thirteen children, nine of whom are living. They are, Earl King of South Dakota, Frank King and Mrs. Miranda Morris of Blue Springs; Mrs. Nannie Cummins of Oak Grove, Mrs. Julia Sweeney of Independence; Walter King of Buckner; Dean, Oscar and Robert King of Grain Valley. He is survived by one brother, Samuel King of Centropolis and one sister, Mrs. Kate Badson of Sapulpa, Okla.[59]

KATE IN FACT AND FICTION

William Jasper King and America Jane (Snodgrass) King had thirteen children [Kate's nieces and nephews], eleven whom survived to adulthood, and nine of them outlived both of their parents. All but one of these children remained in Missouri, and eight of them lived their entire lives in Jackson County.

Some of Kate's nieces and nephews (children of Kate's brother, William Jasper King) at Independence, Missouri. **Six Siblings,** left to right: **'Frank' William Frank King** (1865-1946); **'Nan' Nancy Evelyn King Young Cummins** (1878-1944); **'Dean' Jona Dean King** (1876-1960); **Julia Lee King Swinney** (1880-1963); **Robert Jasper King** (1889-1973); and, **Miranda Jane King Morris** (1885-1971). Not Shown: **Lucy A. King Young** (1868-1911).

i. Frank William (26 May 1865 in Lexington, Lafayette County, Missouri-9 January 1946 at two miles north of Blue Springs, Jackson County, Missouri) married Jennie Elizabeth Anderson on 23 May 1893 (date license was issued) in Jackson County, Missouri. Frank and Jennie had five children.

ii. Lucy A. (14 May 1868 in Blue Springs, Jackson County, Missouri-21 February 1911 in Pleasant Hill, Cass County, Missouri) married Daniel W. Young, as his second wife, on 24 November 1895 in Blue Springs, Jackson County, Missouri. Lucy and Daniel left Jackson County sometime after June 1900, but Daniel returned to Jackson County, with a third wife, before January 1920. Lucy and Daniel had four sons; Daniel had five children with his first wife and no children with his third wife.

iii. Earl R. Monroe (15 September 1873 in Jackson County, Missouri-5 March 1963 in Silverton, Marion County, Oregon) married Mary Isabela Heisinger on 30 May 1892 in Independence, Jackson County, Missouri. Earl R. Monroe King left Jackson County, Missouri, and moved his family to South Dakota around 1912. Earl and Mary Isabella had ten children.

Earl R. Monroe King

- iv. Child (died young).

- v. 'Dean' Jona Dean (23 October 1876 near Blue Springs, Missouri-- 7 March 1960, in County Hospital, Jackson County, Missouri) married first Bertha Adela Branch on 10 August 1904 in Jackson County, Missouri, and married second Anna E. Baines on 20 December 1921 in Jackson County, Missouri. Dean and Bertha had two children. Dean and Anna had no children.

- vi. 'Nan' Nannie/Nancy Evelyn (12 August 1878 in Blue Springs, Missouri-30 May 1944 in Kansas City Hospital, Jackson County, Missouri) married first James M. Young on 22 December 1894 in Blue Springs, Missouri; after being widowed in 1904, she married second Jesse Lewis Cummins, as his second wife, on 26 February 1908 in Jackson County, Missouri. Jesse Lewis Cummins' first wife 'Gertie' Mary Gertrude Snodgrass (1874-1904) was Nan's first cousin (Nan's mother and Gertie's father were siblings). Nan and James had four children, two of which died in infancy. Nan and Jessie had two daughters. Jessie and Gertie had two children who were Nan's step children.

- vii. Julia Lee (23 March 1880 in Blue Springs, Missouri-27 January 1963 in Independence, Missouri) married Rolla Lewis Swinney, 19 August 1903, in Independence, Missouri. Julia and Rolla had one son, Rolla Lewis, Jr.

Walter R. King

Oscar King

viii. Walter R. (Twin) (5 August 1882 in Grain Valley,Missouri-September 1971 Independence, Missouri) married Maud May Rolen on 27 January 1971 in Missouri. Walter and Maud had five children.

ix. Oscar (Twin) (5 August 1882 in Grain Valley, Missouri [crippled at birth]-11 December 1939 in Independence, Missouri) never married.

x. Miranda Jane (19 February 1885 in Jackson County, Missouri-18 May 1971 in Independence, Missouri) married 'Jack' Richard Jackson Morris on 16 December 1903 in Independence, Missouri. Miranda and Jack had a son and a daughter.

xi. Robert Jasper (2 September 1889 in Jackson County, Missouri-17 May 1973 in Independence, Jackson County, Missouri) married Ethel Shrout on 2 September 1909 in Independence, Jackson County, Missouri. Robert and Ethel had six children.

xii. Parmer (Twin-Died young)

xiii. Samuel (Twin-Died young)

Martha Jane King

The second daughter of Robert L. King and Malinda Rebecca (Stringer) King was Martha Jane King, born in Polk County, Missouri, on 18 June 1842 (she was six years older than Kate). After Nancy died, Martha was Kate's only sister. According to her obituary, Martha came to Jackson County with her parents at age seven, which would have been in about 1849; however it should be noted that the family was still in Polk County on 15 October 1850, for the census. She was with her parents in Sni-a-Bar Township, Jackson County, Missouri, at age 18, on 19 July 1860. Then sometime in 1860, obviously after the census was taken on 19 July and supposedly in Jackson County, Missouri, Martha Jane married John Oath Ragland. No marriage documents for this couple have been found in Jackson County records. Perhaps they crossed the state line and got married in Kansas since their marriage has not been found in any marriage records for the entire state of Missouri.

John Oath Ragland [Kate's only brother-in-law], a son of David Ragland (1815-before 1880) and 'Susan' Susanna [--?--] (about 1816-before 1860), was born in Barren County, Kentucky, on 21 June 1842. His parents moved to Washington County, Illinois in 1847, where John's mother died. David and Susanna Ragland had seven children.[60] David Ragland moved to Jackson County, Missouri, in about 1854, where he married Elizabeth Hendricks and they produced four more children.[61]

John Oath Ragland came to Jackson County, Missouri, with his father in 1854.

John Oath Ragland and Martha Jane King Ragland remained in Jackson County after their marriage until at least the Civil War was well underway. John Ragland signed a promissory note to J. T. Henderson for $7.25 in Jackson County, Missouri on 1 January 1862. John failed to appear in Jackson County Court as summoned on 27 April 1867, and the court ruled in favor of the plaintiff plus interest for a total cost of $11.81 against him. John obviously had not returned to Jackson County following the forced exodus of General Order No. 11 in 1863. John reportedly served as a private in the 77th Missouri Militia for three months before being discharged in January 1863, with a disability. If John did, indeed, serve in the Union Militia, it is especially noteworthy that his daughter, Georgeanna, later (more than three decades later in 1897) married 'Babe' (William Napoleon) Hudspeth, a documented Bushwhacker who rode with Quantrill. This would be another example of where both 'Northern/Union/Yankee' sympathizers and 'Southern/Confederate/Rebel' sympathizers were found within the same immediate family, albeit 30 years later.

It was not documented exactly when this family left Missouri, but in the 1870 Federal Census, the Ragland family (listed in error with the name of 'Ragdale') was in the gold fields of California (in Township 3, Placer County) on 27 July 1870, where John was a lime burner. Although they are listed in the 1870 Federal Census with the surname 'Ragdale', the given names and ages of the children and parents fit this family, which was listed only four pages from the listings for Martha's parents and brothers. They were surrounded by miners and many Chinese.

They returned to Missouri and were on the census in Blue Springs, Jackson County, on 1 June 1880.[62] They lived near Lake City in Ft. Osage Township, Jackson County, Missouri, on 8 December 1883, when their youngest child was born and John was a stone mason. They were living in a hotel in Independence in Jackson County, Missouri, on 12 June 1900. John Oath died in Jackson County, Missouri, on 12 February 1905. He was buried in Woodlawn Cemetery,

Independence, Jackson County, Missouri. The widowed Martha Jane King Ragland was living with her daughter and son-in-law, Dora and William Burrus, at 3014 E. 20th Street, Kansas City, Jackson County, Missouri, on 23 April 1910. Martha Jane died at 1003 Prospect, Kansas City, Jackson County, Missouri at 75 years, 10 months, 26 days on 14 May 1918, from apoplexy compounded by Bright's disease. She was buried in Woodlawn Cemetery, Independence, Jackson County, Missouri, on 16 May 1918. The brief obituary for Martha Jane failed to mention her surviving brothers (William J. and Samuel R.) or sister, Kate:

Ragland

 Mrs. Martha Jane Ragland died yesterday at her home, 1003 Prospect Avenue. Mrs. Ragland was born in Polk County, Missouri and had lived in Jackson County since she was 7 years old. Her husband, John O. Ragland, who died 13 years ago, was formerly in business in Independence. Mrs. Ragland was 75 years old.

 She is survived by two daughters, Mrs. Annie Hudspeth of the home address and Mrs. William L. Burrus, 3420 Bellefontaine Avenue, and three sons, J. M. Ragland, 3118 Benton Boulevard; R. H. Ragland, 1128 Montgall Avenue and Charles Ragland, Independence.

 The funeral will be at 2:30 o'clock tomorrow at the home of Charles Ragland, 123 East Kansas Street, Independence. Burial will be in Woodlawn cemetery.[63]

John Oath Ragland and Martha Jane King Ragland had eight known children [Kate's nieces and nephews] all born in Jackson County, Missouri, but only five survived their mother:

i. William Robert (29 December 1861-20 June 1902 in Jackson County, Missouri) married Mary Eliza Rider on 25 June 1896, in Jackson County, Missouri. William Robert and Mary had three children, one of whom died in infancy, before William Robert's untimely death.

ii. 'Annie' Georgeanna R. (20 March 1864-11 February 1929 in Kansas City Hospital, Jackson County, Missouri) married 'Babe' William Napoleon Hudspeth on 5 February 1897, in Jackson County, Missouri. This unhappy marriage produced no children. Annie left Babe and when he died he named his nephews as his beneficiaries in his Will; Annie went to court and 'broke' the Will, much to the displeasure of the Hudspeth family.[64]

iii. John Marion (20 May 1865-14 June 1939 in Kansas City, Jackson County, Missouri) married Mary H. Carmody on 27 November 1895, in Jackson County, Missouri. John Marion and Mary had one daughter and one son. John Marion Ragland, listed as 'Jack' Ragland, was guardian of his aunt Kate, listed as Sarah Head in 1929.[65]

iv. Charles H. (20 March 1869-24 January 1959 in Encino, Los Angeles, California) married 'Nellie' Nell W. Jones about 1896 in Jackson County, Missouri. Charles and Nellie had three children and lived in Jackson County until at least 1940. Although Charles died in California, he was buried in Independence, Jackson County, Missouri.

v. Rufus Hudspeth (29 September 1872-10 November 1927 in Kansas City, Jackson County, Missouri) married first Edna Carpenter, and married second Eugenia Marie Louapre on 2 December 1908, in Kansas City, Jackson County, Missouri. Rufus Hudspeth Ragland had no known children.

vi. Child (Died young) (before 1883 [Dora was the eighth child]-??)

vii. 'Vady' Guy (Died as Child) (about 28 April 1879-7 October 1892 in Jackson County, Missouri).

viii. Dora Hazel (8 December 1883-8 February 1956 in San Bernardino County, California) married 'Shad' William Louthan Burrus 8 September 1902 in Jackson County, Missouri. Dora Hazel and William had three children.

Francis Marion King

A second son of Robert L. King and Malinda Rebecca (Stringer) King, named Francis Marion King, was born near Bolivar in Polk County, Missouri on 25 September 1845 (only three years before Kate was born). He was on the census with his parents in both 1850 and 1860. On 15 November 1864, Francis Marion married Eveline Lynch, in Lafayette County, Missouri.[66]

Eveline Lynch King [Kate's sister-in-law] was born in Missouri on 15 January 1847, the youngest child of William Lynch (between 1801 and 1810-before 1850) and his second wife Rebecca Ginans (about 1804-before 1860). Eveline's parents had three daughters.[67] William Lynch and Rebecca Ginans Waldo Lynch also had children from each of their first marriages;[68] the marriage of Eveline's half-brother would connect her and her sister-in-law, America Jane (Snodgrass) King, by yet another intermarriage.[69]

The marriage between Francis Marion King and Eveline Lynch was performed by Rev. W. B. McFarland, who was a pastor of the Methodist Episcopal Church and served many churches in Missouri after his arrival from Virginia. During the winter of 1862, Rev. McFarland was the only minister allowed by the Union forces to preach in Lexington, Lafayette County, Missouri. Rev. McFarland neglected to record the marriage until seven months later in June 1865. This long delay between the actual marriage and the recording of the marriage may account for some of the erroneous information recorded but poor spelling, bad penmanship and general carelessness also may have contributed to some errors.[70]

Francis Marion and Eveline apparently moved to Lafayette County with their respective families sometime soon after General Order No. 11 was executed. How long they remained there after their marriage was not known. On 4 August 1870, they were living near Auburn, Township 3, Placer County, California, with their three-year-old son Anson. Francis was listed on the 1870 Federal Census as a farmer in a dwelling next to his parents. When the family moved to California and how long they stayed there was also unknown.

They obviously had left Missouri because of the dangerous situation that existed during the armed conflict there and the repercussions that followed.

They left California and were back on the King family farm in Sni-a-Bar Township, Jackson County, Missouri for the Federal census on 18 June 1880. Francis had purchased this farm from his father in March of 1880, three months after his mother died. Francis and Eveline were still at this location for the 1900 census.[71] They were not located on the census in 1910; there was no known reason why the family would not be found on their own property. Was it simple oversight on the part of the census taker? Did the family intentionally avoid the census taker? Had they temporarily relocated? There is no documentation to support one option over another; but, it was presumed that they were living on the family farm in 1910 and were 'missed' in the enumeration by the census taker.

Francis was living in Blue Springs, Jackson County, Missouri, in July 1912, when he was the informant on Eveline's death certificate. Eveline died on 20 July 1912, in Sni-a-Bar Township, Jackson County, Missouri, aged 64 years, 7 months, 25 days, from rheumatism with endocarditis.

Reportedly Kate came to keep house for her brother after Eveline died:

> "You could honestly say that from 1912 until 1920 she kept house for her brother and nephew on the same farm where she furnished the money to build the house and it stands today three miles south from Lake City."[72]

This implication that Kate was in Jackson County continuously from 1912 to 1920 conflicts with her documented residence (as Sarah C. Batson) in Sapulpa, Creek County, Oklahoma in 1911 and 1916 in city directories, and in the Federal census on 8 January 1920.

Kate was listed as Sarah C. Batson on legal papers in Blue Springs, Jackson County, Missouri in July of 1920.

Two days before his death Francis transferred the King family farm to his son Anson for $1.00 and 'Love & Affection' by a warranty deed dated 5 May 1916. Francis Marion King died of chronic bronchitis on 7 May 1916. He was buried next to both his wife and his parents in Slaughter Cemetery. His obituary appeared in the *Sni-a-Bar Voice*:

> Francis Marion King was born September 23, 1845, near Bolivar, Missouri. He was married to Eveline Lynch Dec 15, 1864. To this union one son was born, Anson Marion, who survives him. He was converted and joined the Cumberland Presbyterian Church in the seventies and soon after was made an elder which position he faithfully filled to the day of his death which occurred May 7, 1966. His faithful wife preceded him some four years ago. He has two brothers and two sisters yet living. The brothers are Samuel R. and William Jasper. The sisters are Martha Jane and Sarah Katherine. Certainly a good man is gone.
>
> The funeral was conducted by his pastor Rev. Geo. W. Petty, at Little Blue Church May 9, to a large concourse of neighbors and friends. He was laid to rest by the side of his wife in the Slaughter burying ground.[73]

Francis Marion and Eveline were the parents of an only son [Kate's nephew] who survived them, Anson Marion King (31 July 1867 in presumably Jackson County, Missouri-29 May 1920 on the King family farm near Blue Springs, Jackson County, Missouri). When Anson died suddenly and unexpectedly on his front porch from a ruptured aortic aneurism on 29 May 1920, he left no spouse, no descendants and no will. His heirs included all of his mother's siblings and half siblings, or their descendants, as well as the legitimate King family members.[74] The time and expense of identifying, locating, and contacting all of the individuals reduced the value of the estate and delayed the settlement. The division of the estate into 2,625 shares for 59 'heirs at law' left little monetary allotment for any individual after the mortgage, taxes, legal fees, debts, and other expenses were paid.

Sarah Catherine King (later, Kate Clarke)

Sarah Catherine King, the subject of this biography, was the third daughter and fifth child of Robert L. King and Malinda Rebecca (Stringer) King. She was listed as Rebecca, age 2, in the 1850 Federal census with her parents in Polk County, Missouri. She was probably born in Polk County as were her two older siblings.[75] Kate was listed as Sarah, age 12, with her parents in Sni-a-Bar Township in Jackson County, Missouri, on 19 July 1860, in the Federal census. Kate's story began the following year in 1861.

Samuel Robert King

The youngest child of Robert L. King and Malinda Rebecca (Stringer) King, and Kate's only younger sibling, Samuel Robert King, was born 19 October 1852 (about four years after Kate was born) in Lake City, Jackson County, Missouri. He was on the census with his parents in 1860. In the 1870 Federal census, he was recorded as 17 years old, 'at school,' and in the same Township in Placer County, California as his parents. However, he was listed in the household of Henry Wilson, probably working as a hired hand.

On 7 September 1879, Samuel Robert King married Elizabeth L. Davenport, the daughter of Samuel Davenport (about 1811-before 1880) and Mary Ann Aldon/Alder (about 1822-unknown). They were married at the home of R. Hill, who also performed the marriage ceremony, in Independence, Jackson County, Missouri.

Elizabeth L. Davenport King Davidson [Kate's only sister-in-law to outlive her] was born 30 April 1858. Her birthplace was listed as Jackson County, Missouri, on her death certificate; but, she was with her parents, Samuel and Mary Ann (Aldon/Alder) Davenport, as a two-year-old in Shawnee Township in Johnson County, Kansas, on 13 August 1860. Elizabeth's parents had been in Boyle County, Kentucky, on 10 August 1850. And, they were in Westport in Jackson County, Missouri, on 2 August 1870.

KATE IN FACT AND FICTION

On 1 July 1874, sixteen-year-old Elizabeth had delivered an illegitimate daughter, Mary Ann "Mamie," named after her maternal grandmother. The child's biological father is unknown; she was raised by Samuel Robert King, as Mary Ann "Mamie" King.

Elizabeth's father, Samuel Davenport, was not in the 1880 census when her mother, Mary Ann, was living with their youngest daughter, Florence Davenport Brett, in Westport, Jackson County, Missouri, on 8 June 1880. The census data indicated that the eight older children[76] of Samuel and Mary Ann were born in Kentucky, probably Boyle County, while the three younger daughters[77] were born in Missouri (despite the location of the family in Kansas in 1860). Elizabeth's older sister Mary Ann Davenport married the Irish immigrant 'Pat' Patrick Powers on 18 September 1864 in Jackson County, Missouri, and they later purchased 40 acres (southwest quarter or south east quarter in Section 7) adjacent to the King family farm. When Samuel Robert King married Elizabeth Davenport, his neighbors became his in-laws.

In the 1880 Federal census, Samuel King, age 27, was listed with his father[78] in Blue Springs Election District in Jackson County, Missouri, on 19 June. Samuel's wife, Elizabeth, was not named on this census, unless erroneously listed as Sarah, in the household of her father-in-law.

**Robert King in the 1880 Census,
Blue Springs, Jackson County, Missouri**

This census was taken six months after Kate's mother, Malinda Rebecca (Stringer) King died, and one week after Kate was listed in the census in St. Louis as Kate Clark. Listed with his father is Kate's brother, Samuel. The census taker mistakenly recorded Samuel's wife's name as "Sarah" rather than "Elizabeth." Myrty appears to be Samuel's step daughter, 'Mamie' Mary Ann, born five years before Samuel married her mother. Errors in this enumeration make interpretation difficult.

In December of 1884, Samuel and Elizabeth were in Ft. Osage Township, Jackson County, Missouri, when and where their son Arthur was born. They are together in Independence, Jackson County, Missouri, in the census on 8 June 1900. In March 1904, Samuel lived in Independence, Jackson County, Missouri, when he signed the marriage license application for his son Arthur. In 1910, Samuel and Elizabeth were in two separate households; Samuel, listed as S.R. and designated as 'widowed', was in Sni-a-Bar Township, Jackson County, Missouri on 26 April with his son Joseph, and Elizabeth was listed as a 'widowed' 'housekeeper' with Frank Davidson in Independence, Jackson County, Missouri on 27 April.

In the next census, on 12 January 1920, Samuel was listed alone and divorced, living at 1408 Oakland in Kansas City, Jackson County, Missouri, and on 17 January 1920, Elizabeth was listed as a single boarder at a hotel on 3736 Broadway Boulevard in Kansas City.

In 1921, Samuel R. was living with his son Arthur at 105 West Riley in Independence, Jackson County, Missouri, where he died on 18 June. He was buried in Woodlawn Cemetery in Independence, Jackson County, Missouri, on 20 June 1921. Samuel was the only child of Robert and Malinda who did not outlive their spouse. A brief obituary for Samuel Robert King appeared in the *Independence Examiner*:

SAMUEL R. KING DEAD.

Formerly a Farmer, but Later Worked at Bolt & Nut Factory.

Samuel R. King, 68 years old, who was born in Jackson County and spent all his life here, died Saturday afternoon at the Independence sanitarium. He was most of his life a farmer, but he was employed for some years at the Kansas City Bolt and Nut Works.

Surviving are his widow, Mrs Elizabeth King, 1133 West Elm street; three sons, Arthur King, 105 West Ruby street; George King, Sugar Creek; Joseph King, Arcadia, Neb.; and a sister, Mrs. Kate Barson, Lee's Summit.

Funeral services were held at 3 o'clock this afternoon at the home of Arthur King, 105 West Ruby street. Burial was at Woodlawn Cemetery.[79]

Since Elizabeth was listed as Samuel's widow both on his death certificate and in his obituary, perhaps they were separated, but not divorced.

Arthur Cleveland King, the eldest son of Samuel and Elizabeth, was the informant on Samuel Robert King's death certificate. Samuel was listed as 'married', not widowed or divorced, and Elizabeth King was listed as his wife on the death certificate.

She lived at 1133 W. Elm Street in Independence, Jackson Co, Missouri, per Samuel's obituary. On 4 August 1921, Elizabeth swore in court that Samuel's estate was worth less than $150 and on 8 August she refused administration of the estate due to insufficient property. The next month, on September 20, 1921, she received $123.08 as widow for Samuel's share of the estate of his nephew Anson King.

Sometime before the 1930 census on 8 April, Elizabeth married the widowed 'Frank' Francis Alexander Davidson, for whom she had kept house in 1910. Elizabeth was with Frank at 501 South Grand Avenue in Independence, Jackson County, Missouri on 8 April 1930. Frank died at this address on 3 June 1931 at the age of 74 years, 2 months and 14 days.[80]

Elizabeth continued to live in the same house and was at 501 South Grand Avenue in Independence on 10 April 1930. Her son, George Samuel King, and his family were living with her. Elizabeth outlived her second husband by a dozen years and died on 24 October 1943.

She was buried as Elizabeth Davidson in the Davidson plot at Woodlawn Cemetery in Independence, Jackson County, Missouri.

Samuel Robert King and Elizabeth L. Davenport King had four children [Kate's nieces and nephews], in addition to the daughter Elizabeth had before their marriage, born in Jackson County, Missouri:

i.   'Mamie' Mary Ann (1 July 1874 - 25 July 1946 in Independence, Jackson County, Missouri) was born when her mother was only sixteen. She married Newton Benton Nicolas Keck on 12 September 1893, in Independence, Jackson County, Missouri. They had five sons and five daughters. 'Mamie' was not mentioned in Samuel's obituary. Although Samuel raised her, Mamie's paternity has not been determined, or located.

ii. Nellie M. (September 1882 - before 1921) was not mentioned in her father Samuel's obituary, but she was listed twice in the 1900 census: once with her parents on June 8th and earlier on June 5th as a servant with Frederick and Annie Child. No further information regarding Nellie has been found.

iii. Arthur Cleveland (6 December 1884 - 10 October 1936 in Kansas City, Jackson County, Missouri) The birth record of Arthur Cleveland indicated that he was the third child of his mother; he married Cora Belle Warren on 3 March 1904 in Independence, Jackson County, Missouri. They had one son and one daughter.

iv. George Samuel (4 July 1888 - January 1970 in Veterans' Hospital at Knoxville, Marion County, Iowa, but buried in Greenlawn Cemetery in Jackson County, Missouri) married first Emma J. Gleason Wade in about 1918; no marriage record has been located in Missouri and Emma may have abandoned her four children, born between 1905 and 1915, with their father John Henry Wade. George Samuel and Emma J. had three children. George Samuel married second on 20 May 1904 in Bolivar, Polk County, Missouri, to a divorcee, Laura F. Fugate Barker, after Emma died on 24 March 1938. George Samuel and Laura F. had no children. George Samuel King had seven stepchildren -- four Wade children and three Barker children.

v. Joseph Edward (12 January 1899 - 23 February 1970 in El Dorado Springs, Cedar County, Missouri) married first the widowed Opal E. Dora Webb Turvey on 6 March 1920 in Lowry City, Nebraska. Joseph Edward and Opal E. Dora had two sons and Joseph Edward adopted Opal's two daughters from her first marriage before they separated. Opal E. Dora married Edward Harrison and Joseph Edward married second Bessie Taylor on 12 April 1940 in Clay County, Missouri. Joseph Edward and Bessie had no children.

Sarah Catherine King outlived all of her siblings, and was the last surviving child of Robert L. King and Malinda Rebecca (Stringer) King after 1921. She obviously maintained contact with her family throughout her life.

Sarah Catherine King, as Sarah C. Batson

This image, reproduced from a photograph in *Earl M. King Family Record*, was identified as, "Sister of Jasper Monroe King," Kate's brother, William Jasper King, through his son, Earl R. Monroe King, who left Missouri and went to South Dakota around 1912. This is further proof of communication between Kate and her relatives throughout her life.

Kate reportedly rebuilt in 1869 her parent's homestead after the original buildings were destroyed during the enforcement of General Order No. 11 in 1863.[81]

Barn on former King Family Farm, Blue Springs, Missouri
This barn (and the King home, not pictured), both still standing in 2014 on the former King family farm, were owned by Mr. and Mrs. Leonard F. Davis in 1965; and, by Mrs. "Mimo" Davis in 1992.

Kate was named in each of her brother's obituaries. The brief obituary of her sister, Martha, did not mention Kate. She reportedly kept house for her brother, Francis Marion King, after his wife died, and later for her nephew, Anson King, after his father died.[82]

Kate was documented living in Sapulpa, Oklahoma, in 1916, 1919, and 1920. Kate may have kept house for her brother and his son after Eveline died; but, Kate definitely left Jackson County after her brother died.

If she kept house for her nephew, Anson, after his father died, she had left and returned to Oklahoma before January of 1920, when she was enumerated in the Sapulpa, Creek County, Oklahoma, Federal census.

Fred Ford also reported that Kate later lived with another nephew, Frank King ['Frank' William Frank, son of

Kate's brother, William Jasper King], in Jackson County, Missouri.

Thus, it was strange and very sad that none of her relatives were willing to step forward to claim her body for a decent funeral and family burial after her death. Her siblings had predeceased Kate, and only a remarried sister-in-law survived her. There were many nieces and nephews still living in Jackson County at the time of her death. Why was Kate's daughter, who lived in Oklahoma in 1930, not contacted? Perhaps there were health, financial and/or personal issues which prevented Bertha from responding . . . presuming she was even notified.

There were only a few people present at Kate's graveside burial, which took place almost a month after she died. A lengthy article in the *Kansas City Times* on 5 February 1930, repeated much of the information from the 1926 article in the *Kansas City Star,* and then noted that relatives had been located and funeral arrangements were pending.

Her many nieces and nephews, even those no longer living in Jackson County, Missouri, plus the dozen still living in Jackson County, Missouri in 1930, all knew 'Aunt Kate.'[83] Personal communication with various descendants of Kate's brother, William Jasper King, involved a general hesitancy to discuss Kate Clarke; but, all acknowledged her association with the family.[84] The daughter of Kate's niece, Miranda Jane King Morris, wrote:

> "Aunt Kate King was Quantrill's girl friend I guess (it was before my time). I know my mother wasn't very proud to have relatives like her."[85]

While many of her relatives might have been ashamed of her profession, at least some apparently accepted the benefits of such ill-begotten gains from Kate.

> "She also started several relatives in businesses in different parts of the country. An old neighbor told about what she did for the family; she herself said nothing about it."[86]

In addition, each of the descendants were aware of some personal memento from Kate passed down in their respective family (as evidenced by the Towle "Old Colonial" dessert place spoon referenced earlier).

Kate's nephew, Joseph Edward King (son of her brother, Samuel Robert King) visited his aunt from Nebraska when she lived at the Jackson County Home. Although Kate does not have appeared to discuss her past with her nephew, Joseph Edward King shared family stories with his granddaughter.[87]

None of the King descendants had a full comprehension of Kate (*e.g.*, no one mentioned Kate's daughter or grandson). But, they all knew there were things about her that, "were never discussed." Fred Ford noted in several letters to Don Hale that Kate's nieces and nephews knew a great deal about her. And, Ford mentioned a story written by her niece, Miranda Jane King Morris, more than once. Unfortunately, this story has not been discovered by the authors. Nor has it been published, or otherwise documented.

We cannot choose our relatives. But, obviously we can choose whether or not to acknowledge them during their life time, or after their death. Blood is thicker than water; but, life with its complex and complicated situations can and does weaken family ties.

KATE IN FACT AND FICTION

CHAPTER 4

Kate's Life with Quantrill:
The Emergence of Kate Clarke

"To be, or not to be: that is the question:
Whether 'tis nobler in the mind to suffer
The slings and arrows of outrageous fortune,
Or to take arms against a sea of troubles,
And by opposing end them?"
William Shakespeare (Hamlet)

If Shakespeare were to have written this about Kate, he might have said 'Mistress or wife? Eloped or kidnapped? Those are the questions.' However, in the end, both outlaws and common laws have in-laws.

Sarah Catherine King first met William Clarke Quantrill when he and his band of guerrilla bushwhackers were encamped near her father's farm in Sni-a-Bar Township in Jackson County, Missouri. A reporter's interpretation of her own story, as told to him by her sixty-five years after the fact, is the most comprehensive record of this event and is the basis for all subsequent descriptions of their meeting.[88] The reporter who authored this article after interviewing Kate has never been identified; but, it has been repeated in whole or in part, or quoted with and without reference by a number of writers, including: Donald R. Hale,

William Clarke Quantrill

Jackson County and Quantrill historian and author; Francis E. Vaughn, Historian General of United Daughters of the Confederacy; Adrienne T. Christopher; and, Edward E. Leslie, author of a 1996 biography of Quantrill. More recently this article was repeated with proper recognition given to the original source by Carolyn Bartels.[89]

Kate and Quantrill first encountered each other in 1861 (as per her own recollections 65-years later) when she was only 13-years-old. But, she did not 'run off' with Quantrill until 1863 when she was 15-years-old. The published recollections of Quantrill's men support the date 1863 as the first year they were aware of Quantrill's involvement with Kate. Connelley's book cites Charles F. Taylor, Quantrill's cohort, who described the date as "summer of 1863."[90] Also, other recollections by Quantrill's men noted that 1863 was the time when he was noticeably distracted from guerrilla warfare and they attributed his distraction to his relationship with Kate. An Internet website lists the date of their secret marriage as August 21, 1863; but, it provides no source or citation for authentication. In fact, this is highly suspicious and erroneous, given that that is the date of Quantrill's raid on Lawrence, Kansas.[91] If an exact date of the marriage were known, there should also be an indication of where and by whom it was performed.

The duration of their marriage was shorter than the three-and-a-half-years mentioned in the 1926 newspaper article. There were certainly many events that occurred in Kate and Quantrill's lives in 1863. Whether marriage was one of them, remains elusive.

Missouri was in a state of turmoil when Kate met Quantrill. The border conflict between Kansas and Missouri commenced seven years before the Civil War began.

The skirmishes between the Kansas Jayhawkers and the Missouri Bushwhackers were in full tilt. Yet, the majority of Missouri's population were moderates who favored staying with the Union provided that the government did not interfere with state's rights, especially regarding slavery . . . even though less than three per cent of the households in the state owned slaves. Missourians maintained that they supported, "neither union-splitters nor rail-splitters."[92]

In June 1861, this delicate balance was upset and neutrality was no longer an option. A meeting between Captain Nathaniel Lyon, Claiborne Fox Jackson, Frank Blair, and Sterling Price, to discuss the role of Missouri's government in the Civil War, disintegrated into a confrontation that lead to open hostilities between the pro-Union and pro-Confederate forces that defeated the elected state government. From this point on it became impossible for the citizens of Missouri to remain neutral "hell, secession and neutrality were largely synonymous terms."[93] It was on this background that Kate and Quantrill first met, Quantrill having already made his first entrance upon the stage of Missouri guerrilla warfare.

Kate's first meeting with Quantrill, as described by Kate to the reporter of the *Kansas City Star* in May 1926, has been re-told many times. This meeting began as Kate returned home from school one day, and she saw a young man talking to her father on the front porch. She immediately noticed the young man's smile, clear blue eyes, scraggly mustache and handsome face. She later learned that he was William Clarke Quantrill, the controversial former teacher from Ohio with conflicting stories regarding his checkered past.

Quantrill had made his mark in Jackson County only a year earlier, and had yet to fully establish his reputation as a fabled guerrilla leader, authorized by the Confederacy, and sought by the Union troops. Quantrill was 11 years Kate's senior. Still, he was apparently smitten with the beautiful young girl of 13, who appeared to be at least four years older.

According to old family stories, Kate's father, Robert L. King, was known for raising fine horses. His stock originated from Kentucky, the state of his nativity. Robert's grandson, Joseph Edward King, told his granddaughter, Bonnie Royal of Kansas City, that Robert brought his horses from Kentucky to Missouri.[94] It was Robert King's reputation for having good horses that attracted Quantrill to the King family farm initially. It was Kate that brought him back time and time again. It was quipped that Quantrill went to get horses; but, wound up with Kate as well.[95]

Quantrill's visits to the farm after school became more frequent, and he and Kate would go on long horse rides together. Kate was a good, but daring, rider and she impressed Quantrill with her riding ability. Kate had begun riding her father's fine horses early in life. She reportedly especially enjoyed riding mounts that showed spirit, liveliness and speed.

When her parents became aware of the growing attachment between their daughter and her suitor, they demanded she stop seeing him. In defiance of her parents' demands, the two young lovers continued to meet in secret only to be observed and reported by neighbors to her father.

What did Kate's siblings think of her affair with a known guerrilla, and her defiance of their parents? Kate's sister Martha had already married and left home at this time; perhaps she was not even aware of the family turmoil. Kate's older brothers, William Jasper, who had reached the age of majority, and Francis Marion, who was also a teenager only two years older than Kate, may have had differing views of their sister's rebellious and disobedient behavior. Kate's younger brother, Samuel Robert, was not yet a teenager; but, he would know whether Kate was at school or not, and where and how she spent her time away from her parents.

Whatever Kate's siblings thought or may have said to her, Kate continued to meet Quantrill secretly. The tales and yarns Quantrill told her added to her infatuation and the two continued to meet clandestinely.

Robert did learn that his teenage daughter was defying his edict to end the meetings with her suitor. Out of fear of her father's anger, Kate decided to tell Quantrill that they could no longer see each other. Kate may have had good reason to be fearful of her father. Kate's father was very strict and abusive towards his family.[96] Robert L. King also suffered from very painful migraine headaches that eventually lead to his suicide.[97]

Kate skipped school one day and rode to Quantrill's camp to tell him that she was too afraid to continue meeting him. There, at his camp, Quantrill was able to persuade her to go with him to a country preacher and get married. They obviously had little time for this action as Kate's absence from school and home would be immediately apparent.

Not everyone believes that the couple was married.

Those unsympathetic to the rebel cause and who view Quantrill as a villain or psychopathic killer tend to believe that Quantrill ruined an innocent girl and made her his mistress.

Unfortunately, no marriage record is known to exist, and Kate's belated claim 65 years after-the-fact is the only evidence of their marriage. However, Paul R. Petersen, a modern-day Quantrill scholar and author, noted that, "many of Quantrill's men attested to the marriage," and even suggested that the minister who performed the marriage was Rev. Hiram Bowman of Oak Grove (a small town in Jackson County, Missouri), since he officiated at the marriages for several of the men who rode with Quantrill.[98]

Rev. Hiram Bowman and his wife, Isabell N. (Hoblet) Bowman, had a large family of 11 children before Isabell died in 1851. Hiram married the widowed Elizabeth Webb on 18 February 1855. He was in Sni-a-Bar Township, Jackson County, Missouri on the 1850 and 1860 census. Hiram was born in New Jersey, married in Ohio and had children born in Illinois and Missouri.[99] It was impossible to determine if he was pro-Union or pro-Confederate based on his geographic origin. Many people changed from a stand of neutrality to anti-Union, and certainly pro-guerrilla, because of antagonistic actions against the local population by Union troops, the Jayhawkers, and the Red Legs.

Hiram Bowman was the pastor of the Oak Grove Baptist Church.[100] He conducted the funeral service for Gabriel William George, who rode with Quantrill. Hiram's daughter Elizabeth married John Koger, who also rode with Quantrill.

Bowman died in Grain Valley, Jackson County, Missouri, on 30 January 1877, after being blind for the last nine years of his life. He was buried next to his wife, Isabell, in Perdee Cemetery. Perdee Cemetery, located in Section 9, Township 49, Range 30 near Grain Valley. This was also the burial site of Kate's brother, William Jasper King, and his wife, America Jane (Snodgrass) King, as well as many of her siblings.

It is a definite possibility that Rev. Hiram Bowman was the country minister who willingly performed the marriage of Kate and William Quantrill.

KATE IN FACT AND FICTION

On the other side of the discussion, a much less sympathetic author claimed that Quantrill, "kidnapped a girl named Kate Clarke," and forced her to be his mistress. Author William Elsey Connelley stated that, "others (without a reference as to whom these "others" might be) said that Quantrill kidnapped the girl and doomed her to an immoral life;" but, "that she became infatuated with him, even wearing a man's clothing and riding in the ranks to be near him."[101] In 1926, Kate, then known as Sarah Head, said she was always safer dressed as a woman, and she never dressed as a man.

Connelley presented an extremely unsympathetic portrayal of Quantrill. He used Charles Taylor as a major source, and Edward Leslie points out that Taylor had a falling out with Quantrill and took every opportunity to denigrate him.

Considering Kate's story told in 1926, it seemed unlikely that she was kidnapped. A letter by Taylor, as reported by Connelley, stated that he lent Quantrill his gray mare for Kate to ride when she left home, and that she went willingly. Kate's story was that she left home alone riding her father's horse. Whether she rode a borrowed horse or her own steed (actually, probably her father's horse), Kate most likely fled willingly into Quantrill's arms. She was definitely under-age and, according to today's standards and current law, her paramour committed a criminal act, even if she consented.

It was during this time when Sarah Catherine King first assumed the alias 'Kate Clarke,' the name by which Quantrill's men knew her, and a name she used for the next two decades.

According to Kate, an alias was advised by Quantrill to protect her identity if questioned by the Union military. One major reason to use an alias would be for her protection from any reprisals against Quantrill. Such was the fate of Mrs. Bill Owens, who was tortured by Confederate soldiers to extract the location of her husband, a Union guerrilla.[102] Bill Owens of North Carolina deserted the Confederate Army two months after he volunteered. He became a leader of other dissenters and led them on raids against the Confederacy. A Confederate posse found his wife and infant son and tortured her to tell them where Bill Owens was located. When the posse later captured a seriously wounded Bill Owens and jailed him to await trial, a vigilante mob forcibly removed Owens from jail and shot him to death. This case involved a Union guerrilla on Confederate soil; but, a guerrilla, and anyone sympathetic to or associated with a guerrilla, is still a guerrilla. Kate was wise to choose an alias.

Additional reasons to hide her identity were to protect her family from scandal, as well as Union reprisal, and certainly to protect her from her family's disapproval, or her father's anger. Many accounts mentioned her fear of her father's wrath; but, again, the original source was the 1926 article based on Kate's recollections many years after the fact. According to Fred A. Ford, who knew Kate as 'Aunt Kate,' and who was an ardent collector of Quantrill memorabilia, wrote the following:

> "The reason for the name Clarke. It would have been sueascide [suicide] to have been married to Quantrill, and she knew it. The Union Army wanted his scalp more than any one man in the State of Missouri, as well as the eastern half of Kansas. Aunt Kate couldent [couldn't] very well claim his name. It would have been poision [poison] to her family."[103]

Clarke was Quantrill's middle name, his mother's maiden name. Kate, the diminutive of her middle name Catherine, was probably the nickname her family and friends called her. The strong feelings of the residents of Missouri regarding Union versus Confederate and Bushwhackers versus Jayhawkers provided further incentive to take an alias.

In addition, it protected her family from the social stigma of the scandal of her fall from grace. Her parent's friends and neighbors certainly disapproved of her behavior regardless of their political sympathies and her family was still hurt and angry with her for running away.

Such continuing disapproval may have been part of the reason it was suggested she used the alias of Mrs. R. J. Claiborne when she visited her family four years after the war:

> "The country people had little to do with the King family at that time on account of the talk regarding the girl." [*i.e.*, Kate].[104]

The social disapproval of her lifestyle and her tarnished reputation as the notorious madam of St. Louis, Kate Clarke, would also have been reason enough to assume another name.

Perhaps this may be the origin of her use as 'Batson' either by marriage, appropriation or confiscation, around the turn of the century, and to keep her true identity secret when she returned to Jackson County, Missouri.

The 1926 newspaper article was the only extant record of Kate's life with Quantrill. Kate recalled those times fondly as ideally tranquil and romantic when filtered through time and memory.

The cabin in which she reportedly resided in those early days survived through the late-1960s, when it was sold and dismantled.[105]

'Wedding Cabin,' Sni-a-Bar Township, Jackson County, Missouri
The images on this two-page spread show the cabin that was reportedly where Kate and Quantrill stayed after their clandestine marriage in 1863. The cabin was located on the northwest corner of Section 19 of Township 49, Range 30, about a mile and a half south and a mile west of the Robert L. King farm in Section 7. [See map of Sni-a-Bar Township, Jackson County, Missouri.]

Between 1862-1864, Kate and Quantrill supposedly lived and traveled together wandering through the Missouri countryside in the summer, sleeping in tents; and, reportedly traveling south in the winter. Still, there is no evidence that Kate ever went to Texas.

She reportedly rode with Quantrill either in front of or behind the band of guerrillas as they moved from campsite to campsite. She remained in camp during the guerrilla raids and

KATE IN FACT AND FICTION

planned battles. There was always the threat of having to make a sudden unplanned departure from camp. She did not mingle with the men, although they always treated her with great respect.

Their domestic, nomadic life together was set against a series of events along the Missouri/Kansas border. Indeed, major escalation of the hostilities between the Union forces and the guerrillas began on 13 March 1862, when Major General Henry W. Halleck (1815-1872) issued General Order No. 2.

General Orders were commands issued by the Military Commander, under Martial Law. Martial Law then, as now, superseded civilian law. The Military Commander and his Provost Marshals determined law and order in the district under their military control. General Orders were numbered according to the sequence in which they were issued.

General Order No. 2 declared that any captured guerrilla would be executed as an outlaw and would not be treated as a prisoner of war. This 'no-quarter order' was issued in retaliation for the execution of a captured Union officer by the guerrillas, after a previously captured guerrilla had been executed by firing squad instead of being exchanged of as a prisoner of war as had been requested by Quantrill.

Lieutenant Levi Copeland was executed after Perry Hoy was shot by a Union firing squad at Fort Leavenworth on 28 July 1862. In retaliation to Order No. 2, Quantrill led a raid across the border into Olathe, Kansas, on 7 September 1862, killing ten men and looting the city.

The reprisals and counter-retributions between the two sides continued to escalate throughout the year, leading to the appointment of Brigadier General Thomas Ewing, Jr., as district commander. Thomas Ewing, a foster brother and brother-in-law of William Tecumseh Sherman from Lancaster, Ohio, increased field operations against the guerrillas and at the same time instituted a serious offensive against the civilians supporting them.

The local civilian population, especially the women and even the children, were a huge help to the guerrillas. It was they who bought the ammunition, supplied food, clothing, shelter and even horses, and acted as spies and messengers.

Most did this willingly because they were either neighbors, friends (at least acquaintances) or relatives of one or more of the guerrillas' families. Others did so out of fear of violence or that such things would be taken by force anyhow if refused.

Starting in April of 1863 and continuing through August, the Federal authorities tried to erode the guerrillas' base of support from local citizens by putting additional pressure on the civilian population. Daily life for the King family, as for all rural families in Jackson County, became increasingly difficult under these added constrictions.

Beginning in July of 1863, the female relatives of known or suspected guerrillas were arrested by Federal troops and imprisoned in downtown Kansas City. The use of an alias by Kate apparently protected her female relatives from this ordeal. Some women brought their small children or younger sisters with them. As the number of prisoners increased the facilities for holding them became overcrowded and the women had to be moved.

Initially, the Union Hotel at 6th and Main was used to house the women prisoners. They were then moved to a bank building at the corner of Delaware and Commercial. Finally, some of the women prisoners were moved into the Thomas building on Grand Avenue between 14th and 15th Streets. This building was originally two stories tall; but, the Missouri artist, George Caleb Bingham, had added a third story for a studio. On 13 August 1863, the Thomas building collapsed and five of the women prisoners were killed and many seriously injured.

Among the dead were two sisters, Armenia Crawford Selvey and Susan Jane Crawford Whitsett Vandever, who, as noted earlier, were 'shirt-tail relation' to Kate due to complex intermarriages. Extensive interfamilial connections of those involved with promissory-note lawsuits explained the amplified guerrilla activity in this part of Missouri as compared to other border regions.[106] These webs of interrelationships connecting families insured that everyone was enmeshed in the border conflict in one way or another.

The collapse of the building and the death of the women certainly was a blemish on the Union commanders and lead to much speculation as to cause of the collapse, including intentional sabotage by the Union troops. It was eventually determined that the collapse was attributed to removal of supporting walls by Federal troops on the first floor of the adjacent two-story building causing the third story to topple over onto that weakened structure.

While shockwaves of the tragedy of the collapse were still very much reverberating among the local citizens, General Ewing added insult to injury and deepened the discontent and estrangement just four days later. On 18 August 1863, Ewing issued General Order No. 10 declaring that the wives and children of any guerrilla plus any citizen found guilty of willingly providing aid to the guerrillas was to be arrested and then banished from the state. A transcript of Order No. 10 is in the Appendix of this work.

This order seemingly offered the Bushwhackers an opportunity to turn themselves in, provided they accepted the 'direction' of the Union Command, but they were still liable to be prosecuted for treason. Jim Lane obviously had a hand in encouraging this order and unfortunately the Kansas Red Legs, commanded by Lane, and the Jayhawkers helped to implement the order despite the directives which prohibited destruction of personal property (except blacksmithing facilities) and prohibited vigilante enforcement of this order. The 'do not destroy property' directive was completely ignored when commanders specifically instructed the destruction of personal property of Confederate sympathizers while implementing this order. The intentional destruction of blacksmith shops in an attempt to prevent the guerrillas from finding places for shoeing their horses, emphasized the role the horse played in guerrilla warfare. This indirectly reflected the role that citizens like Robert L. King and his inventory of good horses played in the conflict.

With the grievances of the death of female relatives, plus the harshness of the new military command heaped upon them back to back, many men in Missouri joined Quantrill and his gang of guerrillas to raid Lawrence, Kansas in retaliation.

At this time Quantrill and Kate were said to have shared a cabin near Blue Springs, Jackson County, Missouri (illustrated previously).[107]

Quantrill had first presented this plan to his council of commanders of allied bands on 10 August 1863. Lawrence was the cradle of the Kansas abolitionists, the headquarters of the Red Legs and the hated Jim Lane, and held all the plunder stolen from Missouri by the marauding Jayhawkers. By the time the entire force was assembled, 450 men rode into the town of Lawrence, Kansas, on the morning of 21 August 1863, and the burning, pillaging and killing began. (See Western Missouri / Eastern Kansas map on page 44.)

The Lawrence raid involved, "the largest such force ever assembled under one command during the entire Civil War," and the atrocities committed there by the guerrilla raiders wrote Quantrill's name indelibly into history as a bloodthirsty, cold-blooded heartless killer.[108] It was one of the bloodiest massacres of civilians in American history and certainly the worse in the Civil War. Lawrence was nearly completely destroyed. The entire business district and 200 houses were damaged or destroyed by fire. While no women were killed, 85 were widowed and 250 children were orphaned. Estimates of the number of men and boys killed ranged between 150 and 200. But, the hated Jim Lane escaped from the revenge seekers. Damage estimates, including extensive looting by the raiders, fluctuated between $1.5 and $2.5 million in 1865 dollars (equivalent to between $22.2 and $37 million in U.S. currency using the 2012 Consumer Price Index comparison).

All the raiders, except one, initially survived the sacking of Lawrence, since there was little resistance to the attack. A single drunken straggler named Larkin Skaggs failed to leave Lawrence on time, and was mobbed by the survivors. At least three of the raiders were wounded.

The retreating raiders were hotly pursued by both Union troops and a hastily organized and poorly armed posse of Kansas civilians, as they made a desperate attempt to return to Missouri. Much of the heavier and bulkier items ransacked by the looters, especially furniture, were abandoned by them during the pursuit. The three wounded men were also abandoned, and later found by the pursuers and shot. After finally reaching their home territory, Quantrill's band split up and went their separate individual ways. During the next week along the Missouri border, raiders and anyone suspected of being involved in the attack on Lawrence were sought out by gangs of Red Legs, civilian vigilantes, Federal troops, and Home Guard units and mercilessly killed with no questions asked; no prisoners were taken. Suspects, including anyone wearing a new suit, or any gathering of two or more men, whether loitering or traveling, were shot or hung on the spot. Well over 100 men were killed in retribution and whether they were innocent or guilty did not matter. Houses found with any items from Lawrence were destroyed without any criteria for separating goods legally purchased from those that were plundered, along with the houses of known guerrillas.

Kate's assertion in 1926 that she rode to meet the returning raiders may not be true. None of the memoirs by Quantrill's men mentioned a woman meeting them during their return from Lawrence. Such a memorable event as a woman riding upon the scene certainly would have been noteworthy. If Kate was in Jackson County at this time, she most likely remained at their last camp waiting and worrying during the entire raid and pursuit.

The Lawrence raid and the subsequent retaliations to it certainly marked a change in Kate's life and ended her perception of the idyllic life as the bride of a guerrilla living in tents in the bush. As the hunt for Quantrill intensified, life in the bush became more and more dangerous.

Another monumental consequence of the Lawrence raid was General Order No. 11, enacted to depopulate the entire border region of Missouri. After being harassed, coerced, exhorted, and threatened by an angry and vengeful Jim Lane, General Thomas Ewing drafted Order No. 11 to appease and placate Lane enough to sustain Ewing's future political aspirations.[109] Order No. 11 was published three days after Ewing's encounter with Lane on 25 August 1863.

General Order No. 11 devastated the Missouri border counties. This military decree inflicted the most severe punitive punishment upon its own citizens by a government in the history of this country, only approached by the earlier 'Trail of Tears,' and the later internment of the Japanese during World

War II. The banished consisted of women, children, and old men. All the able-bodied men were gone, either killed, in the military or had joined the guerrillas. In addition, all the good horses, mules and dray livestock were gone, either requisitioned by Union troops, stolen by Red Legs, pilfered by Jayhawkers, or confiscated by Bushwhackers.

People had to take whatever personal property they could with them, as there was no time or market to sell it. What remained would be destroyed. The old, feeble, sick, and very young were squeezed in amongst the few portable belongings that could be conveyed in whatever type of wagon or cart that remained for the exiles, sometimes drawn by a scrawny dairy cow. Others could take only what they were able to carry.

Meanwhile, the enforcers of the edict abused their authority and acted immediately; they did not wait the prescribed 15 days. Marauding Red Legs and other avengers from Kansas also preyed upon the banished by looting and burning before those affected had time to gather their possessions and flee as refugees.

Within two weeks, the only structures left standing in the 'Burnt District' were lone chimneys amongst charred ruins. Over 20,000 families within an area of 30,000 square miles, 85-miles long and 50-miles wide, were uprooted and displaced with no safe place to go. Some people went to adjacent counties in Missouri beyond the jurisdiction of the edict, such as Lafayette, Saline, or, Howard Counties. Two of Kate's brothers were in Lafayette County in 1864 where they married.

However, the refugees were not welcome wherever they went because there were no places to stay, they had little if any money, and no means to support themselves. They were even more unwelcome on the Kansas side of the border. Some people quit the state entirely and headed for Arkansas, Oklahoma, Texas or California. Kate's parents and at least three of her siblings went to California.

The severity of Order No. 11 further polarized the entire region, state, and beyond, and stirred much heated debate. Because of Order No. 11, Ewing was held in contempt long after the war ended. His name was despised in western Missouri for generations. George Caleb Bingham, the Missouri artist who was then Missouri State Treasurer, traveled from Jefferson City to Kansas City to confront Ewing to try to persuade him to rescind the order. After a heated exchange, Ewing refused and ordered Bingham out of his office. Bingham swore retribution upon Ewing for this terrible directive.

Bingham was true to his promise. He painted the well known painting, 'Martial Law,' or, 'Order No. 11,' depicting the horror and hardship of this order. So popular, he had a commission for a second copy. Both post-Civil War-era genre paintings hang in public galleries today. His first painting executed on a gingham table cloth, is prominently on display at the State Historical Society of Missouri in Columbia, Missouri. The second commission is property of the Cincinnati Art Museum.

After the war, General Thomas Ewing returned to the state of his birth. He was born in Lancaster, Ohio. Twice when Ewing tried for the nomination of governor of Ohio, Bingham supplied scathing letters, pamphlets and engravings of his painting to successively defeat Ewing.

Even after his death in 1879, Bingham's postmortem letter may have been the factor in the defeat of then Senator Ewing's bid for governor. Ewing was narrowly defeated in his bid for the governorship of Ohio in 1880.

Ewing lost that election by less than three per cent of the vote. Whether Order No. 11 adversely affected the outcome of that election has been debated without resolution, but the well-known painting "General Order No. 11" by George Caleb Bingham was widely disseminated throughout the state during the campaign against Ewing.

Martial Law (or, Order No. 11) by George Caleb Bingham
The above is an engraving based on Bingham's original, 56" x 78" oil painting executed on a stretched gingham table cloth; today it is at the State Historical Society of Missouri, Columbia, Missouri.

George C. Bingham painted this, one of two extant renditions (the second copy is in the Cincinnati Art Museum), in his studio at his Jackson County residence in 1868 or 1869 to show, "*the desolation of the border counties of Missouri, during the enforcement of military orders, issued by Brigadier General Ewing, of the Union Army, from his Head Quarters, Kansas City, Augt. 25th 1863.*"

Many engravings of this painting were made and widely distributed throughout the United States. The painting itself was also displayed and circulated around Ohio when used later against Thomas Ewing during his election campaign for governor of Ohio.

Some Jackson County residents blamed Quantrill for bringing the wrath of the Union down on the people. However Order No. 11 did little to change the loyalties of the majority of the guerrilla sympathizers. It did little to stop the activities of the guerrillas. The main reason the border quieted down was that the guerrillas either went south for the winter or moved the location of their raiding interests to other parts of the state, probably in anticipation of the 1864 invasion by the Confederate troops under General Sterling Price. The lessening of guerrilla activity in the border region, lead to Order No. 20, issued on 20 November 1863, which partly rescinded Order No. 11 by allowing the banished to return, if they could prove their loyalty to the Union and find shelter and a way to make a living off the burned landscape. Of course proving one's loyalty was very difficult especially if former neighbors were vindictive. Very few exiles returned immediately, and some never returned at all. Those that did return had to rebuild and replant without any government assistance or protection.

Exactly where Kate went during Order No. 11 is not documented. Her parents and siblings initially fled into Lafayette County, Missouri, before eventually removing to California.

Kate did not go with her parents; but, remained with Quantrill.

In August of 1870, her parents; brother, Francis Marion King (with his wife); unmarried brother, Samuel Robert King; and, married sister, Martha Jane (King) Ragland, were all living near Auburn, Placer County, California. The families all returned to Jackson County, Missouri, before the 1880 Federal census. The location of Kate's brother, William Jasper King, in 1870 has never been ascertained.

Kate was living in St. Louis, Missouri, under her alias, 'Kate Clarke,' in 1870, and was there as early as October 1863. Apparently, Kate fled to St. Louis to escape the consequences of Order No. 11.

According to Schultz, Kate joined Quantrill in September of 1863—giving no indication of her location before joining him—staying in a one-room log cabin with George Todd and his mistress in their temporary camp on the Stanley farm near Blue Springs in Jackson County, Missouri.[110] The women were sent away to an unspecified place when Union patrols were reported to be approaching. Rather than fight, the guerrillas moved to the Dillingham farm, southwest of Blue Springs, for a more concealed hiding place.

Soon thereafter, it became time for the guerrillas to leave Missouri and head for Texas.[111] When the trees dropped their leaves there was no longer adequate cover in Missouri to avoid detection by the Federal troops. In addition, life in Texas was much easier without the danger of military pursuit and armed clashes. Furthermore, food was plentiful and the climate, both atmospheric and political, was much friendlier to the guerrillas.

Some speculate that Kate went to Texas with Quantrill for the winter, as was the usual practice of some of the guerrillas to take their wives and children with them. However, according to Schultz, Kate only met with the guerrilla leader to say, "Goodbye," before his departure. Kate intended to spend the winter with her parents and rejoin Quantrill after his return in the spring. There is no documentation for this statement by Schultz, who accepted the marriage of Kate and Quantrill as legitimate. He indexed 'Kate King' under 'Kate Quantrill.' If Kate had planned to spend the winter with her parents, it would imply that:

1) Robert L. King had a definite place to stay for the winter after Order No. 11 was instituted and his home was burned, which he did not;

2) Kate had reconciled with her parents after defying them and running away (it was unknown when, or if, her parents forgave her); and,

3) Kate's return would be accepted by her parent's friends and neighbors after ruining her reputation by running off with Quantrill, and that was not the case.

Kate never mentioned going to Texas, and her presence there has not been mentioned by other Quantrill scholars, even recently by Petersen.

Where was Kate during the winter of 1863/1864? Perhaps that was when she first went to St. Louis.[112] A signed statement by 'Kate Clark,' presented before the Provost Marshal in St. Louis on 13 October 1863, disclosed that she resided on Sixth Street near Green, but would be moving very soon, "perhaps tomorrow."[113]

She was identified as the landlady of another female witness in the case of a Union prisoner, Robert Louden. Mr. Louden, a known Confederate mail runner and an accused 'boat burner', had been arrested at Kate's bawdy house six weeks earlier. Based on this case and considering Kate's past and future associations with various "underworlds," Whites suggested that Kate may have been active in the Confederate underground:

> "Precisely because of their marginal public standing, prostitutes like Kate Clark could cover the disloyal activities of southern sympathizers in St. Louis during the war."[114]

A house of prostitution would have a great many men from all walks of life coming and going frequently at all hours of the day or night. It would provide multiple opportunities for the exchange of information between individuals without arousing suspicion or undue attention of the authorities.

Kate went to St. Louis whether Quantrill took her, or sent her, either by herself or with someone else. Moreover, it has never been determined with whom or where exactly she stayed initially. It is obvious that she would have associated with, and been accommodated by people sympathetic to the southern cause. And, even while St. Louis was under Federal control, there were many supporters of the Confederacy in the city before, during, and after the Civil War.[115]

According to Petersen, the guerrillas gathered on 10 September 1863, at Perdee's farm to begin their retreat to Texas. According to Schultz, Quantrill left Perdee's place with about 400 men on October 1. Quantrill was definitely in Sherman, Grayson County, Texas, by late October 1863.[116]

In 1860, 20 per cent of the population of Grayson County was from Missouri, most having arrived within the previous two years. Petersen recorded Quantrill's active participation, at the request of the Confederate military there, to maintain local order, round up deserters and repel at least two invasions of northern Texas by Union forces.

If Kate had accompanied the guerrillas to Sherman, Texas, she would have been housed in the town, as were the other wives and families of the few married guerrillas.

The single men of the command were required to camp at Georgetown about fifteen miles north of Sherman, south of the Red River. Many of the men from Missouri knew friends or had relatives living in Grayson County so there was news from home and people to visit. Kate also had friends and relatives in this county, as well.

Ephraim Snodgrass, a brother of Kate's sister-in-law, America Jane (Snodgrass) King, wrote a letter home to Missouri from Sherman, Texas, on 26 February 1873, a decade after Quantrill was in Sherman, Texas. In the winter of 1863, Ephraim Snodgrass was in the Confederate Army. The significance of the letter was that Kate knew other southern sympathizers, apart from the guerrillas, who had connections to Sherman, Texas. Life in Sherman was easy with plenty of social activities, including dances in various homes, church services at either of two churches, monthly market day, or horse races at the track established by Quantrill and Jim Chiles.

During the winter of 1863-64, Quantrill lost his control over the entire band of guerrillas. For whatever reason, the group splintered into smaller bands, each under a different leader. Various authors have described differing scenarios with varying motives and conflicting interpretations of the events leading up to and causing Quantrill to be usurped and the band divided into smaller factions.

However, none of the events seemed to involve Kate directly. And, apparently none touched on her relationship with Quantrill. The small band that remained with Quantrill headed north out of Texas around the first part of April 1864. Due to weather delays and other factors the group did not arrive in Jackson County, Missouri, until 22 April 1864. The families of the other guerrillas remained in Texas:

> "Their families remained here out of necessity for food and shelter, their homes in Missouri having been destroyed in 1863 when several counties were depopulated."[117]

KATE IN FACT AND FICTION

Kate could not return home to her family at this point. The status of her relationship with her family at this time remained uncertain. But, even if they had reconciled the discord of her defiance and departure, her parents had been banished from Jackson County and their buildings burned. Thus, there was no home for Kate to return. If Kate had been with Quantrill, she would have stayed wherever they set-up camp.

However, it is most likely that Kate was in St. Louis, and while awaiting Quantrill's return from Texas, had become engaged in a career of prostitution.

Because of the increased number of Union troops and expansion of patrols in Jackson County, the guerrillas were under constant harassment. General Thomas Ewing had been reassigned to St. Louis and replaced as commander of the Border District by General Egbert B. Brown of the Missouri State Militia. Besides the greatly increased numbers of soldiers, General Brown added pressure on the guerrillas with troops from Colorado which were much better trained than the poorly prepared Kansas troops previously deployed.

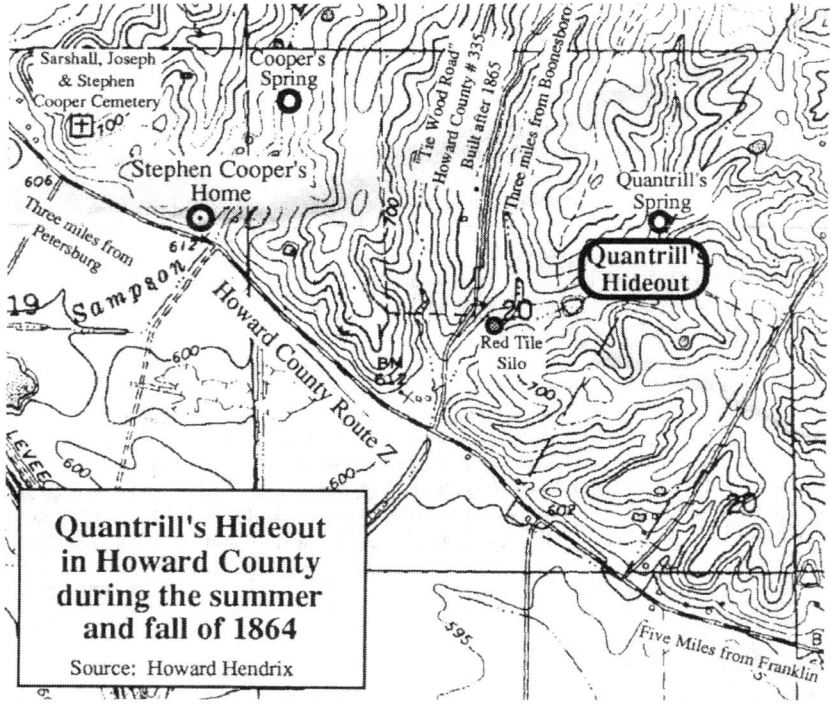

Quantrill's Hideout in Howard County during the summer and fall of 1864
Source: Howard Hendrix

Kate's Life With Quantrill

At the end of May 1864, Quantrill left his band after a disagreement with George Todd, and he reportedly spent the rest of the summer in Howard County, Missouri.[118] There, Quantrill and Kate supposedly lived together in a tent camp in the Howard County countryside.

This was a relatively peaceful respite for the couple. Kate cooked in an attached, shanty kitchen. And, she also learned to smoke a pipe. She and Quantrill spent many quiet, contented hours together. There were reports that Quantrill was ill or recovering from old wounds during this interval. There was a suggestion that he had two of his wisdom teeth removed about that time. Without concrete evidence, Kate appears to have been living in St. Louis; but, may have spent at least part of the summer of 1864 with Quantrill to nurse his wounds and assist in his recovery to health.[119]

At the end of September, Quantrill was well enough to join his small corps of men to merge forces with other guerrilla units for a major assault on a Federal installation in Fayette County, Missouri. On 20 September 1864, a large band of guerrillas, lead by 'Bloody Bill' Anderson, charged a blockhouse resulting in a disastrous defeat. After this fiasco, the large gang again broke-up into individually led units. Quantrill returned to his base camp near Boonesboro, Howard County, Missouri, and from there he engaged in several smaller isolated skirmishes.

The end of October 1864 marked the end of both the Confederacy and the reign of the guerrillas in Missouri. General Sterling Price, commander of the Confederate Army in Missouri, had met with Quantrill, Todd, and Anderson and ordered them to destroy railroads to prevent Federal reinforcements arriving from St. Louis before his invasion into Missouri.

Quantrill was also involved with an action against Federal troops on 15 October in Glasgow, a small town in Howard County, Missouri. While in Glasgow, Quantrill confiscated $21,000 from the bank.

Within a week, events began to deteriorate in rapid succession.

KATE IN FACT AND FICTION

First, George Todd was killed in Independence in Jackson County, Missouri, on 21 October.

Then, General Price was defeated at the Battle of Westport in Jackson County on 23 October.[120]

Finally, 'Bloody Bill' Anderson was killed in Richmond, Ray County, Missouri, on 26 October.

The long friendship and mutual esteem between Quantrill and Todd had deteriorated and dissipated into animosity and hostility by this time. Yet, Quantrill must have felt some remorse at the death of his former friend and colleague, in contrast to the, "feeling of grim satisfaction," attributed to him by Albert Castel. Surely, Kate must have felt the loss, as she had known Todd since childhood, and had the closest association with him of any of Quantrill's coterie.

The defeat at Westport ended Confederate action in Missouri, as the rebel forces were pushed back into Arkansas. On 8 November 1864, General Price began the retreat of his remaining troops into Texas.

Quantrill decided to go to Virginia with others to join General Lee's army, hoping to surrender with better terms at the end of the war as soldiers. They knew if they surrendered in Missouri they would be shot as outlaws. Quantrill left Missouri and headed south on 13 November 1864.

Kate was in St. Louis by the end of October before Quantrill left:

> "Toward the end of October, Quantrill said good-bye to **Kate, who would remain in St. Louis**, and returned to the Sni-a-Bar region, where he had planned his past successes."[121]

Note that Schutz gave no indication of when Kate had arrived in St. Louis initially. She may have gone to St. Louis at least a year earlier.[122]

Quantrill did not get his small party of thirty-three men assembled to leave for Kentucky until early December, and did not cross the Mississippi River into Tennessee until the night of 1 January 1865.[123]

Kate was in St. Louis, supposedly at a boarding house—more likely operating a bawdy house—when she was notified that Quantrill had been severely wounded on 10 May 1865, at the farm of James H. Wakefield, located five miles south of Taylorsville in Spencer County, Kentucky. Quantrill was paralyzed from the bullet in his back and had been left at the Wakefield farm, under the assumed name of Captain Clarke, after bribing Edwin Terrill,[124] the man hired by the Federals to hunt down Quantrill dead or alive. While staying at the Wakefield home, Quantrill was visited by some of the men who had accompanied him to Kentucky. They had arrived ready to rescue him. But, Quantrill refused to leave to prevent repercussions from Terrill against James Wakefield, who had had vouched for Quantrill's promise that he would not leave.

Also, the doctor, Isaac McClasky, summoned by Wakefield, had already informed Quantrill that his wound was fatal.[125] It was during this time that Quantrill confided to Wakefield that the money he had left with a Mrs. Olivia D. Cooper of Missouri should be sent to his mother and sister in Dover, Ohio. This reference to his sister indicated that Quantrill was not aware that she had died in 1863, and provided evidence that he had not been in Ohio visiting his mother earlier during the summer as suggested by one author.

Two days later Terrill, having discovered that his captive was Quantrill, returned, loaded the wounded man into a wagon and transported him to a military prison infirmary in Louisville, Jefferson County, Kentucky. Finally, on 13 May 1865, Quantrill arrived at the prison in Louisville, and was transferred into official military custody.

While he was in the infirmary, Father Michael Power, a priest called from Louisville, converted Quantrill to Catholicism and administered the last rites.[126] Quantrill requested Father Power to contact Mrs. Olivia Cooper in order that some of the money she held for Quantrill should be given to the priest to buy a cemetery plot and a headstone for Quantrill. The rest of the money was to be given to Kate King.[127] Apparently, Cooper had relocated to Spencer County, Kentucky, from Jackson County, Missouri, during Order No. 11.[128]

KATE IN FACT AND FICTION

On 6 June 1865, twenty-seven days after being shot in the back and paralyzed from the shoulders down, William Clarke Quantrill died.[129]

Father Michael Power did purchase a cemetery plot in what was then St. Mary's Cemetery;[130] but, he did not erect a tombstone as per Quantrill's deathbed request. Instead, fearing grave robbers, Father Power instructed the sexton, Patrick Shelly, and his wife, Bridget,[131] who were present at the burial, to completely obscure the grave which was only 10 paces from their cottage so it could be vigilantly guarded against disruption.[132]

The irony of Power's precautions was that Quantrill's remains were disinterred by his own mother within a dozen years of his burial. On December 7, 1887, "Mrs. Quantrill persuaded Bridget Shelly, who upon her husband's death had replaced him as sexton, to allow the grave to be opened ...."[133] W. W. Scott then paid to have the grave dug up the next day.[134] Another irony is that the grave of the most notorious Confederate guerrilla Quantrill was 'safeguarded' by a former Union soldier. Patrick Shelly was in Co. G, 15th Kentucky Infantry, and had applied for (on 1 April 1872) and received a pension. Bridget applied for (on 7 July 1885) and received a widow's pension.

Many reports of Quantrill surviving his wound, subsequent escape, and assumption of another secret identity began immediately after his death and continues today. All such published reports have proven to be undocumented.[135] Kate claimed she had rushed to his bedside three days before his death (*i.e.*, arriving on 3 June) and was present, "as he breathed his last." Kate had become a widow at the age of 17.

If Kate were present at Quantrill's death bed, she would have stayed in Louisville to be at his graveside as well. No date has been recorded for Quantrill's burial, which would have occurred as soon after his death (on June 6) as the necessary arrangements could be made by Father Power.

Only a very small group of people gathered mere steps from the sexton's cottage at (then) St. Mary's Cemetery for the somber, clandestine, internment into a hastily dug grave. Those reported to be present at this graveside service were the

Catholic priest, Father Power; sexton, Patrick Shelly, and his wife, Bridget Enright Shelly; and, undertaker, John C. King, who had supplied the coffin and presumably the embalming.[136]

Quantrill's Original Gravesite in Kentucky

The original, unmarked, partially empty grave of William Clarke Quantrill is just inside the gate (above), to the left, in Lot 624. This gate faces Duncan Street today (2014). But, at the time of Quantrill's 1865 death, this was the location near the caretaker or sexton's house; the main entrance was off present-day 26th Street to the north. Below: Kate likely stood before Quantrill's open grave. His clandestine internment took place in middle foreground of this image. Images courtesy Max McCoy.

In addition to Kate—who only claimed to be at her husband's bed side and never his graveside—there were, perhaps, one or two other men and women who supported the guerrilla cause, were in Louisville, and knew of Quantrill's demise.[137]

The absence of public awareness of Quantrill's capture and subsequent death, coupled with the earlier deaths of Quantrill's men and the surrender of his surviving companions, plus the need for secrecy demonstrated by Father Power, insured that the number of attendees would be very small. Due to the priest's concerns, the burial may have occurred at night under the cover of darkness. Perhaps the gravedigger(s) or other cemetery or undertaker employees observed the lowering of the coffin before they hurriedly filled in the unmarked grave. No one other than the four first named attendees ever claimed to have witnessed the initial burial of William Clarke Quantrill.

Some time later, there were at least three women who claimed to have been with Quantrill just before, or at his death:

1) Olivia Cooper, who had been banished from Missouri and was reported by McCorkle to have been in Kentucky then;[138]

2) Mrs. Neville Ross, who had also been banished by Order No. 11, and whose son was with Quantrill in Kentucky;[139] and,

3) Kate, who later claimed she had been there.

The four weeks between Quantrill's capture and his death was certainly an adequate interval for Kate to travel from St. Louis to Louisville. More than one antagonistic author has implied that Kate's visit to Quantrill's death bed was the reason she received the bequest of the money rather than his poor mother, implying the beautiful young woman beguiled a dying man to change his mind. Certainly, it should be noted here that a wife's right to inheritance from her husband took legal precedence over that of his mother.

However, it is peculiar that Quantrill never sent for his mother, nor at least notified her of his impending death. His mother could have reached Louisville as quickly and as easily from Ohio as Kate did from St. Louis. In 1900, Mrs. Quantrill claimed that she did not learn of her son's death (and his money) until 10 years after the war.[140]

It's certainly possible that more than one woman visited Quantrill during his incarceration at the infirmary in Louisville. There was no log kept to document his visitors; no reporters were sent to interview him; and, there was no suggestion that he left a written record of any kind.

Only the Catholic priest who listened to and received Quantrill's last confession might have heard truths that many seek today. Father Michael Power, however, never broke his vow of the covenant of that confessional. He took to his grave 14 years later the burdens of many whom he had ushered to the other side, including Quantrill's likely deathbed confession.[141]

It also seems strange that Quantrill's mother, Caroline C. Quantrill, who in her later years was desperate for money for her very subsistence, did not contact Kate to inquire of her son's money, especially to see if any might be left for her benefit. Perhaps Mrs. Caroline C. Quantrill was never aware, and she certainly never acknowledged, that her son, William Clarke Quantrill, left a widow.

Mrs. Quantrill, at age 69, visited Kate's hometown community of Blue Springs, Missouri, on 11 May 1888, and, "remained in Jackson County for some time," through the spring 1889. She visited at the invitation of former members of Quantrill's men, who sent her a railroad ticket. Her desire, or so she said, was to learn about her "lost son." She may also have sought to solve the mystery behind some of her son's money.[142]

While in Jackson County, Mrs. Quantrill expressed her dissatisfaction with another daughter-in-law (the widow of her son, Franklin), and confronted Mrs. Olivia D. Cooper regarding $800 her son had given to Mrs. Cooper before he died in Kentucky.[143]

The notion that Mrs. Cooper was visited by Quantrill in Spencer County, Kentucky, before he was shot, and gave her money to hold for him was given validity when Mrs. Cooper admitted to Caroline Quantrill in 1888 that, yes, she had had the money; but, had given it to Kate King and the priest.[144]

This strongly suggests that no one in Missouri knew the whereabouts of Kate in 1888. If Kate's location were general knowledge, Mrs. Quantrill probably would have sought her out to ask for money.

Even though Kate claimed to be at his side on his death bed, she later denied that Quantrill ever gave her any money or loot from the Lawrence raid. Various reports claimed that she had received either money, jewels or loot from Quantrill, which she used to open either a boarding house or brothel in St. Louis.

The newspaper reporter in 1926 disclosed that Kate had related that one of Quantrill's men gave Quantrill some of the jewelry he had plundered during their return from Lawrence and, that "Quantrill gave Kate seven diamond rings, three pins and four sets of earrings."[145]

This information obviously came directly from the Kansas City Star article on 23 May 1926, which listed the same jewelry "out of the loot" that "Quantrill gave his bride." Fred Ford wrote in his letter to Velma West Sykes on 22 May 1970, that, "Kate said she sold the jewelry Q. gave her from the Lawrence raid," and used that money to rebuild her parent's home after the war. However, Kate denied that she received any jewels or loot from Lawrence.

However, there would be much less blood on the bank funds than on any items from the Lawrence raid. If Kate received money from Quantrill in Kentucky, it would most likely be part of the cash from the $21,000 stolen from the bank in Glasgow, Missouri and not jewelry or other loot from Lawrence, Kansas. If Kate, indeed, received money; but, sought to conceal that truth, her statement rings truthful on the surface because the money would have technically been given to her by Mrs. Cooper. Technically, if Mrs. Cooper turned any money over to Kate, she had not received it directly from Quantrill. Various authors who mention the amount of money described it as being between $800[146] and $4,000.[147]

Kate's Life With Quantrill

In retrospect, it would appear that Kate, despite her denials, did benefit financially either from the spoils of the looting of Lawrence or conceivably whatever cash Quantrill had left with Mrs. Cooper for safe keeping. While her family would have preferred that she opened a boarding house—and perhaps she did much later—Kate did indeed become a well-known madam of one of the two finest 'houses' in St. Louis. The source of her initial investment for this business venture was either the cash she received from Quantrill's death bequest and/or the jewels she received from Quantrill after the Lawrence Raid.

Perhaps Kate ended her "sea of troubles" and used those "slings and arrows of outrageous fortunes" to establish her house of 'social evil' as a surrogate monument for the tombstone that Quantrill had requested on his deathbed.[148]

KATE IN FACT AND FICTION

CHAPTER 5

That 'Other Woman' – Naughty Nancy

*"Ships that pass in the night, and speak each other in passing
only a signal shown, and a distant voice in the darkness;
So on the ocean of life, we pass and speak one another,
only a look and a voice and then darkness again and a silence."*
Henry Wadsworth Longfellow

The handsome and charming William Clarke Quantrill was, not surprisingly, a "ladies man" and rumored to be involved with many women prior to his liaison with Kate King, later known as Kate Clarke. While most were like 'ships passing in the night,' Nancy, also known as Anna Walker, requires additional exploration as the 'other woman' because she has been misconstrued and confused with Kate.

First, Nancy Walker's family was instrumental with Quantrill's presence in Jackson County, Missouri.

'Anna' Walker was born as Nancy Elizabeth Walker in Jackson County, Missouri, on 17 January 1841. She was the youngest of the eleven children of James 'Morgan' Walker and 'Polly' Mary (Cox) Morgan. Other children in the family included her brothers John Riley Walker, Andrew Jackson Walker, and Zachariah Taylor Walker, who would all later ride with Quantrill.[149] Seven-year-old Nancy was with her parents in the census in Blue Township, Jackson County, Missouri, on 31 August 1850.

Nancy's father, James Morgan Walker, usually identified as either James M., or, Morgan Walker, came to Jackson County, Missouri, from Kentucky and had settled in the adjacent section which Kate's family later occupied. As close neighbors, there is no doubt that Kate knew most, if not all, of the Walker children, although she was seven years younger than 'Anna' Nancy Walker.[150]

Morgan Walker

In 1860, the elderly Morgan Walker was a wealthy landowner (about 1,800 acres valued at $37,500), farmer and slave holder (25 slaves which contributed to his personal property valued at $26,500, along with $35,100 in livestock listed as 25 horses, 48 mules, 13 oxen and 35 cows he owned). Thus, it was not surprising that the Walker farm was targeted for a raid, supposedly to free slaves, by a group of Kansas ruffian abolitionists. However, one member of that group, William Clarke Quantrill, betrayed his five companions when he approached John Riley Walker to warn him of the planned raid on the elder Walker's farm. John Riley Walker took Quantrill to his father. Together, they planned an ambush for the raiding party. Quantrill returned to the band of Kansas bandits that night and led them into the ambush on the farm of Morgan Walker on 10 December 1860. This signaled the beginning of Quantrill's reputation as a bushwhacker, established a lasting friendship between him and Andrew J. Walker, and marked the end of Quantrill's days as an abolitionist.

Connelley suggested in 1910 that Quantrill had actually planned the Morgan raid to win the heart of 'Anna' Nancy Walker . . . and her future inheritance of land and slaves.[151] Considering recent research superimposed upon the actual time line of historical events, this suggestion was either pure romantic fluff, or part of the design to discredit Quantrill or anyone associated with him, particularly women. Quantrill might have met Nancy when he was taken to the home of

Morgan Walker by John Riley Walker on the day of the ambush, but the raid was obviously planned well before Quantrill even knew Nancy.

Nancy Walker married 'Riley' William Ryland Slaughter on June 11, 1857, in Jackson County, Missouri.[152] Riley Slaughter, born 25 April 1837, was the son of Josiah and Elizabeth (Koger) Slaughter of Virginia. Both early pioneer families were well-established and well-respected in Jackson County.[153]

Connelley indicated that Nancy Walker was a "fine looking woman," beautiful except for a crooked nose, and with a good figure. A period photograph, currently posted on Ancestry.com and purported to be Nancy Walker, showed no indication of a crooked nose; and if the photo were correctly identified, it illustrates another example of Connelley's negative bias against women associated with Quantrill.

Nancy Walker, identified as Nancy Slaughter, was named in the probate record of her brother, Collins Walker, on 26 January 1858. In the census on 6 July 1860, nineteen-year-old Nancy was with W. R. Slaughter in Sni-a-Bar Township, Jackson County, Missouri. Her husband was a 23-year-old merchant and they had two young children – a two-year-old daughter Sydney Susan (apparently named after Nancy's brother Sidney Clay Walker) and a month-old son Josiah (named after Riley's father). Their young family disintegrated after Riley discovered Nancy's infidelity with a doctor who was boarding with the Slaughters. This indiscretion earned her the moniker 'Naughty Nancy' amongst present-day Jackson County family researchers.[154] Riley immediately divorced his wife, and she returned to the home of her father a short time before the raid on the Morgan Walker farm. Thus, Quantrill would have met Nancy in December 1860, if not before.

Apparently the two Slaughter children went with their mother when she was sent back to her parents. By 1870, 'Riley' William Ryland Slaughter had moved to Chariton County in central Missouri. With two counties between him and his past, he had become a farmer and married the widow, Mary Elizabeth Rudisaile Welker. Riley fathered four more children with his second wife; but, only one daughter, Florence

Elizabeth Slaughter, survived beyond 1910. His second wife, Mary Elizabeth, died in Salisbury, Chariton County, Missouri, on 11 September 1911. Riley married a third wife, Susan E. Thomas Winn, who died 23 February 1926, three years after 'Riley' William Ryland Slaughter died on 18 March 1923. Neither his obituary nor his own life story which he wrote in June 1921, mentioned his marriage to Nancy Walker. Apparently the injured spouse successfully moved on with his life after Nancy did him wrong.

Nancy's behavior did not improve after her divorce. According to Connelley, she took several lovers, including William Clarke Quantrill and George M. Todd, one of Quantrill's captains. In April 1862, she married Joe Vaughn, another Jackson County bushwhacker who also rode with Quantrill for about a year.[155] This was the same Joseph Vaughn mentioned in *Branded as Rebels*, compiled by Joanne C. Eakin and Donald R. Hale, in 1993, except that Joseph G. Vaughn who married Nancy Walker was not killed at the Battle of Pea Ridge, a pivotal battle that saved Missouri for the Union, in March 1862. The marriage of Joe and Nancy occurred after the Battle of Pea Ridge was fought. Nor was he the Joseph L. Vaughn who later claimed to be Frank James living under an alias.

Joseph G. Vaughn was born 5 August 1839, in Sni-a-Bar Township in Jackson County, Missouri, to Albert Vaughn and Minerva Gibson. It is likely that Joe's middle initial 'G.' was for Gibson, his mother's maiden name. Joe's son, Samuel, born in 1886, was given the middle name Gibson. Joe was the second born and second son of eight known children. In 1845, the family moved to Buchanan County, Missouri, where they were living in Bloomington Township in the 1850 census. Joe returned to Jackson County, Missouri, in 1855, with his parents.[156] On 21 July 1860, Joe was 20 years old and living with his parents in Fort Osage Township in Jackson County, Missouri.

The period between this census and his marriage to Nancy Walker was when he rode with the guerrilla band of Quantrill. Following their marriage, Joe and Nancy moved away from Jackson County to somewhere north of the Missouri

River, probably to Clay County, until the end of the Civil War. Joe was never with Quantrill again, nor with the Confederacy after his marriage. The marriage date of April 1862, quoted by Connelley, has not been confirmed by any Missouri marriage record. There is no record of their marriage in Jackson County. However, Nancy was named in her father's probate record, as Nancy Vaughn, on 12 September 1866. A daughter Marie Vaughn, believed to be born about 1863, received a child's share in the probate of James M. Walker. Marie Vaughn probably died young as no further record of this child has been found. After Nancy sold the land she inherited from her father, she sent Joe packing and supposedly moved to Baxter Springs, Kansas, and set-up a bawdy house.[157]

Joseph G. Vaughn married second Sarah Belle Harris, daughter of James 'William' and Nannie (Henry) Harris, in Jackson County, Missouri, on 14 December 1870. Joe and Sarah produced at least nine children, of whom seven were still living in 1900 and 1910. Joe became a successful, but roving dairyman farmer. He was in Grain Valley, Jackson County, Missouri, on 11 Nov 1871 (birth of daughter Josephine); in Kansas in 1884 and 1886 (birth of daughter, Stella Elizabeth, and son, Samuel Gibson, respectively); back in Grain Valley, Jackson County, Missouri, on 21 November 1891 (birth of daughter, Elsie); in Sni-a-Bar Township, Lafayette County, Missouri, on 14 January 1900 (Federal census); and, in Jackson Township, Johnson County, Missouri, on 27 April 1910 (Federal census). Neither he nor his wife Sarah was located on a census in 1920, nor was a Missouri Death Certificate located between 1910 and 1963. They presumably died and were buried somewhere beyond the state of Missouri. Three of their married daughters moved respectively to Montana, Washington and Kansas. Apparently, another injured spouse successfully moved on with his life after "Naughty Nancy" did him wrong.

Whether Nancy Walker ever owned or operated a bawdy house in Baxter Springs, Cherokee County, Kansas, has not been documented. The original reference to Nancy as a madam in a house of prostitution was in a letter from 'Fletch' Charles Fletcher Taylor to Connelley. Nancy Walker, referred to as Anna Walker by Taylor and Connelley, was said to have

KATE IN FACT AND FICTION

opened a house of prostitution in Baxter Springs, Kansas, after she sold the land inherited from her father and sent Joe Vaughn away. Fletch Taylor was a captain in Quantrill's command who had an active part in many of the escapades of the guerrilla band. On 8 August 1864, Fletch's right arm was amputated to save his life after he was badly wounded. He survived the war, served in the Missouri State Legislature and then went to California, where he died in 1912. Eakin and Hale reported that Charles Fletcher Taylor died "between August 1916 and August 1917."[158] As with many of the guerrillas who rode with Quantrill and survived after the war to record their memories, Fletch recorded information after the fact adjusted according to the filter of his best recollections. Then, William E. Connelley added his own perspective on the story when he wrote his book on Quantrill in 1910. Many authors have since repeated statements regarding both Kate and Nancy Walker as fact. It should be noted that Connelley had nothing good to say about any woman associated with Quantrill. He believed all women associated with Quantrill were, or became prostitutes.

To date, there is no evidence that Nancy Walker was ever in Baxter Springs, Cherokee County, Kansas. Fred Ford noted in a letter in 1962 that Nancy "then moved to Baxter Springs, Kansas and did wrong" there.[159] Whether Fred was repeating what Connelley wrote in his book, or if he had another source was not stated; but, Fred had read Connelley's book. There was no evidence that Fred had any direct knowledge of Nancy's occupation or location.

Unfortunately, there was no record of her whereabouts in any document except the 1860 Federal census where she was listed with her first husband, W. R. Slaughter, in Jackson County, Missouri. She was named in her father's probate (as Nancy Vaughn on 12 September 1866) and her mother's will (as Nancy C. Wood on 23 October 1866) in Jackson County, but neither document indicated where she was living at the time.

Her daughter, Sydney Susan Slaughter, identified as "Sidea S. Slauter," in Missouri marriage records, married Samuel J. Lane, on 14 January 1877, in Jasper County, Missouri. Although it was tempting to assume that Sydney, at age about 19, would be living at home with her mother and both were living in Jasper County in 1877, there was no conclusive evidence to support either supposition. Nancy's son, Josiah Slaughter, was reported to have died on 27 October 1881 in Galena, Cherokee County, Kansas.[160]

A biography of David D. Wood in the 1883 *History of Jasper County, Missouri,* mentioned his wife as Mrs. Nancy Slaughter and that:

> "Mrs. Wood was previously married to a Mr. Walker, who deserted her with two children to raise, Sidney and Josiah, who died Oct. 27, 1881, and was buried at Galena, Kan., being twenty-two years old May 9, 1882."[161]

Note Nancy's maiden and married names were reversed and the course of events was 'whitewashed' in her favor, but enough details were provided to indicate that this was, indeed, the same Nancy Walker. This was not evidence that either Josiah or his mother were residents of Cherokee County, Kansas in 1881. Jasper County, Missouri and Cherokee County, Kansas, are adjacent to each other; and, Cherokee County adjoins the northeast corner of Oklahoma. (See Western Missouri / Eastern Kansas map on page 44.)

It was reasonable to assume that Nancy may have been in this general vicinity around 1880. However neither she nor her children have been located in the 1870 or 1880 Federal census nor in any state census around this time.

Careful analysis of 'Fletch' Charles Fletcher Taylor's original letter also indicated a case of switched identities regarding whether Kate or Nancy married a man named D. Wood. Fletch mentioned both Kate and Anna Walker in the same sentence and then used the pronoun 'she' which confused Connelley enough for him to state, in error, that Kate had married a Mr. Wood.[162] It was Anna (*i.e.*, Nancy Walker), not Kate, who married Mr. Wood.

Nancy Walker Slaughter Vaughn married David Dansler Wood on 15 November 1871, but no location was listed.[163] As specified on their death certificates, three of the sons of Nancy and David were born in Missouri; it appears more likely that the parents were married in Missouri, but no marriage record has been found in Missouri records.

Nancy Walker Slaughter Vaughn Wood and David Dansler Wood had the following children:

1) Charles Alexander Wood, born 29 August 1871 in Missouri, was in Weatherford, Parker County, Texas, per Federal census, on 9 June 1900, 28 January 1920, and 18 April 1930, where he died at 61 years, 1 month, and 6 days on 5 October 1932. He married 'Dora' Eudora Frances Andrews on 20 March 1892 and they had six children, all born in Texas.

2) Benjamin F. Wood, born about 1873, died young;[164]

3) Lonzo Wood, born about 1875, died young;[165]

4) 'Dee/Doc/Dock' Dansler Ocho Wood, born 18 September 1876 in Missouri, was in Palo Pinto County, Texas, per Federal census on 10 May 1910, 8 January 1920 and 21 April 1930. He registered for the draft in World War I, at age 47, on 12 September 1918, in Mingus, Palo Pinto County, Texas. He and his wife 'Fannie' Frances Jones were the parents of four daughters. Dansler Ocho Wood died at Mineral Springs in Palo Pinto County, Texas at 82 years, 8 months and 10 days; his death certificate indicated that he was the son of Dane Wood and Nancy Walker.

5) 'Lon' Bess Lonzo W. Wood, born 18 Jan 1880 in Missouri, was in Hill County, Texas, per Federal and state census, on 5 May 1910, 19 January 1920, 2 April 1930, 1935 and 25 April 1940. He registered for the draft in World War I at age 39, as Lonzo Woods, on 12 September 1918. He married 'Monie' Mona Belle Low on 17 July 1904 and they had 10 children. 'Lon' Bess Lonzo W. Wood died in Terrill State Hospital in Kaufman County, Texas, on 23 May 1958; his death certificate listed his parents as Dansler Wood and Mary Elizabeth Walker.

That 'Other Woman'

David Dansler Wood was enumerated in the Federal census in Parker County, Texas, on 15 June 1900, as D. Wood, age 50, widower, living alone. He died on 8 June 1905 in Weatherford in Parker County, Texas. He was buried in Spring Creek Cemetery in Weatherford next to Nancy, whose tombstone indicated she died in 1894.

Thus, the final days of Nancy were as anonymous and ambiguous as those of Kate.

However, the gossip of Nancy's association with Quantrill continued through her granddaughter, a daughter of her daughter, Sydney Slaughter Lane, who was rumored to be Quantrill's granddaughter. Nancy's daughter Sydney was born at least two years before Quantrill could have met Nancy. The rumor that William Clarke Quantrill sired a child with Nancy had no more basis of truth than any of the other unfounded claims of William Clarke Quantrill's paternity.

Although Sydney Slaughter Lane eluded the census takers in 1870 and 1880, it was recorded on the 1900 Federal census that her two daughters were both born in Missouri. On 1 June 1900, the widowed, 50-year-old farmer, S. J. (Samuel J.) Lane, was in Cockrell Township in Chariton County, Missouri, with his daughters, 18-year-old Lula, and six-year-old, Veda (Viola Pearl). With such large intervals between Samuel and Sydney's marriage in 1877, and the birth of their first daughter in 1882, and then the more than a dozen years between the births of the two daughters, there logically could be additional children that may or may not have survived childhood. The only verification of Sydney's fate was a notice which appeared in the *Press Spectator,* in Salisbury, Chariton County, Missouri:

Gone to Rest

Mrs. Sam Lain, who resided near Bynumville, died Wednesday morning of consumption after an illness of six months. Deceased was a good Christian woman, a member of the church, aged about 35 years, and besides a devoted husband, leaves two little girls and many friends. Funeral services were conducted on the following day by Rev. Hise at the McCurry schoolhouse after which remains were laid to rest in the cemetery at that place.[166]

Tragedy continued to stalk Samuel. It started when Samuel's father, Alexander, died when Samuel was only about eight years old. Samuel's mother Julia Ann Tucker was widowed a second time leaving her with six young children. Samuel was the oldest son. Julia Ann's first husband George Corby had died leaving her widowed with a very young daughter Mary Jane Corby born in 1845. Julia Ann then had had five more children born between 1847 and 1858 with Alexander Lane before he died.

On 30 November 1865, Julia Ann married for the third time, David M. Harlan, as his third wife. They had one child, Andrew Oliver Harlan, born 4 June 1868, before David M. died on 2 May 1869, leaving Julia Ann widowed for the third time. David M. Harlan, born about 1804 in Georgia, was one-quarter Cherokee and had been a Commissioner for the Cherokee Treaty in first Arkansas and later in Indian Territory. Julia Ann Tucker Corby Lane was his third wife.

Julia Ann's subsequent marriage, her fourth marriage, to James Monroe Potter ended in divorce because he would not work.

In 1869, when Samuel's step-father, David M. Harlan, died less than four years after his marriage to Samuel's mother, Samuel had not yet reached the age of majority; he was only 19 years old. With the death of his wife, Samuel was left with a teenage daughter and a two-year-old daughter to raise by himself.

Five years later, yet another tragedy for Samuel was reported in three installments in the local newspaper of Salisbury, Missouri:

> One of the saddest accidents that has happened in Hamden for many a year, happened Tuesday eve about 6 o'clock, Mr. Jeff Hammons and Lou Lane were returning from Keytesville where they had been married, and the hard rains of the north had swollen Bee Branch and they drove in the branch at the ford at the residence of Grandma Davis and the buggy was overturned and Mrs. Hammon and her little child were drowned. The bodies have not been recovered. We extend our sympathy to the bereaved ones.[167]

A SAD INCIDENT

> Tuesday Jeff Hammons and Lou Laine of near Hamden came to Salisbury to see A.W. Johnson in regard to the adoption of the woman's little son, aged 18 months. Mr. Johnson wasn't at home and they went on to Keytesville where they were married by Squire Wheeler and seeing Mr. Johnson over there told him they would be in Salisbury the following day to get out paper of adoption for the little boy. In going home from Keytesville they attempted to cross Bee Branch at the old ford near Hamden, but the stream was swollen from recent rain and soon after getting into the water the horses commenced to lunge, turned over the buggy and all were soon in the water. Mr. Hammon caught his wife three times, but finally she sank and he barely got out with his own life. The next morning the babe was found about a mile and a half below and in the afternoon the woman was found a half mile below. Dr. Jennings went up this morning to hold an inquest. There is a peculiar sadness about the accident and our sympathy is extended to all who are distressed.[168]

> In speaking of the death of Mrs. Jeff Hammond by drowning last week we stated that Coroner Jennings had gone to hold an inquest. He informs us that the verdict was accidental drowning and that there was no evidence of foul play, but rather tended to confirm the report that Mr. Hammond did all he could to save his wife and the little child.[169]

The death of his older daughter on her wedding day, as well as the death of his only grandchild, was misfortune piled onto calamity for Samuel. The news articles explained the tragic death of Lou/Lula but there was no clue regarding the father of her eighteen-month-old son. No record of a previous marriage has been found and it could well be that the child was born out of wedlock. The 1900 Federal census indicated that A. W. Johnson was a lawyer in Salisbury, Missouri and apparently was the lawyer chosen to handle the adoption of Lou/Lula's unnamed son by Jeff Hammons.

Jeff Hammons remarried about a year later in Randolph County, which is located immediately east of Chariton County, Missouri. Jeff and his wife Hattie Elizabeth McCart Smith were in the 1910 Federal census at Moberly, Randolph County, Missouri, with their three children plus her three Smith children. Jeff Hammons died 26 June 1955, and was buried in

Moberly, Randolph County, Missouri. His widow died a year later and was buried next to her husband.

The news articles about the drowning death on her wedding day, failed to mention Lou/Lula's father Samuel, who was presumably still in the area, although he was not located on the 1910 census. In the 1920 and 1930 Federal census, Samuel J. Lane was in Sni-a-Bar Township in Jackson County, Missouri, living with his married daughter Viola Pearl Lane Hall. Here he died on 20 November 1931 at 81 years, 9 months and 1 day of age. Samuel J. Lane was buried in Blue Springs Cemetery in Jackson County, Missouri and not beside his wife in McCurry Cemetery in Chariton County.

Viola Pearl Lane married Herbert Lee Hall on 27 February 1917, in Kansas City, Jackson County, Missouri, when she was 22 and he was 26. They lived their entire lives in Jackson County, Missouri, and died there less than three weeks apart; he died on 10 July 1981 and she died on 29 July 1981. They were buried in Blue Springs Cemetery in Jackson County, Missouri. They had no children.

The only survivor named in Viola's obituary was Kenneth Lumbley of Arcadia, Missouri, misidentified as her cousin.[170] It would be interesting to know if Viola knew of or associated with the Wood family connected with her maternal grandmother. Although she apparently had no contact or little association with the family of her paternal grandparent, 'Riley' William Ryland Slaughter, Viola and her husband, Herbert, were active supporters of the Slaughter Cemetery Association.[171]

Viola Pearl Lane Hall was rumored to be Quantrill's granddaughter, which implied that her mother, Sydney Susan Slaughter Lane, was the biological daughter of William Clarke Quantrill. Whether this was speculated by others or an actual claim made by someone was not documented; but, the story has no basis in fact. If a birth year of 1858 for Sydney were estimated from her age of two years on 6 July 1860, in the Federal census, with her mother and 'Riley' William Ryland Slaughter, then Sydney was conceived three years before Quantrill made his first appearance in Jackson County, Missouri, where Nancy Walker lived. Speculation that Viola

That 'Other Woman'

might be Quantrill's granddaughter was idle rumor, nasty hearsay, viscous gossip, or any combination thereof rather than a claim made personally by Viola. Viola was born a year after the death of Nancy Walker Slaughter Vaughn Wood, so she never knew her maternal grandmother, and she was only two-years-old when her mother died. Viola never heard any stories directly from either her mother or grandmother.

William Clarke Quantrill never had any children.

All claims of being a direct descendant of William Clarke Quantrill have been proven to be false.

However, two of the women most closely associated with Quantrill—Kate King and Nancy Walker—each left descendants . . . but, descendants fathered by other men.

Kate had a daughter born ten years after Quantrill died.

Nancy had children born before her affair with Quantrill, as well as children born after his death; but, she had no children with Quantrill. Nancy's affair with Quantrill left no offspring. In 1863, while waiting for his scouting party to return from Lawrence (just before the Lawrence, Kansas raid), Quantrill recounted events in his past, including his romance with Anna (*i.e.* Nancy) Walker.[172] This was during Quantrill's liaison with Kate. No wonder Kate and Nancy are historically confused, and persistent rumors still exist.

The ghost of Nancy Walker continues to wander in the shadow of Quantrill, and to haunt Kate long after all three ships have passed into the night.

KATE IN FACT AND FICTION

CHAPTER 6

Kate's St. Louis Years:
Social Evil and the Great Social Experiment

A girl has gotta do what a girl has gotta do.
[Paraphrased from: John Steinbeck (The Grapes of Wrath)
"Still, a man's got to do what a man's got to do."]
Can a city regulate the world's oldest profession?

Biographers of William Clarke Quantrill and historians of the Kansas/Missouri Border Conflict know that in 1863 he was involved with a young woman by the name of Kate King, later known as Kate Clarke. After Quantrill's murder in June 1865, this 17-year-old ex-consort of the notorious guerrilla leader managed to survive and thrive for another 65 years.

The interval between Quantrill's 1865 demise in Kentucky, and Kate's death in Jackson County, Missouri, in 1930, involved a lifetime of intrigue, scandal and mystery.

Steinbeck's original quote, "a man's got to do what a man's got to do," in *The Grapes of Wrath* referred to catching spiders. But, in Kate's case, it was finding a way to survive on her own in a large city. St. Louis was the fourth largest U.S. city in 1870. During the war, the Union Army controlled St. Louis and there had been no major battles to scar the city.[173] The capture of Camp Jackson in 1861[174] secured Federal authority within St. Louis. The Union Army controlled the city and it became a Federal stronghold.[175] During the war, southern sympathizers had to learn "to live under the watchful eye of the Provost Marshal's office, in a society dominated by Republican thinking."[176] The demand for goods during and after the war kept St. Louis prosperous and it became truly a 'land of opportunity' after the war. After the war, St. Louis was lavish and exciting—a good place for Kate to make a new home for herself. Between 1840 and 1870, the population of St.

KATE IN FACT AND FICTION

Louis increased almost 10 fold from 36,000 to 350,000 and much of this increase was young men. Thus, prostitution was a profitable business for women whose only other opportunities for making a living were as servant, seamstress, laundress or teacher[177]—none of which was near as lucrative as prostitution.[178]

Kate turned to prostitution to make a living as she sought an avenue for economic security. She had enough money to start a business. The 'boarding house' that Kate operated in St. Louis was actually a 'bawdy house.'

The first suggestion of Kate's presence in St. Louis was an unclaimed letter addressed to 'Kate Clark' at the Post Office on 15 August 1863.[179] Her first documented appearance was a statement signed 'Miss Kate Clark' on 13 October 1863.[180]

Kate was the landlady at Sixth Street near Green, of another female witness in the case of Robert Louden.[181] Louden, a known Confederate mail runner and accused 'boat burner' had been arrested at Kate's bawdy house six weeks earlier while visiting the witness. Based on this case and considering Kate's past and future associations with various 'underworlds,' it was suggested that Kate was active in the Confederate underground.[182] A St. Louis City librarian pointed out to the co-author of this biography that Confederate opposition to the Union presence was never underground, but demonstrated openly and defiantly.

Apparently, Kate did well in her chosen profession. On the Federal census on 30 June 1870, 'Kate Clark,' age 22, whose occupation was enumerated as a 'whore,' was in the Fifth Ward of St. Louis.

In 1870, it was 'safe' to publicly list prostitution as a profession. Kate headed a household of twenty-one other prostitutes and three female domestic servants. The 'whores' were all young, ranging in age between 16 and 26, and 'white,' except for one who was 'black.' The domestic servants were older, ages 27 to 31; two were 'black' and one was 'white.' Unless the census taker had made an error in listing the occupation and race for the women, the presence of a black prostitute indicated this was, indeed, a very high class establishment.[183]

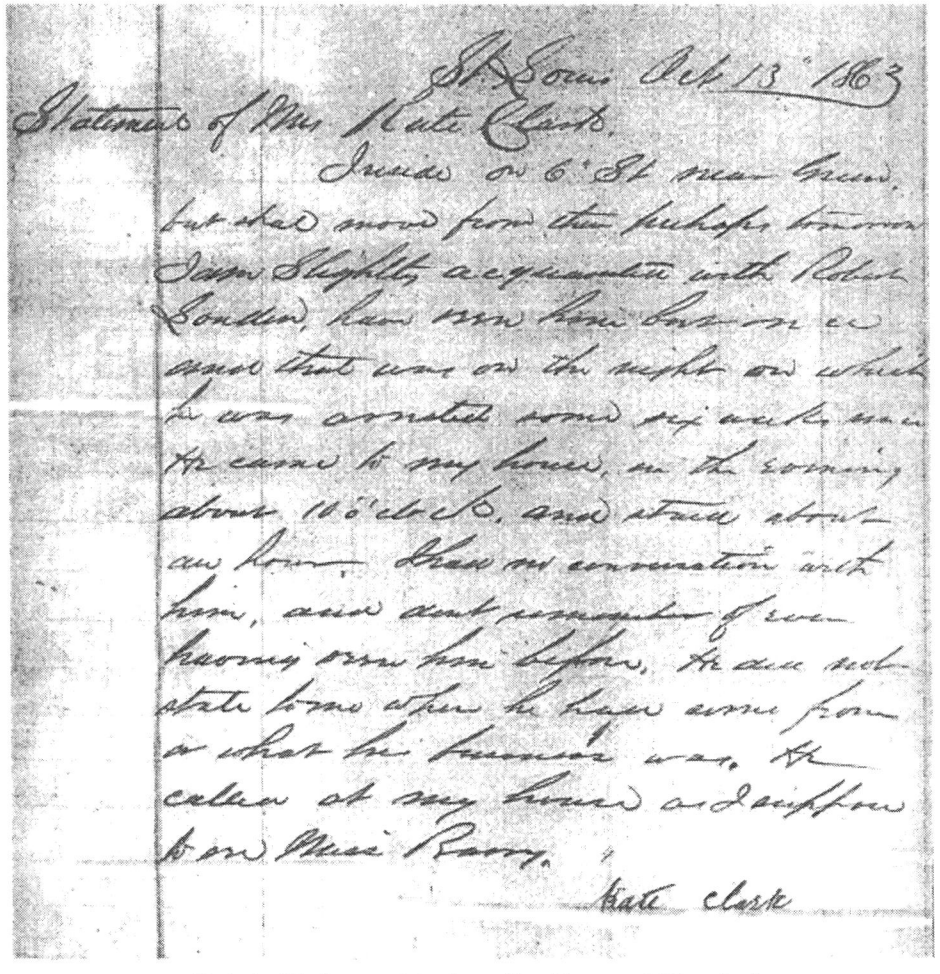

Kate's Statement before the Provost Marshal
St. Louis, Missouri, 13 October 1863

Apparently Robert Louden, the Confederate mail runner and later convicted boat burner, visited one of the women at Kate's house. Kate's occupation provided many opportunities for a variety of men to come and go at her residence frequently.

She states, "I reside on 6th Street near Green but shall move from there perhaps tomorrow. I am slightly acquainted with Robert Louden, have seen him but once, and that was on the night in which he was arrested some six weeks since. He came to my house in the evening about 10 o'clock and stayed about an hour. I had no conversation with him and don't remember of even having seen him before. He did not state to me where he had come from or what his business was. He called at my house as I suppose to see Miss Barry. Kate Clark"

KATE IN FACT AND FICTION

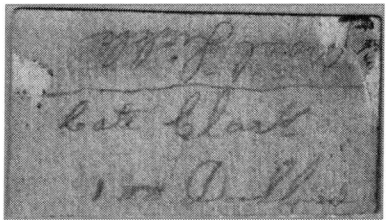 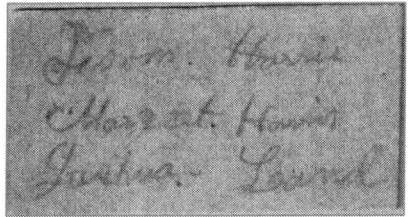

A Peculiar Document Worthy of Scrutiny and Further Study

The foregoing statement offers Kate's authentic signature. Another document presented here for consideration is a supposed promissory note preserved in Jackson County, Missouri, penciled by "Cate Clark." This note for "100 dollars" on a small piece of paperboard was claimed by the donor to have been passed down by a Rogers/Harris family member who had loaned "Cate Clark" the money. The names on the note are: Noel (sic.) Liddle (upside down above Clark's name; and Isom [Isham] Harris, Margaret Harris, and Joshua Land, on the verso.

If this small note's provenance is true and authentic, then it would have been at a time in her life when Kate went by the alias, "Kate Clarke" (or, Cate Clarke, as she may have been known to her 'hometown' creditors . . . those who knew her from childhood as Robert King's daughter, Catherine or Cate . . . and, also as Quantrill's mistress, or wife).

Therefore, this would have been during her years with Quantrill through her life as a prostitute and then madam in St. Louis . . . 1861-1881.

To narrow that timeframe, Kate would have needed money. And, for such a substantial sum ($100 during this time period would be between $2,700 [1861] and $2,326 [1881] in 2014 dollars), what collateral might she have had to provide to guarantee repayment of the debt? This *might* narrow the date of this document to between 1865 (when Quantrill died and Kate was left to her own devices in St. Louis) to 1870 (when Kate became successful and independent enough to manage a bawdy house).

Further, Kate likely would have to have been in her hometown of Blue Springs, Jackson County, Missouri, in order for those loaning her the money to stake their claim.

With that logic stated, observe these inconsistencies or questionable aspects of the document's supposed provenance, however:

1) While in St. Louis, Kate appears to have spelled her name "Kate Clark(e);" an example where she spelled her first name as "Cate" has not been located in any other primary source;

2) All the names on the undated slip were penciled by the same hand, which may or may not be in Kate's handwriting;

3) The senior Isom [Isham] Harris, husband of Margaret Harris, was born in 1823 and <u>died in 1852</u>. Although they did have a son named after his father (no data about the younger Harris located by these authors); and,

4) Joshua Land was born in 1815 and <u>died in 1866. A</u>lthough he, too, had a son named after him. "Josh" Land, age 19, was living with his 60-year-old mother in the 1880 Federal census of Jackson County, Missouri. It is unlikely that he would have been in a position to loan money to "Cate Clark" at this time, or before.

The only other possibility might have been that Kate borrowed $100 from these people near the end of her life when she was again back in Jackson County. At that time, as will be seen, she borrowed $100 against her inheritance of the Anson King's estate. However, by then, Kate was definitely using the name "Mrs. Sarah C. Batson," and hadn't used the alias, "Kate Clark(e)," in nearly 40 years.

To be sure, the Harris, Liddle (Liddel/Liddil) and Land surnames are included among those who supported Quantrill and the guerrilla cause. But, this document and its proposed provenance is terribly weak, and may even have been inadvertently misinterpreted and/or represented.

Still, the reader should know of its existence for further consideration. Jackson County (Mo.) Historical Society Archives, General Collections, Donation ID 72.038.001, Document ID 70F3.

Kate Clark, in the 1870 Federal Census, St. Louis, Missouri

Because of the Social Evil Ordinance in St. Louis, prostitution was regulated and therefore 'legal' and safe to list as an occupation. Here Kate and 21 white women in her house listed their occupation as 'whore,' with three domestic servants (2 former African-American slaves, and 1 white).

The value of Kate's personal property was $7,000 (equivalent to over $125,000 in 2013 currency per the Consumer Price Index) . . . quite a sizable sum, especially at a time when the weekly wage for a seamstress was $1.50 and rooms rented for $3.50 a month.

Kate was obviously very financially successful in 1870, particularly for a young, single woman. If Kate used the money that Quantrill reportedly gave her—whether from the spoils of the looting of Lawrence, Kansas, or cash from the bank robbery in Glasgow, Missouri—to establish her 'House of Social Evil,' it was invested in this venture rather than to procure and set the tombstone Quantrill requested on his deathbed.

In the Federal census, Kate incorrectly, whether intentionally or accidentally, listed her birthplace as Kentucky. The birthplaces reported by the other women with her show that most were born outside the state of Missouri. Only three listed Missouri as their birthplace. Six of them were from southern states: Kentucky, Virginia, and Texas, while the rest were 'Yankees' from New York, Pennsylvania, Ohio, Illinois and Indiana. Apparently not all clients of the brothel were seeking 'Southern Belles.' Four of the women were born outside of the US—three in Baden [Germany]. This reflected not only the smaller percentage of foreign-born prostitutes (18.9%), with Irish and German being the far largest groups,[184] but the fact that immigrate prostitutes worked mainly in the poorer lower-class brothels located along the river front.[185] Kate's establishment was located downtown, and was one of the two finest houses in St. Louis.

At age 22, Kate seemed quite young to be the madam of such a large brothel. It seems doubtful that she began her career in prostitution as a madam rather than 'working her way up' as a courtesan. Levine maintained that Kate and Lizzie Saville (the madam of the other grand palace of sin or pleasure, dependent upon one's view of the Social Evil Ordinance) were successful madams because they were native-born white women and "managers as much as workers."

"The distinction is a difficult one, for while legal documents—and many historians—assume a distinct separation between the brothelkeeper and those who work in the brothel, that distinction becomes less tenable when the managers are women. Many women who managed brothels were women with personal experience in prostitution; the available evidence suggests careers as both managers and prostitutes, a common phenomenon though generally undocumented."[186]

Another historian, with expert knowledge regarding both women's studies and prostitution, agrees with Levine regarding Kate's experiences.[187] However, she achieved it, Kate was operating a profitable business in 1870. Kate was wealthy enough to be a victim of theft and well-known enough for that to be newsworthy when Esther Wise stole a gold locket worth $35 and a gold watch worth $75 from Kate in May 1872.[188]

During the years between 1865 and 1870, the prostitutes of St. Louis experienced frequent and extreme changes in the laws and their enforcement regarding their profession. At times the general attitude was one of tolerance and indifference while at other times a strong push for enforcement would occur resulting in frequent raids and arrests. In 1870 St. Louis took a progressive step forward to deal with prostitution by passing a city ordinance to regulate it; this 'Social Evil Ordinance' was often called the "Social Evil Law."

On 14 March 1870, the governor of Missouri signed Senate Bill No. 362 revising the charter of the City of St. Louis which, among other things, gave the city the power to regulate prostitution. On 5 July 1870, the City Chamber passed the ordinance, by a vote of sixteen to five, designed to bring prostitution in St. Louis under combined medical and police control. Following an example of many European countries, the St. Louis ordinance, the only one of its kind in a large U.S. city, focused on the regulation and not the suppression of prostitution. The law specified registration of prostitutes, reporting changes in their residence, license fees, medical exams, and treatment of disease, plus opportunities for reform. This was to be implemented at no cost to the tax payers.

Owners of bawdy houses were required to pay a fee of $10 per month and each prostitute was charged $1.50 per week. The working women would be examined weekly by a health official, paying a dollar for each examination. The income generated was to create and operate a Social Evil Hospital to provide free treatment for the prostitutes infected with venereal disease (now called sexually transmitted diseases, or STDs). Also a House of Industry, a vocational and rehabilitation school, was proposed as an adjunct to the Social Evil Hospital. Obviously no one wanted the hospital or school built near them. The city boarded patients at a private institution for almost two years, and then eventually built the hospital at a cost of $100,000 on Arsenal Avenue, at the intersection of Manchester Road, outside the city limits near the County Insane Asylum and Poor House.

The Social Evil Hospital, located on 11 acres near the St. Louis County Insane Asylum and the Poor House, opened in the fall of 1872. After the repeal of the Social Evil Ordinance, the hospital continued to operate treating first unwed mothers and patients with sexually transmitted disease, and then as a women's hospital, renamed the Female Hospital. The city of St. Louis operated the hospital until 1910 when the City Hospital took the patients, and the building became an infirmary for the aged from the Poor House until it was razed around 1915. Sublette Park now occupies the location.

The Social Evil Ordinance initially had broad public support; it was expected to both reduce the spread of venereal disease and decrease the public visibility of prostitutes while reforming them.

Kate complied with the new law. Later, Kate was publicly quoted in the newspaper as initially being against the law; but, changed her mind after finding the Ordinance was beneficial in spite of the high cost.[189] On 14 March 1873, she asked for...

> "...a permit to keep the house on the Northwest corner of 6th and Elm Streets for bawdy house purposes. If permitted to occupy the house, I will comply with all the rules and regulations of the ordinance."[190]

Thus, she moved her operations from 112 South Eighth Street to larger quarters at 112 Sixth Street.

On 1 April 1873, Kate leased the mansion, formerly occupied by St. Luke's Hospital at Sixth and Elm, from owner Logan D. Dameron.[191] Thomas Huntington, acting as agent for Dameron, arranged the agreement. The building was rented for $2,000 per year for the first twenty-three months, during the expired term of the lease to St. Luke's Hospital. This would be the equivalent to about $35,714 per year in today's currency, based on the Consumer Price Index. After the first two years, there was an option for Kate to continue renting the building for an additional three years at $2,500 per annum. In 1873, newspaper reporters interviewed Kate directly and saw an actual copy of the lease which was reported as follows:

> "Who did lease the building to Kate Clark?" was the question that first presented itself to the reportorial mind, and in pursuit of the inquiry a visit was paid to the building itself. Kate Clark was announced, by the colored woman who opened the door, to be engaged with her hair-dresser, and a stay consequently had to be made in the parlors of the establishment until the arrival of the landlady. In the course of fifteen minutes she made her appearance, with her head done up in a towel, and in reply to the request of the reporter to see the lease, she said she would bring the paper down in a short time if it could be found. The finding of the paper seemed to occupy considerable time, for it was nearly three-

> quarters of an hour before she returned to the parlor, but the hairdresser had completed her toilet, which, however, a brother reporter present on behalf of the staid old *Republican* remarked, was not near so becoming as the first and more careless costuire.
>
> THE LEASE was given by Thos. Huntington, as agent, and conveyed to her the use of the building at a rental of $2,000 a year for the first two years of her occupancy, and gave her the option of continuing her residence there at a yearly rental of $2,500 for three years longer.
>
> Miss Clark anxiously inquired what would be the result, and seemed to be greatly comforted by the hopeful assurances of the *Republican* man. She went on to say that the house was vacant for several months before she applied for it, and that when she made her application to Mr. Huntington, she frankly told that gentleman for what purpose she wanted it, and that gentleman said that Mr. Dameron did not care who took it so long as it was some responsible party, and that he did not want to figure in it all. Mr. Huntington, she continued, did not ask for any security at all.
>
> Miss Clark remarked in conclusion that she thought the law was a very good one in its effects and that she could not see why any one should want to break it up, and the *Democrat* reporter withdrew in search of Mr. Dameron again.[192]

Note that the $2,000 rental fee was per year, not per month as stated by Barnes.

However, rather than reducing the presence of prostitution the Social Evil Ordinance brought the sex industry to the foreground and the presence of prostitutes became more obvious and obnoxious to the general public.[193] The expanded visibility of prostitution in the city fueled efforts to repeal the law. At the head of the repeal campaign was Reverend William Greenleaf Eliot, a Unitarian minister, founder and Chancellor of Washington University.[194] Rev. Eliot and his supporters argued that the Social Evil Ordinance was bad policy from both a medical and a moral point of view. In addition to the sexism of the double standard applied to the female prostitutes versus their male clients, the opponents objected to the 'foreignness' of the law and its European influence and philosophy.[195] However, the new law generated huge amounts of money for the city.[196] The initial efforts to overturn the Social Evil Ordinance were defeated in the City chambers.

Kate's St. Louis Years

On 6 August 1873, William G. Eliot challenged the constitutionality of the law by filing a complaint against two very prominent St. Louis madams using the state statute forbidding the operation of bawdy houses. The two madams named in Eliot's suit were Kate Clarke and Lizzie Saville whose high-class establishments in elegant mansions at the edge of the inner city, were far removed from the foul slums down on the riverfront or the hovels of 'Wild Cat Chute' north of downtown.[197] Eliot contended that the ordinance was inconsistent with state law and should be repealed. Three days later, trying to raise the same issue, Eliot filed a complaint against Logan D. Dameron, a well-known and highly respected business man in St. Louis, who owned the building that Kate had rented.[198]

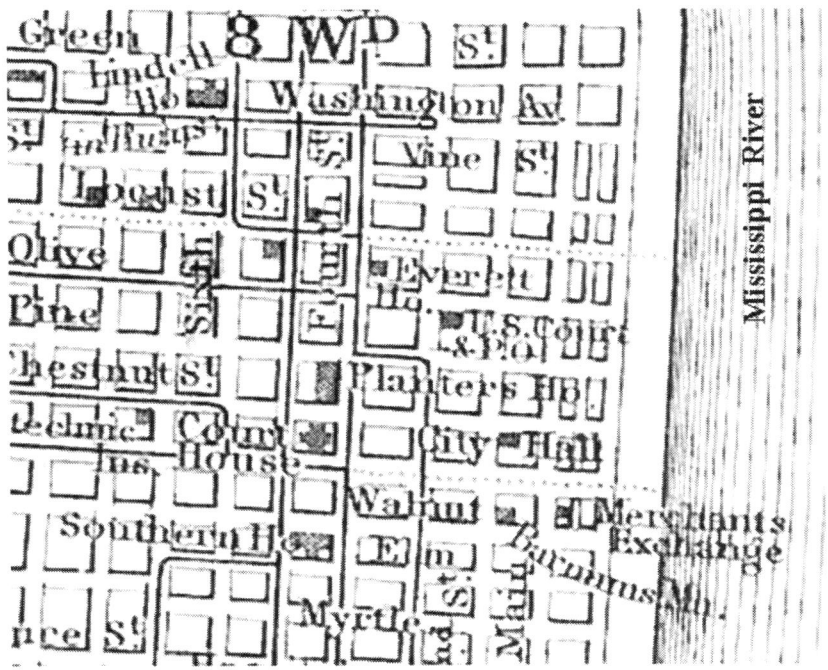

Downtown St. Louis, Missouri, in 1870
Kate Clarke's and Lizzie Saville's establishments were located across the intersection from each other at 6th and Elm Streets. The other, 'less elegant' houses of prostitution were located along the riverfront, down and away from the major downtown area of the city.

Eliot's case against the two women went to court on Saturday, 16 August 1873. Their attorney was none other than J.R. Claiborne.[199] The Sunday edition of the *St. Louis Democrat* published a lengthy article describing the court proceedings of the previous day.[200] Both Kate and Lizzie appeared in court elaborately dressed in silk, linen, lace and jewels. Claiborne defended the madams by pointing out the city was empowered by the Legislature to 'regulate or suppress' prostitution within the city limits and this took precedence over the state law forbidding bawdy houses. Interest in these test cases drew the "largest audiences ever assembled within its walls" of the Court of Criminal Corrections. The debate regarding the 'Great St. Louis Experiment' and the progression of the case through the courts was also actively followed and reported by newspapers[201] throughout the entire country. Following final arguments, Judge John W. Colvin took the case under advisement and rendered a decision the following Saturday.[202]

On 23 August 1873, Judge Colvin of the court of Criminal Records convicted Kate and Lizzie on the basis that the city ordinance was inconsistent with the other state laws and fined them each one hundred dollars. He also stated that the law itself was unjust because it did not apply to both sexes equally. The women appealed to the Missouri State Supreme Court and threatened to sue the city to recover the dues they had paid under the ordinance if it were repealed; when interviewed by a reporter Kate was careful to say:

> It will depend altogether on the way that the case is decided in the Supreme Court. If the case is decided against us, why, of course, all we can do is to ask them to give us back our dues. We paid our money in good faith, and now we are prosecuted for complying with it. It seems pretty hard that we should be fined now, and should be put in the calaboose if we don't pay our dues.[203]

The Missouri State Supreme Court reversed Judge Colvin's decision on December 1, 1873, and declared he had overstepped his authority.[204]

The court ruled on three separate components in this case:

1. Social Evil Ordinance of St. Louis was declared valid indicating that the license issued by the city under this ordinance was valid and should shield the licensee from criminal proceedings by the State.

2. Declaring part of a law unconstitutional did not void the rest of the law meaning that the remainder of the provisions of that law was valid and enforceable.

3. The charter to St. Louis to regulate brothels did not conflict with the state law prohibiting them and thus, declaring that St. Louis' right to regulate brothels was not inconsistent with the state law banning them.

Not all rulings were unanimous and there were dissenting votes. However the outcome was that the court upheld the Social Evil Ordinance and declared that Kate and Lizzie could not be prosecuted for operating a brothel in St. Louis.

On 3 January 1874, the *St. Louis Daily Globe* published an extremely brief item:

Court of Criminal Corrections

Kate Clark and Lizzie Saville; keeping bawdy-houses, dismissed at prosecutor's costs.

This succinct report announced that Kate and Lizzie had defeated the efforts of Eliot and his many allies and could not be charged with the crime of operating a brothel. Two 'ladies of the night' had asserted their rights to the chagrin of the social reformers who felt they were trying to right a social injustice. However the crusade to repeal the ordinance continued.

Local newspapers, especially the *St. Louis Daily Globe* and *St. Louis Democrat*, continued to be the forum for discourse pertaining to the repeal movement. Rev. Eliot's continuing campaign to repeal the ordinance, bolstered by the efforts of prominent women linked to the suffrage and former abolitionist movements, along with 'well connected' local women allies, gained increasing public support. In the February 22, 1874, issue of the *St. Louis Daily Globe*, a reporter visited the Clarke house in hopes of an interview with Kate. Unfortunately for him and for all future scholars of Kate, she was not available for an interview. The reporter accompanied the assemblage of sixteen state legislators who had traveled to St. Louis to tour the brothels so they could "see the social evil law in operation" first hand. The lower dens of infamy along the river front were disregarded and the slums of Almond and Green Streets were avoided.

> The hacks wheeled up Chesnut [Chestnut] to Sixth Street stopping in front of Lizzie Saville's and Kate Clark's, the two crack palaces of sin in that portion of the city.[205]

The delegation visited Lizzie's place first and then progressed to Kate's abode. When the tour was completed only three legislators were left in the group. The *St. Louis Daily Globe* reported the other thirteen fact-finders would "wake up this morning with practical experience of the workings of the social evil system."

The crusade broadened into duels between the political parties at both city and state levels. In January 1874, State Senator McGinnis reintroduced a bill to revoke the power to regulate prostitution from the St. Louis charter. After much political maneuvering, the repeal bill passed on 18 March 1874, by a vote of 19 to 10, a margin of one vote above the 18 required for passage. In April, the St. Louis City council nullified the Social Evil Ordinance. However, the repeal bill did not specifically forbid keeping a house of prostitution and a subsequent court ruling stated that revoking a license did not renew state prohibition against brothels, and thus such establishments, which could not be licensed, were still legal.

Kate's St. Louis Years

A Tour of Kate Clarke's St. Louis

This gallery represents St. Louis sites that were within a three- to four-block radius from the intersections of either Sixth and Elm Streets (where Kate Clarke resided in 1870) or, Seventh and Walnut (717 Walnut; where Kate Clarke resided in 1880). The views are from an 1878 *Tour of St. Louis*, and appear in clockwise order using the map of St. Louis on page 129):

Polytechnic Institute
Seventh and Chestnut Streets

A five-story building constructed between 1858 and 1867. In 1869 the Library was transferred from the private Library Society to the Board of Education and moved to the Polytechnic Building. In 1874, the library opened the reading room and access to references to the general public. Since this was within walking distance from Sixth and Elm Streets (where Kate was in 1870) and from 717 Walnut (where Kate was in 1880), one wonders if Kate, or 'her girls,' ever visited the public reading room of the library.

KATE IN FACT AND FICTION

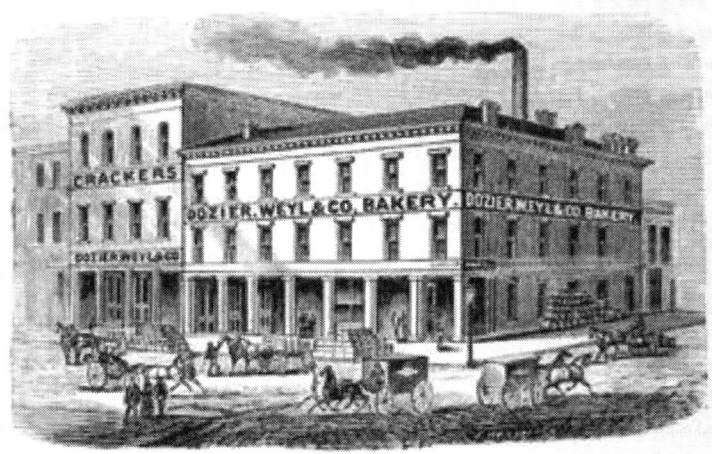

**Dozier, Weyl and Company Bakery
corner of Sixth and Pine Streets**
A three-story building occupying a quarter of the block. The building housed the bakery for breads, crackers and "jumbles," as well as the retail and wholesale departments. Here baked goods of all sorts were produced from the grain of the West to supply an area from Minnesota to the Gulf and from Indiana to the Pacific. What tantalizing smells of fresh baked goods reached Kate's 'palace of sin?'

The Old Jail, Sixth and Chestnut Streets
The corner where "the hacks wheeled up Chestnut to Sixth Street" to stop at Kate's place when the sixteen state legislators visited to "see the social evil law in operation" in February 1874.

Planters House (above)
Fourth Street between Chestnut and Pine Streets

The oldest hotel in St. Louis in 1878. This 300-room, four-story building, built in 1841, was the second of three elegant structures known as the Planters Hotel and was in the block adjacent to the Court House.

Court House (next page, top)
Chestnut and Market Streets
between Fourth and Fifth Streets

The Court House construction spanned from between 1839 to 1862. The dome was completed in 1864. It was built as a combination federal and state courthouse which housed civil, circuit and supreme courts. Kate did not have far to go to appear in the court room during her trial. The case of Dred Scott was also tried in this building. When the city and county governments of St. Louis separated in 1877, the Court House became city property. It was Missouri's tallest building until 1896. In 1940, the city deeded the Courthouse to the Federal Government. Today the "Old Courthouse" is part of the Jefferson National Expansion Memorial Park, and is open to the public free of charge.

**Tony Faust's Oyster House and Saloon
southwest corner of Fifth and Elm Streets**
In 1878 this building was located next to the ruins of the Southern Hotel, which had burned to the ground in 1877. Kate . . . and/or her 'clients' . . . had to have patronized this popular establishment.

**Southern Hotel
Fourth and Walnut Streets**

Southern Hotel was "The Hotel" of St. Louis. Kate saw this six-story Italianate being constructed on the block bounded by Walnut, Fourth, Fifth and Elm Streets. Built in 1865, it was destroyed by fire discovered at 1:20 a.m. on 11 April 1877, with loss of life and with an estimated economic loss of $370,420, ($92,000 over the insurance coverage). Surely, the former St. Luke's Hospital building at Sixth and Elm Streets provided shelter to at least some of the hotel guests who fled the fire in their night clothes. The blackened ruins of the hotel were a sad reminder of the tragedy; but, new construction began in August 1879. On May 11, 1881, a new fire-proof Southern Hotel opened on the same site, just as Kate was leaving St. Louis.

Olympic Theater (not illustrated)

At the southwest corner of Fifth and Walnut Streets, Olympic Theater was one of the three principal theaters in St. Louis, and one that Kate would have frequented.

In downtown St. Louis in 1878, drinking, gambling and crime also were all concentrated within the same general area. Fine wine parlors and many beer halls were situated along Fifth Street between Market and Walnut Streets.

> "The gamblers are here, not in pairs, but in scores and hundreds. They infest the business portion of the city. On Fourth Street are situated some of the finest 'gambling hells' of the city. On Fifth and Sixth streets are numerous houses. . . . These gambling places

KATE IN FACT AND FICTION

are open to the right kind of visitors, both day and night. . . . In the squares adjacent to Sixth and Chestnut, and up Sixth to Olive Street, there are a half dozen or more gambling houses."[206]

"If one determines to spend a night in the street and among the 'all night houses,' it might be well 'to take in' a part of Broadway, Fourth, Fifth, Sixth, Seventh, Eighth and Ninth streets. . . . In this district street-walkers and gamblers do most abound. The vicinity of the large hotels are favorite waiting places for the fallen women who seek their prey on thoroughfares. **Sixth Street, between Washington Avenue and Market Street, is much used by these degraded beings. Chestnut Street, from the Courthouse to Eleventh Street, is also a much traveled highway of bawds after nightfall.**"[207]

Obviously Kate's place catered to a higher class clientele than would be attracted to the offerings available in the immediate surrounding neighborhood. However, this "high crime" environment offers an explanation for some of the many times Kate's name appeared in the local newspaper.

**Gratiot Street Prison
Eighth and Gratiot Streets**
More than three blocks from Kate's place of business was the largest Federal prison in Missouri. Originally built by the Missouri Medical College, the building was converted to a prison in December 1861 and served as mainly a transfer point for Confederate prisoners of war, both men and women Confederate sympathizers, guerilas, spies, 'contraband' slaves, and Federal soldiers accused of crimes, until 1865. It was operated under the command of the Provost Marshal. It had a designated capacity of 1,200; but, at times, accommodated over 2,000 prisoners, including Absolom C. Grimes and Robert Louden. Gratiot Street Prison was demolished in 1878 (so was still standing during much of Kate's residency in St. Louis). Today it is the site of Ralston-Purina Headquarters.

Kate's St. Louis Years

    Kate continued working as a madam after repeal of the Social Evil Ordinance—at least until 4 February 1875, when she 'sold out' her entire inventory. The names of the citizens identified in the farcical narrative about the sale seemed concocted, and the entire story was presented as entertainment, rather than news:

UNDER THE HAMMER

A Bagnio Sold Out by a Reforming Courtesan—A Grand Rally of the Toodles Family in Search of Bargains

    Yesterday the furniture and fixings of Madame Kate Clark's *maison de jore* on Sixth and Elm streets, were sold at auction.

    At 10 o'clock in the morning the auctioneer took his position on the block to sacrifice, as the hand bills say "the most elegant outfit of household furniture, ever offered at public auction." To say that the excitement ran high, and that the crowd was a mixed one would simply be, to draw it mild. Some of the most wealthy of the demiscrips, tried with Mrs. Toodles from uptown for this or that article of *virtu*, not virtue, as they passed in turn beneath the hammer; silks hanging of the most gorgeous patterns, brocateles, that might well grace the salons of the wealthiest merchant princes; plush and rep parlor sets, magnificently carved and inlaid with gold and mother of pearl, representing allegories or some page from Grecian or Roman mythology; dressing case chamber sets of the most bewitching beauty and elegant design; easy chairs and *tete-a-tetes* of foreign manufacture, soft and downy, and inviting enough to seduce an Eastern potentate from the voluptuous blandishments of the *seraglio*; pier glasses reaching from floor to ceiling, in heavy massive, carved and gilded frames; silk, satin and rep lambrequins, Axminster, Moquet and Brussels carpets, soft and velvety, and in which the feet are smothered half an inch; oil paintings, pronounced by judges, admirable works of art, chromos and steel engravings, vases of costly proportions, sparkling chandeliers, came one by one to the block, and were knocked down to Smith, Brown, or Jones, as the case might be.

    Brown smiled and looked happy as he thought of the story he would tell Mrs. B. and the girls, as to where the elegant set came from, and how the Snitkins' across the way would be dying with envy as they saw it delivered at his own proud mansion. Mrs. Thompson thought it a crying shame the stuck-up Jones should have purchased that elegant Brussels, and wondered, in looks, what the world was coming to, but still hopes they won't get that Severis Vase, for if they do she will leaves Jones, who is up to a thing or two, and he has for the past two weeks kept the sale a profound mystery from Mrs. Jones, and winks his eye knowingly, and undergoes the remarkable piece of human torture known as "laughing in his sleeve," as he regrets Mrs. Jones' absence to Mr. Jenkins, whose wife is present, and recklessly bidding on every article that is put up. Jenkins is of a sympathetic nature, and regrets it too, and still the voice of the auctioneer is heard in the frescoed corridors and gilded chambers. "Going, Going" all day long from the hour of 10 a.m. until dark, and the last article of the palace of sin was disposed of.

And why this sale of earthly splendor? Not because the slaves of vice and passion have ceased to patronize this mansion of misery. Not because the wages of sin, of prostitution, of virtue lost never to be regained or souls damned eternally, and bodies given over to paupers coffins and paupers graves, were not still at the command of the sharp and shrewd managers of the place, but because simply she is going to be married. A plain business arrangement has been entered into with a gentleman of New York, the result of which will be a quiet wedding as soon as Madame Clark's affairs shall have been fully settled, and somewhere in an up town neighborhood of Gotham the penates will be set up and Mistress Kate will enter upon her new life.[208]

The listing of furnishings provided further proof of the opulence, grandeur and richness of Kate's establishment and why Kate Clarke was named as one of the defendants by Eliot in his crusade to repeal the Social Evil Law. The timing of this sale (February 1875) was particularly interesting, which, along with Kate's announcement of her impeding marriage, occurred about eight months before the birth of her child in 1875 in St. Louis.[209] Apparently, no other newspaper in St. Louis considered Kate's sale or marriage as newsworthy, since no other news reports were found.

Eliot's complaint against Logan D. Dameron, the owner of the building rented by Kate, was never tried in court, but the public battle between Dameron and St. Luke's Hospital Board continued, and was still newsworthy four years later:[210]

Kate's St. Louis Years

AN OLD TROUBLE REVIVED
In Which a Bawdy House Keeper Figures Prominently

The old suit instituted by Logan D. Dameron, a prominent Methodist, against the managers of St. Luke's Hospital, has been resurrected again for trial. Nearly four years ago the causes which led to the legal proceeding were published at length in the city papers, and created no little interest, hence the time which has elapsed, and the prominence of the case, furnish excuse sufficient for the following recapitulation of the proceedings.

In March, 1870, the Board of Mangers of the St. Luke's Hospital, leased from Mr. Dameron the building situated on the northwest corner of Sixth and Elm streets, and remodeled the house for hospital purposes. Although the lease was for five years, the managers became dissatisfied with the property in December, 1872, and made overtures with Mr. Dameron for a surrender and cancellation of the lease. The defendants, in their answer, allege that such arrangements were made, satisfactory to both parties, and that by the agreement the defendants are not justly indebted to plaintiff in any sum, while plaintiff claims that defendants owe him a balance of $1,306.70.

The chief interest in the case, however, is in connection with the re-letting of the building by Mr. Dameron, shortly after its vacation by the hospital managers, to one Kate Clark, for bawdy-house purposes.

Mr. Dameron was violently assailed by members of the church, at the time, and the contest, considered publicly, was very violent for some time. The north half of the property is now occupied by Madame Saville and her frail blondes, and the south half is a boarding-house.

The case will doubtless be called for trial this afternoon in Circuit Court No. 5, and one of the chief witnesses will be Kate Clark.[211]

In 1877, the building still housed a brothel, "now occupied by Madame Saville and her frail blondes," and Kate was to appear in court as witnesses that afternoon. Logan D. Dameron, and not the Hospital Board, had, indeed, been responsible for renting the building to Kate and the building continued to be used as a brothel even after prostitution was no longer regulated.

The law to repeal the Social Evil Ordinance passed only because of a compromise that prevented police raids on brothels (to prevent harassment of the women who had registered with the city in good faith) and continued the existence of the hospital and reformatory. The House of Industry, never successful in reforming the prostitutes, most of whom resented such attempts, closed very soon. The Social Evil Hospital began to treat unwed mothers as well as women infected with sexually transmitted diseases. When the Social Evil Hospital became part of the municipal health system, Mayor Brown lamented "the only door that was opened by the city for a repentant female has been closed, perhaps forever."[212]

When the Social Evil Hospital became a general hospital for women the name was changed to the Female Hospital. The city of St. Louis discontinued using it as a hospital in 1910 and the building was used as an infirmary for the residents of the poor house until it was razed around 1915.[213]

Because the Missouri State Supreme Court ruling of 1873 left St. Louis in such a legal and legislative quandary, the city came close to 'decriminalizing' prostitution in the years between 1874 and 1879. However in 1879, the state legislature repealed the provisions enacted to protect the brothels in St. Louis from raids or police extortion. The city council of St. Louis then passed an ordinance which made the operation of a brothel a misdemeanor.[214] Thus the great experiment involving the regulation of 'Social Evil' by St. Louis ended and the management of prostitution and brothels was again controlled by the police. Prostitution was again criminalized and the trade and women in the trade moved out of the public eye.

In the 1880 Federal census on 11 June, Kate was still in St. Louis. But, she would soon leave the city.

Kate Clark, in the 1880 Federal Census, St. Louis, Missouri
Because prostitution was no longer regulated in St. Louis, and thus was an illegal activity, Kate now listed her occupation as "Boarding House" keeper.

Kate's St. Louis Years

Kate was located at 717 Walnut Street in a 'boarding house' with eight female boarders. Prostitution and the operation of brothels were no longer legal in St. Louis, and had to be less conspicuous. The women's ages ranged between 19 and 30 years of age; no names of women living with her in the 1870 Federal census appeared with her in the 1880 Federal census. She was operating her business on a much smaller scale than in 1870.

Kate was listed as age 38 and widowed. Of course the census did not indicate when she was widowed or how often she was widowed. Was she a widow from the loss of a husband who died in 1865, or one whom she might have married in 1875? Or, both?

This was the last time "Kate Clarke" appeared on a state or Federal census.

The last document of Kate Clarke's presence in the city of St. Louis was a listing for her in the 1881 city directory at 717 Walnut Street, further solidifying Kate's presence there a year earlier.[215]

Another association of Kate and Lizzie Saville, besides being Madams on the same street[216] and Lizzie later moving into Kate's business location,[217] was that Lizzie lived at the same residence—717 Walnut—in 1885 as where Kate resided in 1880. Lizzie Saville was listed in the St. Louis city directory at 818 North 10th in 1872; in 1877, 1878 and 1881, Lizzie lived at 117 South Sixth.

What finally became of the two establishments on Sixth and Elm is unclear. Busch Stadium is now located on the site were Sixth and Elm were in 1870 and 1880.

Lizzie Saville occupied part of Dameron's building, the former St. Luke's Hospital site, in January of 1877.[218] With the repeal of the Social Evil Law and the deregulation of prostitution, Lizzie had downsized (she only had the north half of the building) when she moved across the street. Lizzie Saville continued working as a madam until at least 1887 when she was fined for keeping a "disreputable house."[219]

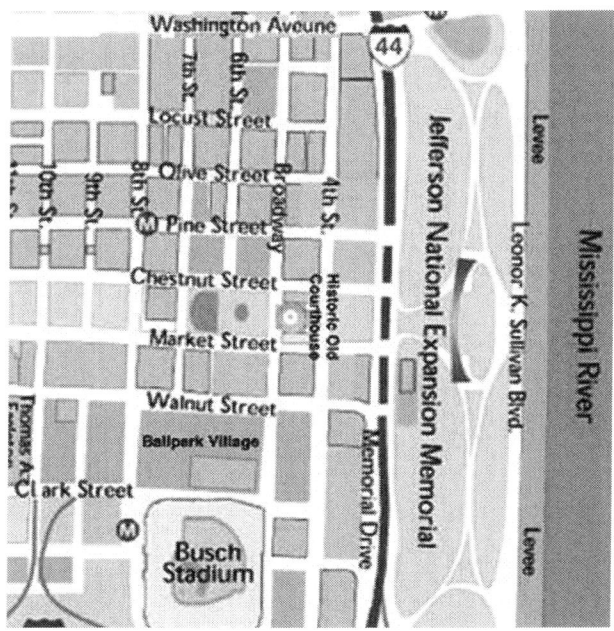

Modern day St. Louis, Missouri
Busch Stadium parking lot is now (2014) located on the site where Kate Clarke's establishment at 6th and Elm Streets had been in 1870; the former baseball stadium on the same city block was situated directly at 6th and Elm. It is a coincidental twist of fate that Elm Street ran parallel to and was not far removed from Clark Street...which was certainly not named after Kate Clarke; but, likely after William Clark, of Lewis and Clark fame.

Had Kate been targeted as an example by W. G. Eliot's lawsuit because she was so conspicuous and a flamboyant spokesperson?[220] Or, did Eliot choose Kate because of her Confederate sympathies, and her past association with Quantrill?[221] Lizzie Saville, equally as obvious and flamboyant as Kate, had also been targeted by Eliot. Nothing is known of Saville's political leanings and activities, but both women certainly had prominent professional profiles. Of particular interest was that when Kate was required to post a $300 bond for the appeal of her case to the Missouri Supreme Court, the bonding company was backed by James R. Claiborne and he was the secretary that handled the account.[222] Although

Claiborne represented Kate in her case before the criminal court in St. Louis, he was not an attorney on the case before the Supreme Court. Could Kate have received moral and financial support from a Confederate underground, including a connection with James R. Claiborne, for her past services during the war? Claiborne's background as a Confederate officer and his active participation in the Confederate Historical and Benevolent Association indicate he held southern sympathies, which obviously did not inhibit his ability to be elected Senator in 1876. However, their professional client/lawyer relationship is the only documented connection between Kate and Claiborne; anything more profound remains purely speculation.

Kate never hesitated to acknowledge her line of work, or to reveal her presence to the public, especially in newspaper reports and in the court room. Professor Whites accused her of 'being hidden' from public view because she wore a veil into court and could not be identified from the witness stand; but, Kate did show her face in the court room by lifting her veil.[223] The other madam, Lizzie Saville, had also been veiled; veils were obviously a fashion statement of the time and the elegant attire of both women was carefully described in the newspapers.

Kate adapted to her circumstances and the ever changing laws, regulations, and enforcement of the city. She had wrestled successfully for years with the forces that tried to inhibit her lifestyle and livelihood.

Kate's daughter, Bertha, was born in St. Louis, in 1875, soon after the Social Evil Law was repealed. With a child approaching school age and prostitution under increasing regulation and prosecution in St. Louis,[224] Kate once again had to 'do what she had to do.' In 1880, Kate left her illegal profession in St. Louis, took Bertha and ran from her sordid past to establish a new identity and a new life, eventually settling in the uncharted frontier Oklahoma Territory.

KATE IN FACT AND FICTION

CHAPTER 7

Kate and Bertha: Motherhood and Beyond

"Mothers are fonder than fathers
of their children because they are
more certain they are their own."
Aristotle (384 B.C. - 322 B.C.)

William Clarke Quantrill left no known children. His consort, Kate, had a child born a decade after he died. Kate had a daughter named Bertha E. Evans. However, Bertha's father remains an enigma. His identity has never been revealed or uncovered. Perhaps the mother, uncertain who her child's father was, chose yet another alias for his name?

Bertha E. Evans was born 6 October 1875, in St. Louis, St. Louis County, Missouri, per her death certificate, as completed on 9 December 1944, from hospital records in Larned, Kansas.

Bertha's birth record is presumed to have been found, although nearly illegible. An online database search provides one, "Bertha E. _____, white female, born in St. Louis, St. Louis County, in 1875."[225]

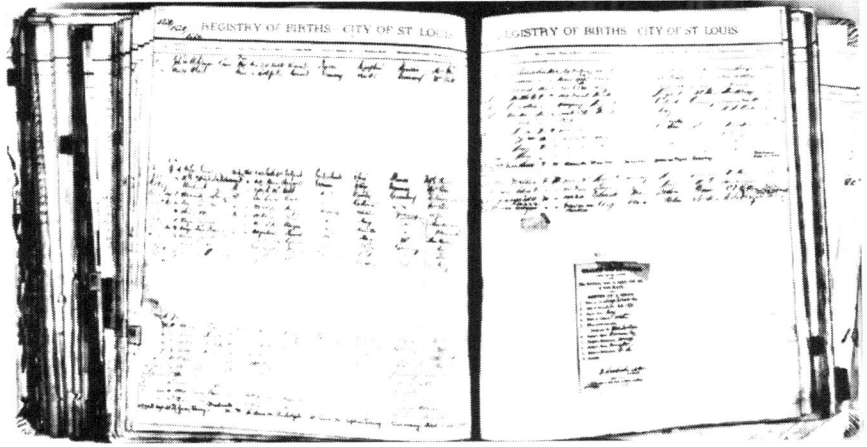

The rest of the page listing the names of parents, places of birth, etc., was illegible.

A birth year of 1877 for Bertha can be estimated from her age on her marriage license issued 21 August of 1899.

Bertha's age listed on the Federal census over 30 years consistently support a birth year of 1877:

1910 (age 34)
1920 (age 43)
1930 (age 53)

Although census records are not a primary source for determination of age, they may often be more accurately relied upon than documentation presented after death, especially if the age is consistent over several decades.[226]

Bertha's middle initial 'E', was ascertained from her marriage documents, which list her as 'B. E. Evans' in one place and as 'B. E. Ivans' in another. The middle initial "E" also appears in the birth registry noted above. Thus, her middle initial represents her actual middle name, rather than her surname, as is sometimes the case in listings for married women.

Given the details in both the birth registration and death certificate, 6 October 1875, was considered the most accurate date of birth for Bertha E. Evans.

On her marriage license, Bertha listed her birthplace as St. Louis, Missouri, and her residence as Harrah, Oklahoma. Bertha's place of residence was listed twice in the marriage documents, once as Harrel, Oklahoma and once as Harrah, Oklahoma. Since Harrel was not found in Oklahoma, Bertha must have been from Harrah, a small town about five- to 10- miles southwest of Oklahoma City.[227]

Kate left St. Louis…left her notoriety there as a madam of a brothel…left her infamy as a guerrilla's sweetheart in Jackson County, Missouri…and eventually went to the anonymity of Oklahoma to protect her daughter from public scorn. This turning point arose immediately after the abrupt change in both the Missouri State and St. Louis City laws and attitudes regarding prostitution in 1879.

The first Federal census in which Bertha *might* appear was 1880, as a 5-year-old child.

Though her mother as 'Kate Clark,' appears as the keeper of a boarding house in the 1880 Federal census in St. Louis, Bertha is noticeably missing from the enumeration.

Without not yet having found Bertha in the 1880 Federal census, one can only speculate her whereabouts. Perhaps she was living with a nearby family. There were only four Bertha Evans of the correct approximate age in the 1880 Federal census of St. Louis, and all four were in households with three other siblings; three of those households listed both parents while one household was headed by a 35-year woman named Kate who was born in Russia.

Kate may have sent Bertha away, even out of state, to a private boarding facility. She certainly had the financial means to do so.[228]

One female child identified as 'Myrty' appears in the 1880 Federal census for Jackson County, Missouri, with Bertha's maternal grandfather, Robert L. King. She is likely a stepdaughter, however, of Kate's brother, Samuel King, who was also enumerated in the household.

Efforts over many years were made to find a connection between Kate and/or Bertha to a man with a surname of Evans, Evins or Ivins. A thorough study of any Robert and/or Martin Evans (names found in the Castanien family record transcribed in this biography) was also made, and to men with those names who were born in either New York (referenced in the article about Kate's business partner / fiancé, who may have been suspected as her baby's father) or, London, England (from the Castanien family record). See pages 35-36, 140, 152-153 for additional mentions of these men.[229]

There is no record of Kate after 1880 until Bertha's marriage in Oklahoma County, Oklahoma, in 1899. The only hint of her whereabouts was offered by W. W. Scott who reported in 1888 that, "*after Quantrill's death, Kate Clark went to Texas, where she still is.*"[230] No record of her in Texas has yet been found.

KATE IN FACT AND FICTION

During this nearly 20-year gap, Kate likely assumed another identity and took Bertha somewhere where they both lived incognito, and she could begin yet another new life to raise her daughter without repercussions from the past.

Considering the lack of evidence she left behind, Kate successfully disappeared, taking Bertha with her, and *eventually* settling in Oklahoma territory, remote and distant from her past.

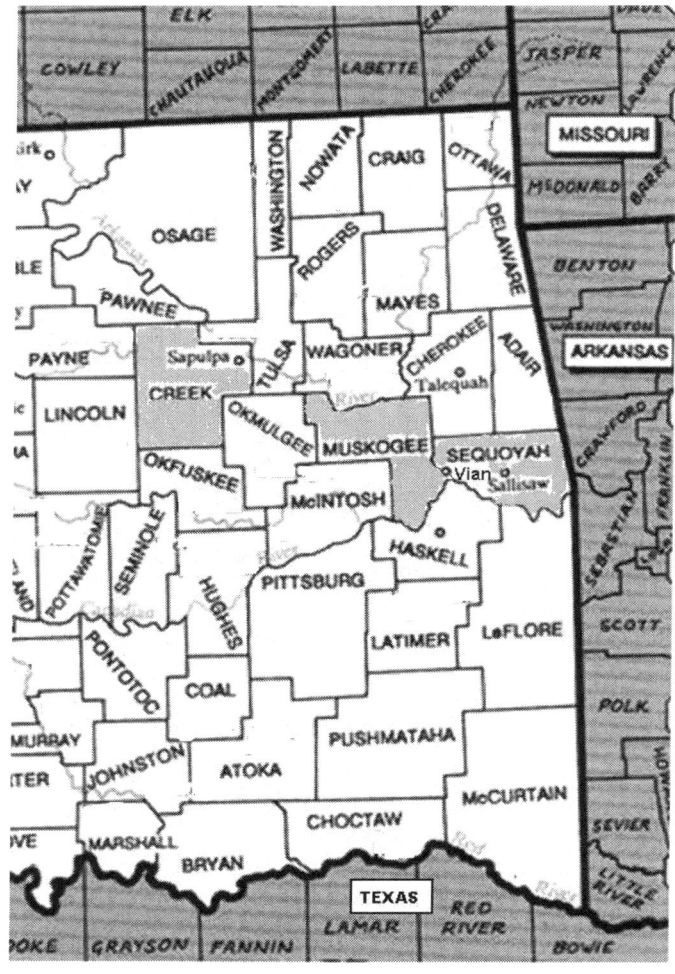

Eastern Oklahoma

Kate and Bertha

Bertha E. Evans married Pliny Mannon Castanien on 21 August 1899, in Oklahoma City, Oklahoma County, Oklahoma.

Marriage Record of Bertha E. Evans Castanien

This was the first and only time that Bertha used a middle initial 'E,' and thus this verifies that 'E' does not relate to her surname. Note that she was named as Ivins in the application; but, was listed as Evins on the license; and, yet later, her son reported her surname to be Evans. The variations in spelling add to the difficulties of locating her in earlier documents. This document provides the places of Bertha's and Pliny's births, and their current residences, as well as where they were married.

KATE IN FACT AND FICTION

Neither Kate nor Pliny and Bertha were found in the 1900 Federal census.

Pliny's personal and family history was thoroughly investigated in hopes of acquiring details to provide some clues regarding where and how they met and their early life together.[231] One artifact, a single mimeographed typed page, contained a brief mention of Bertha which is quoted *verbatim* here, complete with the misspelling of 'descent' and 'imprisonment:'

Bertha's side of family

Mother--Sarah Catherine King, child of George and Mirah Stringer of Louisville, Ken., Scotch desent

Father--Son of Robert Evans of 14 Randolph Road of Sq. London, Eng. Had brother Martin Evans."

Pliny's side (P.M.)

Father--Cyrenus, son of Alexander Castanien, who emigrated from St. Petersburg, Russia, well educated when he left at 18 to escape imprisement for refusal to enter army service, musical, inventive, married Marilles Libendine King, born in Ohio of Holland desent, inherited farm is still there. Three sons of Alexander, John of Ohio 5 sons, Dave, Ohio, three sons, living Alfred; Will and George dead. Cyrenus had nine children, was born in Ohio.

Mother--Ann, her grandfather was a sailor stolen or adopted by a sea captain named Clayton, and became a sea captain and went back to discover parentage, found in Molph, English. Mother's father went by Samuel Clayton's name, giving her name Ann Clayton, settled in Ohio later had 12 children, John and Mary Died, Jane live in Colo and in 1935 was about 80. Mother's father married welsh woman, Cynthia Anna, one child, who married Cyrensus.

Pliny Castanian (P.R.)
   Father--Pliny Mannon Castanian Married Oklahoma City, 1900.
   Mother--Bertha Evans (King)

To this union was first born, Marley, who died at 7 mos.[232]

Kate and Bertha

Home of Robert Evans, 14 Randolph Road, London, England, as it appears today (2014)[233]

This historic 4-5 bedroom house in London's Little Venice includes a grand hallway, communal garden, two reception rooms and other elegant amenities.

KATE IN FACT AND FICTION

The information regarding the Castanien family also included in this document, which has proven to be remarkably accurate, indicated it was supplied by Bertha's son, "Cas" Pliny Raymond Castanien, in about 1935.

The information about Bertha, as supplied by her son, accurately recorded her mother as Sarah Catherine King. And, while it misidentified her maternal grandparents (or, omitted a generation), it included the maternal Stringer surname.

One wonders if Pliny Raymond heard this information from his mother Bertha, or if he heard it directly from his grandmother, Kate. Did Bertha gather such family history stories from only her mother, or did she hear stories from her maternal grandfather, Robert L. King?

Nonetheless, the major significance of this single sheet of paper was the affirmation that Kate, identified as Sarah Catherine King, was the mother of Bertha. Without a birth record or a family Bible, this remained the most conclusive piece of evidence definitively linking Kate and Bertha.

The Federal census listings linked Sarah C. Batson to Bertha as mother and daughter. But, this family note linked daughter, Bertha, directly to her mother, Sarah Catherine King.

Pliny Mannon Castanien was born about 1872, near Upper Sandusky, Pitt Township, Wyandot County, Ohio. He was the eighth child and third and youngest son of Cyrenus Y. Castanien and Cynthia Anna Clayton. Pliny Mannon listed his birth place on his marriage license as Perry County, Ohio, which is a long way from Wyandot County. Pliny's father, Cyrenus, was born and raised in Perry County, Ohio; but, all Castanien researchers indicated that Cyrenus was married and the first eight of his children were born in, Wyandot County, Ohio.

Kate's son-in-law, Pliny Mannon Castanien (right)

The ninth and youngest child was born in Nebraska. As a young boy, Pliny Mannon Castanien moved with his parents to Ninnescah Township in Cowley County, Kansas, where they were on the Federal census on 24 June 1880.

"Phil" M. Castanien participated in the Oklahoma Land Run of 22 April 1889.[234] Pliny Castanien obtained the southeast quarter of Section 2, Township 12, Range 1, in Elk Township, Oklahoma County, Oklahoma Territory.[235] In 1892, Pliny and his two older brothers, Frank and Charles, were in the livery business in Guthrie, Logan County, Oklahoma.[236] The city directory of Guthrie listed both residential and business addresses for P.H. [middle initial "M" mistaken as an "H"] Castanien in 1892 and 'Plynn' Castanien in 1896. By 1896, the parents had joined their three sons in Guthrie, Logan County, Oklahoma. Pliny's father and mother remained in Guthrie until their deaths in 1912 and 1918, respectively.[237]

Strangely, neither Kate nor Bertha and Pliny have yet been found on the 1900 Federal census, which was taken less than a year after Kate and Pliny's marriage in Oklahoma County, Oklahoma. They were not living with or near any of Pliny's siblings who were found in the census.

Bertha and Pliny were in Sapulpa, Creek County, Oklahoma, in December 1902, when their first son, 'Marley' Pliny M. Castanien, was born:

> **Prolific Oklahomans**
> The following from the *Sapulpa Democrat* with [will] be read with a great deal of interest by Guthrie people. Mr. and Mrs. Castanien were at one time residents of this city. That paper says:
> P.M. Castanien, of Castanien Bros., Clothiers, came down to the store Thursday afternoon wearing an all-wool-and-yard-wide smile, and without waiting for the question, he simply repeated: "It's a boy and he weighs 8 pounds." Upon further investigation it was found Mr. C was still of sound mind and that his wife had presented him with an 8-pound boy Thursday morning. Dr. Anderson was in attendance: "Papa" seems to be getting along alright, and Uncle Frank has been purchasing toys for a week, now.[238]

KATE IN FACT AND FICTION

Sapulpa, Indian Territory, 1901

In a 1901 *History of the State of Oklahoma* by L. B. Hill, a surprising description of Sapulpa read as follows: "The railroad reached Sapulpa in 1884 and during the years when it remained a terminus and hence a supply point for nearly all the region to the west of it, this town was a frontier place and a rendezvous of characters the like of which can never again assemble in the state of Oklahoma. A noted place in the history of border days is occupied by the Stockade Hotel, an institution which flourished in Sapulpa. On its dirt floors members of the Dalton gang, the French and James boys, Cole and Bill Younger and other outlaws are said to have danced and caroused." Kate also migrated here from St. Louis, sometime between 1881 and her family's first documented reference to Sapulpa in 1903.

Kate and Bertha

The announcement of the birth of their first child indicated that Pliny and his brother operated a clothing business in Sapulpa at this time, and that Bertha and Pliny had lived in Guthrie before coming to Sapulpa. Tragically, their infant son, Marley, died seven months later on 24 June 1903. He was buried in the Sapulpa cemetery with no marker on his grave.

Sometime between June 1903 and 1908, Bertha and Pliny moved from Sapulpa to Braggs, Oklahoma. Bertha was in Braggs by 23 September 1908, when she was a member of the Board of Directors of the Bank of Braggs, which was owned by her husband and other Castanien family members.[239]

Kate and Bertha both appeared in the 1910 Federal Census, located in different counties in Oklahoma.

Kate, using the name Sarah C. Batson, was in Vian, Sequoyah County, Oklahoma on 21 April 1910.

Kate was enumerated as a 61-year-old, widowed, head-of-household, with one living child from a single birth, in a rented home. Her occupation was 'keeper of a hotel' and she had been unemployed for sixteen weeks during the previous year. One servant, employed at the hotel, lived with Kate; Ella Thompson, age 40, widowed with two living children from four births, was recorded in the same household. Additional research was done to verify if Ella was truly a servant or if she might be a prostitute.[240] Although some details about Ella's life remained vague, she seemed to be employed as a hotel servant and not as a prostitute, so Kate was not operating a brothel passing as a hotel in 1910 (see following pages for additional proof of this assertion). Interestingly, in this census, Kate listed her correct age; but, still reported that she had been born in Kentucky and her parents were born in Virginia. It appeared as if she was operating a legitimate boarding house, but currently had no boarders. There was no other information to suggest that Kate might be operating a bawdy house, although Oklahoma territory and its booming oil fields and other expanding enterprises offered many potential clients.

KATE IN FACT AND FICTION

Kate, as Sarah C. Batson, in the 1910 Federal Census of Vian, Oklahoma

Here Kate was listed as Sarah C. Batson, a Hotel Keeper. There is nothing to indicate that this might be a brothel pretending to be a hotel. The only other person in the household was a servant; there were no young women listed.

Oklahoma became a state on 16 November 1907. Prior to that Oklahoma was known as 'Indiana Territory' from 1803 when it was first included in the Louisiana Land Purchase. In 1812 it was part of the Missouri Territory and in 1819 it was part of the Arkansas Territory. Oklahoma took a Territorial Census in 1890 and 1907; but, neither Kate nor her daughter, Bertha, appear on either of these census returns.

Unfortunately the 1890 Federal census was largely destroyed before public release (public access to the census is restricted for 72 years). The remnants that survive do not list Kate in the indices. Kate's location and occupation in any 1900 Federal census return has not yet been located.

Meanwhile, Bertha, age 34, was in Braggs, Muskogee County, Oklahoma, with her husband Pliny Mannon Castanien and her second-born, infant son, Pliny Raymond Castanien, when the Federal census taker visited their home on 15 April 1910. Less than twenty miles separate the towns of Vian[241] and Braggs;[242] Kate and Bertha were geographically close at this time, and they seemed to move back and forth frequently.

In June 1910, Bertha "formerly of Braggs," visited her mother in Vian. After a week, Pliny joined her, and then he and Bertha left to, "take up their residence," in Sapulpa.[243]

By 1911, both Kate, as Mrs. Sarah C. Batson, and Bertha were living at different addresses in the same town of Sapulpa,[244] in Creek County to the west. And, by February 1913, Kate, "an old time hotel lady," also described as "a former hotel lady of this place," and, "one of the best public cateress' in the state," opened the Monticello Hotel in Braggs.[245]

In the next Federal census in 1920, Kate, still using the name Sarah C. Batson, age 72, was living in the same household with her daughter and son-in-law at 123 West Tompson in Sapulpa, Creek County, Oklahoma, on 8 January 1920. Her grandson, Pliny R., age 11, was with his elders.

Kate had moved to Sapulpa from Vian almost a decade before when she was listed as Mrs. Sarah C. Batson, living at 233 South Main Street, in the 1911 Sapulpa city directory. 'Plinnie' M. and Bertha Castanien were also back in Sapulpa and lived at 407 South Main. He worked for Banner Electric Company. Kate had moved in with Bertha and Pliny before 1916, since the city directory of that year listed Sarah Batson living with Pliny Castanien.

It appears that Bertha and her husband shifted back and forth between several counties in east-central Oklahoma during the early part of the twentieth century, beginning with their marriage in Oklahoma County in 1899.

In 1910, Bertha was located in Braggs in Muskogee County, Oklahoma, on the Federal census. Bertha was back in Sapulpa in Creek County by 25 March 1914, when she purchased property from her husband. Perhaps the Castaniens

KATE IN FACT AND FICTION

left Braggs, Oklahoma, soon after the fire of 4 July 1911, which destroyed the entire business district.[246]

Property records in Sapulpa, Creek County, Oklahoma, were examined for further clarification of when and how long Bertha and Pliny lived in Sapulpa.[247]

Three Generations
Kate, as Sarah E. Batson (mother)
Bertha E. Evans Castanien (daughter)
"Cas" Pliny Raymond Castanien (grandson)
This photograph is estimated to have been taken about 1912 in Oklahoma. It has no visible identification regarding its origin, location or date. 'Cas' Pliny, who was mistakenly identified as a *granddaughter* by Breihan in 1971, was born 9 August 1908, in Braggs, Oklahoma. Pictured here between three- and four-years-old, dates the photograph to about 1912 ± a year or two.
At about this time, both Kate and Bertha were living in Sapulpa, Creek County, Oklahoma.

Pliny, as P. M. Castanien, was involved in a law suit involving property in Sapulpa which originated in Creek County Court on 16 December 1913, and was decided by the Supreme Court of Oklahoma on 26 December 1916.[248]

Pliny Castanien, sometimes with Bertha's name included, was listed in the city directory of Sapulpa annually from 1911 through 1930.

Bertha and her husband, Pliny, were in Sapulpa for the Federal census of 1930 on 7 April, and were still there through 16 September 1931, when she sold the property back to her husband.

Pliny was involved with a variety of different types of business ventures and the various occupations listed for him through the years included:

1) working for a transfer company, in business with his brothers, in 1896;
2) bank director and cashier in 1908 (he, his brothers, and his father owned the Bank);
3) banker on the 1910 census;
4) working for Banner Electric Company in 1911;
5) electrical contractor on the 1920 census;
6) traveling salesman in 1928 and 1937;
7) salesman for an oil supplier on the 1930 census; and,
8) 20-year representative for Baird Manufacturing in 1938, per his obituary.

On the 1930 Federal census, the Castanien family was recorded as living at 123 Werth Street in Sapulpa on 7 April. Their 21-year-old son, Pliny Raymond, was with his parents, Pliny M. (age 57), and Bertha (age 43).

This census was taken three months, almost to the day, *following* Kate's death at the Jackson County Home in Jackson County, Missouri, on January 9, 1930. Kate was buried a month later in Wyandotte County, Kansas, without family present. Did her family not know, or not care she had died? Had they not been notified of her death? What circumstances inhibited her daughter and grandson from attending Kate's funeral? Had they been informed that she had been admitted to the former Jackson County Poor Farm nine years previously? The answers to these questions have been lost to time.

Bertha and Pliny left Sapulpa before 1932; they were not listed in the 1932 Sapulpa phone directory.

In 1937, they were listed at 1305 Fairview Avenue in Wichita, Sedgwick County, Kansas, along with their son and his wife at 327 N. Poplar.[249] 'Cas' Pliny Raymond and Imogene L. (Jones) Castanien were at this address on 28 November 1936, when he completed his application for a social security number.

**Social Security Number Application
Pliny R. Castanien (Kate's grandson)**
The vital record includes his name; birth date and place; parents; residence; employer; and, Pliny's signature. This primary source originated in 1936 after Kate's death in 1930.

However, by October 24, 1937, Pliny Mannon had moved to Hutchinson, Reno County, Kansas, where the local newspaper reported he was building a new home.[250]

Just a couple of weeks prior, Bertha had been admitted as a patient at the Larned Hospital for the Insane in Pawnee County, Kansas, on September 9, 1937. Larned State Hospital continues today (2014) and confirmed that Bertha had been admitted from Sedgwick County, where Wichita is located, although Sedgwick County was not in their 'catchment area.' Reno County adjacent to Sedgwick County was in the hospital's catchment area.

Current privacy regulations prohibited the hospital from providing information about Bertha's diagnosis, or date of onset of her mental illness. Perhaps Pliny, Sr., moved to Hutchinson specifically so that Bertha could be admitted to Larned Hospital . . . or, Bertha was transferred to Larned Hospital because Pliny moved from Wichita.

Bertha's mental state may have deteriorated gradually over a long period, and may explain why the family did not, or could not respond to Kate's dire situation between 1921 and 1930.

It is also possible that Kate's mental condition had also deteriorated earlier, and that combinations of factors lead to a mutual estrangement between mother and daughter.

Kate's nephew, Joseph Edward King, told his granddaughter that when he had visited his aunt Kate at the Jackson County Home, Kate was, "far into dementia," then.[251] The onset of dementia may have been a reason why Kate was initially admitted to the Jackson County Home for the Aged and Infirm in 1921.

Kate's or Bertha's conditions may have had gradual or intermittent onset, and their individual afflictions could have coincided to produce a volatile situation causing alienation and severance of familial ties.

Pliny Mannon Castanien died suddenly and unexpectedly in his new home in Hutchison, Kansas, on November 13, 1938, as announced in two different local papers:[252]

KATE IN FACT AND FICTION

Pliny M. Castanien

Services for Pliny M. Castanien, who died here on Sunday, will be held at 4 o'clock this afternoon in the Lahey and Martin mortuary at Wichita. Burial will be in Wichita Park Cemetery.[253]

[Untitled]

Pliny Mannon Castanien, 70, was found dead in a chair at his home, 1328 East Third, Sunday morning by neighbors who notified police officers. Dr. H. M. Steward, coroner, said he apparently had suffered a heart attack and had been dead a short time.

He was representative of the Baird Manufacturing Company of Tulsa and had lived in Hutchinson about a year. His son, Pliny R. Castanien, police reporter for the Wichita Eagle came and accompanied the body to Wichita for burial.

Funeral services will be held at the Lahey-Martin mortuary tomorrow afternoon at 4 o'clock in Wichita.[254]

Pliny Mannon's obituary appeared in the Wichita paper where his son worked (Reno County is immediately adjacent to Sedgwick County, where Wichita is located):

Oil Salesman is Dead at 67

Pliny Mannon Castanien, 67 years old, father of Pliny R. Castanien, Wichita newspaper reporter, died suddenly in Hutchinson, Kas., Sunday. Mr. Castanien had been residing there for the past year.

Altho he had suffered from heart trouble and had been under treatment in Hutchinson, his death was entirely unexpected.

Mr. Castanien, who was employed by the Baird Manufacturing Company of Tulsa, Okla., had sold oil field products in this section for the past 30 years.

He was born at Upper Sandusky, Ohio and came to Kansas with his parents in 1875. They settled near Udall and he grew to manhood there. He had lived with his son here for several years before going to Hutchinson.

In addition to his son, who resides at 1725 North Vassar Avenue, he is survived by his wife Bertha; five brothers and one sister.

The body was brought to Wichita Saturday night. Funeral services will be conducted from the Lahey and Martin Mortuary at 4 p.m. Tuesday with the Rev. W. E. McCoy officiating.[255]

Kate and Bertha

Bertha was named secondarily possibly to avoid referencing her situation at the state asylum. Imogene, the wife of Pliny R., who was also still living at this time, was not mentioned at all. This oversight or omission suggests that Pliny R. did not write the obituary.

Baird Manufacturing Company of Tulsa, Oklahoma still exists today (2014), and is still involved with oil field (gas and oil fittings, etc.) equipment. His son, Pliny R., arranged for the burial of Pliny M. Castanien in Wichita Park Cemetery in Wichita, Sedgwick County, Kansas.

Bertha remained at Larned State Hospital. She was listed there on April 4 in the 1940 Federal census, and died there on 8 December 1944, at the age of 69 years, 2 months and 1 day, of arteriosclerosis and kidney disease.

Death Certificate of Bertha E. Castanien (Kate's daughter)
Data was supplied by the Larned State Hospital from Bertha's 1937 admittance records. Bertha's "married" status should be "widowed;" her husband died in 1938. Curiously missing is anything about Bertha's mother, listed as "Unknown." Her father's surname, "Evans," and birthplace, England, are recorded.

KATE IN FACT AND FICTION

Bertha had been a resident of Larned State Hospital for seven years and 28 days. Her body was transported to Wichita for burial beside her husband.[256] Bertha and Pliny Castanien's graves remain unmarked.[257]

Bertha's son, "Cas" Pliny Raymond, was stationed in Savannah, Georgia, in the Army when she died,[258] and, thus, the information on her death certificate was abstracted from the Larned State Hospital records. Only the surname Evans, with unknown given name, was listed for Bertha's father on her death certificate. Her mother was listed as unknown. It is strange that hospital records would not include her mother's name. It is unexplainable how her husband, Pliny M., failed to supply better admitting information; he knew and had lived with his mother-in-law.

"Cas" Pliny Raymond Castanien, son of Bertha E. Evans and Pliny Mannon Castanien—and Kate's grandson—blazed a much better marked trail than that left by either his parents or grandmother. Pliny was born 9 August 1908, in Braggs, Muskogee County, Oklahoma. Pliny Raymond was born five years after his parents had buried their first-born infant son, who had been named Pliny Mannon Castanien, Jr., after his father.

Pliny Raymond used the nick name "Cas" during college and throughout his professional life. Perhaps this nickname even originated in childhood to avoid confusion with his father when addressing them at home together.

He was with his parents, as a very young child, in Braggs, Muskogee County, Oklahoma on the Federal census on 15 April 1910.

In the 1920 Federal census, he was with his parents, as an 11-year-old boy, in Sapulpa, Creek County, Oklahoma, on 8 January 1920. His maternal grandmother Kate, using the name, Sarah C. Batson, was also living in the same household. Thus, Pliny knew Kate, had been old enough to remember her, and had had an opportunity to learn about any aspects of her life that she was willing to share with her only grandchild. It is intriguing to speculate how much personal history Kate would have disclosed to an inquisitive grandson.

Cas graduated from high school in Sapulpa, Creek Country, Oklahoma, in 1926. He was pictured as a member of the Junior Class in the 1925 issue of *The Sapulpan*, the year book of Sapulpa High School. He attended Oklahoma Agricultural and Mechanical College, now known as Oklahoma State University, in Stillwater, Oklahoma, from 1926 through 1930, although he may not have attended continuously.[259] He was listed as Pliny Castanien, freshman, living at 307 Knoblock, Stillwater, Oklahoma, in the 1926-1927 college directory.[260]

However, Cas was not recorded in either the 1927-1928 or the 1928-1929 college directories. But, he was listed in the Sapulpa, Oklahoma City directory, as boarding at the same address where his parents lived at 123 West Thompson. 'Musician' was recorded as his occupation in the city directory.

He was again noted in the 1929-1930 college directory as living at 316 Hester in Stillwater, Oklahoma.[261] He was also listed as 'Cas' in the 1930 *Redskin*, year book of Oklahoma Agricultural and Mechanical College published by the Student Association, and was active on the News Staff, in the College Band and in Kappa Kappa Psi.[262]

"Cas" Pliny Raymond probably did not graduate from college with a degree, since when he enlisted in the U.S. Army in 1944, his enlistment record stated that he had three years of college education then. In addition, a biographical note about Pliny in 1993 does not mention any advanced degrees, although it indicated that he had attended institutions of higher learning.[263]

If he had graduated, his degree would be listed and 'graduated' used in the place of 'attended.' The dates of his attendance at Wichita State University were not specified; but, he probably attended classes there while employed at the newspapers in Wichita.

In the 1930 Federal census, Pliny, at age 21, was living at home with his parents in Sapulpa, Oklahoma, on 7 April.

"Cas" Pliny Raymond Castanien began his journalist career as a cub reporter for the *Wichita Beacon* in 1931.[264] His special interest was the police beat and he later worked as a police reporter for the *Wichita Evening Eagle* for nine years.

Besides accounts about crime, accidents and other police reports, Pliny wrote human-interest stories.[265]

"Cas" Pliny Raymond Castanien married Imogene L. Jones in Sedgwick County (probably in Wichita), Kansas, on 6 May 1934.

**Marriage License of Kate's Grandson
"Cas" Pliny Raymond Castanien and Imogene Jones**
This marriage took place in Wichita, Sedgwick County, Kansas, after Kate's death. Kate and her granddaughter-in-law never knew each other.

They lived at 327 North Popular in Wichita, Kansas, on 28 November 1936, when he applied for his Social Security number at age 28.

"Cas" Pliny and Imogene moved to various addresses within Wichita between 1937 and 1948. According to the Wichita city directories, Pliny and Imogene Castanien lived at: 327 N. Popular Av. in 1937; 1347 Lewellen Av. in 1938; 1725 N. Vassar Av. in 1941 and 1943 (also at this address in 1940 Federal census); and, 638 N. Popular in 1948.

They owned the house at 1725 N. Vassar Avenue in Wichita on 5 April 1940, at the time of the Federal census. Present in the household with Pliny and Imogene in this census, and listed as a *daughter*, was 10-year-old Janice Castanien.

However, her place of birth, listed as the state of Washington, which, if correct, and in conjunction with the fact that she was born about four years before Pliny's marriage, indicated that Janice was not a biological child of this couple.

The only other genealogical reference found for Janice was a divorce of Janice L. Castanien from Paul R. Eskildsen in Marin County, California, in August of 1973.

There was a Janet Castanien in the 1930 census in Pitt Township, Wyandot County, Ohio, who was the daughter of Pliny's second cousin, Paul Castanien, and his wife Ruth.

Perhaps Janet, a cousin, was mistakenly listed as a daughter, Janice, by the census taker when Janet was visiting in California. There was no further record of Janice, or her relationship with Pliny and Imogene.

"Cas" Pliny was married to Imogene at the time he enlisted in the Army on 1 March 1944, at Fort Leavenworth, Kansas. During the Second World War, he was assigned to the Kansas Office of War Information as a staff writer. He was located in Savannah, Georgia, when his mother died in December 1944. Whether Imogene accompanied Pliny during his military assignments, or she remained in Wichita during the war, is unknown.

After his discharge from the Army, "Cas" Pliny returned to Wichita, Kansas, and worked for the *Evening Eagle*. He then worked for the *Tulsa World* for a year before moving to California.

From Tulsa, Oklahoma, they moved to San Diego, California. "Cas" Pliny joined the staff of the *San Diego Union* in 1948 and worked as a police reporter at that newspaper for 26 years.[266] He developed an extensive and mutually respectful relationship with the San Diego Police Department which aided both him in his professional career and the police department in their community relations. "Cas" Pliny was the person on which the character, Ben Andrews, in the television series,

"Manhunt," was based. Pliny worked as a technical advisor on "Manhunt," a syndicated crime television drama. 'Manhunt' aired 78 half-hour episodes between 1959 and 1961. Victor Jory starred as San Diego police detective, Lieutenant Howard Finucane. Patrick McVey starred as police reporter, Ben Andrews, whose character was based on Pliny Castanien. *The Chronicle* newspaper in the program was the "stand-in" for the *San Diego Union*. A partial set of episodes from this 50+year-old, black-and-white series are currently available online.

"Cas" Pliny's wife Imogene died in San Diego, California on 3 December 1966. No known children survived this marriage. Two years later in 1968, Pliny married Barbara Ruth Anderson, whom he had met while she worked in the San Diego County Coroner's office. Barbara Ruth was born 9 April 1913, in Eagle Rock, California. Little is known about Barbara other than she made annual voyages between California and Honolulu, Hawaii Territory, from 1936 to 1941.[267]

Pliny Raymond Castanien

After Pliny retired from the *San Diego Union* in 1974, he became the volunteer historian for the San Diego Police Department in the office of the Northern Division. In 1993, his book, *To Protect and Serve: A History of the San Diego Police Department and Its Chiefs, 1889-1989*, was published by the San Diego Historical Society.

Pliny Castanien died on 6 February 1994 and his obituary was published, with a featured byline, in *The San Diego Union-Tribune*, the now merged successor of the newspaper that had employed him for twenty-six years:

Pliny Raymond 'Cass' Castanien, 85, author and longtime police reporter

by Dee Anne Traitel, Staff Writer

Pliny Raymond 'Cass' Castanien, a former police reporter for *The San Diego Union* and author of a book published last year on the history of the San Diego Police Department, died Sunday of cardiac arrest at Kaiser Permanente Hospital. He was 85.

Mr. Castanien, who was named for a Roman scholar, Pliny the Elder, was hired to cover the police beat for the *Union* in 1948. By the time he retired in 1974, he had covered the city's Police Department for 26 years and had worked with eight city editors.

Considered a classic police-beat reporter, he was known throughout the ranks of the Police Department, from new recruits up to the chief. There was even a television character based on the San Diego newsman.

Mr. Castanien was the prototype for the newspaper reporter in the 1959-1960 television series, "Manhunt," which was based on the San Diego Police Department. Actor Pat McVey portrayed Mr. Castanien, who worked as a technical adviser for the series. As a journalist, he wrote about mayhem, felonies, accidents and fires. But he always kept an eye out for the gripping human-interest stories that cross the police blotter. He also wrote extensively about the challenges and problems faced by the cop on the beat.

He is credited with establishing a police-academy program to promote good relations between police and the news media. He was honored by the Police Department for fair and accurate reporting.

After retiring from the *Union*, Mr. Castanien was asked to work as an unpaid historian for the Police Department. In an office at the department's Northern Division, he wrote, *To Protect and Serve: A History of the San Diego Police Department and Its Chiefs, 1889-1989*. The book was published in 1993.

At the time of his death, he was at work on a book of trivia about the Police Department.

Mr. Castanien attended Oklahoma A&M College and Wichita University, majoring in journalism. He got his start as a police reporter at the *Wichita Beacon* in 1931. He subsequently worked as a police reporter for the *Wichita Evening Eagle* for nine years. He worked for a year for the *Tulsa World* before joining the *Union*.

During World War II, he was a staff member of the Office of War Information assigned to the state of Kansas. He also served in the Army Air Corps as an undercover investigator.

Mr. Castanien's first wife, Imogene, died in 1967. He married Barbara Anderson, a former employee of the county Coroner's Office, in 1968. They met while he was covering police stories. The couple traveled widely in retirement, mainly in Mexico. She is his only survivor.

There will be no funeral services. Contributions to the San Diego Humane Society may be made in his name.[268]

Much of the information in this obituary was taken from an article, entitled, "Police Beat Reporter Plans Travel," published in the *San Diego Union* on 1 January 1974, announcing Pliny's retirement after 25-years as a police reporter at that newspaper.

The authors of this biography, Virgil Hoftiezer and Vicki Beck, did not discover "Cas" Pliny Raymond Castanien until 1996, two years after his death. Pliny's wife, Barbara, continued to live at the same address in San Diego, California, where she and Pliny lived when he died. Barbara Ruth (Anderson) Castanien died in San Diego, California, on September 18, 2009. His widow's wishes not to be contacted were respected.[269]

Unfortunately, any information Pliny knew regarding his parents or his grandmother was lost when he died. He had shared some personal information with some of his paternal relatives; but, he contributed nothing to piece together the last years of his parents' lives or any concrete data regarding his maternal side of the family beyond the verification that Bertha was the daughter of Sarah Catherine King, aka. Kate.

None of Kate's nieces or nephews (or great nieces or nephews), ever knew about their aunt's daughter, Bertha. Although the King descendants knew that their respective parent or grandparent knew "Aunt Kate" and passed down family stories about her, there was never any mention or record of her daughter, Bertha, and thus none were aware of Kate's grandson, "Cas" Pliny Raymond Castanien. Indeed, Kate's family ties completely unraveled once she left her daughter in Oklahoma to return to her hometown of Blue Springs, Missouri.

Pliny Raymond Castanien died without children, leaving only his second spouse to survive him. Bertha was Kate's only child, and Pliny Raymond Castanien was the only child of Bertha that survived beyond infancy.

Consequently, Kate's line of descent ended with her grandson. Past, present, or future claims of being descended from Kate, or of knowing a direct descendant of Kate, have no genealogical foundation, and have no documented basis.

A claim by a self-proclaimed descendant from a son of Kate, supposedly fathered by Quantrill, apparently was a ploy to sell a book and lacked any sort of documentation, despite repeated promises to provide such evidence. As stated previously, William Clarke Quantrill left no known offspring, and certainly none by Kate.

Kate was definitely fonder of her daughter than the elusive father was. Perhaps Bertha's biological father never even knew of her existence. Bertha apparently did not know his given name—or at least her son never identified his grandfather by name. But photographic evidence (as shown on page 158) proves that Kate claimed Bertha as her daughter. The mother was fonder than the father because she was certain that the child was her own.

KATE IN FACT AND FICTION

CHAPTER 8

Kate's Fate
The End, and Her Final Resting Place

*"Do not go gentle into that good night,
Old age should burn and rave at close of day;
Rage, rage against the dying of the light."*
Dylan Thomas (1951)

    Kate seemed to have anticipated the advice Dylan Thomas, the Welsh poet, wrote for his dying father in the journal *Botteghe Oscure* in 1951. The controversy and mystery generated during her lifetime continued to follow her into death. She changed her name again one last time, and died as 'Sarah Head'. Many questions shrouded her death and even her burial. Two different tombstones, erected in her honor in different cemeteries by different generations of aficionados, illustrate the unorthodoxy and contradictions of her story, both in life and in death.

    Kate Clarke's life in St. Louis, Missouri, was documented up through 1880, after which she disappeared. Kate changed her identify and took her young daughter away from public scrutiny to raise her in complete obscurity. The marriage of her daughter, Bertha E. Evans, in Oklahoma City in 1899, suggested that Kate had eventually moved to the anonymity of Oklahoma Territory.

Kate, as Sarah E. Batson

KATE IN FACT AND FICTION

Kate's intent to avoid public notice was extremely successful. She had adapted the name 'Batson;' but, whether that name was acquired through a marriage, or, if it was just another purloined *nom de plume* has not yet been ascertained.

On the 21 April 1910, Federal census, Kate was using the name 'Sarah C. Batson.' She was enumerated as a 61-year-old widow operating a hotel in Vian Township, Sequoyah County, Oklahoma, with one servant, a 40-year-old widow named Ella Thompson. No boarders were listed with the two women. The census confirmed that Kate was the mother of only one child (unnamed) who was then still living.

A year later, Kate had moved to Sapulpa in Creek County, Oklahoma, where her daughter and son-in-law, Bertha and Pliny Castanien, were also living.[270] Sometime during the next five years (between 1911 and 1916) she moved in with Bertha and Pliny.[271] Whether this move was precipitated by health issues (for her or Bertha), financial considerations, or familial concerns, or a combination of factors, is pure speculation.

Kate may have given up her home at 223 South Main in Sapulpa, Oklahoma (where she was living in 1911) initially to go back to Jackson County Missouri to keep house for her brother, Francis Marion King, after his wife, Eveline Lynch King, died on 20 July 1912. According to Fred A. Ford, Kate returned to the King family farm to keep house for her brother, Francis Marion King, who died on 7 May 1916, two days after bequeathing the King family farm to his son Anson.[272]

Anson King continued to live on the King farm until his sudden and unexpected death four years later. Kate, as Sarah Batson, apparently returned to Sapulpa, Oklahoma, between the deaths of her sister-law, Eveline, in 1912, and her brother, Francis Marion King, in 1916. Sarah C. Batson lived with her daughter, Bertha E. Evans Castanien (and Pliny) at 123 West Thompson in Sapulpa in 1915.[273]

Seventy-two-year-old Kate was still living with her daughter, Bertha, and family in Sapulpa, Creek County, Oklahoma, on 8 January 1920, when the Federal census taker visited their home. During the previous 18 months, Kate had also lost both her oldest brother and her only sister.[274]

Kate's Fate

Kate left Sapulpa, Oklahoma, and returned to Blue Springs, Jackson County, Missouri, sometime between January and July in 1920. This momentous interstate move was probably prompted by the sudden and unexpected death of Kate's nephew, Anson Marion King, on 29 May 1920, from a ruptured aortic aneurism.

On July 2, 1920, Kate was in Blue Springs, Jackson County, Missouri, listed as Sarah C. Batson, now of Blue Springs, in the probate papers for Anson King.[275]

She may have been staying at the home of another nephew, Frank William King, the son of her late oldest brother, William Jasper King. According to the letter of Fred Ford written in 1965, Kate was staying with Frank King at this time.[276] Also according to Fred Ford, he saw Kate in attendance at the Anson King Estate sale on 23 July 1920.

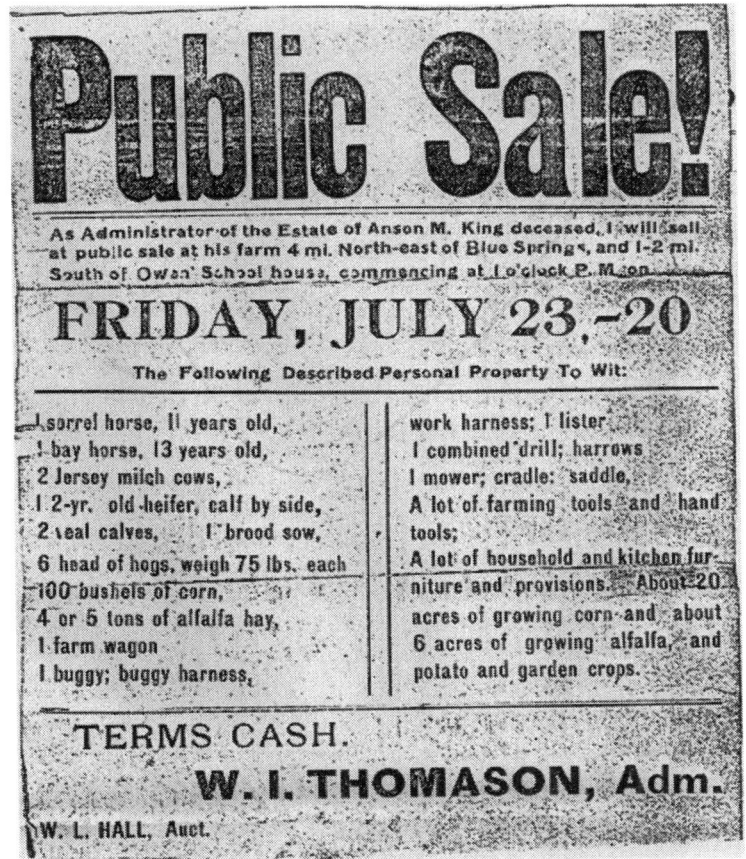

Anson Marion King, the son of Kate's late older brother, Francis Marion King, was only 52 years, 9 months, and 29 days of age, unmarried with no children, and the sole owner of the King family farm. The King family farm, land originally purchased by Kate's father in 1855, was the home where Kate and her siblings had been raised. Kate supposedly paid to have the house and barn rebuilt after the Civil War ended;[277] all the buildings were burned during the Federally-mandated evacuation dictated by General Order No. 11 in August 1863.

Kate would have expected to have a major role in settling the family affairs and sorting the family effects since she and her younger brother, Samuel Robert King, were the only two surviving siblings of that generation...although there were numerous nieces and nephews to be considered. Kate had five nieces and nine nephews living in Jackson County in 1920.[278]

However, the events involving the settlement of the King estate unfolded very differently than expected. Anson King had died intestate, meaning he did not have a Will, and thus, his estate was open to claim by any and all of his relatives, including the siblings and half-siblings of his mother, Eveline Lynch King. Eveline's parents were both married previously and each had had children from their first marriages. These individuals "of the half blood" also made claim upon the estate of Anson M. King.

By the time the estate was settled 17 months later, shares as small as 1/735 were allocated to the 67 heirs-at-law. Kate's last remaining sibling died before the estate was finally settled.[279]

On 20 September 1921, Kate, as Mrs. Sarah C. Batson, received $123.08 as her two-fifteenths (2/15) share of the final settlement of Anson King's estate from W. I. Thomason, administrator of the estate. Her signature on the receipt for the disbursement was witnessed by her nephew Oscar King.

> $123.08 Independence, Mo.
> September 20th 1921.
>
> Received of W.I. Thomason, Administrator of the estate of Anson M.King deceased, late of Jackson County, Missouri, the sum of One Hundred Twenty-three & 8/100 Dollars, being payment in full of my distributive share in said estate, as one of the heirs of said deceased, as shown by the final settlement of said administrator, filed in the Probate Court of Jackson County,Mo. at Independence, on September 14th 1921.
>
> Sarah C. Batson
>
> Attest:-
> Oscar King

Her shaky signature, as Mrs. S. C. Batson, less than two months earlier on 11 July 1921, documents her promise to pay $100 of her anticipated inheritance to John W. Clements (18 January 1856-17 April 1937), a lawyer in Independence, Missouri, who was the attorney for the Anson King estate's administrator, W. I. Thomason.

Kate signed the note, "Mrs. S. C. Batson." Either Clements had provided some sort of legal services for Kate; or, he had advanced her with $100 in cash in anticipation of a larger, forthcoming inheritance as collateral. Whatever the business rationale for this "loan," there was no reference to Kate owing Clements interest.

Sadly, after the repayment of her $100 advance, Kate was left with only $23.08 of her $123.08 inheritance.

> Mr. W.I. Thomason,
> Blue Springs, Mo.
> Dear Sir:-
>   Independence,Mo.
>   July 11th 1921.
>
>   Please pay to Mr.John W.Clements the sum of One Hundred Dollars, out of any money in your hands due me from the estate of Anson M.King deceased, and charge said sum to me as a part of the amount due me as one of the heirs of said Anson M.King from his personal estate.
>
>   Yours very truly,
>   Mrs S. C. Batson

KATE IN FACT AND FICTION

The value of $123.00 in 2013 currency is $1,500 per the Consumer Price Index, and thus $23.00 would be roughly equivalent to about $280, a very small inheritance, indeed, for the sole surviving child of Robert L. and Malinda Rebecca (Stringer) King, and the 160 acres of land they had owned in Sni-a-Bar Township (Section 7, Township 49 north, Range 30 west) of Jackson County, Missouri. Of course, Kate never recouped her costs in rebuilding the King family house and barn after the Civil War.

By the time the Anson King estate was finally settled, Kate had moved into the Jackson County Home for the Aged and Infirm (originally called the Jackson County Poor Farm) where she would reside for the remainder of her life.[280]

Jackson County Home, Little Blue, Missouri, 1933
Jackson County has operated a facility for the indigent at this location since 1852. By 1921, when Kate was admitted, two major services were offered here: 1) the County Hospital (bottom image) and the County Home, a nursing home facility for pauper residents (top image). This historic property today (2014) is still owned by Jackson County, and those same services (and others) continue through a lease with the Truman Medical Center Corporation.

Kate's Fate

Kate's request for admission to the County Home was approved by the Jackson County Court, predecessor of the Jackson County Legislature, on 15 April 1921.[281] She probably moved into the facility soon thereafter.

Who initiated the request for Kate was not stated. It may likely have been her nephew, Jack Ragland, of the Kansas City Live Stock Exchange, who was identified as Kate's guardian in 1929.[282]

John Marion "Jack" Ragland
(20 May 1866-14 Jun 1939)

Jack was the second son and third child of Kate's sister, Martha Jane King Ragland. John Marion, named after his father John O. Ragland and his uncle, Francis Marion King, became a member of the Kansas City Livestock Exchange. He was the informant on his sister, 'Annie' Georgeanna R. Hudspeth's, death certificate, and was Kate's guardian in 1929.

John Marion Ragland and his wife Mary H. Carmody Ragland had two children: Frances Elizabeth (married Robert Charles Swisher) and John C. Ragland. Jack Ragland was Kate's "guardian," or power of attorney, in 1929, and would have been available for claiming Kate's body (and paying her final expenses had he been her executor) in 1930.

KATE IN FACT AND FICTION

During her stay at the County Home, four superintendants directed Kate's well-being and health care:

1) Dr. James William Kinyoun, of Buckner, Missouri, who was superintendant from at least 1919 to 1922;[283]

2) William Henry Carr, 1923 through at least 1926;[284]

3) Lee N. Allen was there for a time during 1925;[285] and,

4) James W. Hostetter by 1930 (through 1935).[286]

In the winter of her years at the County Home, looking back at her teenage love affair, did Kate make any overtures to revive Quantrill? Curiously, in 1922, "a member of the Confederate Veterans of Oklahoma," called upon Huston Quin, the then mayor of Louisville, Kentucky, to locate the body of William Quantrill.[287] Why an envoy from Oklahoma of all places? One might speculate that Kate instigated this search. And, it may have led to a 1926 *Kansas City Star* article about Kate living at the Jackson County Home.[288] Unfortunately the identity of the reporter who authored this often quoted and frequently referenced report has never been revealed. This article has been the quintessential reference for Kate's life.

Nearly all subsequent reports about Kate have utilized, paraphrased, cited, drew upon, and even plagiarized this account.

Unfortunately, the story contains many errors that detract from its credibility as a completely reliable reference. Kate's advanced dementia by this date when she visited with the reporter should also be taken into account.

According to the 1926 article (transcribed and provided as an appendix in this biography), Kate "ran-off" with another County Home inmate named Walter Head:

> Four years ago [1922], when 74 years old, she ran way with an inmate of the home whom she had known for years and was married the fifth time. She and her husband do not live together at the home, for men and women are separated.[289]

Walter Head had been enumerated at the County Home in the 1920 Federal census as a 54-year-old Irishman. In the 1930 Federal census, Walter Head was identified at the Jackson County Home for the Aged and Infirm as a 68-year-old widower, born in Kentucky.

Based on census history, Walter Head would have been about 60 or 64 years old in 1926 . . . 56 or 60 when he "ran away" with Kate. According to various city directories of Kansas City, Missouri, from 1900 to 1912, Walter Head's profession was described was a wood worker working for wagon and carriage makers there from 1900 to 1912.[290] Results of recent research as this biography goes to press suggests that Walter Head was the son of Joseph Franklin Head and Eliza Jane Beall Head of Daviess County, Kentucky, as enumerated on the 1880 Federal census.[291]

No record of any of marriage for Kate—perhaps four, certainly not five—have yet been located in public documents in Missouri or Oklahoma.

However, Kate's surname definitely changed from Batson to Head by 1929 when she was listed as "Mrs. Walter Head, formerly of Independence, Missouri," in the list of inmates of the Jackson County Home.[292] Her husband, Walter

Head, was also listed as an inmate, formerly of 511 Walnut Street, with no one noted as friend, guardian or relative.

Despite the 1926 expose, "none of the inmates of the County Home where she died ever knew her real identity. She seemed content to sit and dream of the past. In her last year, although her mind still seemed to be clear, she rarely spoke to anyone."[293] Kate died on 9 January 1930.

News stories, as well as Kate's death certificate, identified Ketterlin Funeral Home as the party which handled her burial. Ketterlin Funeral Home was paid by Jackson County to perform undertaking services for the indigent. Kate's body was preserved and held in a vault for nearly a month while Ketterlin Funeral Home searched for relatives.[294] The delayed burial was not due to the undertaker abandoning bodies[295] as suggested in 2008.[296] It may seem strange that the funeral home was searching for relatives. However, it may have been part of their contract to make an attempt to contact

---

STILL NO FUNDS FOR BURIAL

No Action by Relatives of Mrs. Sarah Head, Quantrill's Bride

There are still no arrangements for Mrs. Sarah Head, who, as the girl bride of William Clarke Quantrill, famous guerrilla leader and espouser of the Southern cause, was known as Kate Clarke. Relatives who were found by the Ketterlin funeral home have made no move to provide funds for the burial.

Mrs. Head died January 9 at the Jackson County Home for the Aged. She had lived there without letting the other inmates know her real identity. Four years ago she told a representative of the Star the story of her romance, marriage to Quantrill and the thrilling war days before his death, when she was left a widow, 17 years old.

relatives before charging the county for burials. Unfortunately, Ketterlin Funeral Home no longer exists, and their business records have not survived.

Kate had at least a dozen nieces and nephews, including Jack Ragland, her guardian just a year earlier. Her daughter, Bertha Evans Castanien, living in Sapulpa, Oklahoma, at this time, was apparently not notified of her mother's death.

> **QUANTRILL'S BRIDE IS BURIED**
>
> **Only a Few Friends at Grave of Mrs. Sarah Head**
>
> The burial of Mrs. Sarah Head was held yesterday afternoon in the Maple Hill cemetery.
> Mrs. Head was the girl bride of William Clarke Quantrill, famous guerrilla leader of Civil War day. She died January 9 at the Jackson County Home for the Aged. Only a few friends were at the grave.

Almost a month after her death, Kate was buried. Her body was interred in Grave 6, Lot 63, Block 5, in Maple Hill Cemetery in Kansas City, Wyandotte County, Kansas. This cemetery apparently had a contract to receive indigent burials at this time. Two consecutive newspaper reports (presented here) announced Kate's death.[297]

Unfortunately, no records exist that identify which relatives were finally contacted, and what "friends" were at Kate's graveside. The reasons Kate's relatives failed to step forward and/or declined to pay for her burial expenses . . . or, to attend the funeral services remain a mystery.

Since she was buried in Maple Hill Cemetery instead of a family-owned plot elsewhere, however, it is presumed that Jackson County, Missouri's 'pauper fund' (at one time called the 'Poor House Fund') was used to cover Kate's funeral and burial expenses. Patient records from the Jackson County Home were destroyed from broken water pipes.[298]

KATE IN FACT AND FICTION

The 6 February 1930 *Kansas City Times* newspaper clearly stated that Kate's burial was in Maple Hill Cemetery. Over the years, the loss of this historical factoid led to a great deal of confusion and controversy regarding the location of Kate's grave.

Kate's death certificate was completed by informant J. W. Hostetter, superintendent of the Jackson County Home at that time, who used Kate's admission data which explains why most of her personal data is incomplete, estimated, or marked "unknown." The "place of burial" on Kate's death certificate was written by a different hand in different ink (or pencil) than other parts of the document, and was nearly illegible on the digitized copy available from the Missouri State Archives' online death certificate database.

Four years after Kate died, her widower, Walter Head, died at the Jackson County Home.

Ketterlin Funeral Home handled his arrangements, too.

And, as with Kate's death certificate, J. W. Hostetter, Jackson County Home Superintendent, relied on County Home admission records to partially complete Head's death certificate.

Walter Head was also buried in Maple Hill Cemetery in an unmarked grave, Grave 1, Lot 53, Block 7, about 50 yards northwest of Kate's grave.

Years later as interest in Kate resurfaced among local scholars, many assumed, erroneously, that Kate was buried in an unmarked grave in the "Potter's Field" maintained at the Jackson County Home.[299] The 'Potter's Field' remains on the property of the former Jackson County Home for the Aged and Infirm. As of 2014, the square-acre is still owned by Jackson County, as is the remainder of the 250+acre tract that is leased to Truman Medical Center Corporation as the Truman Medical Center-Lakewood.

However, there are no known extant burial records for the 750+grave-cemetery in the now overgrown parcel of sacred space at the southwestern corner of the property. And, no pauper graves were ever known to have been marked.[300]

Others believed, also in error, that Kate was buried (or subsequently re-interred) in an unmarked grave next to her parents in Slaughter Cemetery in Jackson County, Missouri.[301]

A memorial marker in honor of Kate was erected in Slaughter Cemetery in 1971.

This monument to Kate, situated next to the grave of Kate's mother, Malinda (Stringer) King, reads:

KATE KING QUANTRILL
1848   1930
AGE 82
Erected by Fred Ford & Arthur Dealy
1971

Fred A. Ford and Arthur D. Dealy may have been neighbors to each other and to the King family; but, they were not related to each other, and neither of them is known to be related to Kate. Dealy certainly was NOT Kate's nephew as previously published.[302] Nor did Kate ever live with Dealy. She certainly _never_, "stayed with Dealy until she was quite elderly, when she was put in the Jackson County Home for the Aged."[303] Dealy was involved with placing the memorial marker because of his interest in Slaughter Cemetery and Jackson County history, not because of any family ties to Kate. Arthur D. Dealy died in 1973 while removing tree limbs from Slaughter Cemetery, still continuing to work on his 'labor of love' which he begin in 1965.[304] Another neighbor, Josie Potts King, was also not related to Kate, despite Fred Ford's mistaken statement in one of his letters.[305]

Kate's memorial marker; looking northeast

Fred Allen Ford was also born and raised in the Blue Springs area of Jackson County, Missouri. He had an active interest in Quantrill and the Kansas/Missouri Border War and acquired a vast amount of information through extensive research.[306] Fred also claimed to have known Kate, whom he called, 'Aunt Kate," and attended the auction sale of the King estate, when and where he saw Kate, and bought some of King family's personal property.[307]

Whether Fred A. Ford and Arthur David Dealy believed that Kate was buried in an unmarked grave in Slaughter Cemetery[308] or if they thought Kate was buried in the Potter's Field of the County Home,[309] the memorial monument they erected in her honor was not intended to mark her grave site. Ford and Dealy had no role in Kate's burial. They *never* retrieved Kate's body from the funeral home, *nor* did they secretly bury it in Slaughter Cemetery, as recently suggested.[310]

Arthur Dealy died in 1973; Fred Ford died in 1976. Shortly after Ford's death, Donald R. Hale, confirmed and verified in writing the burial site for, "Kate King, Quantrill's wife, who died under the name of Sara Head:"

```
                                    Independence, Mo.
                                    September 21, 1976

Mrs. Dorothy Butler
C/O THE BANNER
Oak Grove, Missouri 64075

Mrs. Butler:

        I recently decided to try to verify that Kate King,
Quantrill's wife, who died under the name of Sara Head,
was buried at the Jackson County "Old Folks" Home near
Lee's Summit. I had taken Fred Ford's word some years
ago that she was there. He told me that the records
were missing for that time (1930).

        I went out there last week and tried to find some
record of her burial and information on the cemetery
there. After being told by one person that there wasn't
a cemetery there and by another that the location was
unknown, I decided to check downtown at the courthouse.
Incidently, I did find out from a neighbor near the
Home, that the cemetery is there and the approximate
location.

        But to get back to Kate King.
After talking to a few people down there over the phone
I found Kate King. I mentioned the name Maple Hill being
the burial site listed on the death certificate. I had
believed that this Maple Hill was an area in the "Farm"
cemetery.

        Lo and Behold. She is buried at Maple Hill......
Maple Hill Cemetery, 2301 South 34th street, Kansas City,
Kansas. A phone call from me verified this. Who would
have thought. Why there? I plan to visit the site.

        Anything new? There is a lesson to learn about
this episode. Don't take anybody's word. Check it out
yourself.

                                    Sincerely,


                                    Donald R. Hale
                                    500 E. College
                                    Indep. Mo. 64050
```

Kate's Fate

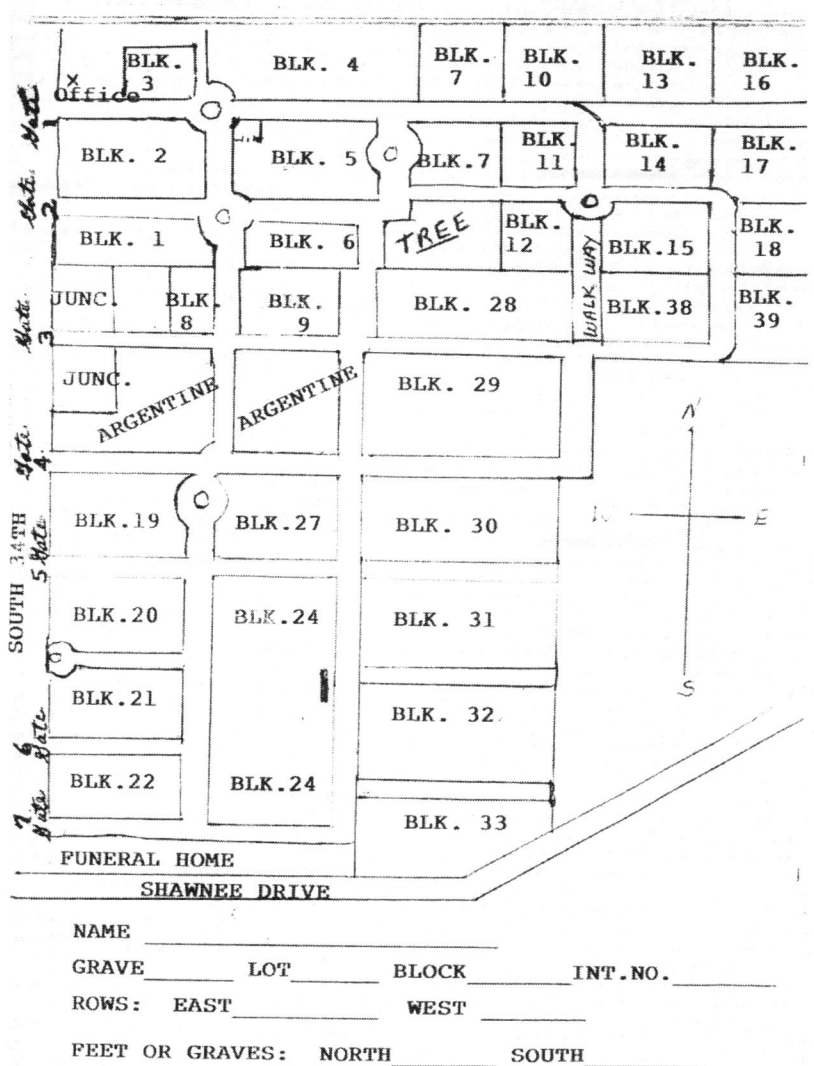

Sarah Head (aka. Kate) is buried in Block 5. Walter Head is interred in Block 7, Maple Hill Cemetery, Kansas City, Kansas

KATE IN FACT AND FICTION

    Hale confirmed in 1976 that Kate was buried in "Maple Hill Cemetery, 2301 South 34th Street, Kansas City, Kansas," rather than at the Jackson County Home in Jackson County, Missouri.[311] However, Kate's grave in Maple Hill Cemetery originally had a tombstone for "Sarah T. Ready," who also died in January 1930, which added to the confusion regarding Kate's exact burial location. Sarah Ready was buried five graves to the south; but, the headstone for her was initially placed, instead, on Kate's grave.[312] Hale rectified this in 1992.

#74   #5

BURIAL RECORD

Date	Name of Person	Grave No.
	LENA SMITH	1-25-1930
	PEARL EDWARDS	1-22-1930
	JAMES F. DELK	1-20-1930
9841	George Ready	Jan 4 1933
	SARAH T. READY *marker*	1-11-1930
	HERMAN SCOTT	1-10-1930

Sarah Ready marker is on Sarah Heads grave ? g 6 - lot 63 Blk 5

Sarah Ready marker should be on grave 5 lot 74 - Blk 5

6-27-92

192

Then, in 1997, Hale and Virgil Hoftiezer split the cost of a small headstone for "Sarah Head;" they used her childhood nickname to mark Kate's burial (Grave 6, Lot 63, Block 5):

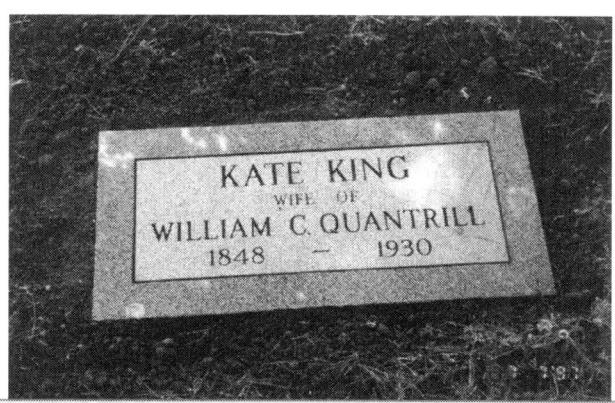

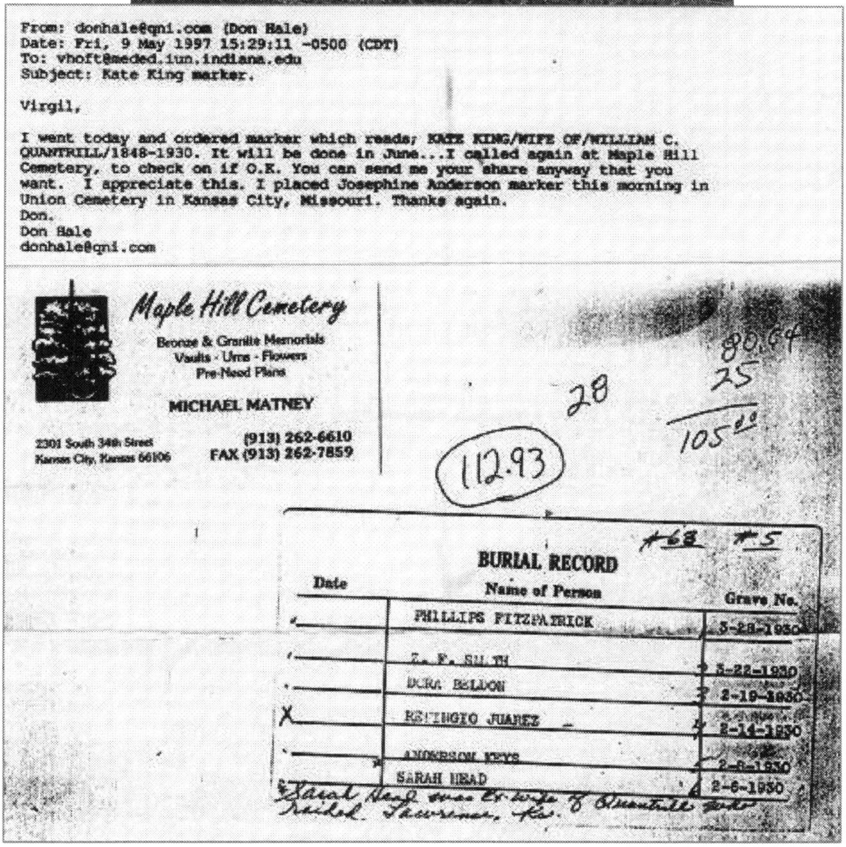

From: donhale@gni.com (Don Hale)
Date: Fri, 9 May 1997 15:29:11 -0500 (CDT)
To: vhoft@meded.iun.indiana.edu
Subject: Kate King marker.

Virgil,

I went today and ordered marker which reads; KATE KING/WIFE OF/WILLIAM C. QUANTRILL/1848-1930. It will be done in June...I called again at Maple Hill Cemetery, to check on if O.K. You can send me your share anyway that you want. I appreciate this. I placed Josephine Anderson marker this morning in Union Cemetery in Kansas City, Missouri. Thanks again.
Don.
Don Hale
donhale@gni.com

Maple Hill Cemetery
Bronze & Granite Memorials
Vaults · Urns · Flowers
Pre-Need Plans
MICHAEL MATNEY
2301 South 34th Street
Kansas City, Kansas 66106
(913) 262-6610
FAX (913) 262-7859

28
80.64
25
105.00
112.93

#63 #5

BURIAL RECORD

Date	Name of Person	Grave No.
	PHILLIPS FITZPATRICK	3-28-1930
	Z. F. SMITH	3-22-1930
	DORA BELDON	2-19-1930
X	REFINGIO JUAREZ	2-14-1930
	ANDERSON KEYS	2-8-1930
	SARAH HEAD	2-6-1930

Sarah Head was Ex-wife of Quantrill who raided Lawrence, Ks.

KATE IN FACT AND FICTION

The confusion over Kate's final resting place, which persisted for over eight decades seemed due to poor scholarship, oversight, or, intentional disregard. Clearly, Kate's authentic burial site has been accurately documented since at least 21 September 1976.

More recently, on 12 October 2010, Paul Petersen had Roger Douthit use dowsing rods to conduct an examination of the grave sites at both the Slaughter and Maple Hill cemeteries in an attempt to determine if there were burials in those plots.[313]

According to Douthit, the dowsing rods indicated a female body between 4'9" and 5'1" tall buried in Grave 6, Lot 63, Block 5, in Maple Hill Cemetery. This is the grave marked by Donald R. Hale and Virgil Hoftiezer.

In Slaughter Cemetery, Douthit's dowsing rods indicated that the spot marked by the memorial marker to Kate did *not* contain a buried body (i.e., the ground has never been disturbed). This finding substantiated the contention that the monument was never meant to be a grave marker; it was erected as a memorial to her memory only.[314]

Petersen further reported that the graves of Kate's parents, to the left (north) of the monument showed positive results for two burials.[315]

During a personal visit to Slaughter Cemetery in 1995, Hoftiezer observed that Kate's memorial marker was immediately to the right (south) of her mother Malinda Stringer King's tombstone. Immediately adjacent on the left (or, north) of Malinda's stone is that of Robert's tombstone; continuing with the graves of Nancy Chism; her daughters, Malinda and Eliza Chism;[316] and, finally, Sarah Dooley (at the far north of the family plot). In front of (or, west) of this row is a tombstone marking the burials of Francis Marion King and Eveline (Lynch) King, his wife.

Three unmarked graves are on either side of them (to the north and south). Any one of those graves may contain the remains of Anson Marion King (son of Francis M. and Eveline) who was buried in 'Slaughter Grave Yard' according to his death certificate, but has no marker.[317] See the diagram of Slaughter Cemetery on the following page.[318]

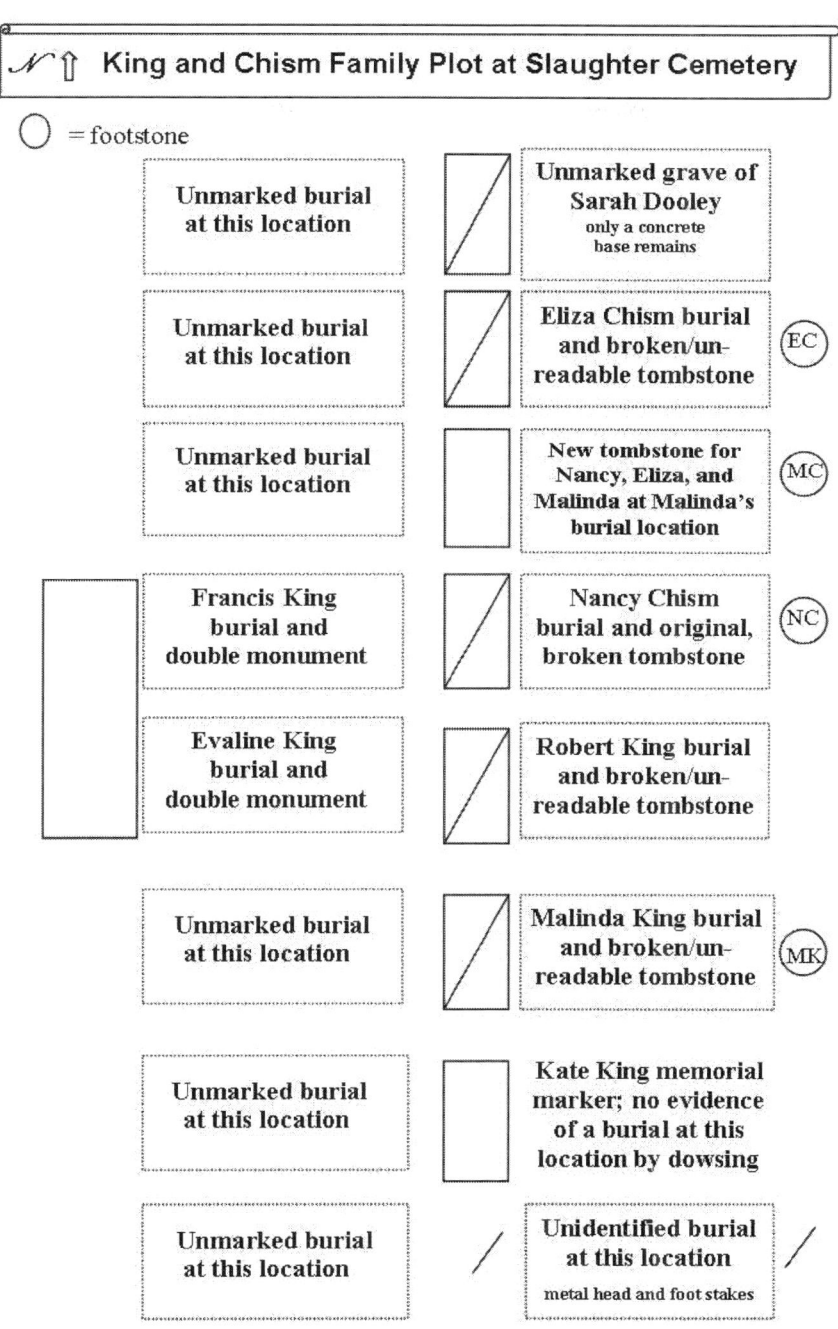

From an on-site survey and dowsing process by David W. Jackson, Aug 2014

KATE IN FACT AND FICTION

Images illustrating the deterioration and destruction of Robert and Malinda King's tombstones over time. Above is Donald R. Hale's image (1960s). Below is Vicki Beck's photo documentation (1992). As of 2014, they have disappeared altogether, as seen in the photo on page 189.

Kate's Fate

There is no question that Kate has two tombstones in two different cemeteries in two different states placed by two different parties at two different times.

This paradigm illustrates the importance of this biography to re-examine and more properly record Kate's story, as urged by Donald R. Hale in 1976.

It mirrors the dichotomy of the woman and the multiple facets of her life.

The life and legacy of Sarah Catherine King, a.k.a. Kate Clarke, continues to stir the imagination, provoke debate and kindle strong feelings.

Hopefully, Kate's true story presented here for the first time in a comprehensive fashion will stimulate continued research and uncover new documentation to further elucidate an incredibly complex and interesting woman.

There is enough fiction surrounding Kate, while the facts are far more interesting and equally intriguing.

Vicki P. Beck with the late William Clarke Quantrill expert, Donald R. "Don" Hale, at Kate King's grave, Maple Hill Cemetery, Kansas City, Kansas

Kate, *i.e.*, Sarah Catherine (King) Quantrill-Evans-Batson-Head, a.k.a. Kate Clarke, did not "go gentle into that good night" of history. But, she did "rage, rage against the dying of the light."

KATE IN FACT AND FICTION

ENDNOTES

[1] "The Strange Romance of Quantrill's Bride: Kate King, Ending Her Days in an Alms House, Recalls Her Life with the Famous Guerilla Leader," *Kansas City (Mo.) Star*, 23 May 1926. For a complete transcript of this article based on an interview with Sarah Head, formerly Kate King, consult the Appendix of this publication.

[2] Royal, Bonnie King. Personal communication with V. Hoftiezer, September and October 2012.

[3] Whites, LeeAnn. The Tale of Three Kates: Outlaw Women, Loyalty, and Missouri's Long Civil War." *Weirding the War,* Stephen Berry, ed. (Athens, Ga.: University of Georgia Press, 2011), 73-94. [Article the outgrowth of Whites' lecture, "The Tale of Three Kates: Prostitution, Loyalty and Missouri's Long Guerilla War," presented multiple times and locations, 2007-2011.].

[4] Sneddeker, Duane R. "Regulating Vice: Prostitution and the St. Louis Social Evil Ordinance, 1870-1874." *Gateway Heritage* (Fall 1990).

[5] Castanien, Pliny. *To Protect and Serve: A History of the San Diego Police Department and Its Chiefs 1889-1989*. (San Diego, Ca.: San Diego Historical Society, 1993).

[6] Jackson County, Missouri, Probate Court Records.

[7] Whites, LeeAnn. *Gender Matters: Civil War, Reconstruction, and the Making of the New South.* (New York: Palgrave Macmillan, 2005).

[8] The obituary for Martha King (Kate's sister) stated that she came to Jackson County at age seven. Martha was born in 1842.

[9] The same list is recorded by the State Archives on 5 Nov. 1864. National Archives and Records Administration. Union Provost Marshal Papers. Online database to a Series of this Record Group provided through the Missouri State Archives. (Cole County). Microfilm F1660, Missouri State Archives, Jefferson City, Mo.

[10] Harris, Charles F. "Catalyst for Terror: The Collapse of the Women's Prison in Kansas City" *Missouri Historical Review* (April 1995), 290-306.

[11] "List of Letters Uncalled for in the Post Office at St. Louis, Missouri on Saturday, August 15 1863; Ladies List," *Daily Missouri Republican* (St. Louis, MO), 15 Aug. 1863, p. 1. [Kate Clark]

[12] Olwine, Margaret. "True Story of Quantrill's Raiders is Too Close to Home to Be Revealed," *Kansas City (Mo.) Times*, 26 Oct. 1967. The Howard County Recorder of Deeds does not have said marriage on record. "Missouri Marriage Project." Howard County. http://usgwarchives.net/marriages/missouri/howard.htm.

[13] *Kansas City Star*, 1926.

[14] Lutz, J. J. "Quantrell, the Guerilla Chief." *Midland Monthly Magazine.* (Jan.-Jun 1897): 7:509-520.

[15] Leslie, 302. Also, Petersen, Quantrill in Texas, 192. Otho Offutt, a Quantrill follower, reminisced in 1903 about a time when he and six companions, "*camped on Pershy Creek about seven miles above Columbia, in Howard County, Missouri. It was a good hiding place and they had an abundance of provisions sent in to them by friends in the neighborhood. They slept on the open ground in their blankets.*" Although this moment in Offutt's story was in February 1865—after he was no longer in league with Quantrill—it adds visual reliability to Kate and Quantrill's fabled campsite. "Giant of the Guerrillas," *Kansas City Star*, 11 Oct. 1903, p. 17.

[16] The same list is recorded by the State Archives on 16 Jul 1862. National Archives and Records Administration. Union Provost Marshal Papers. Online database to a Series of this Record Group provided through the Missouri State Archives. (Unidentified County). Microfilm F1660, Missouri State Archives, Jefferson City, Mo.

[17] Quantrill did end up in Kentucky, but at least some of his men reported that they were en route to Virginia to surrender with the Confederate troops there. Surrendering in Missouri, they would be recognized as guerrillas, and not as confederate soldiers. Thus, presumably Quantrill left for Virginia; but, only got as far as Kentucky.

[18] Ford, Anna Scrapbook. "When Quantrill's Mother Came to Blue Springs," *Westport Historical Quarterly*. (June 1968): 4:2:16-20. Anna Ford was a sister of Fred A. Ford. Also noted in Leslie, 410-411; *Iola Register*, 18 May 1888; and, Wellman, Paul I. "She remembers when Quantrill's Mother Came to Blue Springs," *Kansas City Star*, 30 Aug. 1942 (relaying a recollection of Miss Narra Lewis; a copy of this and other clippings about Lewis are located at the Jackson County (Mo.) Historical Society Archives, Document ID 103F5-6.)

[19] Kansas State Historical Society. "Secretary's Annual Report." *Transactions of the Kansas State Historical Society* (1904):8:124.

[20] Social Security number application.

[21] Consult the William E. Connelley Collection at the University of Oklahoma Libraries, Western History Collections.

[22] Christopher, Adrienne Tinker. "Kate King Clarke: Quantrill's Forgotten Girl Bride," *Westport Historical Quarterly*. (June 1968): 4:2: 21-22. The bedroom furniture was in the King house (supposedly the one Kate built for her parents) and was sold as part of the King estate after Anson died. Presumably, the furniture was sold with the house when Robert (Kate's father) sold the farm to his son, Francis, who then willed it to his son, Anson. This was the furniture involved with the news article that prompted Fred Ford's letter to Josie Potts King.

[23] Kansas City *Star*, 1926.

[24] Kansas City *Star*, 1926.
[25] Kansas City *Star*, 1926.
[26] Geiger, Mark W. "Indebtedness and the Origins of Guerrilla Violence in Civil War Missouri." *The Journal of Southern History* (February 2009): LXXV: 1.
[27] Ancestry.com has over 180 listings relating to the ancestry of Malinda's father as of March 2014. All but a handful include the same erroneous information listing a son born before his parents were born; thus, breaking the chain of descent. It was suggested, without documentation, that the Stringer family originated in Ireland.
[28] Malinda's maternal line can also be traced back to Virginia, but through North Carolina and perhaps to Scotland.
[29] The widowed Limeledge Stringer did post an earlier marriage bond to wed Jenny Reed in Lincoln County, Kentucky on 2 January 1798, but no marriage was licensed or recorded; thus the marriage to Elizabeth Scott a year and a half later was considered to be Limeledge's second marriage.
[30] Betsy's eldest daughter Rachel Stringer (Malinda's older sister)[Kate's maternal aunt] married her stepbrother Anderson Rigney on 23 October 1820 in Green County, Kentucky. Anderson Rigney was the son of Jesse Rigney (second husband of Betsy) from his first marriage to Elizabeth Linthicum. Anderson Rigney and Rachel Stringer remained and died in Kentucky. At least two of the children of Anderson and Rachel moved to Texas and a son died in Gentry County, Missouri.
[31] Levi Stringer [Kate's maternal uncle] moved to Madison County, Illinois where he married Louisa Dunnagan on 4 January 1827. They had four children, one of whom-Joseph E. Stringer-married his first cousin Lousia S. Edwards. Levi was in Madison County, Illinois for both the 1830 and 1840 census; his widow with four children was listed there in the 1850 census.
[32] Sarah A. Stringer [Kate's maternal aunt] married Samuel Ralston on 27 February 1821 in Green County, Kentucky. The bondsman to her marriage was Anderson Rigney who was both her step brother and her brother-in-law.
[33] William M. Stringer [Kate's maternal uncle] went first to Madison County, Illinois with his uncle in 1817, then returned to Kentucky when his stepfather Jesse Rigney died in 1823. Following his marriage in Kentucky, William M. brought his wife, mother and siblings to Illinois, settling first near Winchester in then Morgan (now Scott) County in 1829, and then moving to Greene County, Illinois in 1832.
[34] Ann Stringer [Kate's maternal aunt] married Lewis Bryant Edwards on 21 October 1830 in Casey County, Kentucky. Many Stringer descendants believe that Ann Stringer was the daughter of William

Stringer, a brother of Limeledge Stringer, because William's will names a daughter Anna. Unfortunately Limeledge did not identify his six younger children by name in his will. However, based on the location of Ann's marriage (in Casey County rather than Montgomery County, Kentucky) and the subsequent locations of Ann and Lewis, it appeared more likely that Ann was the daughter of Limeledge Stringer and 'Betsy' Elizabeth Scott Stringer. Ann and Lewis lived in Greene County, Illinois before moving to first Hickory County and then Henry County, Missouri. They raised eight children, one of whom — Louisa J. Edwards — married Joseph E. Stringer, son of Levi Stringer. If Ann was the daughter of Limeledge and Elizabeth this was a marriage between first cousins.

[35] Donnelly, Gassette and Lloyd. *History of Greene County, Illinois.* (Chicago, Il.: Donnelly, Gassette and Lloyd, 1879). 724-725.

[36] A birth date of 23 January 1810 has been calculated from the death date listed on Robert's tombstone.

[37] Robert L. King's birth in Kentucky (according to later census data), his 1837 marriage in Greene County, Illinois, and his 15 February 1836 purchase of 80 acres of land in Section 4 (east half of southeast quarter of Section 4, Township 9, Range 11) in Greene County, Illinois, were circumstantial evidence used to identify William James King as a possible father of Robert. This circumstantial evidence includes William James' location in Greene County, Illinois during the correct time, and the fact that Robert named his first-born son William. To date no evidence has been found to disprove a relationship between Robert and William James, but the will of William James King did not name a son Robert; although this will named the four sons from William James' marriage to Mary Anne Cadwell, it did not name his daughter from his last marriage to Rachel Smith Marshall. Since most of the other King families in Greene County, Illinois, have been proven to be unrelated, William James remains the most likely candidate by default. There were several, seemingly unrelated, King families located in Greene County during the 1830 to 1840 period. For example, Alexander King was the Justice of Peace who performed the marriage ceremony for Robert King and Malinda Stringe [Kate's parents]; a thorough review of the genealogy of Alexander King does include another Robert King that has no known relationship to Robert L. King [Kate's father]. While the age of William James King (born 30 June 1788) would fit for him to be the father of Robert, but only if he were married to Robert's mother before his two later marriages to Mary Anne Cadwell (on 30 June 1825 in Jacksonville, Morgan County, Illinois) and Rachel Smith Marshall (on 15 February 1844 in Lynville, Morgan County, Illinois). It should be noted that Morgan County was formed in 1823 from Greene County where William James King first

purchased land in 1822. The probate of William James King's estate mentions the children from both his marriages in Morgan County.

[38] Robert was nearly an adult when William married Mary Anne Caldwell in 1825. Robert bought land in Greene County, Illinois in 1836 which he sold before moving to Missouri. If his father had provided Robert the money to purchase land in 1836, and then Robert subsequently left Illinois, William James King may not have felt it necessary to mention his son in his will over a decade later. If William James King can be proven to be the father of Robert, this lineage can be traced directly back beyond Kentucky and Illinois to Pickering in Yorkshire, England.

[39] Nancy and her children were in the same counties in both Illinois and Missouri, during the same times, as Robert. They were both in District 71 of Polk County, Missouri, in the 1850 Federal census; Robert was in his own household (with Malinda and five of their children), while Nancy and her four children were with Isham Edwards, the father-in-law of her sister-in-law. Isham Edwards, Sr., born in Virginia between 1775 and 1784, married 'Patsy' Margaret Witt in Patrick County, Virginia, on 8 October 1804. They had eight children and then moved to Kentucky where their son Lewis Bryant Edwards married Ann Stringer [Malinda's sister and Kate's maternal aunt] on 21 Oct 1830 in Liberty, Casey County, Kentucky. Thus, Nancy King Chism was living in 1850 with the father-in-law of her sister-in-law. Unfortunately many people have erroneously assumed Nancy to be the daughter of Isham Edwards because she is with him in 1870. Isham Edwards was probably in Greene County, Illinois with his son Lewis Bryant Edwards in 1840 before he went to Polk County, Missouri in 1850. In the 1856 state census, Isham was living in Yellow Springs, Des Moines County, Iowa, with his married daughter Catherine Edwards Clark. Isham Edwards died on 27 May 1859 in Brownville, Nemaha County, Nebraska Territory, where his son Taulbird Habel Edwards lived. And finally, Nancy King Chism was in Ft. Osage Township in Jackson County, Missouri, in 1860, 1870 and 1880 census, while Robert was in Sni-a-Bar Township, Jackson County, Missouri, in 1860 & 1880 (Robert was in California during the 1870 census).

[40] In addition to shared geographic locations, the naming patterns of their children suggest Robert and Nancy are related. Nancy's children included William (same name as her brother, Robert's, first-born son perhaps both named after the paternal grandfather?) and Malinda (perhaps named after Robert's wife). Robert named a daughter Nancy, presumably after his sister. Nancy and both her unmarried daughters Eliza Chism and Malinda Chism were buried in the adjacent grave plots next to Robert and Malinda in Slaughter Cemetery in Jackson County, Missouri. Nancy's oldest son William

Chism [Kate's cousin] married Agnes Dalton-whose brother Lewis was the father of several members of the infamous Dalton gang; the Dalton Gang included three sons of Lewis Dalton. The Dalton brothers were first cousins of the Younger brothers who were affiliated with another notable gang of outlaws, as well as former guerrillas with Quantrill.

[41] Robert purchased 80 acres (the east half of the southeast quarter) in Section 4, Township 9, range 11 for $100 on 15 February 1836; he received a land patent for this property on 2 December 1839.

[42] Malinda did not sign the Mortgage Bond; was it because the land was purchased before their marriage or did wives not sign Mortgage Bonds although their signatures are required to sell land? Did Robert mortgage this land in order to purchase additional land? Luther Tunnel (26 September 1793-3 August 1865) was a large land owner in Greene County, Illinois, having purchased his first 80 acres there on 9 October 1823. Luther married his wife Louisa Parks on 22 November 1825 in Greene County, Illinois. Although they had nine children, including two sons—one of which produced two grandsons—there were no Tunnel descendants to carry on the family name beyond that generation.

[43] On 9 January 1855, Robert L. King bought 40 acres (the southwest quarter of the southeast quarter) in Section 7, Township 49, Range 30, in Jackson County, Missouri (the patent for this land was issued two years later on 1 April 1857). Three months later, he bought 40 acres in adjacent section 18 (the northeast quarter of the northeast quarter) for $500 from John and Eleanor Cummins. Two years after the initial purchase, on 1 April 1857, he bought 40 more acres (the northwest quarter of the southeast quarter) in Section 7 of Jackson County (the patent for this land was issued four years later on 1 June 1859).

[44] Robert acquired 80 acres of land (east half of the southeast quarter of Section 7 in Township 49 north, Range 30 west) in Jackson County (the patent for this property was issued on 1 May 1857) which became the King family farm. This land remained in Robert's possession until he sold it to their son Francis Marion King for $600 on 5 March 1880 after Malinda had died. Francis Marion King later transferred the title to this property to his son Anson for $1.00 plus 'love and affection' on 5 May 1916 two days before he died. When Anson died intestate in June 1920, there was a long legal dispute to settle the estate. This land passed out of the possession of the King family on 28 January 1921 when it was sold to John J. Flynn for $6,129.20 to settle the estate. [This would be equal to $77,000.00 in today's dollars according to the 2011 Consumer Price Index.] John Flynn still owned this property in 1931.

Endnotes

[45] Patrick Powers, was a brother-in-law to Samuel Robert King [Kate's brother and son of Robert and Malinda]. Patrick was born in Dumore, County Waterford, Ireland on 11 Jun 1834, and married Mary Ann Davenport, born December 1847 in Kentucky, on 18 September 1864 in Jackson County, Missouri, apparently soon after Patrick immigrated the same year (immigration date per 1900 census). Mary Ann Davenport was a sister of Elizabeth L. Davenport, wife of Samuel Robert King. All ten of Patrick's and Mary Ann's children (who were first cousins to the children of Samuel Robert King through their mothers] have been identified: Maria or Margaret (born 24 November 1864), John H. (born 7 February 1866 and died 13 April 1935 in Kansas City), William (born 9 July 1869), Samuel J. (born 15 Jan 1871 and died 14 August 1947 in St. Joseph, Buchanan County, Missouri, but buried in Woodlawn Cemetery in Independence, Missouri), James (born 12 August 1872), and Richard Matthew (born 11 July 1874 and died 27 October 1952 in Independence) who were all baptized at St. Mary's Church in Independence, Jackson County, Missouri, plus Thomas (born about 1877), Mary E. (born about January 1880), Walter (born November 1884) and Albert P. (born February 1886). Patrick and Mary A. Powers were listed with their family very near the King family farm in the Blue Springs Election District of Sni-a-Bar Township in Jackson County, Missouri, on June first in both 1880 and 1900 Federal census. Patrick Powers died 9 July 1905 at 71 years of age and buried in Woodlawn Cemetery in Independence, Missouri. The widowed Mary A. Davenport Powers died on 15 January 1916 in Kansas City, Jackson County, Missouri and was buried next to her husband. Patrick Powers apparently purchased the southwest quarter of the southeast quarter in Section 7, Township 49, Range 30 in Sni-a-Bar Township in Jackson County, Missouri, sometime between 1864 and 1877.

[46] Thomas Torpey, age 65 and born in Ireland, and his wife Mary, age 58 also born in Ireland, with children all born in Missouri: Thomas, Jr. age 26, Maggie age 20, Michael age 18, and James age 7, were listed next to William Jasper King in the 1880 census in Blue Springs Election District, Jackson County, Missouri, on 1 June. Both Thomas, Sr. and Mary died before the 1900 census; him in 1888 and her in 1872 (per Ancestry.com). Thomas Henry Torpey, born 4 December 1854 in Independence, and Lucy Hutchings, born 10 July 1960 in Jackson County, were married in about 1882 probably in Jackson County, Missouri. Lucy was the daughter of another close neighbor of the King's -Thomas C. Hutchings and his first wife Serilda Cummins (she was also the much older half sister of Porter Hutchings). Thomas Henry and Lucy were listed next to Francis Marion King in Sni-a-Bar Township, Jackson County, Missouri, in the

1900 census on 13 June. They had no children after 18 years of marriage. Thomas Henry Torpey and Lucy Hutchings Torpey both died in Blue Springs, Jackson County, Missouri; he died on 31 October 1932 and she died 2 July 1938. They were both buried in Blue Springs Cemetery, Jackson County, Missouri. Jackson County land records need to be checked to determine when Thomas Torpey purchased the northwest quarter of the southeast quarter in Section 7, Township 49, Range 30 in Sni-a-Bar Township of Jackson County, Missouri.

[47] William Jasper King [Kate's older brother] purchased the 40 acres in Section 18 (northeast quarter of the northeast quarter) from his parents on 1 March 1870 for $500. This was the same price Robert L. paid for this land fifteen years earlier when purchased in 1855. Robert and Malinda probably sold this land to their eldest son at considerably less than market value, because they sold another 40 acres nearby (the northwest quarter of southeast quarter of Section 7) on the same day to John N. Speck for $700, which is 40% more for the same acreage. When the last remaining parcel (southwest quarter of the southeast quarter of Section 7) was sold has not been determined.

[48] Auburn, the county seat of Placer County, is located northeast of Sacramento. Placer County abuts the Nevada border at Lake Tahoe and is immediately south of Donner's Pass where the famous Donner Party was trapped during the winter of 1846-1847.

[49] How and when these families arrived in California was not apparent. Robert and Malinda sold two parcels of land in Jackson County, Missouri, on 1 March 1870. Was this in order to obtain funds to finance the trip to California? Their son William Jasper King [Kate's brother], who purchased one of the land parcels, presumably stayed on that property in Jackson County, Missouri, but avoided the census there; William Jasper and his family were not located on any census in 1870.

[50] California Voter Registration Lists. This would explain why John Ragland failed to appear in Jackson County Court in Missouri when summoned on 27 April 1867 for an overdue note for $7.25 he signed on 1 January 1862 to J.T. Henderson; perhaps John took his family to California in early 1863 after he was discharged with a disability in January from the 77th MO Militia. Ancestry.com reported John Oath Ragland's story which also recounted that in the 1870's John and his family traveled by wagon train to California where they farmed and prospected for gold for about three years before returning to Jackson County, Missouri in the late 1870's. The time frame outlined was shortened and shifted. John was listed on the Voter Registration Lists for seven years from 1866 to 1873. The latter time frame fits better with the date of General Order No. 11.

[51] This was a very confused listing, including the age recorded for the widowed Robert as 58 years which was 12 years too young-a huge discrepancy.

[52] Geiger.

[53] When the building used to house the jailed female relatives of guerrillas arrested by the Federal troops collapsed, among the women killed were two sisters-Armenia Crawford Selvey and Susan Jane Crawford Whitsett Vandever, two daughters of the sixteen children of Jeptha M. Crawford and Ann Elizabeth Harris-who were 'shirttail relation' to Kate. The names of these two women were reported incorrectly as 'Mrs. Selby' and 'Mrs. Vandiver' by the *Daily Journal* of Kansas City on 15 August 1863. Subsequent reports by others made additional errors in these names. Leslie recorded the names correctly.

For more details about this tragic event, see *Lost Souls of the Lost Township: Untold Life Stories of the People Buried in the Davis-Smith Cemetery, Kansas City, Jackson County, Missouri*, by Paul R. Petersen and David W. Jackson.

Armenia's seven-year old son Jeptha was imprisoned with her, but he escaped serious injury when his mother was killed.

Charles Selvey, the husband of Armenia Crawford Selvey, was a first cousin to America Jane Snodgrass King [Kate's sister-in-law, the wife of brother William Jasper King] (their mothers were sisters). In the 1870 census, all three sons of Armenia Crawford and Charles Selvey were with their double uncle and aunt John B. Selvey and Ann Elizabeth Crawford Selvey in Blue Township, Jackson County, Missouri. It is thought that Armenia was widowed before July 1860 since Charles is not found in that or any later census.

John B. Selvey, a brother of Charles Selvey and thus another cousin to America Jane Snodgrass King [Kate's sister-in-law], was married to Ann Elizabeth Crawford, a sister of Armenia Crawford Selvey.

Another Selvey brother, Lewis, married his first cousin Nancy E. Snodgrass, a sister of America Jane Snodgrass King [Kate's sister-in-law].

Another Crawford sister, Laura Francis Crawford had married Stewart Whitsett, a brother of William Noland Whitsett who had been the first husband of Susan Jane Crawford Whitsett Vandever.

Mary Whitsett, a sister of Stewart and William Whitsett, married William A. Snodgrass, a brother of America Jane Snodgrass King [Kate's sister-in-law].

Riley Crawford, the younger brother of Armenia and Susan, was a guerrilla who rode with Quantrill and was the reason these women were arrested.

[54] Miranda Ann Snodgrass, an older sister of America Jane Snodgrass [Kate's sister-in-law, wife of brother William Jasper King],

married Elijah Lynch in Jackson County, Missouri on 24 Oct 1852. Elijah Lynch was a half-brother to Eveline Lynch [Kate's sister-in-law, married to Kate's brother Francis Marion King]. The sibs and half-sibs of Eveline Lynch King and Elijah Lynch (or their heirs) eventually made claims on the estate of Kate's nephew and greatly reduced all the shares.

[55] There was a recent report that Charles A. Longacre, a young man who joined Quantrill's Guerrilla band in January 1863, was a distant relative of Kate King. (Petersen, 2011) Petersen provided no source for this statement other than "Historians have noted" without specifying which historians or when and where it was noted. A brief search of the genealogy of Charles A. Longacre documented that he was the son of John Longacre (11 July 1802 in Jefferson County, Tennessee-17 July 1862 in Johnson County, Missouri) who, with his son Benjamin W. Longacre, was killed by Union soldiers. John's widow (Charles' mother) was Phoebe Thurlton Longacre (1880-1891). She and a daughter were jailed in St. Louis after being severely ill-treated by Jayhawkers. Preliminary research revealed no genealogical links between either Kate's maternal Stringer/Scott line or paternal King line and the Longacre/Thurlton/Carter/Ireson/Cock families. If a relationship between Charles A. Longacre and Kate were established it might provide additional genealogical clues about Kate's ancestry. However, Charles A. Longacre certainly had incentive enough to become a guerrilla without a familial connection to Kate.

[56] William A. (28 August 1835-21 February 1913), Miranda Ann (18 November 1836-21 October 1923), James Newton (24 September 1838-22 December 1918), Ephraim (26 February 1842-20 December 1876) and Nancy E. (2 December 1843-27 June 1889).

[57] Isaac (about 1844-before July 1860), Henry (about 1846-supposedly died during the Civil War), America Jane 12 August 1847-30 October 1908), Bartley Allen (9 April 1849-25 October 1916), 'Lee' Leander A. (1851-1895), John Charles (10 October 1854-15 December 1931) and Parmer (17 April 1856-13 March 1930).

[58] This was the 40 acres (northeast quarter of northeast quarter of Section 18) of land directly south of the King family farm in Jackson County, Missouri, purchased by Robert L. King in April 1855 for $500 from John and Eleanor Cummins. William Jasper paid the same amount for this land in 1870 as his father paid fifteen years earlier.

[59] *Jackson* (Independence, Mo.) *Examiner*, 4 Apr. 1919. 'Kate Badson' is Kate, a misspelling of Batson.

[60] Lucy D. Ragland (about 1834-), James Willis Ragland (about 1836-30 January 1870), David Granville Ragland (about 1840-),

John Oath Ragland (21 June 1842-12 February 1905), George M. Dallas Ragland (about 1845-1918), Solomon W. Ragland (about 1848-), and Sarah Ragland (about 1851-).

[61] William R. Ragland, Mary Ragland, Susan Ragland and Millie Ragland.

[62] According to a submission to Ancestry.com the John O. Ragland family had traveled to California for three years, but had returned to Missouri in the late 1870s. This time line conflicted with documentation; John O. Ragland was registered to vote in Auburn, Placer County, California from 1866 through 1873—which is longer than three years.

[63] "Ragland," *Kansas City Star, 15 May 1918.*

[64] Eakin, Joanne Chiles, Personal communication, November 1995.

[65] *Independence Examiner*, 12 Aug. 1929. Jack's Missouri Death Certificate lists the birth date of 20 May 1866. His mother's name is typed as the informant; but, that is an error since she was deceased. The informant should be his wife, Mary H. Jack's trade or occupation was listed as "Livestock Com." John Marion Ragland was listed in several places (city directories, etc.) as J. M. and was definitely affiliated with the Kansas City Stock Yards in the Federal censuses in 1900, 1910, 1920, and 1930. He was 73 at the time of his death in June 1939.

[66] Lafayette County, Missouri, Marriage records, Book 6, Page 162.

[67] Sarah Ann Lynch Bolger Dooley (about 1836-11 April 1891), Lavina Lynch Iske (about 1843-6 December 1922) and Eveline Lynch King (15 January 1847-20 July 1912).

[68] William and an unknown first wife had a son Elijah Lynch (24 July 1829-20 July 1918) who married Miranda Snodgrass. After his service in the Confederate army, Elijah Lynch became a bushwhacker with Quantrill, adding yet another link to Kate.

Rebecca and Alfred Waldo had Irvin Waldo (about 1804-before 1860), Nathaniel Waldo (about 1827-), James Wesley Waldo (8 April 1827-7 September 1902) and Anson Waldo (28 May 1829-before December 1920).

Later, these half siblings of Eveline successfully claimed a share in the inheritance from the King estate.

[69] Elijah Lynch became a brother-in-law to Kate's sister-in-law when he married Miranda Snodgrass, a sister of America Jane Snodgrass who married William Jasper King (Francis' and Kate's older brother). Thus, Eveline and America, who were sisters-in-law by their marriages to the two King brothers, Francis Marion and William Jasper, respectively, were also connected through sibship and marriage, respectively, to Elijah Lynch.

[70] Rev. McFarland recorded this as a marriage between Emeline Linch [instead of Eveline Lynch] and William King [instead of Francis King].
[71] On 5 March 1880, Robert King sold to F.M. King (his son Francis Marion]) the east half of the southeast quarter of Section 7, Township 49 of Range 30 for $600. This was the land Robert King bought in 1855 and received the patent for on 1 May 1857.
[72] Ford, Fred A. Letter, 6 March 1963.
[73] *Sni-a-Bar Voice*, 12 May 1916.
[74] The probate of this estate was not completed until the autumn of 1921 and involved extensive legal paper work, which also required selling the King family farm. The relationship of all the heirs of Anson were specified in these documents. The final settlement presented at the September 1921 Term in the Probate Court of Jackson County Missouri illustrated the complex family relationships recognized by the court and clearly reveals the extent to which 'blood', and even 'half blood' ties, bind families together. See Appendices.

There is no record of whether the claims to Anson King's estate by his mother's sibs and half-sibs were viewed as inequitable by the King heirs, but it seemed unjustified. The dissection of the King estate proved to be a 'genealogical gold mine' for family historians; the application for Letters of Administration filed in Jackson County, Missouri, Probate Court in May of 1920 listed the heirs, their relationship to the deceased Anson M. King, and their current city of residence for each. Indeed, a treasure trove of family heritage, but an extensive and expensive delay in settlement of the estate.

[75] The obituaries of both Martha and Francis each indicated that they were born in Polk County, Missouri; in Francis' obituary it said he was born near Bolivar, Missouri, which is the county seat of Polk County.
[76] Sarah A. (about 1840-), Henry J. (about 1841-), John (about 1844-), Mary Ann (about 1846-1916), Martha Ann (about 1849-before 1876), 'Polly' (April 1850-), Priscilla L. (March 1851-1916 in Linn County, Kansas) and Laura Belle (25 December 1852-16 October 1936 in Independence, Jackson County, Missouri).
[77] Sarah E. (about 1857-), Elizabeth L. (30 April 1858-27 October 1943) and Florence (about 1860-).
[78] This was a confused listing. Robert's age was listed as much too young. But, Samuel, listed as his son, appeared to be the correct age, with his occupation listed as "with father" and his state of birth was listed as Kentucky rather than Missouri (a common error often seen in the census). The other two people listed in the same household were Sarah, age 25, keeping house, and her daughter, Myrty, age 6. Elizabeth L. Davenport had a daughter 'Mamie' Mary Ann King born 1 Jul 1874, five years before Samuel and Elizabeth

were married. Perhaps 6-year-old Myrty is 'Mamie' Mary Ann with her mother and Samuel visiting his father in the 1880 census. That Elizabeth was enumerated as 'Sarah' is an apparent Census enumerator's recording error.

[79] "Samuel R. King Dead," *Independence Examiner*, 20 June 1921. Note: 'Kate Barson' is Kate, with a misspelling of Batson. The Independence sanitarium was the local hospital, later known as the Independence Regional Health Center, as per letter from Mid-Continent Library. It is now defunct and its services transferred to Centerpoint Health Center. The librarian also noted that Sugar Creek (the residence of son, George) is a small town north west of Independence along the Missouri River.

[80] 'Frank' Francis Alexander Davidson was married first to Sebrina Mullin who died in 1906 leaving eight children: Oscar (1885-1934), Clarence M. (1886-1910), Effie (1888-1971), John (1889-1959), Wilbert (1891-1919), Lucy (1893-1965) and Ralph Basil (1896-1943). All of these children were buried in the same cemetery as their parents, Woodlawn Cemetery in Independence, and at least some were buried in the same section 11. All six sons registered for the draft for World War I. His WWI draft registration was the last documented record for Wilbert before his burial in 1919. Clarence died of stab wounds and both Oscar and Ralph died of acute alcoholism. This family was subjected to more than its share of tragedy.

[81] Ford letters. Fred Ford may have only repeated, from the original newspaper source, that Kate rebuilt her parents' house and barn (along present-day Argo and Owens School Roads). An image of the rear of the King home was previously published (with an incorrect address) by Carl Breihan in *Real West* magazine. A silhouette of the house and barn appeared in Margaret Olwine's *Kansas City Times* article. Fred Ford, who claimed to be related to Kate through the marriage of her niece, Georgeanna Ragland, to his cousin, Babe Hudspeth, and thus called her 'Aunt Kate,' wrote a letter in 1963 that reported Kate built and furnished a house to replace her parents home that was burned by the Red Legs. Fred said he bought at the King estate sale the bedroom furniture that Kate had paid for with money looted from Lawrence, Kansas. The sale of the King estate was held on 23 July 1920. Fred Ford was listed as a purchaser at the Anson King estate sale of several items, including a bed stead.

[82] Fred Ford wrote that 'Aunt Kate,' whom he knew at least by sight, kept house for her brother Francis Marion and nephew Anson, both of whom he identified by name; Francis Marion's wife Eveline Lynch King died in 1912 and he died in 1916. Fred Ford's letter of 30 May 1962 to Mr. & Mrs. Floyd King of Blue Springs, Missouri, stated that Kate lived with Marion King [Kate's brother Frank Marion King], and

Anson King, her nephew for about six years. Fred also stated that Kate was there when Anson died in June 1920. If the latter statement were true, it may have indicated that Kate left Oklahoma to attend the funeral and then remained in Jackson County for a while longer. Also, in this letter Fred noted that "Aunt Kate came to live with Mr. & Mrs. Frank King."

[83] The children of Kate's siblings still alive in 1930 included:

1) nine children of her brother William Jasper King: 'Frank' William Franklin King, Earl R. Monroe King, 'Dean' Jona Dean King, 'Nan' Nannie Evelyn King Young Cummins, Julia Lee King Swinney, Walter R. King, Oscar King and Miranda Jane King Morris; eight of these nieces and nephews lived in Jackson County—Earl had moved to South Dakota in about 1912;

2) three children of her sister Martha Jane King Ragland: John Marion Ragland, Charles H. Ragland, and Dora Hazel Ragland Burrus were still alive and all three of them lived in Jackson County; in 1926 Jack Ragland (presumably John Marion) was listed as guardian of Sarah Head in the Jackson County Home; and

3) three sons of her brother Samuel Robert King: Arthur Cleveland King and George Samuel King both lived in Jackson County; Joseph Edward King lived in Nebraska in 1930, but moved to Jackson County by 1940; Samuel Robert King's stepdaughter 'Mamie' Mary Ann King Keck also lived in Jackson County in 1930.

[84] Boman, Halys Morris. Personal communication, 1990-2000. Dick, Audrey Lee, compiler. *Earl M. King Family Record*, 1985. Hostetter, Dorothy Bell King. Personal communication, 1995. King, 'Peg" Lillie L. Lage. Personal communication, 2000. Thompson, Mary Louise King Thompson Waldron Roberts. Personal communication, 1995.

[85] Boman.

[86] *Kansas City Star,* 23 May 1926.

[87] Royal.

[88] *Kansas City Star*, 23 May 1926.

[89] Bartels, Carolyn M. *Bitter Tears: Missouri Women and Civil War: Their Stories.* "The Strange Romance of Quantrill's Bride." (Harrisonville, Mo.: Burnt District Press, 2002).

[90] Connelley, William Elsey. *Quantrill and the Border Wars.* (Cedar Rapids, Ia: Torch Press, 1910), 282-283. An extract of notes from Charles Fletcher Taylor to W. W. Scott in 1879 is as follows (punctuation added): *"Never married I believe. Kate Clark who keeps a fancy house in St. Louis now (1879), and is a noted woman there, lived in Jackson County and the night Q. took her from home, he borrowed my gray mare for her to ride on, and from that time on he never did much fighting. He kept her that summer, and that winter we went south and he left her. The next summer he went back and got with her and staid in the brush until he started to Ky. where he was*

killed. He never took on much after the women but rather shunned them, while quartered in Sherman, Texas. He staid in camp most all the time while the rest of his officers were having a good time riding in Gen. Blunt's buggy and ambulance we captured on the trip out to Texas." Kansas State Historical Society, Topeka, Kansas. William Elsey Connelley Papers [Also found in the KSHS Connelley papers are William W. Scott materials (Scott's widow sold her husband's materials to Connelley). See also Connelley-related materials in the KSHS John Lutz Papers].

[91] http://www.millersparanormalresearch.com/Pages/Quantrill.htm.

[92] Phillips, Christopher, "Missouri's War Within the War." DISUNION Blog on Opinionator- Exclusive Online Commentary from *The New York Times*, May 2011. (http://opinionator.blogs.nytimes.com/category/disunion).

[93] Phillips.

[94] Royal.

[95] Royal.

[96] This according to his grandson, Joseph Edward King, who was born after Robert L. King died. So, the story must have originated from his father, Samuel Robert King, telling his children anecdotes.

[97] Royal.

[98] Petersen, Paul R. *Quantrill in Texas: The Forgotten Campaign.* (Nashville, Tn.: Cumberland House, 2007), in photograph section, 128-129.

[99] Judging from the best possible online information about Bowman, much of which fails to identify original, primary source material. http://trees.ancestry.com/tree/22655651/person/1277040225?ssrc=&ml_rpos=3

[100] Petersen, *Quantrill at Lawrence*.

[101] Connelley.

[102] Myers, Barton A. "Dissecting the Torture of Mrs. Owens: The Story of a Civil War Atrocity." *Weirding The War.* (Athens, Ga.: University of Georgia Press, 2011), 141-159.

[103] Fred Ford Letters, 1963.

[104] *Kansas City Star*, 23 May 1926.

[105] Fred A. Ford claimed "they never occupied the log house on the W. H. Dayton farm overlooking the spring where they met.... Contrary to legend, which declares that the couple spent their honeymoon there and that Kate returned for her declining years, the house was build and occupied by the Flynn family." Olwine, Margaret, "True Story of Quantrill's Raiders is Too Close to Home to Be Revealed," *Kansas City* (Mo.) *Times*, 26 Oct. 1967. At the time of the article the cabin could "be seen on Argo Road, about a mile east of the old Lobb Church." In the late-1960s, this cabin was sold to the Jackson County Parks Department for $50, dissembled, and the

pieces used to repair other period buildings at Missouri Town 1855, an architectural preservation effort by the Jackson County Parks Department.
[106] Geiger. Also, Petersen and Jackson, *Lost Souls of the Lost Township*.
[107] *Kansas City Star*, 1926. Also, Leslie, 302, and Petersen, *Quantrill in Texas*, 192.
[108] Castel, Albert. *William Clarke Quantrill: His Life and Times*. (Norman, Ok.: University of Oklahoma Press, 1962), 125.
[109] Leslie, Edward E. *The Devil Knows How to Ride*. (New York: Random House, 1996), 257-258.
[110] Schultz, Duane. *Quantrill's War: The Life and Times of William Clarke Quantrill:1837-1865*. (New York: St. Martin's Press, 1996), 254.
[111] Petersen, *Quantrill in Texas*.
[112] Whites.
[113] National Archives and Records Administration. Union Provost Marshal Papers. Online database to a Series of this Record Group provided through the Missouri State Archives. (St. Louis County). Microfilm F1195, Missouri State Archives, Jefferson City, Mo. Kate may have been there even sooner: The first suggestion of Kate's presence in St. Louis was an unclaimed letter addressed to 'Kate Clark' at the Post Office on 15 August 1863. "Ladies List of Letters Remaining Uncalled for at the Post Office at St. Louis, Missouri, on Saturday, August 15, 1863," *Daily Missouri Republican* (St. Louis, MO), 15 Aug. 1863, p.1.
[114] Whites.
[115] Gerteis, Louis S. *Civil War St. Louis*. (Lawrence, Ks.: University Press of Kansas, 2001).
[116] Leslie, 285; Petersen, "Quantrill in Texas," 127; Schultz, 264; and, Castel, 155. All these authors note that while in 'deep Indian territory,' Quantrill wrote a report to General Price on October 13 while in the camp of General Douglas H. Cooper and a 'few days later' the band crossed the Red River into Grayson County, Texas. Petersen says Quantrill rode to Sherman after all his men crossed the river, "by October, 1863."
[117] Petersen, *Quantrill in Texas*, 184.
[118] Correspondence from William D. Day, Fayette, Missouri, to Vicki P. Beck, 2007. A one-page leaflet titled, "William Quantrill in Howard County," contained this graphic, "Quantrill's Hideout in Howard County During the Summer and Fall of 1864." It was derived from data supplied by Howard Hendrix, whose grandfather came from Indiana to the Boonesboro area in 1869, when Hendrix's father was seven-years-old. He later passed down the family tradition: The Hendrix family *"lived in a log cabin about a mile north of Quantrill's*

camp.... Quantrill had camped in a secluded hollow up the east branch of a creek lying east of the Tie Wood Road. The hills south of Boonesboro had a fine stand of white oak timber and during the railroad boom in the 1880s a flourishing rail road tie industry was located in this area and the loggers employed there caused at least two taverns to be located in Boonesboro. The Tie Wood Road was built during this time. Quantrill may have chose this location near Stephen Cooper since Cooper was a Confederate Colonel in the Missouri Brigade and Cooper's family may have been sympathetic to Quantrill and his followers."

Edwards, in *Noted Guerrillas*, states that Quantrill, sick, wounded, barely able to ride and worn from long pain and exposure, arrived in Howard County about the 10th of July of 1864. He spent the first few weeks with his old refugee friends from Jackson County, Evan Hall, Reuben Harris and Samuel Sanders. Connelley stated that Quantrill broke up with George Todd in the summer of 1864 and sought his mistress, Kate Clarke, then took up refuge in Howard County. Castel, in his notes to John McCorkle's book, *Three Years with Quantrill*, restated that Quantrill, while in Howard County, spent most of the summer hiding out with his teenage mistress, Kate King.

[119] Leslie, 302. Also, Petersen, *Quantrill in Texas*, 192.

[120] Westport is now a part of Kansas City, Missouri (Kansas City annexed Westport in 1899). However it was initially a separate town, settled in 1831, that prospered when it displaced Independence, Missouri, as the starting point west for traders, trappers and wagon trails, especially from 1854 to 1860. During the Civil War, there were many skirmishes between Union and Confederate groups in the area, causing trade to fall off.

[121] Schultz, 293; bold typeface added for emphasis.

[122] National Archives.

[123] Schultz.

[124] The surname of this Union guerrilla/outlaw hired to hunt down Quantrill, is also spelled "Terrell" by Leslie. On the internet, the spelling most frequently encountered is "Terrill."

[125] Connelley identified the doctor that examined Quantrill at Wakefield's farm as only 'McClasky' (p. 476). Leslie identified him as Isaac McClasky (p. 366).

Isaac McClasky (5 Sep 1826 - 21 Aug 1883) practiced medicine in Nelson County, Kentucky, his entire career. He, with his wife, Margaret Clay Thomas McClasky, lived in Nelson County at each of the 1850, 1860, 1870 and 1880 Federal census. Two different medical students were with the family in 1850 and 1860.

After Isaac McClasky died and was buried in Big Springs Cemetery, Bloomfield County, Kentucky, his widow, Margaret, went to live with their son Benjamin and his family in Spencer County,

Kentucky, as per the 1900 Federal census. By 1910, Benjamin McClasky had moved to Louisville, Kentucky, and practiced medicine there until his death on 23 September 1923.

[126] Louisville, Kentucky, city directories list Rev. Michael Power:
1865: Rev. Michael Power, residence at 5th between Green and Walnut
1870: Father Michael Power, pastor, residence at 126 Brook
1875: Rev. Michael Power, residence at 126 Brook near Market
1876:   "   "   "   "   "
1878: Rev. Michael Power, pastor St. Michael's Church,
       residence 126 Brook near Jefferson

[127] Olivia Cooper was the wife of Zachariah Green Cooper and the daughter of Thomas Dawson and Nancy Sanders, who were both born in Virginia. Olivia was born in Bloomfield, Nelson County, Kentucky on 27 March 1820. She and Zachariah had at least six children born in Missouri between 1850 and 1861. They were in Jackson County, Missouri in each Federal census from 1850 through 1900. Olivia died in Jackson County, Missouri, on 16 October 1910 at 90 years, 6 months, 21 days. She was buried in Lee's Summit, Missouri.

McCorkle reported that a 'Miss Eliza Saunders' had told him about the money Quantrill gave to Mrs. Cooper.(Barton) Considering the maiden name of Olivia's mother, it is possible that Olivia was related to Eliza Saunders and perhaps provide a clue as to why Mrs. Cooper removed to this particular location during Order No. 11.

[128] Barton, O.S. *Three Years with Quantrill: A True Story Told by His Scout John McCorkle*. (Norman, Ok.: University of Oklahoma Press, 1992); according to McCorkle who was in Kentucky with Quantrill.

[129] Colonel Richard J. Hinton tells of Quantrill's last days, and General Blunt's travel to Louisville to discover Quantrill had recently died: "Stories of Quantrill," *Ligonier* (In.) *Leader,* 11 Dec. 1890, p. 7.

[130] St. Mary's Cemetery, located between 26th and 28th on Duncan Street in Louisville, Kentucky, was established in 1849 by Rev. Karl Boeswald, pastor of St. Mary's Immaculate Conception Church. Following the first burial in 1851, the cemetery became the burial ground for many German and Irish immigrants. The name of this cemetery eventually changed to St. John's Cemetery. This name change occurred before 1884 when W. W. Scott *first* visited Louisville and initially referred to it as the Portland Catholic Cemetery, probably because it was often referred to locally as the 'German Catholic cemetery near Portland.' According to Connelley, Scott made two trips to Louisville - the first time in Spring 1884 when he spoke with both Patrick and Bridget. The second visit with Mrs. Quantrill was in December 1887 after Patrick died and then the grave was opened. (Connelley)

Endnotes

[131] In the 1870 Federal census (21 June 1870) of Louisville, Jefferson County, Kentucky, the Irish-born, 35-year-old, Patrick Shelly, was listed as Sexton of St. John's Cemetery. The city directories of Louisville, Kentucky, in 1869 and 1876 also listed Patrick Shelly as Sexton of St. John's Cemetery. In the 1880 Federal census (2 June 1880) Patrick Shelly, with his wife Bridgett, five children and mother-in-law, Margaret Enright, were listed in Louisville; Patrick's occupation was Cemetery Sexton; but, the cemetery was not identified. Patrick Shelly died on 19 May 1885, at age 48, and was buried in St. John's Cemetery (Kentucky Death Index and findagrave.com).

The widowed Bridget Shelly continued the family's association with the cemetery. In the 1887, 1888 and 1889 city directories for Louisville, Kentucky, Bridget Shelly was noted as sexton of St. John's Cemetery at residence 2639 Duncan. In the 1900 census (4 June 1900) Bridget's occupation was Superintendent of Cemetery. It was Bridget that directed W. W. Scott to Quantrill's grave in December 1887 after Mrs. Quantrill convinced her that "the grave might be opened." (Connelley)

[132] No records exist to mark the exact location of Quantrill's grave. The sexton's cottage has been torn down and a new entrance road constructed further obliterating the exact location of the grave. An old cemetery map of "uncertain accuracy" does indicate where the sexton's cottage was located. (Thies, personal communication from Leslie.)

[133] Leslie, *The Devil Knows How to Ride*.

[134] Connelley (*Quantrill and the Border Wars*, p. 35) quotes W. W. Scott's notes regarding his two visits to the cemetery in spring 1884 and in December 1887, the latter visit occurred after the death of Patrick Shelly. Scott consistently misspelled the names of both Patrick Shelly (as Scally) and Father Power (as Powers). Scott paid Bridget $2.50 for locating the grave and paid Louis Wertz, the employee who did the actual digging, 'a dollar extra.'

[135] Leslie, Edward E. "Quantrill's Bones," *American Heritage* (July-August 1995), as viewed online at http://wesclark.com/jw/quantril.html. Leslie states that there are at least 14 families claiming linear descent from Quantrill, including a fellow claiming to be a great-great grandson at the burial of Quantrill's bones; but, Leslie adds, "there is no hint of evidence that he [Quantrill] sired any children."

[136] Connelley noted that, "John C. King, undertaker, coroner, Third and Jefferson streets, Louisville, Ky.," had furnished the coffin and attended the burial.

Kentucky Death Records note that John C. King, age 75, died March 7, 1894, of uremia of 9 days duration; born Kentucky;

residence at 719 W. Walnut; buried March 9 in Cave Hill Cemetery; attending physician, Dr. Wilson; undertaker Wyatt.

John C. King has no known genealogical connection to Kate's family.

John C. King was listed with his wife Ann and children (Robert Emmet, Eliza and John), as an Undertaker in Louisville, Kentucky on 17 July 1860, on 7 July 1870 and 10 June 1880. He was listed in the Louisville city directory as an embalmer or undertaker at 80 W. Jefferson in 1869, 1878, 1886 and 1892. In 1850 he was a carpenter living in Scott County, Kentucky.

John C. King and his wife Ann Eliza Thomason (1827-1904) had three known children, including Robert Emmet King (1848-1921) who was the first Republican mayor of Louisville, but for only 17 days (January 14th through January 31st) in 1896 when he was appointed mayor pro tem after Henry S. Tyler died in office. (http://trees.ancestry.com/tree/31688964/person/ 1810043067/mediax/1?pgnum=1&pg=0&pgpl=pid|pgNum).

[137] "He Had a History: The Man Who Killed Quantrill, the Guerilla, Died Peacefully in Missouri," *Emporia* (Ks.) *Gazette*, 30 April 1910. A St. Joseph newspaper syndicated John Langford's obituary that stated he died in Albany, Missouri. "Langford said he saw the wounded man there [in the hospital] where he lay on a bed, very pale and suffering in intense agony. Langford claimed to have been present when Quantrill died."

[138] Barton.

[139] Mrs. Neville Ross was Harriet E. Ross, the widow of Lawrence N. Ross, who died in October 1856 in Jackson County, Missouri. Neville was most likely the middle name of Lawrence based on the use of the name by his widow in 1865. And, a grandson born about 1870 was named Neville R. Lobb. Harriet and Lawrence had four children: Charles N., John L., Ella N. and James born between 1841 and 1850 in Missouri. Their son John was with Quantrill in Kentucky. Mrs. Ross was in Kentucky, the state of her birth, in 1865 because of Order No 11. She was in Jackson County, Missouri in the 1850, 1860, 1870 and 1880 census; for the last three census she was in Blue Township, the Township in which Independence is located. On 30 November 1871, Harriet married Jacquilin A. Lobb in Jackson County, Missouri. Jacquilin A. Lobb was the father of her son-in-law John L. Lobb who was married to her daughter Ella N. (*i.e.*, Harriet married her daughter's father-in-law). "Quantrill's Ride to Doom: Last Comrade [Allen Palmer] to See Him Alive Tells Story," *Kansas City* (Mo.) *Star*, 15 Sept. 1918.

[140] If Quantrill did try to contact his mother, the communiqué have not surfaced. The manner and nature in which Mrs. Quantrill later inquired about her "lost son," lends credibility to the fact that Quantrill

did not initiate any messages from his deathbed. And, her recollection in 1900 solidifies this theory. "Quantrill's Hard Heart Melted When He Thought of Mother: Sent Money to Her as Long as he Lived: She Enters Odd Fellows Home," *Indianapolis Sun*, 13 Dec. 1900.

[141] Kentucky Death Records list: Michael Power, male, white, single, age 52, died 7 January 1879 of Volvilus [sic., Volvulus, a twisted loop of bowel which can lead to obstruction and ischemia], born Ireland, residence Brook - Market & Jefferson, buried 9th January in St. Louis by undertaker M. Regan. Father Michael Power died just 14 years after he administered the final rites to Quantrill.

Also note that Patrick Shelly died only six years after Michael Power died.

Both the priest and sexton involved with Quantrill's burial died relatively young within two decades after the burial, and were dead before Quantrill's original grave was disturbed in 1887.

[142] Ford, Anna Scrapbook. "When Quantrill's Mother Came to Blue Springs," Westport Historical Quarterly. (June 1968): 4:2:16-20. Also noted in *Iola Register*, 18 May 1888; Leslie, "Quantrill's Bones," 410-411; and, Wellman, Paul I. "She remembers when Quantrill's Mother Came to Blue Springs," *Kansas City Star*, 30 Aug. 1942 (relaying a recollection of Miss Narra Lewis; a copy of this and other clippings about Lewis are located at the Jackson County (Mo.) Historical Society Archives, Document ID 103F5-6.)

[143] Leslie, 411-413.

[144] Leslie, 413.

[145] Hale, Donald R., *We Rode with Quantrill: Quantrill and the Guerrilla War as Told by the Men and Women Who Were with Him, with a True Sketch of Quantrill's Life.* (Lee's Summit, Mo.: Donald R. Hale, 1992), 1992, 124.

[146] Castel.

[147] Schultz.

[148] Quantrill's grave sites were eventually marked; but, only after his remains had been re-interred . . . more than once and in at least two different locations. His skull, arm and leg bones had been separated and exhibited as trophies for many years. For thorough coverage of the ultimate fate of Quantrill's bones, consult Ralph Monaco's, *Scattered to the Four Winds: General Order No. 11 and Martial Law in Jackson County, Missouri, 1863.* (Independence, Mo.: Jackson County Historical Society, 2013), 194-200. In the Kansas State Historical Society's official "Secretary's Annual Report," published in the *Transactions of the Kansas State Historical Society* (1904):8:124:

"Since May, 1888, this Society has had possession of the two shin bones and of a lock of hair of William Clark Quantrill. They have not been entered among the accessions or exposed to the public because of an obligation not to do so until after the death of the mother. "Mrs. Quantrill died Monday, November 23, [1903] at an Odd Fellows' home in Springfield, Ohio, aged eighty years. These relics of the most historic devil developed by the civil war were taken from his grave in Kentucky by W. W. Scott, of Canal Dover, Ohio, assisted by Mrs. Quantrill. The grave was opened to satisfy the mother of his death. Mr. Scott found two men who were with Quantrill when he was wounded in a fight with federal guerrillas, about June 1, 1865, one having been with him since leaving Kansas and who was in the massacre at Lawrence. Mr. Scott was a schoolmate of Quantrill, and spent twenty-five years in the study of his life. A response received November 30 from Mrs. Scott informs us that Mr. Scott died about a year ago, and thus is lost the most elaborate work concerning the famous guerrilla. In one of his letters Mr. Scott says that all the correspondence and papers accumulated in his investigation shall come to the Historical Society." Connelley later purchased Scott's materials from the widow, and the Kansas State Historical Society also acquired Quantrill's skull; which has since been repatriated and buried in the Quantrill family plot in the Fourth Street Cemetery at Dover, Ohio. O'Connor, Bill. "A burial of shame? The skull of Quantrill of the Civil War raider is interred in Dover, but the jury's still out on whether the man who terrorized Kansas was a hero or a scoundrel", *Akron* (Oh.) *Beacon Journal*, 22 Nov. 1992, B1, 2.

[149] Eakin and Hale.

[150] Morgan Walker settled on Section 18, Township 49, Range 30 in Sni-a-Bar Township directly south of Section 7, Township 49, Range 30 which Robert L. King later purchased.

[151] Connelley, 197-198.

[152] Connelley.

[153] Kate's parents, brother and other relatives are buried in Slaughter Cemetery. Kate was 'related' to the Slaughter family through the marriage of her brother William Jasper King to America Jane Snodgrass, the sister-in-law of Josiah's and Elizabeth's granddaughter Sarah Frances Potts; Sarah Frances Potts, daughter of Sina Emily Slaughter, a daughter of Josiah and Elizabeth, and Levi Potts, married Parmer Snodgrass, a brother of America Jane Snodgrass King.

[154] Harris, Jon, personal communication, 2000-2014.

[155] Connelley.

[156] Eakin and Hale.

[157] Ford.

[158] Eakin and Hale, 423. Several Ancestry.com posts for Charles Fletcher Taylor have included a clipping of his obituary dated 1912.

[159] Fred Ford letter to Don Hale.

Endnotes

[160] Livingston, Joel Thomas. *History of Jasper County, Missouri, and Its People*. (Chicago, Il.: Lewis Publishing Co., 1888).
[161] Livingston, biography of David D. Wood, 1029.
[162] Connelley.
[163] Livingston, biography of David D. Wood, 1029. The Yell County, Arkansas, location listed for their marriage on Ancestry.com was incorrect; that record was for a marriage between a Nancy Wood and a T. J. Vaughn.
[164] As per a Family Tree posted by Joyce Castor of Aubrey, Texas: http://trees.ancestry.com/tree/16621491/person/18009851629.
[165] Ibid.
[166] *Press Spectator*, 13 Aug. 1897.
[167] *Press Spectator*, 13 May 1902.
[168] *Press Spectator*, 16 May 1902.
[169] *Press Spectator*, 23 May 1902.
[170] Kenneth was actually a half first cousin once removed to Viola though her father's half sister Mary Jane Corby. The parents of Kenneth Lumbley were William Green Lumbley and Mary Alice Eakman; William G. Lumbley was the son of William L. Lumbley and Mary Jane Corby. Mary Jane was a half sister of Samuel Lane through the first marriage of his mother. The Lumbley family was in Baxter Springs, involved with lead and zinc mining from 1925 through 1940. They were also in Lowell Township, Cherokee County, Kansas, where Samuel was with his mother in 1870. Apparently Viola grew up more associated with her Lane relatives than with the Walker or Slaughter sides of her family.
[171] Hale, *KC Star*, 1968; *Sentinel*, 1970.
[172] Leslie, 201.
[173] The city of St. Louis had weathered the war with only one minor military incident at Camp Jackson in 1861, which set the stage for a balance of power during the remainder of the war. (Arenson, Gerteis) The presence of many German and Irish immigrants and the influence of financial investors from New England linked the city to the Union. The proximity of St. Louis to surrounding free states made it a center for conflicting views regarding the slavery issue, such as the Dred Scott case. (Gerteis)
[174] In 1861, William Tecumseh Sherman, then president of the Fifth Street Railroad, and his seven-year-old son Willy were eye witnesses when Federal soldiers, escorting captured troops from Camp Jackson, fired into the civilian crowd. William T. Sherman was one of three Civil War Generals to live in St. Louis at some time:
1) Ulysses S. Grant lived in the city from 1854 until 1860; he was married in St. Louis and his wife returned to the city from 1850 to 1852 while he was stationed in Michigan.

2) Confederate General John S. Bowen returned to St. Louis in 1857 and became involved in the Missouri militia; General Bowen was chosen to ask Grant to discuss the terms of surrender at Vicksburg, but Grant refused to see Bowen. Bowen died in 1863 and his widow was exiled in Atlanta until Sherman ordered civilians out of that city and then Mrs. Bowen returned to St. Louis.

3) William Tecumseh Sherman was in St. Louis from 1850 until 1852 and then returned in 1861 until 1862 and again in 1874 to 1886. General William T. Sherman was buried in Calvary Cemetery in St. Louis in February 1891. (Winter)

[175] James Buchanan Eads contracted with the War Department to build the first seven ironclad gunboats for the Union's river navy necessary to gain and keep control of Mississippi River during the war; this stimulated ship building and iron works and foundries throughout the city. Railroad connections to the city and industrial activity increased after the war. St. Louis exploded with commerce and riverfront traffic and shipping resumed full tilt, while construction began on Eads Bridge. James B. Eads designed this St. Louis railroad bridge across the Mississippi River in 1868 and the bridge opened in 1874. (Gerteis) Eads Bridge is now a National Historical Landmark and still in use today.

[176] Gerteis.

[177] Single women with some education could possibly secure a teaching position. Kate had no education, having left school when in her early teens. The oldest profession in the world required no advanced education and relatively little capital investment.

[178] Interestingly, a survey of prostitutes found that two-thirds of them entered the trade by choice, while only eighteen per cent reported that poverty drove them into the business; a surprising fourteen per cent were married and one-third were servants while another one-third were unemployed when they entered the profession. Corbett, Katherine T. *In Her Place: A Guide to St. Louis Women's History.* (St. Louis, Mo.: Missouri Historical Society Press, 1999).

Many young women entered the trade, but not all became as rich and famous as Eliza C. Haycraft, the "Queen of Almond Street." Eliza came to St. Louis in 1840 as a nineteen year refugee, cast out by her family, with an abusive husband, from Callaway County, Missouri. During the next thirty years, she worked her way up from a 'single working girl' to the madam and owner of five brothels and much St. Louis real estate. She rented some of her property to other madams and became known for her charity to the poor—the classical stereotypic "whore with a heart of gold"—it was even reported that she was born on Valentine's Day. Although she could not read or write (she signed all her legal documents with an 'X'), she was a very astute business woman. Eliza retired from the business in

1870 just as the city passed the short-lived 'Social Evil Ordinance' to regulate prostitution. At her death in December of 1871 she left an estate of a quarter of a million dollars (worth $28 million in 2006 dollars) to her six sisters, specifically excluding any interests of the respective husbands (a highly unusual stipulation for women's inheritances at that time in history). Eliza C. Haycraft was buried in Bellefontaine Cemetery in St. Louis, alone in huge 21-grave plot with no marker—a provision imposed by the cemetery to reluctantly allow a 'soiled dove' burial in hallowed ground. Shepley, Carol Ferring. *Movers and Shakers, Scalawags and Suffragettes: Tales from Bellefontaine Cemetery.* (St. Louis, Mo.: Missouri History Museum, 2008), 153-155.

[179] "Ladies List of Letters Remaining Uncalled for at the Post Office at St. Louis, Missouri, on Saturday, August 15, 1863," *Daily Missouri Republican* (St. Louis, MO), 15 Aug. 1863, p.1.

[180] National Archives and Records Administration. Missouri Union Provost Marshal Records.

[181] The case of Robert Louden, gleaned from an online index (Missouri Digital Heritage) to the National Archives and Records Administration, "Missouri's Union Provost Marshal Papers: 1861-1866," insinuates a tantalizing, but murky tale. There were eight people who each presented a "sworn statement about Robert Louden" before the Provost Marshal in St. Louis around mid October in 1863. Two statements were sworn on 28 September, while three were made on 13 October, two on 14 October, and one on 12 October:

Name	Subject	Date
Barry, Mary	Sworn statement about Robert Louden	10-13-1863
Clark, Kate	" " " "	10-13-1863
Donovan, Frances J.	" " "	10-14-1863
Engle, Theodore	" " "	09-28-1863
King, John	" " " "	10-13-1863
McSoley, Brenna	" " "	09-28-1863
Skilling, Anna	" " "	10-14-1863
Tallon, Peter	" " " "	10-12-1863
Danf, Joseph	Orders on what to do about the escapee [after Robert Louden's escape]	10-04-1864

Unfortunately the website displayed only subject topics with an index to the actual microfilmed transcripts. Access to the actual statements might be more enlightening; but, were not readily available to the author.

Five of the witnesses, including Kate Clark, were women, and each made only one statement before the Provost Marshal. Based on

Kate's statement, the women's 'depositions' would verify the association of Louden to each of the women, and perhaps confirm his location at various time periods. It would be interesting to know how the others were associated with Louden. They may well have been involved with the 'Confederate underground,' without being prostitutes.

The men, except Theodore Engle, all made multiple appearances before the Provost Marshal during a two-year period of time between 1863 and 1865. Joseph Danf was apparently attached to the military and his 77 statements indexed in this collection concerned releases, paroles and reception of prisoners at Gratiot Street Prison. Peter Tallon was referred to as St. Louis Chief of Police and also as U.S. Chief of Police; his 92 statements indexed in this collection involved surveillance reports of multiple suspects including guerrillas, rebels and even Quantrill sightings. Whether the single statement by Theodore Engle was related to Theobold Engle, a revenue aid held prisoner for several months because he was on board a steamship with Louden when Louden passed Confederate mail to the ship's captain, is pure speculation at this point in time.

John King was interviewed in regards to Louden on the same day as Kate and Mary Barry/Berry. He garnered particular attention because of his surname and any possible connection to Kate's family. John King appeared before the Provost Marshal at least six times between 1862 and 1865 before he was jailed in Gratiot Street Prison once again. Separate index listings for John B. King appeared 19 times in 1864 and 1865. John King, owner of a drinking house and proprietor of a saloon, was charged with aiding spies and escaped prisoners, as well as selling liquor to soldiers. John B. King was charged with impersonating a detective and as a deserter. Both John and John B. were noted as prisoners at Gratiot Street Prison. Neither John King nor John B. King (if they are one and the same, or separate individuals) are believed to be related to Kate King.

[182] Whites, 2007.

[183] Whites, LeeAnn. Personal communication, 1996-2014. There were black women in the sex trade in St. Louis; but, they were a distinct minority, comprising only 12% of the registered prostitutes. Yet, they were more prone to arrest. Only 12% of registered prostitutes were black; but 72% of the prostitutes arrested for prostitution after the repeal of the "Social Evil Ordinance" were black. Disproportionate numbers of black women were prostitutes when compared to the general population in St. Louis where blacks compromised less than five percent of the total population. Black women's access to decent paying work was even more limited than that of black men. There was no evidence that white cliental expressed a preference for or against black prostitutes in St. Louis.

Levine, Philippa and Susan R. Grayzel, eds. "Race and the Regulation of Prostitution: Comparing Public Health in the U.S. and Greater Britain." Chapter 4. *Gender, Labour, War and Empire: Essays on Modern Britain.* (London: Palgrave Macmillan, 2009), 51-71.

[184] By 1860, about 40% of the population of St. Louis was German and Irish immigrants. (Levine) Apparently a larger immigrant population base provided better job opportunities for immigrant women in other professions than prostitution than were available for black women.

[185] Levine.

[186] Levine, 69 (footnote 41).

[187] Whites, personal communication.

[188] *Missouri Republican*, 4 May 1872.

[189] *St. Louis Democrat*, 10 Aug. 1873.

[190] Wunsch, James. "The Social Evil Ordinance." *American Heritage Magazine.* (February/March 1982): 33: 2.

[191] St. Luke's Hospital, named for the patron saint of physicians, was organized in 1865 by leaders of the Episcopal Church and several doctors who were concerned about the lack of medical care in St. Louis. St. Luke's first opened as a twenty-five room facility with eight physicians at Ohio and Sumner Streets in the spring of 1866 and was immediately tested by the cholera epidemic that swept through the city that year. Cholera patients were treated free of charge supported by the Episcopal Church and the community. The hospital encountered financial difficulties and it was decided in September of 1867 that the hospital was located too far from the center of population; the hospital moved to 6th and Elm in March 1870 and then again to Pine Street between 9th and 10th Streets in June 1873. The hospital was debt free by 1874. In June of 1881, a new building at Washington Avenue and 19th Street was erected for $41,000. Hyde, William, and Howard L. Conrad, eds. *Encyclopedia of the History of St. Louis.* Vol. I. (St. Louis, Mo.: The Southern History Company, 1899).

In 1870 there were seven hospitals in St. Louis:
1) City Hospital at Lafayette Avenue on the northwest corner of Linn,
2) German Lutheran Hospital at 2612 South 7th,
3) Good Samaritan Hospital at Dayton on the corner of Jefferson Avenue,
4) Marine Hospital at Marine Avenue south of the US Arsenal,
5) St. Louis Hospital at Spruce on the corner of 4th,
6) St. Joseph's Hospital at Jefferson Avenue on the northwest corner of Osage, and
7) St. Luke's Hospital at Elm on the southwest corner of 6th.

Ten years later in 1880 there were eight hospitals in St. Louis: St. Joseph's Hospital was no longer listed, St. Louis Hospital had another location under construction at Montgomery near Grand Avenue in addition to the one at Spruce and 4th, the Social Evil Hospital had been built near the Arsenal on Manchester Road, and St. Luke's Hospital had moved to 913 Pine. "St. Louis: Pages in Time." (http://members.tripod.com/~Vide_Poche/map.html).

[192] *St. Louis Democrat*, 10 Aug. 1873.

[193] The Ordinance nearly overwhelmed the enforcement officials; within the first eight months the city registered 1,284 prostitutes, 136 brothels, nine houses of assignment and 243 single rooms. (Wunsch) Initially the number of prostitutes (estimated to be 5,000) seemed to decrease, but there was a net increase as more of them were forced from single rooms into brothels which also increased in number from ninety-nine in 1871 to 133 two years later. In addition, there was a huge increase in their mobility with over 6,000 change of residence permits issued by March 1873; there had been 821 applications to move in 1871, which increased to 5,662 in 1872.

[194] William Greenleaf Eliot was the Chancellor of Washington University at the time of the law suit until his death in 1887. Rev. Eliot was born in New Bedford, Massachusetts and attended Columbia College in Washington, D.C—now George Washington University. After graduate work at Harvard Divinity School he was ordained as a Unitarian minister in 1834 and then went to St. Louis where he formed the First Unitarian Church. When the church building was nearing completion, he returned to Washington, D.C. in 1837 to marry 'Abby' Abigail Adams Cranch whose father was a nephew of Abigail Adams. William G. Eliot's father, mother and wife were all first cousins to each other because their mothers were sisters (as well as sisters of Rebecca Greenleaf who married Noah Webster). They were a very distinguished family. William G. and Abby produced 14 children, but not all survived until adulthood. William G. Eliot was very active in public life; his actions helped to keep Missouri in the Union at the onset of the Civil War; he founded the St. Louis Public Schools, St. Louis Art Museum, Mission Free School, South Side Day Nursery, Mary Institute and the Western Sanitary Commission which provided medical care and supplies during the war. He also contributed to the founding of the Colored Orphans' Home, Soldiers' Orphans' Home, Memorial Home, Blind Girls' Home, Women's Christian Home and other good works; he was also the grandfather of T. S. Eliot–Thomas Sterns Eliot (1888-1965), playwright, literary critic, and important 20th century poet who received the Nobel Prize in Literature in 1948, was born in the United States, but moved to the United Kingdom and became a British citizen in 1927.

In 1869, William Greenleaf Eliot resigned as minister of the Unitarian Church and congregation he founded to become chancellor of Washington University which he had co-founded. Rev. Eliot continued his devotion to social reform and led the battle to repeal the Social Evil Ordinance. Eliot, Charlotte C., "William Greenleaf Eliot (1811-1887)." Vol. III. The Preachers. *Heralds of a Liberal Faith*, edited by Samuel A. Eliot, American Unitarian Association, Boston, MA, 1910, p. 90-98. (http://harvardsquarelibrary.org/Heralds/William-Greenleaf-Eliot.php).

[195] Levine.

[196] During the first ten months of operation the Ordinance generated $26,544 in fees, which more than doubled to $56,190 the next year and in 1873 the income rose to almost $63,000. Expenses for the Ordinance did increase over time, especially when another floor was added to the hospital. The surplus of $13,000 left in the social evil fund after the law was repealed had to be offset by $21,000 from the general fund required to complete the initial projects. Although the experiment was not self-sustaining financially as originally proposed, it probably could have been if it had continued to function longer. (Sneddeker)

[197] Barnes, Harper, "The Madame Years: Our City's Brief Embrace of the "The Social Evil," St. Louis Magazine, February 2009. (http://www.stlmag.com/St-Louis-Magazine/February-209/The-Madame-Years/).

[198] Logan Douglas Dameron was born 31 October 1827 in North Carolina to George Ball Dameron and Mary Worsham Moore. The family came West in 1833. Logan D. had steamboating interests on the Missouri and Mississippi Rivers and settled in St. Louis in 1859. He was married first to Mary E. Chappel on 4 May 1852 in Randolph County, MO. He remarried second to Elizabeth McCombs and third to Cornelia Jackson Turner. In 1870 he lived around 17th Street in St. Louis with his second wife and daughter; the family had three white female servants and a coachman living with them. In 1880 he was with his third wife, an adult son and his daughter from the second marriage; no servants were in the household. His occupation on each census was listed as a book dealer and publisher. In the 1881 and 1890 City Directory, Logan D. Dameron was listed at 913 Pine as manager of Advocate Publishing House (he was publisher of the "St. Louis Christian Advocate"); his residence was 3142 Olive. Logan Dameron died 21 May 1891 in Lexington in Lafayette County, Missouri. (Hyde and Conrad, Vol. II) His will, dated 4 July 1887, was filed for probate and published in the *St. Louis Post-Dispatch* on 31 May 1891.

[199] James Robert Claiborne was a prominent lawyer in St. Louis who represented Kate in St. Louis city court in 1873. Kate's alleged

marriage to J.R. Claiborne was reported in a 1926 newspaper article, in the eighth paragraph from the end: "Four years after the war, when things had quieted down along the border, she returned to visit her family as Mrs. J.R. Claiborne." *(Kansas City Star,* 23 May 1926) Kate and Claiborne never married. Three years after the court case, James Robert Claiborne was elected a Missouri State Senator. If he had married Kate, this marriage would certainly have been brought forth and discussed during the election campaign. There was no record of a Kate or a Sarah marrying Claiborne; the only marriage recorded for James R. Claiborne was to Miss Fannie Moore in 1879 in Cooper County, Missouri. It is presumed that any subsequent references to a marriage between Claiborne and Kate came from this erroneous report in 1926.

[200] *St. Louis Democrat*, 17 Aug. 1873.

[201] *Buffalo Daily Courier,* Buffalo, NY, August 1873; *Chicago Daily Tribune*, Chicago, IL, August 24, 1873; *Daily Ohio State Journal,* Columbus, OH, August 6, 1873; *The Deseret News,* Salt Lake City, UT, August 20, 1873; *Dubuque Herald*, Dubuque, IA, August 24, 1873; *The Leavenworth Weekly Times*, Leavenworth, KS, August 21, 1873; *Memphis Daily Appeal*, Memphis, TN, August 6, 1873 and August 24, 1873; *The New York Times*, New York, NY, December 2, 1873; *St. Louis Democrat*, St. Louis, MO, August 17, 1873; *Sandusky Daily Register*, Sandusky, OH, August 6, 1873.)

[202] John W. Colvin, Judge of St. Louis Criminal Court, was born in Virginia about 1817, had been a lawyer in St. Louis prior to his appointment as Judge and he and his wife Mary Elizabeth Strode lived at various addresses throughout St. Louis per city directories from 1863 to 1867. Judge John W. Colvin died in St. Louis of heart and lung congestion on 21 April 1876 — less than three years after he ruled on Kate's case.

[203] *St. Louis Democrat*, 29 Aug. 1873.

[204] Post, Truman A., Reporter. "State of Missouri, Respondent, v. Kate Clarke, Appellant." *Reports of Cases Argued and Determined in the Supreme Court of the State of Missouri.* (1874): LIV: 17-45. [The Judges: David Wagner, Wash Adams, H.M. Vories, T.A. Sherwood and W.B Napton.].

[205] *St. Louis Daily Globe*, 22 Feb. 1874.

[206] Dacus and Buel, 474.

[207] Ibid., 465-66, bolded font added for emphasis by the author.

[208] *St. Louis Dispatch*, 4 Feb. 1875, p. 4. This entertaining article required an understanding of the 'classical' furnishings of a house of iill-repute, such as: georgous = misspelling of gorgeous; virtu = valued for beauty, antiquity or quality of workmanship; brocatele [sp. brocatelle] = brocade with design woven in high relief; rep = 'ribbed' cloth woven in cords (can be silk, wool or cotton); bserglio [sp.

seraglio] = part of a Muslin palace where the harem is secluded; pier glass = framed mirror(s) on walls between windows; lambrequin = short drapery covering upper part of an opening (e.g. door, window) or shelf, etc.; and chromos = chromolithographs, i.e., colored pictures made by lithography.

[209] Registry of Births, City of St. Louis, "Missouri Birth Records, 1851-1910," p. 209, database on Ancestry.com, from film by the Missouri State Archives, Jefferson City, Missouri. The original "Pre-1910 Birth Register Entry, St. Louis City Births," was not available from the City of St. Louis Recorder of Deeds & Vital Records Office. Hoftiezer was referred to the Bureau of Vital Records at the Missouri Department of Health and Senior Services in Jefferson City, Missouri, which could not locate the original record viewable on Ancestry.com.

[210] Dameron denied that Huntington acted on his behalf and claimed that the Board of St. Luke's Hospital was responsible for the lease of the building to Kate. According to him, when the hospital moved, Dameron had been offered a fifty per cent increase in rent if the building could be used as a bawdy house which he refused; he also alleged that the rental agent, Thomas Huntington, then arranged with the members of St. Luke's board, including C.F. Robertson, the Episcopal Bishop of Missouri, to sublet the building to a 'landlady' at the increased price. The Hospital Board adamantly denied knowledge and responsibility for the sublease of the building. (*St. Louis Democrat*, 10 August 1873) (*St. Louis Democrat,* 13 August 1873) and (*St. Louis Democrat,* 29 August 1873)

[211] *St. Louis Dispatch*, 25 Jan. 1877.

[212] Lindenbusch, John. "The Social Evil Ordinance: Legalized Vice (and Vice Versa)." *St. Louis* (June 1980): 12, 18-19.

[213] "The House of Industry," Women in Health Sciences, Washington University, St. Louis. (beckerexhibits.wustl.edu/mowihsp/win/TimelineSocialEvilHospital.htm)

[214] Wunsch.

[215] A lag period of several months to a year may have been necessary between canvassing, publication and distribution of city directories. On 23 April 1881, W.W. Scott wrote a letter addressed to, "Miss Kate Clark, or Mrs. Kate Quantrill" in St. Louis. The letter was returned to him by the U.S. Post Office stating that it was undeliverable to those names. Kate's days in St. Louis apparently ended abruptly. Letter at the University of Kansas, Kenneth Spencer Research Library, in the William Clarke Quantrill Collection, for which a detailed, online, finding aid is available at: http://etext.ku.edu/data/ksrlead/pdf/ksrl.kc.quantrillwilliam.ead.pdf.

[216] *St. Louis Daily Globe*, 22 Feb. 1874.

[217] *St. Louis Dispatch*, 25 Jan. 1877.

[218] *St. Louis Dispatch*, 25 Jan. 1877.

[219] *St. Louis Post-Dispatch*, 28 June 1887.
[220] Levine.
[221] Whites.
[222] Petersen, Paul R. Personal communication, 28 November 2008.
[223] *St. Louis Democrat*, 17 Aug. 1873.
[224] *St. Louis Post Dispatch*, 8 Sept. 1874, and 24 Feb. 1882.
[225] Registry of Births, City of St. Louis, "Missouri Birth Records, 1851-1910," p. 209, database on ancestry.com, from film by the Missouri State Archives, Jefferson City, Missouri. The original "Pre-1910 Birth Register Entry, St. Louis City Births," was not available from the City of St. Louis Recorder of Deeds & Vital Records Office. Hoftiezer was referred to the Bureau of Vital Records at the Missouri Department of Health and Senior Services in Jefferson City, Missouri, which could not locate the original record viewable on Ancestry.com.
[226] A search of the Missouri State Archives' online index to Missouri births using all combinations of names for Bertha or her mother, as well as birth dates from 1875 through 1877, failed to locate any other appropriate listings.
[227] Harrah, Oklahoma, is located in the extreme southeast corner of Oklahoma County at a ford in the North Canadian River. The town was formerly known as Sweeney, but was renamed Harrah on 22 December 1898 in honor of the entrepreneur Frank Harrah who developed the town in the 1890's.
[228] Another possibility to consider was that Kate, who had reconciled with her parents when she returned to Blue Springs after the Civil War and rebuilt their house and barn, had left the infant Bertha in the care of the maternal grandparents. But, when Kate's mother, Malinda Rebecca (Stringer) King, died on 18 January 1880, it would have left young Bertha, who was then about five years old, without a female caregiver. Perhaps, then, Kate returned to Blue Springs at that time to reconnect with her daughter and family.
[229] Of the dozen individuals named Evans in the First Ward of the 1880 Federal census of St. Louis (Kate's neighborhood), only half of those were male. The older ones were married, and the younger ones, as boarders or roomers, could not have enticed a woman like Kate to sell her business to a New York business partner / fiancé.

St. Louis city-wide, there were an additional dozen individuals named Evans who were born in New York (on the presumption that Kate's business partner may have been Mr. Evans, as alluded to in the newspaper on page 140 of this biography); only four of those were male, and none could be connected by the authors of this biography to Kate and/or Bertha.

St. Louis city-wide, there were 15 individuals named Evans who were born in England (based on the "Cass" Pliny Raymond Castanien family record reproduced in this biography); nine were male, and none were in Kate's neighborhood and therefore could not be connected by the authors to Kate and/or Bertha.

There were no Evins or Ivins enumerated in St. Louis in 1880 (the alternate spellings the author found for Bertha's father's surname).

Regarding Evins, there were 61 individuals by that surname born in New York who lived throughout the U.S. None were named Martin and only one named Richard was too far distant to connect to Kate and/or Bertha. There were 18 individuals indexed by Evins who were born in England. None lived in Missouri; none were named Martin; only one was named Richard, but there were no details about him that could be connected to Kate and/or Bertha.

Regarding the Ivins surname, there were 24 born in New York who lived throughout the U.S. None were named Martin or Richard. There were six individuals indexed as Ivins who were born in England. None lived in Missouri; and, none were named Martin or Richard."

[230] Scott, William W. "W. C. Quantrill: The Name Recalls a Bloody History," *Lawrence Gazette*, 30 Aug. 1888, p. 4. Might she have retreated to Quantrill's old stomping grounds? No record of her has yet been uncovered.

[231] All known persons with the surname Castanien in the United States were contacted in 1996 seeking information regarding Pliny Castanien and Bertha. An amazing number of these people replied sending family histories, genealogical data or recommendations of additional relatives, who would share such information. No one knew much about Pliny, but most knew of his existence. Amongst the volume of information received were copies of the same identical mimeographed sheet of information from two independent respondents (and referenced by many others who responded) who noted information regarding Bertha's genealogy. This information, written in 1935, could only have come from Pliny's and Bertha's son Pliny Raymond Castanien; there are several references to communication with 'Plin' in their family records.

[232] Snyder, Jean Castanien, North Carolina/New Jersey. Personal communication, 22 April 1996. [Jean also provided the photo of Pliny Mannon Castanien with his nephew.] Also, Castanien, Donald G., Davis, California. Personal communication, 16 March 1996.

[233] Various online sources point to this historic structure, from which the images on this page derive: http://gohistoric.com/places/635577; http://www.zoopla.co.uk/property/9-randolph-road/london/w9-1an/25109274. Edouard Mendes de Costa, from The Netherlands, lived at this house in 1905, according to *The London Gazette*, 1 Dec. 1905, p. 8659, which provided a list of naturalizations from the previous month. By 1912, Arthur Dones lived at this house, according to John Parker's *Who's Who in the Theatre*. Volume 3. (Boston, Ma.: Small, Maynard and Co., 1912), 128. Tragically, on

December 6, 1941, five members of the Wils family were killed by a parachute mine during World War II. Four of them died at the home (http://www.cwgc.org/find-war-dead/casualty/3115474/ WILLS,%20VERA; and, http://www.doverwarmemorialproject.org.uk/ Casualties/Civilians/SurnamesUtoZ.htm). By 1958, Dr. P. R. Masek lived at this address (http://www.iafss.org/publications/frn/350/- 1/view). And, the owner as of 2014 is Paul Weiland, a member of Venrex Ii LLP (https://www.opencompany.co.uk/company/ OC309270/venrex-ii-llp).

[234] The Oklahoma Land Run began the disposal of Federal unassigned public domain land in Oklahoma whereby two million acres, left vacant post-Civil War to create Indian Reservations, were proclaimed open for settlement on 23 March 1889 by President Benjamin Harrison. Over 50,000 people gathered at 'boomer camps' at the boundaries of Oklahoma Territory to await the dash for land; settlers could claim 160 acres and, after five years of homesteading it, could receive title to it. Entrepreneurs seeking potential business and investment opportunities mingled with the land seekers; some 'jumped the gun' and these 'sooners' eventually lead to many lawsuits. Towns sprang up overnight. Oklahoma Territory was incorporated in 1890 and Oklahoma became the 46th state in 1907.

[235] This land in Section 2 is located three miles north of Harrah, OK and one mile west of the Lincoln County, OK line. Harrah, OK was the residence Bertha E. Evans listed on her marriage record in August 1899, ten years after Pliny made his land run claim.

[236] Holmes, Helen F., ed. *Logan County History, 1889-1977: Logan County, Oklahoma*, Volume 1: The Families. Cyrenus Castanien Family. (Guthrie, Okla.: History Committee, Logan County Extension Homemakers Council, 1980).

[237] Pliny's brother Frank stayed in Guthrie until at least 1900, but moved to Le Flore County, Oklahoma by 1920, while his brother Charles did not leave Guthrie until after 1910, when he moved to California. Two of Pliny's sisters, Sarah Elizabeth and Annie, died as children in Ohio, whereas his other three sisters survived to adulthood and married: 1) Mary Jane Castanien married Charles Henry Wisner and died in Guthrie, Logan County, Oklahoma in about 1942; 2)' Clara' Clarissa Carolyne Castanien married Morris P. Roe and died in Sonoma County, California in 1947; and 3) Iva J. Castanien married Tom Malone late in her life in 1935, after having previously lived singly in Guthrie, Oklahoma. She died on 22 January 1963 in Ramah, El Paso County, Colorado.

[238] *The Southwest World*, 20 Dec. 1902.

[239] Bank Commissioner of the State of Oklahoma. "The Bank of Braggs, Oklahoma" *Annual Report of the Bank Commissioner of the*

Endnotes

State of Oklahoma. (Bank Commissioner of the State of Oklahoma,1908), 31.

[240] In the 1910 census, Ella was listed as born in Texas, father born in Arkansas, mother born in Alabama, unemployed for five weeks the previous year, and was able to read and write.

Ancestry.com listed Ella Jackson, daughter of Andrew Caldwell Jackson, married to Samuel Duly Thompson (1877-1909), born and died in Vian, Sequoyah County, Oklahoma. According to Find-A-Grave both Samuel Duly, Sr. and Jr. were buried in Round Mountain Cemetery in Gore, Sequoyah County Oklahoma. Ella's and Samuel Duly's son Samuel Duly Thompson, Jr. was born 3 March 1901 and died April of 1985.

On 9 July 1900 census, Ella Thompson, age 30 (born November 1869 in Texas, mother of one living child from two births, father born in Missouri, mother born in Alabama) was on the census with her new younger husband, Dooley Thompson, age 22 (born November 1877 in Arkansas, parents' birthplaces both unknown, farm laborer) in Flint Township 12 N, Range 23 E, Cherokee Nation, Indian Territory (now Oklahoma).

In the 1910 census, when Ella was in Vian as a servant with Kate, Ella's son Samuel Thompson, age 9 (born in Oklahoma, father born in Arkansas and mother born in Texas) was also in Sequoyah County, Oklahoma, with the family of William O. and Minerva C. Miller and their five children. Also with the family was Andy Thompson, age 6, born in Oklahoma. Perhaps Andy was Ella's second living child and was named after his maternal grandfather, *i.e.*, Ella's father, Andrew Caldwell Jackson.

Ella was not located on the 1920 or 1930 census; no Thompson family member was found in 1920. On 10 April 1930, Samuel D. Thompson (Jr.), age 29, born in Oklahoma was a laborer on the state highway in Fort Gibson, Muskogee County, Oklahoma with his wife Bertha and infant son Samuel. In 1940, this family was in Nash Township, Muskogee County, Oklahoma. Sam D. was a farm laborer.

Also in the 1940 census on April 15th, there was an unnamed female Thompson with Homer M. and Athena Simons and their three children in Hobart, Kiowa County, Oklahoma. This 70 year old widow, born in Texas, with an eighth grade education was in Kiowa County in 1935 and was identified as the grandmother-in-law of Homer. Perhaps this unnamed woman was Ella living with her granddaughter.

There was no indication that Ella was a prostitute at any point in her life.

[241] Vian, Oklahoma was established in Sequoyah County in 1902, taking its name from the Big Vian and Little Vian Creeks. It began as

a trading post in the Cherokee Nation and acquired its first post office in 1886. Rapid growth occurred after the railroad came through in 1888 and Vian became the center for shipping the cotton grown in the area.

[242] Braggs, Oklahoma, located about ten miles south of Ft. Gibson, was originally named Patrick, after John J. Patrick; he built the first store and post office by the Arkansas River and operated Smith Ferry, but moved the post office to the current site of Braggs when the St. Louis and Iron Mountain Railroad arrived. Patrick owned the first cotton gin and died in 1927. On 10 September 1888, the town was renamed Braggs after Solomon Braggs who owned the grist mill until he died in 1907. In 1907 the population was 330 and between 1910 and 1913 three gin mills, three banks, a church, school and cemetery were established. Note that the Castanien family owned and operated The Bank of Braggs before these three new banks were established. Beginning in 1942 (WWII), the Federal Government bought 32,000 acres of Cherokee land and the War Department built Camp Gruber which was a POW camp until 1946 when it was closed. Braggs declined then as well.

[243] "Vian Notes (from Sequoyah County Democrat)," *Star Gazette* (Sallisaw, Ok.), 24 June 1910. The newspaper had reported on 18 Mar. 1910, that Kate and Mrs. East were giving up charge of the Northern Hotel in Vian to Mrs. Bohnam.

[244] Sapulpa, Oklahoma, the county seat of Creek County, was incorporated on 16 May 1898. Sapulpa is 15 miles southwest of Tulsa, OK where the land has been under the control of five countries (Spain, France, England, Mexico and the U.S.) and the Choctaw Indian Nation (during the Civil War). A spur of the St. Louis-San Francisco Railroad passed through Sapulpa in 1886 and the post office was acquired in 1889, almost a decade before Sapulpa was chartered. The first major industry was walnuts until brick making rose to prominence in 1898. Sapulpa was a major railroad yard beginning in 1900. The glass industry began in 1912 and Sapulpa became known as the 'Crystal City of the South West."

[245] A cateress is a female caterer. "Hotel Changes Hands," *Braggs Bugle*, 20 Feb. 1913; "Personal and Local," 27 Feb. 1913, where Miss Anna Martin was named as the head waitress; and, "Braggs Briefly Reviewed," 6 Mar. 1913.

[246] "Braggs, OK Fire, Jul 1911," GenDisasters: Genealogy in Tragedy, Disasters, Fires, Floods (http://www3.gendiasters.com/oklahoma/9608/braggs-ok-fire-jul-1911).

[247] The land records for "The West fifty (50) feet of Lot numbered Six (6) and the West fifty (50) feet of the South fifty-six and 6/10 (56.6)

feet of Lot numbered Three (3) in Block numbered sixty-eight (68) in Sapulpa Oklahoma.":
a) 16 April 1913: Pliny purchased it by warranty deed from George A. and Ella S. Smith of Sapulpa for $1,000.
b) 25 March 1914: Pliny of Sapulpa sold it by warranty deed to his wife Bertha for $3,000.
c) 16 September 1931: Bertha sold it by warranty deed back to Pliny for $1.00.
d) 1 August 1941: Creek County Board of Commissioners sold it to the highest bidder, R.F. Henshaw of Tulsa, OK, for $256.00, following his initial offer of $75.00 on 20 June 1941.
e) There were several undated mortgage transactions on it involving Standard Savings & Loan Association, Oklahoma Savings & Loan Association and Local B & L Association. No reasons for the multiple financial transactions were given.

[248] _____, "Tankersley v Castanien," 1916 OK 1051, 162P. 191, 63 Okla. 18, Case Number: 6800, Oklahoma Supreme Court Cases, Wyoming State Law Library.

[249] City directory, Wichita, Kansas, 1937.

[250] *Hutchinson News Herald*, 24 Oct. 1937, 19.

[251] Royal.

[252] In 1996, two replies in response to the mass mailing to all known Castanien descendants had suggested that Pliny, Sr. had died in 1937, perhaps in a car accident in California:
1) Jean L. Castanien Snyder, of both North Carolina and New Jersey, mentioned in a letter dated 22 April 1996, that "Pliny Mannon Castanien married Bertha Evans King in Oklahoma in 1900 -- Later to California."
2) a copy of one page of an undated letter (but obviously written while Pliny, Jr. was living in San Diego, CA) from Jean Shirtzer to an unknown recipient (but perhaps Jean L. Castanien), which said: "I called Pliny tonight to try to get the information on his dad but he said he'd have to look up records. He thought his dad died in 1937 but he didn't remember when he was born. Anyway I'll do the best I can with records I have here and what mother had told me."
Perhaps Jean Synder repeated general information that had confused the timing and the generation of whether it was the Senior or Junior Pliny Castanien in California. Both Pliny Sr. and Jr. were In Wichita, Sedgwick County, Kansas in 1937. Apparently Pliny, Jr. was not the most reliable family historian if he could not provide an accurate date of his father's death. It has now been documented that Pliny, Sr. died in 1938 in Kansas.

[253] *The Hutchinson News*, 15 Nov. 1938, p. 10.

[254] *The Hutchinson News*, 14 Nov. 1938, p. 6.

[255] *Wichita Eagle*, 14 Nov. 1938.

[256] Bertha's body was embalmed at Beckwith Funeral Home (by the grandfather of the current funeral director) in Larned for transport to the Lahey Funeral home in Wichita. Beckwith Funeral Home, Larned, Ks. Personal communication via. telephone.
Bertha and Pliny M. were buried in Lot 2 of Memorial Garden D in graves 5 and 6, but the cemetery receptionist could not provide any additional information, not even dates of burial, only verified the years of burial; she said she was prohibited from providing additional information by law. Wichita Park Cemetery, Wichita, Ks. Personal communication.

[257] Randall Morell, Morell Funeral Home, Larned, Kansas, have no Castanien records. Mr. Morell volunteered to check at Wichita Park Cemetery for tombstones on the graves of Pliny and Bertha for the author, Virgil Hoftiezer. Morell reported that their graves were both unmarked. Morell, Randal. Morell Funeral Home, Larned, Ks. Personal communication, with the author's appreciation.
The Lahey Funeral Home in Wichita was unable to accurately read an electronic record for Bertha Castanien, but the information appeared to be the same as shown on Bertha's death certificate.
A special thank you to Jeanne Reed, Librarian at Mid-Continent Library in Excelsior Springs, MO, for locating the news articles about Pliny Castanien and then for obtaining phone numbers to the funeral homes in Larned, KS, which lead to the series of events that provided this valuable information and documentation. Her response to e-mail inquiries have always been prompt, polite, and above all productive. Her diligence and professionalism is greatly appreciated.

[258] Lahey (now Downey and Lahey) Funeral Home, Wichita, Ks. Personal communication.

[259] Oklahoma Territorial Agricultural and Mechanical College was founded in 1890 in Stillwater as the public, land-grant, co-educational institution of the Territory. When Oklahoma attained statehood in 1907, 'Territorial' was dropped from the name. In 1957 the name was changed to Oklahoma State University of Agriculture and Applied Sciences. Finally, in 1980 the ending of the name was dropped and the institution became known as Oklahoma State University.

[260] Briggs, Edwin W., ed. *Directory of the Greater Oklahoma Agricultural and Mechanical College, 1926-1927*. Class of 1927. (n.p.: Y.M.C.A. and Y.W.C.A., 1927).

[261] Payne, William Howard, ed. *Directory of the Oklahoma Agricultural and Mechanical College, 1929-30*. (n.p.: Y.M.C.A. and Y.W.C.A. and A. and M. Printing Department,1930), 27.

[262] Kappa Kappa Psi is a national honorary band fraternity founded by ten members of Oklahoma Agricultural and Mechanical College on 27 November 1919. It was and still is headquartered in Stillwater, Oklahoma.

[263] Castanien, 121.

[264] The *Wichita Beacon* began publishing in October 1872. The *Wichita Eagle*, which started publication in the spring of 1872, was its chief competitor for 88 years. In 1960 the *Beacon* was purchased by the *Eagle*; the *Beacon* was published as a evening edition and the *Eagle* was the morning edition. Ridder Publications purchased both newspapers in 1973. Ridder and Knight merged the following year in 1974. In 1980, Ridder-Knight combined the two newspapers into the *Wichita Eagle-Beacon*. Beacon was dropped from the name in 1989 and the newspaper became known as *The Wichita Eagle*. Pliny worked for these newspapers while they were independent rivals before the era of the mergers.

[265] An internet search located several newspaper articles authored by Pliny on a variety of topics, including:
1) Seven families of Amish farmers have moved from their frontier homesteads at Yoder (now an oil producing center) to Iowa. In an interview with members of the settlement Pliny Castanien, *Wichita Eagle* newsman, related in the Sunday *Eagle* of March 22, 1936, that "Tractors, Not Oil, Cause Kansas Amish to Migrate."
2) Castanien, Pliny, "Wichita Man Pays Tribute to His Father, A Civil War Hero," *Wichita Eagle* (Morning), 13 February 1938. Efforts to obtain copies of these articles, especially the second one, continue, but have proven fruitless to date.

[266] The *San Diego Union* was founded 10 October 1868. In 1928 Copley Press acquired both the *San Diego Union* and the *Evening Tribune*, another San Diego newspaper founded on 2 December 1895 which had merged with the *San Diego Sun* in 1939. The *San Diego Sun* had been founded in 1861. Copley Press merged the *Union* and the *Tribune* into *The San Diego Union-Tribune* on 2 February 1992. On 18 March 2009 the merged newspaper was sold to the private group, Platinum Equity of Beverly Hills.

[267] Barbara Anderson, of appropriate age and correct birth place when included, appeared on the passenger lists of the following ships and voyages with inclusive dates of the voyage:
Monterey, San Francisco, CA to Honolulu, HI, 3 March 1936 to 6 March 1936;
Monterey, Los Angeles, CA to Honolulu, HI, 10 February 1937 to 15 February 1937;
Lurline, Honolulu, HI to Los Angeles, CA, 18 November 1938 to 26 November 1938;
Matsonia, Los Angeles, CA to Honolulu, HI, 4 May 1939 to 10 May 1939;
Chaumont, Honolulu, HI to San Pedro, CA, 14 May 1940 to 22 May 1940; and,

Matsonia, Honolulu, HI to Los Angeles, CA, 13 June 1941 to 18 June 1941.

[268] Traitel, Dee Annne, "Pliny Raymond 'Cass' Castanien, 85; author and longtime police reporter," Obituaries, *The San Diego Union-Tribune*, 8 February 1994. Much information taken from "Police Beat Reporter Plans Travel," *San Diego Union,* 1 January 1974, which announced Pliny's retirement after twenty-five years as a police reporter at that newspaper.

[269] JaCoby, Alfred, Director, San Diego Union History Project (Copley Newspapers), 7776 Ivanhoe Avenue, LaJolla, Ca. Personal communication to Vicki Beck, 21 March 1996.

[270] Sapulpa city directory.

[271] Sapulpa city directory.

[272] Ford and Hale personal communications. Through his mother Ella Bell Hudspeth Ford, Fred Allen Ford was related to the several Hudspeth men associated with Quantrill and the rebel cause (Eakin and Hale), including 'Babe' William Napoleon Hudspeth who married 'Annie' Georgeanna Ragland, Kate's niece, on 5 February 1897. This marriage ended in separation and Annie returned to her parent's home before Babe died on 24 May 1907. Although Fred called Babe Hudspeth his 'cousin', they were actually second cousins once removed. It was through this unhappy marriage of his 'cousin' to Kate's niece, that Fred Ford claimed relationship to 'Aunt Kate'.

[273] Sapulpa city directory, 1916.

[274] William Jasper King died at the home of his brother-in-law Parmer Snodgrass near Grain Valley in Sni-a-Bar Township in Jackson County, Missouri, on 26 March 1919; Martha Jane King Ragland died on 14 May 1918 at the home of her daughter in Kansas City, Jackson County, Missouri. William Jasper's obituary noted a surviving sister, "Mrs. Kate Badson" [note misspelling of Batson] of Sapulpa, Oklahoma. Obviously Kate's relatives in Jackson County, Missouri, knew her whereabouts in 1919, but did they know Kate's daughter Bertha Castanien was also in Sapulpa, Oklahoma?

[275] Jackson County, Missouri, Probate Court. Case File I4432 for Anson M. King.

[276] Ford.

[277] Ford.

[278] 1) The surviving children of Kate's brother William Jasper King still living in Jackson County, Missouri in 1920 were: Frank William King, 'Dean' Jona Dean King, Nannie Evelyn King Young Cummins, Julia Lee King Swinney, Walter R. King, Oscar King, Miranda Jane King Morris, and Robert Jasper King; William Jasper's daughter, Lucy A. King Young, had predeceased her father in 1911 and his son, Earl R. Monroe King, had moved to South Dakota in 1912.

Endnotes

2) The surviving children of Kate's sister Martha Jane King Ragland were all in Jackson County in 1920; they were: 'Annie' Georgeanna R. Ragland Hudspeth, John Marion Ragland, Charles H. Ragland, Rufus Hudspeth Ragland, and Dora Hazel Ragland Burrus; two of Martha Jane's sons, William Robert and Guy, had predeceased their mother in 1902 and 1892, respectively.

3) Kate's brother Francis Marion King had had an only child, Anson, who died in 1920 and was not included in the tally of nephews above.

4) And Kate's younger brother Samuel Robert King had three sons, two of which -- Arthur Cleveland King and George Samuel King -- lived in Jackson County, Missouri in 1920. Joseph Edward King did not live in Jackson County in 1920 and thus was not included in the above tally of nephews; however Joseph Edward King visited Kate sometime between 1921 and 1930 and then he moved back to Jackson County before 1935.

[279] Samuel Robert King died 18 June 1921 in an Independence hospital; his estranged widow Elizabeth P. Davenport King received Samuel's share of the King estate even though she refused the administration of his estate on August 8, 1921. Kate was listed as "a sister Mrs. Kate Barson of Lee's Summit" in Jackson County, Missouri, in Samuel's obituary published 19 June 1921 in *The Independence Examiner*, which misspelled 'Batson' and referred to her as 'Kate' rather than the 'Sarah C.' of her legal signature; her family obviously referred to her as Kate.

[280] Formerly known as the Jackson County Poor Farm, the Jackson County Home for the Aged and Infirm was established by the Jackson County Court for the indigent elderly. The initial facility was the 160-acre farm of Henry Washington Younger (father of the infamous Cole Younger) purchased for $1000. The Poor Farm, was a large working farm overlooking the scenic valley of the Little Blue River. The property expanded to more than 300 acres with several institutional buildings by 1852. In July 1908, a new building was added—and still operated today—as a long-term care facility. In 1928, Harry S. Truman was Presiding Judge of the Jackson County Court and passed a bond issue to construct two, three-story wings and a four-story hospital addition. In the years that followed, conditions deteriorated. Operational control of the hospital eventually was relinquished to the Kansas City General Hospital and Medical Center Corporation, a nonprofit corporation. In 1976, the Jackson County Legislature officially changed the name of the Jackson County Hospital and County Home to Truman Medical Center. Today, Truman Medical Center, Inc., manages the expansively beautiful, forested property at Lee's Summit Road and Gregory Boulevard. (Jackson)

[281] Petersen, Paul R. Personal communication, 28 November 2008.

[282] *Independence Examiner*, 12 Aug. 1929. Jack is presumed to be Kate's nephew, John Marion Ragland (1865 -1939), the second oldest son of Kate's sister, Martha Jane King Ragland. Kate's brother-in-law, John Oath Ragland, husband to Martha Jane, had died previously in February of 1905. The oldest son of Martha Jane King and John Oath Ragland, William Robert Ragland, had died in Jackson County, Missouri, on 20 June 1902, leaving a widow and two minor children. Thus, the second son, John Marion Ragland, would be the 'next in line' to handle family affairs. Another son, Rufus Hudspeth Ragland, died on 12 Nov 1927. But another son, Charles H. Ragland, was also in Jackson County in 1929.

[283] James William Kinyoun (3 Feb 1859 - 4 Mar 1942) was 'Head' and Doctor at Jackson County Home when the 1920 Federal census (10 Feb) was conducted. Kinyoun, age 60, was born in North Carolina. His third wife, Anna L., 26, born in Missouri, was Matron. Kinyoun had married Anna Laura Smith, age 18, on 15 Aug 1917, in Kansas City, Jackson County, Missouri. Also listed were 18 staff (including cooks, fireman, baker, seamstress, engineer and nurse), and 446 inmates, including Walter Head. [This was a huge increase in the number of inmates from the previous decennial census.]

James Kinyoun's first wife had been Mary Belle Akers (11 Oct 1858 - 10 Jun 1914), daughter of Sylvester Akers, who, as fate would have it, had ridden with Quantrill. Mary Belle (Akers) Kinyoun is buried in Buckner Hill Cemetery, as is James Kinyoun.

Kinyoun married a second time to another woman also named Mary B., whose surname was Hollingsworth, on 19 June 1890, in Independence, Missouri.

In the 1900 Federal census (2 Jun) James Kinyoun, was listed as age 41, born Feb 1859 in North Carolina. He had been married to his second wife for 9 years and they had no children. His wife, Mary B., age 39, born Oct 1860 in Missouri. In the 1901 *Missouri History Encyclopedia*, James William Kinyoun, as well as his brother, John Vance Kinyoun, had published biographies. James W. was mayor of Buckner for several terms, and medical examiner for several insurance companies and three social organizations.

In the 1910 Federal census, J. W. Kinyoun, age 51, was listed in Buckner, Ft. Osage Township, Jackson County, Missouri with wife, Mary B., age 47. They had no children. According to this enumeration, this was the second marriage for both partners, and they had been married for only 14 years. He was still in general practice.

City Directories list James W. Kinyoun as physician: in Kansas City in 1921; in Independence with Laura in 1924 and 1930; and, alone in Independence in 1938.

Endnotes

[284] William Henry Carr (9 Aug 1859 - 21 Apr 1912) was Superintendent of the Alms House for two separate terms: at least from 1899-1901; and, again at least from 1923-1926.

In the 1880 Federal census (Jun), 20-year-old William Carr was with his parents in Blue twp, Jackson County, Missouri. About 1885, William H. Carr married Frances Ella Luttrell (1862 - 1948), a granddaughter of James Lewis Dalton. They had two children: Myra F. and William Henry Carr.

When the 1900 Federal census was taken. Carr, who was born in Baltimore, Maryland, was 40 years old. He had been married for 15 years to Frances E., born in Missouri, Feb 1862. She was a 38-year-old Matron of the Home. Their 13-year-old daughter, Myra F., born Jan 1887, in Missouri, lived with them and 11 employees (including engineer, librarian and laundry man). There were 149 inmates (including 29 African-Americans).

In 1910 Federal census (15 Apr) William H. Carr, age 50, was a laborer in Independence with his wife, Frances E., and 2 children. The Carrs were buried in the Luttrell Cemetery.

[285] Lee N. Allen was named as the County Home superintendent over 29 employees when the book, *Jackson County, Missouri: Opportunities and Resources* was published in 1926.

[286] James W. Hostetter (21 Jul 1878 - 5 Jul 1948) was Superintendent of Jackson County Home for the Aged and Infirm.

In the 1930 Federal census (16 Apr) James W. Hostetter, age 51, enumerated with wife, Hattie M., age 52, Matron, and daughter, Lela M., 22-year-old bookkeeper. Only five other staff were listed (a farmer, matron, nurse, steward and another matron) with 657 inmates, including Walter Head. [Note another huge increase in the number of inmates, but a noticeable reduction in staff.]

James W. Hostetter, at 22, married Hattie May Mann, age 23, on 7 Feb 1910, in Jackson County, Missouri.

In the 1910 Federal census, James W. Hostetter, age 31, had been married 9 years. He lived with his wife, Hattie, and three children, ages 2 to 8, in Buckner, Ft. Osage Township, Jackson County, Missouri. James W. was a Liveryman.

In the 1936 Independence City Directory, James W. Hostetter was listed as Judge of the Jackson County Court (akin to today's Jackson County Legislature).

In the 1940 Federal census (10 Apr) James W. Hostetter, age 60, was listed with an 8th grade education, lived in Independence (in the same house he lived at in 1935), and was a Jackson County Court Investigator. His wife, Hattie M., was 63, had a year of college. Their married daughter and son-in-law lived with them.

[287] "To Locate the Body of W. C. Quantrill," *Bismark* (N.D.) *Tribune*, 13 May 1922. Why would a Confederate Veteran envoy in Oklahoma have made such a request?

[288] *Kansas City Star,* 23 May 1926.

[289] *Kansas City Star,* 23 May 1926.

[290] Kansas City, Missouri, city directories have only a single listing for Walter Head for the years listed below, except for one year which listed two persons by this name:

    1900: Blacksmith, Std. W & C Co. [presume that 'W & C' refers to Wagon and Carriage]
    1903: Wagon maker
    1904: Helper at Carriage & Wagon Works
    1905: Woodworker; Washing Machine & Manufacturing Co.
    1909: Shoer at Virginia House
    1910: Woodworker
    1912: Wagon Maker, Nelson Johnson

Walter Head was not found on a Federal census for Jackson County, Missouri, in 1900 or 1910. Head was admitted to the County Home between 1912 and 1920.

[291] 1880 census (5 July), Knottsville, Daviess County, Kentucky, lists 15-year-old Walter Head with his parents: Joseph Head 61, farmer, born in Kentucky, father born in Maryland, mother born in Kentucky; and, Jane Head, 58, born in Kentucky, father born in Virginia, mother born in Kentucky; and, sisters: Lydia Head, age 14, Jenny Head age 18, and widowed Margaret Duncan, age 25, with her two children: Walter (named after his uncle, Walter Head) age 12, and, Lilly age 7, all born in Kentucky.

    Joseph F. Head (1 Sep 1817 - 14 Jan 1899) and Eliza Jane Head (7 Dec 1820 - 18 Mar 1896) are both buried in South Hampton Church Cemetery in Owensboro, Daviess County, Kentucky (findagrave.com).

    Eliza Jane, the daughter of Hilliary Beal (1791-1877) and Margaret Adams (1787-1852), married Joseph F. Head on 6 Dec 1816, in Daviess County, Kentucky.

    Joseph Franklin Head is the son of Henry Robert Head (1784-1850) and Elizabeth Henry (1786-1831). Joseph's brother, William B. Head, married Eliza Jane's sister, Margaret.
(ancestry.com/tree/48236838/person/12868215250)

    The Joseph F. Head family was not located on the 1870 Federal census.

    Joseph H. Head, 38, and Eliza J., 38, with children: Margaret E. 15; S.L. (male), 14; Hilry (male) 7; Elizabeth, 2; and, John 1, were in Daviess Co, Kentucky in the 5 Jul 1860 Federal census.

    Relevant information from the Kentucky Birth and Death Indices was suggestive, but not conclusive:

Endnotes

1) Death record of Margaret E. Duncan (1845-1933) in Ensor, Daviess County, Kentucky (buried in Scythia, Daviess County, Kentucky), listed her as the daughter of Joseph Head and Josephine;
2) Birth record of Hillary Head listed him as son of Joseph Head and Elizabeth J. Beall, on 6 April 1854, in Daviess County, Kentucky (Hillary was named after his maternal grandfather; but, Elizabeth was listed instead of Eliza;
3) Birth record of Little Head listed him as son of J. F. Head and Eliza J. Bell, on 3 Jul 1856, in Daviess Co, Kentucky (Bell a misspelling of Beal);
4) Death record of Cecilius L. Head listed him as son of Joseph F. Head and Eliza J. Bell, in 1927 in Louisville, Kentucky (Bell another misspelling of Beall; it is likely that the S. L. in the 1860 Federal census is a misunderstanding of C. L.)

[292] *Independence Examiner*, 12 Aug. 1929.

[293] "Widow of Noted Guerilla Dead," *Hutchinson* (Ks.) *News*, 5 Feb. 1930. Also, "Quantrill's Bride Dead," *Kansas City Star*, 5 Feb. 1930.

[294] *Kansas City Times*, 5 Feb. 1930.

[295] Kate's body was not left in the funeral home when the mortician left suddenly. Ketterlin Funeral Home continued to operate for many years after 1930. The son of the original owner was involved in an incident in 1948-1949--eighteen years after Kate's burial--when unburied, embalmed bodies were found stacked in his garage and basement. Mr. Ketterlin had become despondent after his wife died and became an alcoholic. After discovery, he closed the business and moved to Warsaw, Missouri. The funeral home's records were most likely destroyed.

[296] Petersen, Paul R. "Solved! The Mystery of Kate King's Two Graves." (quantrillsguerrillas.com/en/articles/108-sloved-the-mystery-of- kate-king-s-two-graves-article.html).

[297] *Kansas City Times*, 5 Feb. 1930; and, *Kansas City Times*, 6 Feb. 1930.

[298] Rabas, Charles. Personal communication, 2007.

[299] Hale, Donald R. Personal communication, 1996-1997.

[300] Jackson, David W. "Jackson County's Poor Farm Transformed into a Rich Healthcare Center." *Jackson County Historical Society Journal* (Spring 2004): 45: 1: 8-13. Also, Schofield, Matthew, "Obscure cemetery reminder of Jackson County poor farm," *Kansas City Star*, 13 June 1984. This article quotes Leon Younger, Director of Jackson County Parks and Recreation, and Clifford Brown, Administrator of Truman Medical Center in 1984.

[301] "Complete restoration of Slaughter cemetery", Sentinel (Blue Springs, Mo.) 5 Mar 1970. This article gives a complete history of the cemetery started in 1848. A monument to the cemetery was erected

in 1966. The article includes a brief listing of the people buried in the cemetery, and erroneously names, Kate King Quantrill, "buried there in an unmarked grave next to her parents." In addition the members of the Slaughter Cemetery Assoc. are listed and include Herbert L. Hall, president and board member Mrs. Viola Hall. See chapter about, 'The other woman,' as this Viola Hall is the granddaughter of Nancy Walker. Also, Petersen, Paul R. "Solved! The Mystery of Kate King's Two Graves." (quantrillsguerrillas.com/en/articles/108-sloved-the-mystery-of-kate-king-s-two-graves-article.html); and, Petersen, Paul R., "The Mysterious Life of Sarah Catherine "Kate" King Quantrill."(quantrillsguerrillas.com/en/articles/149-the-mysterious-life-of-sarah-catherine-kate-king-quantrill-article.html)

[302] Petersen, *Quantrill in Texas*. Arthur Dealy was born and raised in Jackson County, Missouri. As a descendant of pioneer families of Jackson County, *i.e.,* Slaughter and Koger, and grandson of Levi Potts and Sina Emily Slaughter, Arthur had an active role in restoring the Slaughter Cemetery. (Hale, 1968; *The Sentinel*, 5 March 1970) Sadly, repeated, senseless vandalism has destroyed many of the gravestones in this cemetery. Arthur was treasurer of the Slaughter Cemetery Association in 1970. Although Arthur's great-great-grandmother (four generations back) was a Mary King, there is no known genealogical connection between Arthur Dealy and Kate. Therefore, Arthur D. Dealy was not known to be related to Kate; he certainly was NOT her nephew, as reported by Petersen.

[303] Petersen. *Quantrill in Missouri*. Also, Rabas, Charles. Personal communication, 2007.

[304] Werts, *Examiner*. This news story from 1982 listed Arthur's death date in error as 1972; his tombstone and the Social Security Death Index entry indicate a death date of 1973.

[305] Ford. Josie Potts, also a granddaughter of Levi Potts and Sina Emily Slaughter, also had Mary King as a great-great-grandmother as did Arthur Dealy. In addition, Josie Belle Potts married Floyd Earl King, son of Thomas Riley King, but again this was a different King family and no known direct genealogical connection exists between the three different King families. Josie Potts was a half-grandniece of America Snodgrass King, who married William Jasper King, and so was Kate's sister-in-law. However, Josie had no known blood relation to Sarah Catherine King a.k.a. Kate Clarke. Perhaps a distant in-law association by marriage was the basis for Josie's claim of a relationship.

[306] Olwine, Margaret. "True Story of Quantrill's Raiders Is Too Close to Home to be Revealed," *Kansas City* (Mo.) *Times*, 26 Oct. 1967.

[307] Fred Ford Letter to Don Hale. Also, Anson King probate case file.

[308] *The Sentinel*, 5 Mar. 1970.

[309] Hale, 1968; Hale, 1976; and Hale, Donald R., "After Six Decades, a Claimant to Role of Quantrill's 13-Year-Old Bride," *Kansas City Times*, 6 Apr. 1963, p. 42.

[310] Petersen. *Quantrill in Missouri*. Rabas, Charles. Personal communication, 2007. Also, Petersen, Paul. "Solved!"

[311] Hale, 1976. And, Hale, Donald R., "After Six Decades, a Claimant to Role of Quantrill's 13-Year-Old Bride," *Kansas City Times*, 6 Apr. 1963, p. 42. This cemetery began in 1865 as, "Arlington Cemetery," ironically, for Union soldiers. A cemetery association was founded in 1905 and it was renamed Maple Hill Cemetery, Inc. The Ketterlin Funeral Home and/or Maple Hill Cemetery, Inc., must have had a low-bid contract with Jackson County governance to take responsibility for pauper, or indigent burials.

[312] Hale, 1992.

[313] Petersen, Paul. "Solved! The Mystery of Kate King's Two Graves." http://quantrillsguerrillas.com/en/articles/108-sloved-the-mystery-of-kate-king-s-two-graves-article.html.

[314] Confirmed by David W. Jackson in August 2014.

[315] Confirmed by David W. Jackson in August 2014.

[316] Nancy Chism is believed to be the sister of Robert L. King. Sarah Dooley was a sister of Eveline Lynch King. Francis Marion King was Kate's brother.

[317] Confirmed by David W. Jackson in August 2014. Since 1995, the King/Chism tombstones have been broken over time (naturally or intentionally) and most pieces are missing. Even so, remaining remnants are hardly readable anyway due to general deterioration of the limestone tablets.

[318] Daughters of the American Revolution—Kansas City Chapter. *Vital Historical Records, Jackson County, Missouri, 1826-1876*. Reprinted and expanded with a full name- and subject-index by Suzanne Vinduska and David W. Jackson. (Independence, Mo.: Jackson County Historical Society, 2009), 349.

The first burial in Slaughter Cemetery was in 1848. It was started by Josiah Slaughter, who came to Jackson County from Virginia in 1832 and owned the land surrounding this family burying ground. In addition to Kate's relatives, several Civil War and Quantrill's Raiders are buried there. The cemetery was deeded to the public in 1872.

Kate's cousin, Eliza Chism's burial in 1921 was the last known burial there for 50 years. When the Daughters of the American Revolution—Kansas City Chapter, surveyed this cemetery in 1933 and published their findings the next year, they transcribed the following names from tombstones then visible. In the ensuing years, stones have deteriorated; been vandalized; and, a select few have been replaced with newer monuments.

As of 2014, burials have and continue to take place occasionally in Slaughter cemetery, which is at the far rear of the newer Swan Lake Memorial Gardens Cemetery at Slaughter Road and Valor/Slaughter Cemetery Road.

Chism, Eliza (1843-1922);
Chism, Malinda (1845-1921);
Chism, Nancy (1806-1881);
Dooley, Sarah;
Gibson, Elizabeth;
Gibson, Silas;
Gosner, A;
Gosner, Mary A;
Gosner, Rachel;
Hutchings, Dora M;
Hutchings, Thomas C;
King, Eveline (1847-1912);
King, Francis M (1845-1916);
King, Malinda (1809-1880);
King, Robert (1810-1891);
Lacy, G W and R A, son of;
Potts, Levi;
Potts, Sinia E;
Slaughter, Elizabeth;
Slaughter, James R;
Slaughter, John H;
Slaughter, Josiah;
Slaughter, Mary J;
Slaughter, Sarah A;
Webb, Claiborne; and,
Webb, Elizabeth L.

Appendix A

General Order No. 2
[the 'No Quarter' Order]

St. Louis, MO., March 13, 1862

1. Martial law has never been legally declared in Missouri except in the city of St. Louis, and on and in the immediate vicinity of the railroads and telegraph lines and even in these localities military offices are specially directed not to interfere with lawful process of any loyal civil court. It is believed that the time will soon come when the rebellion in Missouri may be considered terminated, and when even the partial and temporary military restraint which has been exercised in particular places, may be entirely withdrawn. By none is this more desired than by the General commanding.

2. It must, however, be borne in mind that in all places subject to the incursions of the enemy, or to the depredations of insurgents and guerrilla bands, the military are authorized, without any formal declaration of martial law, to adopt such measures as may be necessary to restore the authority of the Government, and punish all violations of the laws of war. This power will be exercised only where the peace of the country and the success of the Union cause absolutely require it.

3. Evidence has been received at these Headquarters that Major General Sterling Price has issued commissions or licenses to certain bandits in this State authorizing them to raise "Guerrilla forces," for the purpose of plunder and marauding. Gen. Price ought to know that such a course is contrary to the rules of civilized warfare, and that every man that enlists in such an organization forfeits his life, and becomes an outlaw. All persons are hereby warned that, if they join any guerrilla band, they will not, if captured, be treated as ordinary prisoners of war, but will be hung as robbers and murderers. Their lives shall atone for the barbarity of their General.

By Command of Major General Halleck
N. H. McLean, Assistant Adjutant General

KATE IN FACT AND FICTION

Appendix B

General Order No. 10

Headquarters District of the Border
Kansas City, Missouri, August 18, 1863

I. Officers commanding companies and detachments, will give escort and subsistence, as far as practicable, through that part of Missouri included in the District, to all loyal free persons desiring to remove to the state of Kansas or to a permanent military station in Missouri -- including all persons who have been ascertained, in the Manor provided in General Order No 9 of this District, to have been the slaves of persons engaged in aiding the rebellion since July 17, 1862. Where necessary, the teams of persons engaged in aiding the rebellion since July 23, 1862, will be taken to help such removal and after being used for that purpose, will be turned over to the officer commanding the nearest military station, who will at once report them to an Assistant Provost Marshal, or to the District Provost Marshal and hold them subject to this order.

II. Such officers will arrest and send to the District Provost Marshal for punishment, all men (and all women, not heads of families) who willfully aid and encourage guerrillas; with a written statement of the names and residence of such persons and of the proof against them. They will discriminate as carefully as possible between those who are compelled by threats or fears to aid the rebels and those who aid them from disloyal motives.

The wives and the children of known guerrillas, and also women who are head of families and are willfully engaged in aiding guerrillas, will be notified by such officers to move out of this district and out of the State of Missouri forthwith. They will be permitted to take unmolested, their stock, provisions and household goods. If they fail to remove promptly they will be sent by such officers under escort to Kansas City for shipment South, with their cloths and such necessary household furniture as may be worth removing.

KATE IN FACT AND FICTION

III. Persons who have borne arms against the Government and voluntarily lay them down and surrender themselves at a military station, will be sent under escort to the District Provost Marshal at these Head Quarters. Such persons will be banished with their families to such State or district of this department as the General commanding the Department may direct, and will there remain exempt from other military punishment or account of their past disloyalty, but not exempt from civil trial for treason.

IV. No officer or enlisted man, without special instruction from these Head Quarters will burn or destroy any buildings, fences, crops or other property. But all furnaces and fixtures of blacksmith shops in that part of Missouri included in the District, not at military stations, will be destroyed and the tools either removed to such stations or destroyed.

V. Commanders of companies and detachments serving in Missouri will not allow persons not in the military service of the United Sates to accompany them on duty except when employed as guides, and will be held responsible for the good conduct of such men employed as guides and for their obedience to orders.

VI. Officers and enlisted men belonging to regiment or companies, organized or unorganized, are prohibited going from Kansas to the District of Northern Missouri without written permission or order from these Head Quarters or from the Assistant Provost Marshal at Leavenworth City or the Commanding officer at Fort Leavenworth or some Officer commanding a military station in the District of Northern Missouri.

By Order of Brigadier General Ewing
P.B. Plumb, Major and Chief of Staff

Appendix C

General Order No. 11
Headquarters District of the Border
Kansas City, Missouri, August 25, 1863

First. All persons living in Cass, Jackson and Bates counties, Missouri, and in that part of Vernon including in this district, except those living within one mile of the limits of Independence, Hickman's Mills, Pleasant Hill and Harrisonville, and except those in that part of Kaw Township, Jackson county, north of Brush Creek and west of the Big Blue, embracing Kansas City and Westport, are hereby ordered to remove from their present places of residence within fifteen days from the date hereof.

Those who, within that time, establish their loyalty to the satisfaction of the commanding officer of the military station nearest their present places of residence, will receive from him certificates stating the fact of their loyalty, and the names of the witnesses by whom it can be shown. All who receive such certificate will be permitted to remove to any military station in this district, or to any part of the State of Kansas, except the counties on the eastern borders of the State. All others shall remove out of this district. Officers commanding companies and detachments serving in the counties named, will see that this paragraph is promptly obeyed.

Second. All grain and hay in the field, or under shelter, in the district from which the inhabitants are required to remove within reach of military stations, after the 9th day of September next, will be taken to such stations and turned over to the proper officers there, and report of the amount so turned over made to district headquarters, specifying the names of all loyal owners and the amount of such produce taken from them. All grain and hay found in such district after the 9th day of September next, not convenient to such stations, will be destroyed.

Third. The provisions of General Order No. 10, from these headquarters, will at once be vigorously executed by officers commanding in parts of the district, and at the stations not subject to the operations of paragraph First of this Order-and especially in the towns of Independence, Westport and Kansas City.

Fourth. Paragraph 3, General Order No. 10, is revoked as to all who have borne arms against the government in the district since August 20, 1863.

By Order of Brigadier General Ewing.
H. Hannahs, Adjutant.

KATE IN FACT AND FICTION

Appendix D

St. Louis Democrat
17 August 1873 (Sunday Edition)

The microfilm reproduction was extremely difficult to read. Thus, only portions of this long article were transcribed in "quotes," interspersed with summarized sections [in brackets].

Kate Clark's Case

Testing the Validity of the Social Evil Law
The Evidence and Arguments—Judge Colvin Takes the Case Under Advisement
The bawdy house cases of Kate Clark and Lizzie Saville came up yesterday in the Court of Criminal Correction

THE QUESTION involved is the constitutionality of the whole social evil system of St. Louis, which will be perpetuated or blotted out, [according?] to the final decision of the case and the contest is a matter of [interest?] to the other great cities of the country, which have watched the experiment in St. Louis with interest. The earnest reformers, men and women, seemed not to have been discouraged or disheartened in the least by the failure of their efforts on the Legislature and City last winter, and have appealed to the courts . . ."
[The social activists believe their side is right and will take the case to the Supreme Court if necessary. Interest in these test cases drew the "largest audiences ever assembled within its walls" of the Court of Criminal Corrections.] . . .
"Kate Clark and Lizzie Saville were early on hand, surrounded by two or three of their "girls," and with their lavish display of jewelry and elegant dresses attracted a great deal of attention. Kate Clark wore a white gauze veil over her face, which contrasted well with a handsome black silk dress, slashed with black lace and set off by a gray linen overdress. A heavy pair of ear-rings were suspended from her ears and her wrists were encircled with heavy gold bracelets."
[Lizzie Saville was even more elegantly dressed, wearing a veiled hat with a feather, a diamond pin and expensive rings on her fingers. Two men accompanied them whose apparel was gaudy, but did not "require detailed description."]

KATE IN FACT AND FICTION

"THE CASES did not come up until about 11 o'clock, when the names of the defendants were called, and some fifteen witnesses for the prosecution. No response was made to the call of "W. G. Eliot," but Kate Clark came forward from the witnesses' room and took her seat behind her legal protector in the contest, J.R. Claiborne. The latter was assisted by Joseph H. Lodge; while the state was represented by Prosecutor Attorney Hogan and Assistant Prosecuting Attorney Taafe. For the purpose of putting the case in a better shape for the appeal to the Supreme Court, it was determined by counsel that no agreed statement should be made out, but that the case should be heard [illegible]."

[The lawyers agreed that the two cases should be heard separately. The complaint against Kate Clarke was read and the first witness called was George Gavin, the Secretary of the Board of Police Commissioners, who read out the application of Kate Clark for a permit to keep a bawdy house on the northwest corner of Sixth and Elm Streets. The permit was granted. Upon cross examination, Mr. Gavin did not recognize the defendant [Kate] as the person who applied for the permit. Dr. O'Brien, Clerk of the Board of Health testified that Kate kept a house of prostitution at 117 South Sixth, but he could not recognize the defendant because of her veil. The veil covering her face was raised with a laugh, which was echoed by the audience. But Dr. O'Brien could not testify if she actually was the person keeping the house. Many other witnesses were called to testify with Claiborne objecting to questions regarding actual or reputed activities of the women, who may or may not be living in the house in question and whether they knew this information from firsthand personal knowledge. No one knew from their personal experience, but they had heard they were prostitutes. Dr. Hunt testified]

"that at the house at which Kate Clark is registered on the books of the Board of Health, 112 Sixth Street, he had never seen her, but had at the house referred so to the complaint, 119. She did not seem to be doing anything, but he would say that she stands as the housekeeper of the place. He understood the house to go as Kate Clark's."

[A police officer whose beat was between Fourth and Sixth and Myrtle and Market testified that he knew Kate Clark and had seen her at the house a dozen times, but he did not know who managed the home. Another officer testified that he knew Kate Clark and that she keeps a house of prostitution whose resident are prostitutes because she told him so while he was investigating the thief of some ice cream from this establishment. After the prosecution finally rested its case and Lizzie Saville's case was submitted, Claiborne presented the case for the defense which was reiteration of the sequence of legislative events leading to the passage of the Social Evil Ordinance. Following final arguments,]

"Judge Colvin announced that he would take the case under advisement, and render a decision on next Saturday."

Appendix E

St. Louis Daily Globe
22 February 1874

SOCIAL INVESTIGATION

A Friendly Visit from the Sages of Jefferson

They Would See for Themselves the Advantages of the Social-evil Law — A Tour by Gas-Light

Of course it was all right.

If the social evil law is to come up before the Legislature on Monday, why the members ought to know something about its operations, and how could they understand its practical workings unless they visited the places in which it was in active operation. Hence the members of the Legislature, who were down in St. Louis last evening, need feel no hesitation in acknowledging to their families and constituents that they took advantage of the opportunity to

Make the Rounds

of the public houses of prostitution in St. Louis, acting as they were purely in an official and legislative capacity.

To some extent the visit was made at the suggestion of Mayor Brown and Police Commissioner Armstrong, who have been button-holing the rural members of the Legislature in the city, and with persuasive accents pointing out the merits of the law.

So a detective was secured on application to the police authorities, and carriages ordered from a prominent livery-stable, which will send in its bill — and it will be a pretty large one — to the Mayor tomorrow, and the Mayor will credit it to

The "Social-Evil Fund,"

or "contingent expenses," unless he is generous and public spirited enough to foot the bill himself. Mayor Brown was never more clerical in appearance than while making his way, with meekly bowed head, along the corridors of the Planters' House, which was the starting-point for the party. Detective Hughey O'Neil made his appearance shortly after 8 o'clock,

Reticent and Watchful.

Gradually the members gathered in the Planters' House parlor, whiling away the interim before starting in discussing their afternoon visit to the Social-evil Hospital. An hour or more was spent in waiting, and firing up at the bar. It was 9 o'clock before the member took their seats in the hacks, which wheeled off in succession, as if they were at a funeral at which the hearse hand ran away with the corpse.

The Route

The hacks wheeled up Chesnut street to Sixth, and down which they drove, hauling up in front of Lizzie Saville's and Kate Clark's, the two crack palaces of sin in that portion of the city. They filled the two parlors in Saville's, and were entertained by the golden-haired landlady in person, assisted by a bevy of soiled doves. After a short stay of about fifteen minutes an adjournment as effected to Clark's. Here they were welcomed by Fannie Devlin and some ten or fifteen of the girls. An elderly and gray-haired Senator from the southern part of the State lolled on the sofa, with a girl by his side, who warmly reciprocated his manifestations of affection.

A St. Louis Representative

held an animated discussion with the housekeeper, Fanny Devlin, was was exclaiming, in a hurt way, at the want of Christian charity, to which, thank God, she was not indebted in the insignificant sum of five cents, and loudly proclaiming her independence of the Christian women who were always telling the girls what to do, but who would refuse to put work in their hands which would give them a decent livelihood. As to

The Social-Evil Law,

she thought it was a good thing for us girls, and took occasion to renew her declaration of independence, for which she would sacrifice her life. She wanted several of the legislators to listen to her words with grave attention, but their effect was lost on a couple of country members, who were making love in a manner which showed how far they had lost all sense of their legislative dignity. Expressing their regret that Miss Kate Clark was not at home, the party left and made their way to

The Castle of Vic de Bar,

on the opposite side of the street. "Miss Debar. Here are the Grangers" "How are you Grangers" was all the informal introduction that was passed. The landlady expressed her abhorrence of the old system under which they were raided by the police. She spoke of her own experience on one occasion in the station house, and denounced the system as one under which they were exposed to the extortions of shysters and loafers, who would cause raids by the police in case their demands were not acceded to.

She Was Asked Her Opinion

if a recent speech from a St. Louis gentleman on the subject of the social-evil law. In reply she expressed the belief that it did not represent the sentiments of his heart — his pocket must have been touched in some way. The "Grangers" laughed. Did she know him? She admitted that she had the honor of knowing the gentleman by sight, with a raising of the eyes that was extremely suggestive.

Then the party went to Lillie Merrill's. The inmates were either "not at home" to the members of the Legislature or they were all away from their posts, as the "Tyler" stated to the leader of the party.

Disappointed,

they wended their way back to the carriage, refusing the invitation of one member, who explained that Clara Smith kept a nice house, and invited the whole party over to see the establishment.

Prescott's was given the go-by, and the party were transferred in carriages to Green Street. Madame Stillman received them princely, dressed in black silk, trimmed with velvet, which made her look like the lady manager of

A Charitable Association.

She was strongly in favor of the present regulation system. She denounced the old as one where she was fleeced by judges, shysters and the police. While she lived in Chicago she was black-mailed all the time until she left for St. Louis. She said the present law was got up by physicians who were were deprived of the exorbitant fees upon which they formerly thrived. The present regulations have diminished sickness more than one half. The girls were perfectly willing to go out to the hospital, and she did not believe the insinuation that had been cast on its management by the last grand jury. A short visit was then paid to Madame Niedderreuther, who, however, was sick and unable to receive her distinguished guests.

The Final Call

was made upon Sallie Lewis, who, remarked a Senator with the party who was acquainted with her, is "one of the smartest women in St. Louis." That she was a woman of superior education and ability was evident in her conversation. She read a card she wrote on the subject, which was published about a year ago, and in which she gave her views on the question as suggested and verified by her experience. Facts that had come to her knowledge since the 1st of January had formed the basis of a letter which she had dispatched to a member of the St. Louis delegation. The member expressed his regret at not having received it.

When the Party Left Lewis,

it consisted of but three of the original sixteen which started out on the trip. The rest had been left by the wayside. Several of them will wake up this morning, with practical experience of the workings of the social evil system.

Throughout the visit, the lower dens of infamy were ignored, and the slums of Almond and Green streets were taboed.

Appendix F

Final Settlement of the Estate of Anson M. King

The final settlement of the Estate of Anson M. King, presented at the September 1921 Term of the Probate Court of Jackson County, Missouri, in Independence, distributed the sum of $923.17 now in the hand of this administrator and the amounts to which they are respectively entitled are as follows:

Sarah C. Batson, an aunt of the whole blood of decedent is entitled to the sum of $123.08 she being entitled to an undivided 2/15ths part of said estate.

Lavina Iske, an aunt of the whole blood of decd. is entitled to 2/15ths or the sum of $123.08

The heirs of Samuel R. King, recently deceased, he being an uncle of the whole blood to said decd. are entitled to 2/15ths or $123.08

The following named heirs of Martha J. Ragland, a deceased aunt of the whole blood of said decd. are entitled to 2/15th of said fund, the same being divided among them as follows:

John M. Ragland, a son of said Martha J.	1/45th, or	$20.51
Chas. H. Ragland, " "	1/45th, "	20.51
Rufus H. Ragland, " "	1/45th, "	20.51
Annie R. Hudspeth, daughter " "	1/45th, "	20.51
Dora Burrus " "	1/45th, "	20.51
Jack R. Ragland, grandson " "	1/90th, "	10.25
Ruth Ragland, grand dhtr " "	1/90th, "	10.25

The following named heirs of William J. King an uncle of the whole blood of said decd. are entitled to 2/15th of said fund, the same being divided among them as follows:

Frank King, a son of said Wm. J. King,	1/75th, or	$12.30
Earl King, " " "	1/75th, or	12.30
Walter King, " " "	1/75th, or	12.30
Dean King, " " "	1/75th, or	12.30
Oscar King, " " "	1/75th, or	12.30

KATE IN FACT AND FICTION

Robt King,	"	"	"	$1/75^{th}$, or	12.30
Nannie E. Cummins, dhtr	"	"		$1/75^{th}$, or	12.30
Julia Swinney	"	"	"	$1/75^{th}$, or	12.30
Miranda Morris	"	"	"	$1/75^{th}$, or	12.30
Willis L. Young, grandson		"		$1/300^{th}$, or	3.07
Jesse W. Young,	"	"	"	$1/300^{th}$, or	3.07
Danl E. Young,	"	"	"	$1/300^{th}$, or	3.07
Homer J. Young	"	"	"	$1/300^{th}$, or	3.07

The following named heirs of Elijah Lynch, a deceased uncle of the half blood of said deceased are entitled to 1/15th of said estate, the same being divided among them as follows:

Willis Lynch, a son of said Elijah Lynch,			$1/90^{th}$, or $10.25
Henry Lynch	"	"	"	$1/90^{th}$, or	10.25
James Lynch	"	"	"	$1/90^{th}$, or	10.25
Alice Russell	"	"	"	$1/90^{th}$, or	10.25
Schuyler G. Hill grandson	"	"		$1/270^{th}$, "	3.41
Miranda Daniel granddhtr	"	"		$1/270^{th}$, "	3.41
Normal F. Warren grandson	"	"		$1/270^{th}$, "	3.41
Wm. A. Warren grandson	"	"		$1/270^{th}$, "	3.41

The following named heirs of Kate Dooley, a deceased aunt of the whole blood of said decedent are entitled to 2/15th of said estate, the same being divided among them as follows:

Peter Bolger, a son of said Kate Dooley,			$1/30^{th}$, or $30.77
John Bolger,	"	"	"	$1/30^{th}$, or 30.77
Ellen Carrigg, daughter	"	"		$1/30^{th}$, or 30.77
Kate Spader	"	"	"	$1/30^{th}$, or 30.77

The following named heirs of Anson Waldo, a deceased uncle of the half blood of said deceased are entitled to 1/15th of said estate, the same being divided between them as follows:

Ella Carpenter, a daughter of said Anson Waldo,			$1/30^{th}$, or 30.77
Anson H. Waldo, a son	"	"	"	$1/30^{th}$, or 30.77

And finally, the heirs of James Waldo, a deceased uncle of the half blood of said deceased are entitled to 1/15th of said estate, the same being divided among them as follows:

Appendix F

John W. Waldo, a son of said James Waldo,			$1/105^{th}$,	or $8.79
Wm. B. Waldo,	"	"	"	$1/105^{th}$,	8.79
Anson S. Waldo,	"	"	"	$1/105^{th}$,	8.79
Elizabeth Weece, daughter	"	"	$1/105^{th}$,	8.79
Lethie Fuson	"	"	"	$1/105^{th}$,	8.79

The heirs of Albert Waldo, a deceased son of said James Waldo, 1/105th to be divided among them as follows, to-wit:

Jesse J. Waldo, son of said Albert Waldo,		$1/525^{th}$, or	$1.76
Della McClelland, daughter	"	$1/525^{th}$, or	1.76
Lottie Arrington	"	"	$1/525^{th}$, or	1.76
Lillie Phillips	"	"	$1/525^{th}$, or	1.76

And the five small children of Leroy N. Waldo, a deceased son of said Albert Waldo, to wit:

Edith Waldo, Esther Waldo, Robert Waldo, Richard Waldo and Royce Waldo, each 1/2625, or jointly $1/525^{th}$, or $1.76

The heirs of Rufus Waldo, a deceased son of said James Waldo, 1/105th to be divided among them as follows to wit:

Lula Kirk, daughter of said Rufus Waldo		$1/735^{th}$, or	$1.25
Dora Stratton	"	"	"	$1/735^{th}$,	1.25
Charley Waldo son	"	"	$1/735^{th}$,	1.25
Ottie L. Waldo	"	"	"	$1/735^{th}$,	1.25
Lillie Donaldson, dahtr	"	"	$1/735^{th}$,	1.25
Chester Waldo, son	"	"	$1/735^{th}$,	1.25

And, the two small children of W. H. Waldo, a deceased son of said Rufus Waldo, their names being:

Mary and Murrell Waldo, 1/735th part jointly, or 1/1470th to each of them, thus giving them jointly the sum of $1.25.

Admr. says that said Daniel E. Young and Homer Young are minors and have no guardian except their father, Daniel W. Young who is their natural guardian and resides in Jackson County, Missouri.

That said Mary Waldo and Murrell Waldo are but very small children and have no guardian, except their mother, Minnie Waldo who is their natural guardian and resides at Carterville, Mo.

That said Edith Waldo, Esther Waldo, Robert Waldo, Richard Waldo and Royce Waldo are all small children and have no guardian, except their mother, Essie Phillips of Fairfax, Okla. who is their natural guardian.

That said Samuel R. King died intestate in Jackson County, Mo. on June 18th 1921, leaving a widow Elizabeth King. That this Court on August 8th 1921 ordered that no letters of administration be issued on the estate of said Samuel R. King and this said widow is therefore entitled to receive his share in this estate.

Appendix G

Heirs Identified in Anson M. King's Estate

Anson M. King was Kate's nephew, the only son of her brother, Francis Marion King. Anson M. King was the grandson of Robert L. King, Kate's father, who initially purchased the land that became the King Family Farm that Robert L. King sold to his son, Francis Marion King, in 1881. Anson inherited this land from his father in 1916. Anson died suddenly and without a Will on 29 May 1920.

The persons identified below as children of Robert L. King were Kate's siblings, and all of Anson's paternal cousins were Kate's nieces and nephews. None of Anson's maternal relatives have any blood relationship to Kate or Robert L. King. However, some were related by marriage to Kate's siblings.

The names appearing below are in the order and as they were listed in the King probate/estate file (with their actual…and sometimes corrected…name(s) in parenthesis):

- **Sarah C. Batson (Sarah Catherine "Kate" (King) Quantrill-Evans-Batson-Head)**-Anson's paternal aunt, daughter of Robert L. King. Sarah received an undivided share of two-fifteenths (2/15) = $123.08.

- **Lavina Iske (Lavina Lynch Iske)**-Anson's maternal aunt, a full sister to his mother, daughter of William Lynch and Rebecca Ginans Waldo Lynch (William and Rebecca had each been married before). Even though the widowed Lavina was an inmate in a State Hospital, she received her full two-fifteenths (2/15) share.

- **Samuel R. King (Samuel Robert King)**-Anson's paternal uncle, son of Robert L. King. Samuel died intestate just prior to the final settlement so his estranged widow (Anson's paternal aunt by marriage) Elizabeth L. Davenport King received Samuel's full share.

- **Martha J. Ragland (Martha Jane King Ragland)**-Anson's paternal aunt, daughter of Robert L. King. Martha died in 1918 so her heirs inherited her share. Martha's surviving children (Anson's paternal cousins and Robert L. King's grandchildren) — John M. (John Marion) Ragland, Chas. (Charles) H. Ragland, Rufus H. (Hudspeth) Ragland, Annie R. ('Annie' Georgeanna R. Ragland) Hudspeth, Dora (Dora Hazel Ragland) Burrus — and two grandchildren, the children of her deceased son William Robert Ragland (Anson's paternal first cousin once removed): Jack R. ('Jack' John Rider) Ragland and Ruth (Ruth Malinda) Ragland — all divided Martha's share amongst them.

- **William J. King (William Jasper King)**-Anson's paternal uncle, son of Robert L. King died in 1919 so his heirs inherited his share. William's surviving children (Anson's paternal cousins and Robert L. King's grandchildren) -- Frank (Frank William) King, Earl (Earl R. Monroe) King, Walter (Walter R.) King, Dean ('Dean' Jona Dean) King, Oscar King, Robt (Robert Jasper) King, Nannie E. Cummins ('Nannie' Nancy Evelyn King Young Cummins), Julia Swinney (Julia Lee King Swinney), Miranda Morris (Miranda Jane King Morris) — and four grandsons (Anson's paternal first cousins once removed), the children of his deceased daughter Lucy A. King Young: Willis L. Young, Jesse W. Young, Danl E. ('Buck' Elbert Daniel) Young, and Homer J. Young received his share. Daniel E. Young and Homer Young were minors who resided with their father Daniel W. Young in Jackson County, Missouri.

- **Elijah Lynch**-Anson's maternal half-uncle, a half brother to his mother, son of William Lynch and an unknown first wife. Elijah Lynch married Miranda Ann Snodgrass and they had eight children. Miranda Ann Snodgrass Lynch was a full sister to America Jane Snodgrass King, the wife of William Jasper King and thus was a sister-in-law to Kate and a daughter-in-law to Robert L. King. As a brother-in-law of Robert's daughter-in-law, Elijah was no blood relation to anyone in the King family except a half-uncle to Anson on his mother's side. Elijah died in 1918 and his share was split amongst his surviving heirs, including his children (Anson's maternal half-cousins) — sons Willis Lynch, Henry (Henry N.) Lynch, James (James L.) Lynch and daughter Alice Russell (Alice Lynch Russell), his grandchildren (*i.e.*, the children of his deceased daughter Lucy B. Lynch Warren, who were Anson's maternal half-cousins once removed): Miranda Daniel (Miranda E. Warren Daniel), Normal F. Warren (James Normal Warren), and Wm. (William A.) Warren, and even his great grandchild Schuyler G. ('Sky' Schuyler Gregg) Hill, the son of Elijah's deceased granddaughter Alta Gregg Hill, who was the only child of Elijah's oldest daughter Sarah Jane Lynch Gregg who died in 1887; this child was Anson's maternal half-cousin twice removed.

- **Kate Dooley**-this must be Sarah Ann Lynch Bolger Dooley, Anson's deceased maternal aunt, a full sister of his mother, daughter of William Lynch and his second wife Rebecca Ginans Waldo Lynch, who died in 1891. Only four of her children were named as her heirs which indicated that four of her children (Martin Bolger, Margaritam Bolger, John Dooley and Rose Dooley) had died before 1920. Her surviving children (Anson's maternal cousins) divided her share — Peter Bolger (who was living with Anson as a hired hand in the 1920 census), John Bolger, Ellen Carrigg ('Ellen' Elleonoram Annam Bolger Carrigg/Carig), and Kate Spader (Kate Bolger Spader Williams).

- **Anson Waldo**-Anson King's deceased maternal half-uncle, a half brother of his mother, son of Rebecca Ginans and her first husband Alfred Waldo. Apparently Anson King was named for his mother's half brother. Anson Waldo's children (Anson King's maternal cousins), Ella Carpenter (Mary Ella Waldo Carpenter) and Anson H.(Anson Henry) Waldo, inherited his share.

- **James Waldo**-another deceased maternal half uncle of Anson's, a half brother of his mother, son of Rebecca Ginans and her first husband Alfred Waldo. James' heirs included:

1) his children (Anson's maternal cousins): John W. (John Wesley) Waldo, Wm. (William) B. Waldo, Anson S. (Saxton) Waldo, Elizabeth Weece (Elizabeth Waldo Weece), and Lethie Fuson ('Leathie' Letha Waldo Fuson);

2) his grandchildren (Anson's maternal cousins once removed):

a) the children of James' deceased son Albert (Albert Ross) Waldo: Jesse J. Waldo, Della McClelland (Della Waldo McClellan), Lottie Arrington (Lottie Waldo Arlington), and Lillie Phillips (Lillie Waldo Phillips) plus

b) the children of James' other deceased son Rufus (Rufus McCorkle) Waldo: Lula Kirk (Lulu Waldo Kirk), Dora Stratton (Dora Waldo Stratton), Charley (Charles) Waldo, Ottie (Otis) L. Waldo, Lillie Donaldson (Lillie May Waldo Donaldson), and Chester Waldo; and

3) his great grandchildren (Anson's maternal cousins twice removed):
   a) the five young children of Leroy N. Waldo, a deceased son of James' son Albert (Albert R.) Waldo, to wit: Edith Waldo, Esther Waldo, Robert Waldo, Richard Waldo and Royce Waldo, who had their mother Essie Phillips of Fairfax, Oklahoma, as their natural guardian, and
   b) the two small children of W. H. Waldo (William H. Waldo) a deceased son of James's son Rufus (Rufus McCorkle) Waldo, to wit: Mary Waldo and Murrell Waldo, who had their mother Minnie Waldo of Caterville, Missouri as their natural guardian.

The division of the Anson King estate was a gold mine for genealogical research but a financial disaster for the heirs. Some of the heirs received shares as small as one two-thousand-six-hundred-twenty-fifth (1/2625) part and amounts as little as eighty-eight cents or even sixty-two and a half cents each.

Kate, as the only surviving paternal aunt, was one of only three heirs that received an "undivided share," the maximum $123.08.

With 71 separate individual heirs located in multiple states; plus, the need to sell the mortgaged land and personal property it was surprising that Anson's estate could be settled and the probate closed within a year and three months after Anson's death.

The question remains if the maternal heirs, especially those of the "half blood," and those two- and three-generations removed, had a justifiable claim to the estate.

KATE IN FACT AND FICTION

Appendix H

Kansas City Star
23 May 1926

Unfortunately the identity of the reporter, who authored this often quoted and frequently referenced article, has never been revealed. This article has been the quintessential reference for Kate's life. Nearly all subsequent reports about Kate have utilized, paraphrased, cited, drawn upon, or even plagiarized, this article. Unfortunately, it is impossible to ascertain what information was taken directly from the interview and that derived from other background sources by the reporter.

According to Kate's nephew, Joseph Edward King, who visited Kate while she was at the Jackson County Poor Farm, Kate was "far in to dementia" at the time. How much of this article was Kate's memories, and how much was "journalistic license" is open to debate.

The unabridged article is reproduced here because of its significance to Kate's story, in fact and fiction.

The Strange Romance of Quantrill's Bride
Kate King, Ending Her Days in an Alms House,
Recalls Her Life with the Famous Guerrilla Leader

The existence of a reputed sweetheart of William Clarke Quantrill—and if his bride she proves to be—it all is a matter of dispute among old-time Southerners along the Civil War border. Many persons, particularly his own men, knew that a young girl, known to them as Kate Clarke, held the guerrilla's love and confidence.

That Quantrill's bride, now a woman 78 years old, still is alive will seem almost unbelievable to those who have heard the accumulation of Quantrill lore nearly all their lives. Kate Clarke, as she was known, effaced herself so completely from the guerrilla's history after his death in Kentucky that there is scarcely any mention of the young and beautiful Missouri girl in the data that has been collected on Quantrill.

Since the day she saw her young husband die from the effect of a bullet wound, she has held his memory so sacred that she has never cared to talk to outsiders about him. This is the first time she has told her story for publication. It was told only after a promise that her presence in a Missouri county home for the poor should not be revealed.

Many inmates of the home are men and women who felt the iron hand of Quantrill's men, and others were friends of the guerrillas. To start another Civil War there would be an easy matter. Kate Clarke is aware of this and holds her peace.

"Well, they wouldn't believe it anyhow," she said in telling her story.

Kate Clarke is mentioned by both William Elsey Connelley and John N. Edwards, respectively, Kansas and Missouri historians. Her true name, Kate King, has been known to only a few. In verification of her story, old county records were examined and her memory was found to be accurate on all points. Two Quantrill sympathizers, now professional men, who knew the girl in their youth, verify the story and say she is the woman associated with Quantrill. And relatives living near her childhood home admit she was the guerrilla's sweetheart.

It was about sixty-five years ago that Kate King, approaching her home near Blue Springs, Mo., from a schoolhouse one mile away, saw a young man talking to her father on the King's front porch. The girl, not (but) 13 years old, was struck instantly with the young man's straight and graceful stature. As she entered the yard carrying her lunch pail and books, her eyes were riveted upon the tall young man who, she later learned, was William Clarke Quantrill.

As her father greeted the returning schoolgirl the young man smiled and Kate returned the pleasant greeting. He had clear cut features and a complexion inclined to be pale, which was beginning now to show a fixed outdoor color. He was 25 years old, but looked a few years younger

Kate, going indoors, put her books and pail away and returned to stand by while the two men continued the conversation. She was a buxom girl, of sturdy build and well developed for her years. Anyone seeing her for the first time would have taken her to be about 16 years old. She was lively and jolly; a disposition which years of turmoil and suffering since have not changed. Old-timers who knew her say she was pretty beyond question. The farm life, spent mostly outdoors and a great deal of time on horseback, had given her health and vigor and rosy cheeks. She could ride a horse like one born to the saddle. Ever since she was old enough to hold a rein her father had provided her with a mount, one that she could call her own.

Quantrill Her Ideal

As she stood listening to the men, the young gallant complimented her looks. He was a polished young man, debonair and polite. Several years before he had taught school in Kansas. Now he was a dauntless and daring guerilla chief, leading more than a hundred men encamped near the King farm. He had left Gen. Sterling Price's army a few months before to organize an outfit to protect the children and women left by the men who had gone to fight for the south. The Kansas Redlegs, under Colonel Jennison, had been plundering Southerners' homes in Missouri, and an outfit was needed close to Independence that could protect the people from these border raiders.

When Quantrill left the King home that afternoon he must have carried back the happy smile of the young miss, for he returned the next day on the pretext of talking to her father. He followed this visit by others a few days apart and at times when he was quite sure Kate would be at home. On most of these calls he would bring the girl some small remembrance.

Robert King, Kate's father had settled on his 80-acre tract some twenty years before. His place near Blue Springs was close to the Morgan Walker farm, where Quantrill's name first had been brought into prominence. That was a year before Kate and the guerila met. She had heard how this dashing young man had brought three Jayhawkers along with him from Kansas to raid the Walker place and liberate the slaves and how he had informed the Walkers of the Jayhawkers' intentions so that the three men might be clipped off while he aided the Walkers to do it.

Parents Failed to End Courtship

Kate was a "rebel" and she admired the young man's daring deed as did all other Southerners about her. So after a few weeks of acquaintance, when the two began riding around the country on horseback, she idolized the young Southern hero more than ever.

Her daring astride a horse as well as her beauty must have charmed the young outlaw, as he was declared to be by the Federal government. Kate never hesitated to take a fence or jump a creek. The two rode around the countryside daily as the friendship ripened. He would be on hand to greet her when she returned from school. On these jaunts, Quantrill would hold her horse's rein at times. He was uneasy about her ability in the saddle when she spurred the horse on daringly. Then again he would dismount to keep her horse from rearing, a trick Kate delighted to do to receive her suitor's attention. The higher she could get a horse to rear the more she thought of it. She had one horse that fought to keep her off its back: so much did the animal dread her mastery. Once on this mount, however, there was no better roan, she recalls.

There came a day when Kate's parents objected to her growing familiarity with the raider. Their daily rides were stopped by her father and she was forbidden to go anywhere with him. But, as is so often the case, the parental ban only served to deepen her regard for the young gallant. She continued to meet him, but in secret, and instead of keeping to the roads they rambled off into the woods, jumping brush, fence and creek.

Some neighbors saw the two riding about. Mr. King was told about it and the girl received a severe scolding. She trembled for days afterwards whenever she thought of her father's wrath. Yet, trembling with fear, she

KATE IN FACT AND FICTION

continued to meet the guerrilla far away from possible detection. At these meetings, they would sit on a creek bank and talk.

Told How He Became a Slayer

Quantrill told her how he became a rebel. He had been born in the North and his family were all abolitionists. An aunt of his, Mary A. Quantrill, was later to furnish Whittier with the instance of waving the Stars and Stripes in Stonewall Jackson's face for the poem "Barbara Frietchie."

Quantrill himself had left Ohio and traveled overland to Kansas. There he had taught school until a brother joined him, he said. Quantrill told Kate in those late spring afternoons how he and this brother had started for Colorado and how on the way his party had been attacked by Jayhawkers, his brother killed and he left to die. He told how he lay quiet for twenty-four hours amid the howlings of coyotes until, sure the assailants had left, he had crawled to the Kaw River and quenched his thirst. There beside the stream he nursed his wound, regained his strength and started back to Lawrence, Kas., a vengeful man.

Kate listened sympathetically as he related how he had joined Capt. James Montgomery's band of Freestaters, the band that had attacked him and his brother. Then as a member of it, he had marked man after man who had been in the assault, later to lure them to some out-of-way spot, where he killed them. These men were always found dead with a shot through the middle of the forehead. This sort of wound, according to John N. Edwards, later became the sign of death at the hand of the guerillas.

When Quantrill had "marked off" all but three men who were among the attackers, he was suspected of treason. Montgomery's men cornered him and he came near being "strung up." He plead with the Free-soilers to give him one real chance to prove himself an abolitionist and he argued so convincingly that he was permitted to lead the raid on Morgan Walker's farm. He told Kate King he had promised the Jayhawkers that he would pay with his own life if Morgan Walkers slaves were not brought to Kansas and freed.

Married to Her Hero

Then when he had gone to the Walker farm with the three men, he had duped the Kansans. The Jayhawkers, hearing of this event, sent out orders to get him dead or alive, and until his death he was the most sought after bushwhacker of the strife. But Quantrill told the young girl he had no fear of being caught by the Kansans. As a "home-guard" he was fired with a desire to protect southern property and to get reprisals for outrages committed on Missouri soil.

One day when Kate had remained away from home until dark listening to her hero's tales, her father suspected that she had met the young guerilla secretly. In dread of getting another scolding she stole away from the house and went to a neighbor's for the night. In the morning after her father had gone to the field, she returned home, took her horse and told her folks she was off for school. Instead of going there she rode into the guerrilla's camp and told Quantrill she feared to meet him any more.

He persuaded her to go for a ride, presenting her a new saddle at the time, and on the way he induced her to go with him to a country preacher's home six miles away. Kate was too young to know what marriage meant. She only knew that she had a blind worship for the young gallant. After the ceremony they rode about the countryside until dark, gathering some food for their first meal together, but not knowing where it was to be. Then starting back towards Kate's home, they stopped at a vacant shanty by the wayside. Still trembling the young bride prepared a meal. Afterwards she rode off by herself to a school friend's home and borrowed a blanket. She was afraid to go elsewhere than to this one home, where she swore her friend to secrecy about the marriage.

Liked Life in Guerilla Camps

Quantrill and his bride slept on the floor that night. Their first breakfast was at the home where she had borrowed the blanket and to which they went to return it. The first day of her married life found her shorn of all timidity; she was no longer the trembling girl of the day before. As Quantrill's mate she was ready to follow fearlessly wherever he led.

Kate King found marriage to the intrepid warrior ideal; she was perfectly contented to be by his side at all times. And he in turn was ready to satisfy every whim of hers. The terrifying guerrilla others knew was easily led by her and she had little difficulty exacting whatever she wanted from him. He was a great one to "josh" her, and half the time she never knew whether he was in earnest or not, she recalls.

The three and one-half years of their married life were spent mostly in tents near his men during the summers and in wandering from place to place in the South during the winters. She never rode beside him in a fight under the black flag or assumed a man's outfit, she declared, as some reports about her have had it. She was always safer dressed, as the girl that she was. Whenever she moved with Quantrill to another camp, the guerrilla sent scouts in advance to see if the road was cleared. Then she followed along with him and at times George Todd would be with them. Quantrill's men would follow at some distance back. Other times the men preceded the young couple on a march. During any raids or fights Kate Quantrill stayed at camp waiting impatient for her husband's return and uneasy about his welfare.

Few of their days together were ever spent with the full assurance that he would not have to make a hasty departure. He was fully armed at all times, prepared to fight his way out of any trap. Many nights their slumber was interrupted by marauders from Kansas out searching for Quantrill's

KATE IN FACT AND FICTION

head. The Jayhawkers hated him unrelentingly. As a bride, Kate paid dearly in anxiety for her attachment to the guerilla chief.

Heard Lawrence Raid Planned

At the time of the Lawrence massacre Kate lay awake the two nights before, worrying over how her husband would fare. Quantrill, Todd and William H. Gregg had planned the raid as she listened to the arrangements. Then the men had gone to prepare the way. The night of the raid Kate was particularly uneasy and, after tossing about in her bed, she decided to go to Quantrill early in the morning. Ninety miles separated the girl from her husband. Before daybreak, without breakfast, she was urging her horse on. Five hours late, she was near Lawrence when she broke into the guerrilla's retreat.

A lookout on Mt. Oread, from where the surrounding country could be seen for miles, had reported troops far off on the march into the city. The guerrillas took their time getting out, however, as the troops were far off. The guerillas were tired after the raid: some of them were drunk and they left behind a terrible wreck of homes and business houses. They had been on a rampage in which murder was nothing to them; they had plundered the wealthier homes and they started their retreat laden with loot.

Quantrill was aghast to meet Kate under the circumstances. They retreated together. Meantime the citizens of Lawrence had come out from their hiding places and the scene of desolation wrung the hearts of all. Women wailed, screamed and wrung their hands as they beheld loved ones dead and severely wounded. The massacre was without parallel in the country's annals. It represented the apogee of border hatred, revealing only factional passion and being of no military merit to a cause.

With the Fugitive Guerilla

Senator James H. Lane organized a few men for whom arms could be found an a pursuit was started before the incoming troops, yet some miles away from the city, could be of any service. It was a poor attempt, as Lane had only a handful of men. But Quantrill and his disorganized outfit were driven from point to point, standing their own at times and driving the pursuers back. Re-enforced by Federal troops, the trail became hot for the guerrillas and they retreated faster. There were several encounters in the night with union forces and a few of the guerrillas were killed.

These outlaws were desperate fighters and seldom lost men in battle; the enemy was always a heavier sufferer. The rebel yells and their boldness terrified, and their horsemanship was perfect; they rode with an ease and abandon acquired only by a life spent in the saddle.

The guerrillas disbanded the second day of the pursuit from Lawrence, some going into hiding in small bands, others taking to the woods alone. Kate and Quantrill hid out in the brush during the day and that night made for a Missouri retreat. During all this fighting for miles on the road out of Lawrence, the girl kept out of gun fire, advancing cautiously along so as to be near whatever happened. Her youth and innocent appearance dispelled all suspicion of her.

For four days and night that time the young girl went without sleep. Once when safely hidden in the Kansas brush the two had no more than lain down to rest when a scouting party passed within three feet of them. One of Quantrill's men had turned over to his chief the jewelry he collected as plunder at Lawrence. The night they reached a safe Missouri haven, Quantrill gave his bride seven diamond rings, three pins and four sets of earrings out of the loot, she relates.

A Tent Their "Permanent" Home

Near the end of Quantrill's Missouri career he had a break with his men over some minor matter that concerned Todd as one of the guerrilla leaders. Quantrill joined Kate, and they went to Howard County. He put up a tent and Kate had a kitchen built onto the place. It was as near a permanent home as the two ever had. He had taught her to smoke, and they wiled away many hours beside the stove, planning the future while he puffed a cigar and she a pipe.

One day while she was preparing a meal outside this tent she spied four Redlegs coming up the road. Quantrill was lounging inside when she hastily informed him. Ready for a fight, as he always was, he dashed out and yelled: "What do you want?"

"Who are you?' one of them shot back.

"I'll show you who I am." the guerilla replied, and in a split second had his pistol out, sending a volley into their midst. He wounded two: then, taking to his horse tethered to a nearby pole, he held the others at bay and made his escape into the woods. He reconnoitered the land and found more Redlegs farther back on the road, so he stayed away from his tent. The Redlegs questioned the girl, but she gave out nothing useful to them in their search. They were out to get Quantrill and had heard he was in the locality. Again it was Kate's youthful appearance that threw off suspicion.

"Kate Clarke" to Quantrill's Men

About 4 o'clock the following morning, when Quantrill was sure there were no head-hunters about his tent, he returned to the girl. She was awake and knew his approach by the sound of his horse, and the two left the neighborhood for a quieter retreat.

Before Quantrill's break with his men, Kate Clarke, as she was known by them, was treated with great respect. She met few of them personally as Quantrill never invited any of them into his tent. Kate had known the guerila, Todd, as a small child and he was her best friend among the men. All the time that Kate was about the camps she declares she never heard a word spoken out of place. After the break, Todd's men spoke jocularly of the "military discipline of Kate Clarke."

There has been a mystery as to how the name Clarke became attached to her. One version was that she adopted this name as it was Quantrill's middle one, for reasons only known to herself. She asserts the truth is that she took the name under Quantrill's advice so that, if she were ever questioned and identified by other, the name would help to throw off suspicion as to her real identity.

Before Quantrill made the fatal expedition into Kentucky he took his bride to St. Louis, rounding up on the way a few of the faithful survivors of his earlier bands. Some of the men who broke with him after the Todd dispute, also joined the party. Quantrill seemed to have a hypnotic influence over them and they were ready to lay down their lives for him. His personal supervision of them was responsible for this, Kate King avers. He was known to go among them at night to see if all went well and at times even to stand guard over the sleeping men. Such faithfulness endeared him greatly.

At Her Husband's Death Bed

When he left Kate in St. Louis it was in the expectancy that he would be back in two months. It was their first long separation. She was left well provided with cash to tide her over, she says. In addition she had her jewels; they had been added to from time to time. She was stopping at a boarding house, where a priest brought word one day that the guerilla chief had been wounded in a scuffle on a farm and was not expected to live.

She hastily prepared for the journey to him. Meantime he had been moved to a government hospital in Louisville. Kate arrived at his bedside three days before the end and she stood beside her husband as he breathed his last. He had been shot nearly a month earlier and the tenacity with which he held to life amazed the doctors.

If the guerilla ever left Kate King any money, as the rumors have it, she denies she ever received it. His men took whatever there was and she returned to St. Louis alone. She was only 17 at the time and had no place to turn for comfort. The war was still on and hatred flamed strongly near her home. Her parents had disapproved of her running away and she was held in disrepute among the old neighbors. A short time after returning to St Louis she sold some of her jewels and opened a boarding house.

To the Aid of Her Parents

Four years after the war, when things had quieted down along the border, she returned to visit her family as Mrs. J. R. Claiborne. The country people had little to do with the King family at that time on account of the talk regarding the girl. Kate's father was having a difficult time: his house had been burned in one of the Free Soilers' raid into Missouri and all he had been able to put up was a temporary shack. Other homes had been rebuilt in part through community support, but not his.

To make up, in part, for the disgrace she had brought upon the family, Kate built them a suitable place. She had married a man of wealth and she contributed regularly to her parents' support after her return to St. Louis. She also started several relatives in businesses in different parts of the country. An old neighbor told about what she did for the family; she herself said nothing about it.

Later Kate King married men by the name of Evans and Wood. Four years ago, when 74 years old, she ran away with an inmate of the home whom she had known for years and was married the fifth time. She and her husband do not live together at the home, for the men and women are separated. She usually spends her days in bed, as it is the most comfortable place she has. Propped against a pillow, she reads and looks out into the hall from her room. She does not mingle with the inmates to give them a chance to pry into her history, but by preference keeps to herself.

Time has left her sturdy and well preserved. She has a clear mind for all that she went through and she bears no malice for the many bitter things said about her. She does not claim any glory for the guerrilla's bloody deeds; she feels they were committed in war to avenge outrages against him. She loved him devotedly, much more, she avers, than any of the other men she married. If historians deny that Quantrill ever had a brother killed by Jayhawkers, she does not care; he told her he had, and his word was enough for her.

A Kind and Gentle Man, She Says

When first approached and told by the writer that he understood she was a good friend of Quantrill in her young day, she followed the questioner's words intently, leaning closer and closer to him as he finished the sentence. Then relaxing with a sigh, as though it might have been something far worse that was sought, she replied slowly:

"Yes, I knew him, but I was only a girl at the time and I didn't have much sense." Then after a moment of recollection her face brightened and she continued more spiritedly, "I never knew a kinder, more considerate and -- and -- and gentler man."

She described the guerilla as extremely handsome, with a clear complexion and a scraggly mustache. He was almost six feet tall and carried himself well. The usual picture one sees of him, she says, scarcely looks like him. It may be that her eyes have idealized the desperado with whom Jesse and Frank James first fought. Some of his opponents say he slunk along, making himself hated by this gait; others say he had peculiar eyes of violet hue, which changed color at times. His eyes were blue, according to Kate King; she never remembers seeing them any other color, she says.

KATE IN FACT AND FICTION

These are the memories that she has to cherish today as she as she wiles away time. She is satisfied to live with them and continue her quiet life as though atonement for the past.

Appendix I

Letters from Fred A. Ford

(from Josie (Potts) King and Donald R. Hale Collection of William Quantrill Society Records)

Vicki Beck of Buckner, Missouri, obtained copies of letters written by Fred A. Ford from the collection of Josie (Potts) King archived at the Blue Springs Historical Society, Blue Springs, Missouri; and, from materials archived at the Jackson County (Mo.) Historical Society Archives, Independence, Missouri, including the William Clarke Quantrill Society Records, originated and largely comprising of materials donated by Donald R. Hale.

Capitalization and punctuation were corrected during transcription for ease of reading. Spelling corrections, missing words and brief corrections or explanations were added in [brackets] by Virgil Hoftiezer as transcriptionist.

1. 30 May 1962 to Mr. and Mrs. Floyd and Josie King

2. 10 June 1962 to Donald R. Hale

3. January 1963 to Donald R. Hale

4. 27 February 1963 to Donald R. Hale

5. 6 March 1963 to Donald R. Hale

6. 11 October 1963 to Josie (Potts) King

7. 22 May 1970 to Velma West Sykes

KATE IN FACT AND FICTION

Letter No. 1

30 May 1962
To Mr. and Mrs. Floyd King
7 numbered pages (5.5" x 8" sheets)

Blue Springs, MO
May 30, '62

Mr. and Mrs. Floyd King
309 South 15th St
Blue Springs, MO

Dear Friends –

This I'm going to write to you about has bothered me so much I'm almost sick. The Saturday March 31 Examiner ran the story that Edward D. Moore wrote.
 Mr. & Mrs. L.F. Davis and Mr. E.D. Moore made us a visit almost six years ago to talk about the King Family and Quantrill and etc. I had never seen Mr. Moore before nor have I ever seen him since. I told them that Marion [Francis Marion] King was Aunt Kate's brother and Anson her nephew and both belonged or were members of Lobb Church-and that she had made her home their [there].
 For about six years, for my mother-in-law Mrs. Ragsdale [Fred's mother-in-law was not Mrs. Ragsdale; impossible to determine why he would have thought this to be the case] had lived on the ajoining [adjoining] farm for about five years and she had been gone for three years. Mrs. Ragsdale and Aunt Kate were good friends and were together quite a bit and she told me that Aunt Kate liked to talk about Quantrill.
 I said when Anson King died in June 1920 Aunt Kate was their [there]. The administrator was Irvin Thompson [W.I. Thomason] of Blue Springs Bank. He called for me to help appraise the things but [I] was away. Mug Boman & Porter Huthens were two of the three that did.
 The sale was in August. I bought most of the furniture. It was walnut and something about it that I liked. I knew I was going to move on a farm in the spring.
 After the sale Aunt Kate came to live with Mr. & Mrs. Frank King. They lived the first house west of the Government Grain Bins on Pink Hill Road, and in a half mile of where my folks lived.
 During the winter my brother and I rented a 253 acre farm from Grace Kenney. Her husband's name [was] James T. Kenney. We moved their [there] in the spring, and with us the Anson King furniture. The Kenneys wanted to know where I got the walnut furniture, so they traded me a lot of

furniture for the bed and I think maby [maybe] another small table or something. I told them I got the furniture at Anson King's sale.

Now mind you Mrs. Kenney was born across the Road from the King farm. She was the daughter of Dr. Surface who practiced medicine their [there] and I suspect during the Civil War.

Anyway after I had traded with them, Dr. [James T. was a dentist and probably used the title 'Dr.'] Kenney told me this, that his father-in-law Dr. Surface told him that Quantrill had gave [given] the furniture to his bride or sweetheart-I can't remember which.

Now Mrs. Grace Kenney is living today in K.C. [Kansas City], MO.
[1 line space]
Mr. Moore gives me quite a build up for a purpose that I don't care about. I did talk about the James boys and Quantrill twice in Lexington, MO, and no other place. You see how some writers can exeragate [exaggerate].

Now this is what I told Mr. Moore and no more. About three weeks before the story was published Mr. Moore called me by phone and told me who he was and that he was going to publish the story, and didn't I get a pretty big price for the bed. I told him I did, but I wanted to see him before the story was published. He said he did not know but would try to see me.

Well, I hadent [hadn't] planed [planned] to write a story, but supose [suppose] I'll haf [have] to.

I hope people won't feel to [too] bad towards me.

I assure you this reporter, now retired, that wrote the story used a lot of blue sky.

Sincerely
Fred A. Ford

Letter No. 2

10 June, 1962
To Donald R. Hale
9 pages

[Obviously this letter is in response to a letter from Donald R. Hale; page 1 of Fred's letter begins at the bottom of page 8 of Don's letter with a distinct change in penmanship.]

Blue Springs, MO
June 10, '62

Quantrill & Border.
page 8
William E. Connelly [Connelley]
816 Lincoln Street
Topeka, Kansas
July 3, 1909
Tells of pictures of Quantrill.

[Fred's letter begins here] I have this book.

[two line space]

Mrs. Strode-I'm sure will go along with you. [Obviously in response to a comment made in the preceding letter.]

[7 line space]

Josie King called me recently and she is not

[end of page 1; this refers to the above letter to Josie Potts King]

mad at me. Yes she is related to Aunt Kate King, [Fred is absolutely incorrect in this statement; whether this was his belief or actually based on such a claim by Josie is unknown.] and say by the way, Babe Hudspeth married Aunt Kate King's niece-name Annie Ragsdale [Ragland, Fred confused Ragland and Ragsdale-see above letter] before marriage to Babe. Babe [is] my relation and I remember them well.

Now Aunt Kate <u>Quantrill</u>-we will call her. Kate's Dad's name was Jasper [Robert was Kate's father, William Jasper was one of Kate's brothers] King and one son was Francis Marion, and Marion's son was Anson.

Another son was Samuel R.

Another son Jasper-name sake. [William Jasper was obviously not named for his father Robert].
Daughter Martha, sister of Kate, and older.
Now Martha was older than Kate and married a Ragsdale [Ragland] and it was her daughter Annie that married Babe Hudspeth [Annie Ragland did marry Babe Hudspeth] who helped burn Lawrence.
Now less [let's] go to Jasper [William Jasper] King, brother of Aunt Kate Quantrill. This Jasper [William Jasper] had a son living in Indep. [Independence], MO name[d] Walter King [living at] 625 East Walnut.
And Walter has a sister name[d] Randy Morris [Miranda Jane King Morris] that could tell you a lot. I have known her for years. If Walter won't tell you where she is living I can. Now this Randy Morris had a sister name[d] Lucy Young [Lucy A. King Young]. I knew them both. They could have been Anson King's sisters [they were Anson King's first cousins]. I'm not sure but Josie will tell me. Find out where she is in Indep. [Independence], MO. She is up on things and has a good memory.

[4 line space]

Now the Davis farm. I'm the guy that told Davis about the civil war happenings their [there]. You see the Kansas Red Legs burned the Jasper [Robert] King's home and etc. to the ground. Quantrill said Lawrence, KS money would haf [have] to pay or build it back so at the close of the war Quantrill gave the money for same.
Now I think I can back this up that is if you will let me help you write this short part.
You see I had this furniture 10 months. I bought at Anson King's sale before I knew where the money came from to buy furniture and build the house now standing where Davis now lives. Even tho I bought the furniture for a song, anyone could tell it wasn't cheap. It was then 55 years old and had been in that house all the time. You see I had rented a farm from Mr. & Mrs. James T. Kenney and moved their [there] the spring of 1921. Mrs. Kenney wanted this walnut furniture and ask me where I got it. It so happened she was born across the road [from] the Jasper [Robert] King farm. Her Dad was a Dr. during Civil War and friends of the King family.
After trading me out of some of the furniture they told me of Quantrill giving the Lawrence, KS money to replace what Red Legs had burned.
Yes on page 197 [in <u>Quantrill and the Border Wars</u>, by William E. Connelley] Nannie or Ann Walker has quite a write up. Now her great granddaughter [Viola Lane Hall was Nancy Walker's granddaughter, not her great granddaughter] and nephews live around here-in fact belong to our church [Lobb Church], and rich with money that came through some of Annie Walker's money invested in Okla [Oklahoma] oil sand.
I once knew the Vaughns at Lake City. The books says she maried [married] a man named Slaughter. He left her. She then M [married] in April 1862. She married Joe Vaughn. He took her to Clay Co. to live after

KATE IN FACT AND FICTION

the Civil War. She got her share of her Dad's money and told husband Vaughn to leave. She then moved to Baxter Springs, Kansas and did wrong their [there].

My memory tells me that she left their [there] and settled in Okla [Oklahoma].

Now this great granddaughter [granddaughter] of hers living here now got her money from that Okla [Oklahoma] hills.

Now it could be you could use my name on the King family and Aunt Kate Q. I would rather build her up than to run her down.

Mrs. Nellie Strode is not to [too] well, but loves company. You should visit her again soon.

I'm at your service.

My phone Canal 8.4003
Blue Springs

I'm tired now and want to get this in the mail.

Fred A. Ford
R 1 Box 229
Blue Springs MO

Appendix I

Letter No. 3

Undated [about 13 January 1963]
[Date of letter based on reference to a burial in the fourth paragraph.]
To Donald R. Hale
8 pages

[no salutation, date or place]

Sara [Sarah] Head or Aunt Kate Quantrill

They held her body hoping her daughter would be found or claim her body. The relation knew where she [Kate's daughter] was.

Seckond [Second]

 Aunt Kate's Dad was named Jasper [Robert], and he had a son named Jasper [William Jasper; Fred was consistent in his errors] also that I knew.
 Two weeks ago they buried one of Jasper's [William Jasper's] daughters in Indep. [Independence] that I was aquainted [acquainted] with. [This was Julia Lee King Sweeney, daughter of William Jasper King, who died 27 January 1963 and provides the approximate date this letter was written.]
 Now the Bible tells us, Woe to anyone who seukrth [seekth?] scandal, now I let one lieing [lying] reporter fool me one time. So don't ever let them publish anything without you know [knowing] what will be published. And it makes no difference as to whether it is true or false. The Bible tells us not to do it.
 Now after the Lawrence Raid, she and Quantrill rode to Carrol [Carroll] County and spent some time their [there] and I have his picture taken in Carrol [Carroll] Co. and he is a hAnsone [handsome] man. The Surface family lived across the road from the King family of Aunt Kate Quantrill and they said Quantrill made a vow, that Lawrence, Kansas, had to build a new home for the one they had burned. And they believed Aunt Kate used the Quantrill money to build and furnish it. For they wanted the furniture and I sold it to them not knowing its history. Later they told me why they wanted it.
 You see I bought the furniture at a public sale in Aug 1920. Aunt Kate Quantrill was standing their [there] and I knew her. Very few people did. My mother-in-law Mrs. Ragsdale [Fred's mother-in-law was not Mrs. Ragsdale; impossible to determine why he would have thought this to be the case] lived on joining farms and she became aquainted [acquainted] with

KATE IN FACT AND FICTION

Aunt Kate while picking goose berries about 1913. At that time Aunt Kate was living with her brother Marion [Francis Marion] King and Marion's son Anson. Marion died and Aunt Kate kept house for her nephew Anson on the same farm and the house Quantrill's money and built and it stands today.

Now Aunt Kate, so Mrs. Ragsdale told me, loved to talk about Quantrill, and in KY they say Quantrill gave her his last $500.00 in gold to Kate Quantrill. I was told he had that amount on him when wounded.

Now I have the story here, written by Aunt Kate's relation. I would let you read it, but never her name be connected to the story.

Don't forget Babe Hudspeth married Aunt Kate's neice [niece] Anna Ragsdale [Ragland; Fred consistently confuses Ragland with his 'mother-in-law Ragsdale']. I visited with Anne Ragsdale [Ragland] Hudspeth in 1920. And her husband Babe Hudspeth helped burn Lawrence and went to the Missippi [Mississippi] River with Quantrill's band. I remember Babe Hudspeth well-[he] died in 1915, I think. His uncle Robert Hudspeth gave Babe the 320 acres that the Steuens family have an elevator on now to dry high bred seed corn near Lake City. Babe Hudspeth is my relation.

The reason for the name Clarke. It would have been sueascide [suicide] to have been married to Quantrill, and she knew it. The Union army wanted his scalp more than any one man. In the state of Missouri, as well as the east half of Kansas, Aunt Kate couldent [couldn't] very well claim his name. It would have been poision [poison] to her family.

Now why can't you write a nice story of her. Why condem [condemn] a woman that has been dead 30 years? Why not write something that will please some of these old southern sympathies? Kentucky was good enough to give Quantrill a road side marker. He was given up to be a milatiary genus [military genius]. I can't say as to whether she helped her relation or not. I know where her picture is when young and she was beautiful. I think I'm getting a duplicate of it soon. Don't forget one Kansas City paper tells she had a daughter by Quantrill and that is why the county farm held her body to try [to] locate the daughter.

Sincerely,
Fred A. Ford

Appendix I

Letter No. 4

27 February 1963
To Donald R. Hale
2 pages

Blue Springs, MO
2-27-63

Friend Donald,

Your letter received. Glad to hear from you. I am glad you refreshed my memory that we both feel the same way about the Civil War.
 Please let me say that the newspapers of thirty years ago were just as careless with the truth about things that happened seventy years before.
 Their [There] was a published or in the paper about the body being held for her daughter to claim the body.
Would you like to see the story a realative [relative] of Aunt Kate wrote?
 Say yesterday I rec'd a letter from Crestwood, KY from the grandson of Wakefield. He sent me the picture of the barn where Quantrill and his men were when surprised by the Federals. Also the house where Quantrill spent the night. He has Quantrill's sword.
I suggest you let me send to you this article the relation wrote and should it suit you, you must not mention a realative [relative] wrote it.
I'll finish this in the A.M.
 Good Morning-I still don't know what to say, I probly [probably] have said to [too] much.

Sincerely,
Fred A. Ford

Letter No. 5

6 March 1963
To Donald R. Hale
2 pages

Blue Springs, MO
3-6 – 63

Mr. Donald R. Hale
15907 CTE Lee Rd.

Dear Friend:

  Your last letter was interesting, and I hope I haven't lost it. I'm sending you the story. Please send it back to me when through with it.
  Please remember do not say kin folks wrote it. I don't know how you will word it. You could say it was given to you by a friend of Aunt Kate's and one that lived by her for five years and still lives.
  You could honestly say that from 1912 until 1920 she kept house for her brother and nephew on the same farm where she furnished the money to build the house and it stands today three miles south from Lake City.
  This I know, she and Quantrill spent considerable time in Howard Co. the fall of 1864 and into Jun. 1865.

Sincerely,
Fred A. Ford

Appendix I

Letter No. 6

11 October 1963
To Josie Potts King
2 pages

Blue Springs, MO
Oct 11, 1963

Misses Josie King

Dear Friend:

 A few lines. I am ready to go to see if I can locate Sara Head's marker or place of burial. Will you send me the name of that man that might be able to help [with the] date of her death?
 I would like to borrow your big book on quantrill for a couple of days. I won't let it get lost and should something happen to it you can have mine in place of it.
 A new book is coming out and I want to find the grave.

Sincerely,
Fred Ford

KATE IN FACT AND FICTION

Letter No. 7

22 May 1970
To Velma West Sykes
2 typed pages

[Typed across the top of the letter: (Copy of letter received after my article about Quantrill was published in *The Star* May 19, 1970). Return mailing label pasted at top of letter reads:

Velma West Sykes
Richart Hotel
4th & Oak Streets
Garnett, Kansas 66032

It appears as if Velma W. Sykes typed this copy of Fred's handwritten letter for her files; there are handmade corrections to the typing within the letter.]

Blue Springs, Mo.
5-22-70

Velma West Sykes,

Dear Madam: Your article in the Kansas City Star interests me.

 For years I have wanted to come to Kansas and see where Quantrill taught school and etc., always afraid I could find no one to talk to. Seven years ago I wrote to the postmaster in Bloomfield, Ky, in regard to just how I could locate the farm where Q. was wounded. I sent money to put add [ad] in the paper. No ans., but when with my two sons I arived [arrive], we were more than welcomed. I found Q. sword and today correspond with the son of the man it was gave to about four days before he was wounded. At that time his dad was a eight year old boy coming home from school. When he met the Q band and one of the men handed him the sword. I had three cousins that helped burn Lawrence. And one of them has two children here now.
 I have a nice picture of the Q. band and can name 29 of them. I was acquainted with Kate King or Kate Clark. She often went by. The house and barn still stands that she built for her folks in 1870. The Red Legs had burned her folks home so Q. said Lawrence had to pay. Kate said she sold the jewelry Q. gave her from the Lawrence raid and built this home and furnished it. I bought the furniture in 1919. Aunt Kate was standing their [there]. Part of it was stole from me.
 I call her Aunt Kate because her niece married my cousin who helped burn Lawrence. I wonder how you got wise to her final resting place. I [It] took

Appendix I

us 35 years to find out. She was cremated, we found out through Jefferson City, MO. I live in three miles of the cemetery, same distance from where the James boys robed [robbed] the Glendale train.

I am surprised to know that he had an aunt in Kansas. Is their [there] any relation left in that section? The cave-this cave near here-where Quantrill and Andy Walker hide thirteen kegs of powder in 1860. They got it from a steam boat stranded on a sand bar in Mo. River. The Federals never found it. It was on Morgan Walker's farm where Q. sold the Kansas boys out -- Ball, Southwick, Lispey and etc. Two of them were killed in ¼ mile of where I live. The day after first fight. I do not believe any women and children were killed in the Lawrence raid. The Red Legs spilled a lot of blood here, but no women or child under sixteen that I know of. I have often heard the old men tell of the trip home from Lawrence. The dust saved their lives, they said. Will close. Might give you a picture of the band if you care for it.

I have lived in Ottawa, Kansas, worked in the Santa Fe shops their [there] in 1916. Also ran through Garnett on train twenty years ago. I will soon reach eighty years of age.

Sincerely
Fred A. Ford
R. 1 Box 229
Blue Springs, Mo.
64015

[Second page of typing]

I'm purching (purchasing?) 10 K.C. Mo. Stars papers and will mail your article to Minn., Iowa, Ky., Alabama, Kansas, N.J. and Mo.

> O what regards we owe to the thinking few
> For but few people think that think they do
> Nine out of ten people let some one else do their thinking.

Picked this up at a Chautauqua in 1914. I have been thinking since in some ways it has cost me.

(PHOTOS ENCLOSED) [but not included in copy]

(1) -- Fred A. Ford, white hat, Mr. & Mrs. Henderson, lived on the Wakefield farm. Mrs. Henderson's grandmother sat up with Quantrill. Spot near silo gun was found-taken close to house & barn. I have pictures of them also. (Keep this one if you care to.)

(2) -- One of Q. men lost the gun in the fight with Terries [Edwin Terrell's] men.
Its [It's] still loaded. I have the numbers of it. (Send this back to me.)

KATE IN FACT AND FICTION

(3) -- This sword was gave [given] to a school boy-son of Wakefield, owner of farm, by Quantrill's band a few days before May 10. This school boy gave it to his son, and his son. I have been to his home twice and here is the sword. This is near Ky. I want to buy the sword. Have seen it on two occasions. (Return to Fred A. Ford, Blue Spring, Mo. R 1, Box 229, 64015)

(4) -- This pond saved the lives of two Q. men. They hid behind the rock wall. Its [It's] their [there] today. The spot where he was hit. At that time big sugar maple trees grew their [there]. (Send this back to me.)

Appendix J

Notes Regarding Persons Named in the Letters from Fred A. Ford

(* denotes relatives of Kate identified in "Kate's Family")

Aunt Kate (*Sarah Catherine King, aka Kate Clarke)
    -Letters No. 1, 2, 3 & 7
Mug Boman (William N. Boman)-Letter No. 1
William E. Connelly [Connelley]-Letter No. 2
L. F. Davis (Leonard F. Davis)-Letters No. 1 & 2
Fred A. Ford-author of all seven letters
Donald R. Hale-recipient of Letters No. 2, 3, 4, & 5
Sara Head (aka *Sarah Catherine King)-Letters No. 3 & 6
*Babe Hudspeth-Letters No. 2 & 3
Robert Hudspeth-Letter No. 3
Porter Hutchens (Porter Hutchings)-Letter No. 1
James boys-Letters No. 1 & 7
Grace (Mrs. James T.) Kenney-Letters No. 1 & 2
James T. Kenney-Letters No. 1 & 2
*Anson King-Letters No. 1, 2 & 3
Floyd King-recipient of Letter No. 1
*Frank King-Letter No. 1
Jasper King [*Robert King]-Letters No. 2 & 3
Jasper King [*William Jasper King]-Letter No. 2
Josie (Potts) (Mrs. Floyd) King
    -recipient of Letters No.1 & 6, noted in Letter No. 2
Marion King [*Francis Marion King]-Letter No. 1 & 3
*Martha King Ragland-Letter No. 2
*Samuel R. King-Letter No. 2
*Walter King-Letter No. 2
Edward D. Moore-Letter No. 1
Randy Morris [*Miranda Jane King Morris]-Letter No. 2
*Annie Ragsdale [Ragland]-Letters No. 2 & 3
Mrs. Ragsdale-Letter No. 1 & 3
Mrs. Nellie Strode-Letter No. 2
Dr. Surface-Letters No. 1 & 3
Velma West Sykes-recipient of Letter No. 7
Terrie [Edwin Terrell]-Letter No. 7
Irvin Thompson (W. I. Thomason)-Letter No. 1
Joe Vaughn-Letter No. 2
Wakefield-Letter No. 4
Annie/Nannie Walker-Letter No. 2
Morgan Walker-Letter No. 7
Lucy Young [*Lucy A. King Young]-Letter No. 2

KATE IN FACT AND FICTION

Aunt Kate (Sarah Catherine King, aka Kate Clarke) -Letters No. 1, 2, 3 & 7

Fred always referred to Kate as 'Aunt Kate' because his 'cousin' on his mother's side of the family, 'Babe' William Napoleon Hudspeth, had married Kate's niece 'Annie' Georgeanna R. Ragland (the daughter of Kate's older sister Martha) in 1897. Babe Hudspeth and Fred Ford were actually second cousins once removed; Fred's maternal grandfather Samuel Mumford Hudspeth and Babe's father Joseph William Hudspeth were first cousins.

It is true that Babe and Annie had married, and it is true that Annie was Kate's niece; but, Babe and Fred were second cousins once removed. So it was a bit of a stretch for Fred to claim Kate as his aunt. There certainly were no blood ties between Fred and Kate. And, Fred's connection to Babe was separated by two-and-a-half generations.

Fred was only about six-years-old when Annie and Babe married. In Letter No. 3, Fred mentioned a conversation he had had with Annie in 1920 -- 42 years after the fact. He had a remarkable memory.

Mug Boman (William N. Boman) -Letter No. 1

Mug Boman was identified by Fred as one of the men appointed by the court to appraise the King estate. Kate's nephew, Anson King, died suddenly on 29 May 1920 without leaving a will. No record of a 'Mug' Boman was found, but William N. Boman was listed adjacent to Anson King in the 1920 census, meaning they were very close neighbors. Close neighbors were often chosen to appraise estates.

William Newton Boman was born 16 July 1882 near Norborne in Carroll County, Missouri, and married Mayme Edith Toomay on 5 February 1908 in Carroll County, Missouri. William Newton and Mayme Edith and their five children were in Sni-a-Bar Township of Jackson County, Missouri in the 1920, 1930 and 1940 census. Their children were: Pearl Mae, Joan Ruth, James M., David Cortland and Willa Belle, all born in Missouri between 1911 and 1920. William Newton Boman died in Jackson County, Missouri and 23 February 1959 at age 76. He was buried in Oakland Cemetery in Blue Springs, Jackson County, Missouri.

David Cortland Boman, son of William Newton Boman and Mayme Edith Toomay, married Kate's grandniece Halys Morris. Halys was the daughter of 'Jack' Richard Jackson Morris and Miranda Jane King; Miranda Jane King, the daughter of William Jasper King, was Kate's niece.

William Boman also signed and was the informant on the certificate of death for Anson Marion King in 1920. This neighbor obviously was close to the King family in more ways than only geographic proximity.

William E. Connelly [Connelley] -Letter No. 2

William Elsey Connelley (15 March 1855-15 July 1930) was an avocational historian and author who published the book "Quantrill and the Border Wars" in 1909. William Elsey was born in Kentucky, but spent most of his adult life in Kansas with multiple endeavers in teaching, wholesale lumber and banking. In the 1890's he began researching and writing histories and biographies. From 1914 until his death in 1930 he was Secretary of the Kansas State Historical Society. He focused much of his extensive research on correspondence with other historians and interviews with eye witnesses, but he favored sources that were pro-Union. He strongly favored Kansas over Missouri regarding the Missouri/Kansas border conflict. His book on Quantrill was heavily biased against the southern cause and presented a very negative view of Quantrill and the guerrillas.

L. F. Davis (Leonard F. Davis) -Letters No. 1 & 2

Mr. and Mrs. Leonard F. Davis were the owners of 40 acres of the King family farm in 1962 as noted in the newspaper article by Edward D. Moore (see below). The fate of other half of the original 80 acres owned by Robert L. King was not mentioned in the article and remains unknown.

Fred claimed he was the source of the information to Mr. and Mrs. Leonard F. Davis regarding the history of the house that Kate had had built.

Fred A. Ford
-author of all seven letters

Fred Allen Ford was born 22 June 1891 to John Calvin Ford and 'Ella' Cinderella Belle Hudspeth, who were married 27 February 1890 in Jackson County, Missouri. John Calvin was the son of Edmund Dorrel Ford and Alvina Thomas Cancellor from Kentucky. Ella Belle was the daughter of Samuel Mumford Hudspeth and Sarah Elizabeth Hudspeth from Kentucky. Although both of Ella's parents carried the same surname, there were no interconnection found between the two Hudspeth families for at least three generations back to her great grandparents.

Fred was with his parents, at age nine, in Ft. Osage Township, in Jackson County, Missouri on 18 June 1900. He was with his parents in Sni-a-Bar Township in Jackson County, Missouri, in 1910 and 1920, living near Frank W. King.

Fred married Pearl Hazel Griswold on 24 October 1924 at Leavenworth, Kansas. Pearl was the daughter of Fred Griswold and Susie Hupp. [See Mrs. Ragsdale below for a discussion of Fred's mother-in-law, whom he identified as Mrs. Ragsdale in two separate letters.]

After his marriage, Fred farmed in Jackson Township in Johnson County, Missouri, and was there on 10 April 1930 in the census. However, by the 1940 census on April 9th, Fred and Pearl had moved their family back to Sni-a-Bar Township in Jackson County, Missouri, again near Frank W. King (perhaps back to his father's farm?).

Fred Allen and Pearl Hazel had the following children:

i. Betty Sue Ford, born 6 March 1927
ii. Rhea Jean Ford, born 13 April 1928
iii. Fred Allen Ford, Jr., born 5 December 1929
iv. Robert Pearl Ford, born 5 December 1929

Appendix J

v.　　　William Highbridge Ford, born 21 August 1933.

Fred Ford spent 70 years researching and accumulating information and artifacts about William Clarke Quantrill. A newspaper article about him by Margaret Olwine, entitled "True Story of Quantrill's Raiders Is Too Close to Home to be Revealed," appeared in the *Kansas City Times* on Thursday, 26 October 1967. Fred Allen Ford died in May 1976 and was buried in the Blue Springs Cemetery, Jackson County, Missouri.

Donald R. Hale
-recipient of Letters No. 2, 3, 4, & 5

Donald R. Hale studied Quantrill, the Civil War, and the Missouri/Kansas Border War for 40 years until his death on 24 February 2008 in Jackson County, Missouri. He authored several books, including but not limited to: *They Called Him Bloody Bill; Branded as Rebels* (Volume 1 with Joanne Chiles Eakin, and several additional volumes independently); and, *We Rode With Quantrill;* as well as numerous newspaper and magazine articles.

Don's article, "After Six Decades, A Claimant to Role of Quantrill's 13-Year-Old Bride," on page 42 in the *Kansas City Times* on 6 April 1963, appeared about a month after he received Fred's last letter to him. Fred was not mentioned in this article.

Don was a close friend of co-author Vicki Beck, and a correspondent to co-author Virgil Hoftiezer. Don and Virgil split the cost of the tombstone that Don had placed on the grave of Sarah Catherine "Kate" (King) Quantrill-Evans-Batson-Head in Maple Hill Cemetery.

Sara Head
-Letters No. 3 & 6

Sara [Sarah] Head was the name under which Kate died and was buried. While she was an inmate of the Jackson County Home (former Poor Farm). Kate ran off with and married fellow inmate, Walter Head. Although they never lived together as man and wife, it was Walter's surname by which Kate was known at the time of her death.

*Babe Hudspeth
-Letters No. 2 & 3

'Babe' William Napoleon Hudspeth married Kate's niece 'Annie' Georgeanna R. Ragland on 5 February 1897. Babe, born 15 January 1842 in Ft. Osage Township in Jackson County, Missouri, was the son of Joseph William Hudspeth (1809-1890) and Amanda Beall. Babe did ride with Quantrill. The 'May to December' marriage -- Babe was more than 20 years older than Annie-was not a happy union. The couple separated, but did not divorce. Thus, when Babe died in 1907 (eight years earlier than recalled by Fred) and left his land and estate to his nephews, Annie was able to 'break the will' when the court ruled in her favor and she inherited the Hudspeth land as Babe's widow; the Hudspeth family had bitter feelings about this 'loss of their land,' according to Joanne Chiles Eakin, in personal communication with the author in November 1995.

Fred's claim that Babe was his cousin was the basis for Fred addressing Kate as 'Aunt Kate. Fred and Babe were second cousins once removed.

Robert Hudspeth
-Letter No. 3

Robert Napoleon Hudspeth (1822-1885) was the uncle of Babe Hudspeth. This brother of Joseph William Hudspeth never married and had no children. Robert N. Hudspeth willed his estate to his siblings.

Porter Hutchens (Porter Hutchings)
-Letter No. 1

Porter Hutchings, identified by Fred as Porter Hutchens, was one of the men appointed by the court to appraise Anson King's estate (also see Mug Boman above). Porter Hutchings, the youngest son of Thomas C. Hutchings

Appendix J

and Mary Ann Hackett, was born in Blue Springs, Jackson County, Missouri on 9 October 1881 and lived in Sni-a-Bar Township his entire life.

The 1877 Atlas of Jackson County, Missouri, indicated that "Thos. Hutchins" [Thomas C. Hutchings] owned 100 acres directly north of the King family farm. Thomas C. Hutchings, his first wife Sarilda Cummins (married 12 July 1858 in Jackson County, Missouri) and their daughter Lucy C. were listed in Sni-a-Bar Township in Jackson County, Missouri, immediately adjacent to Robert King in the census on 19 July 1860. On 1 June 1880 Thomas C. Hutching(s) and his second wife Mary A. Hackets (married 8 December 1864 in Jackson County, Missouri) with children: Lucy A., James E., Dora M., Thomas W. and Walter Lee, were in the same neighborhood as the King family farm, with the family of Dr. J. M. Surface and John and Martha King Ragland close by. In the 1900 census, Porter Hutchings, age 18, was listed with his widowed mother Mary and brother Walter one household from Francis Marion King, who was then living on the King family farm. On 15 January 1920, Porter and his wife Lola Maude were listed adjacent to William N. Boman who was listed next to Anson King in the 1920 census. Porter Hutchings died in Blue Springs, Jackson County, Missouri, in 1964.

Lucy C. Hutchings, the older half sister of Porter Hutchings, married Thomas Henry Torpey, the son of the neighbors on the north side of the King family farm. Thomas Torpey, Sr. owned the 40 acres originally purchased by Robert L. King in 1857.

Thus, the Hutchings family and the Robert L. King family were very close neighbors. Close neighbors were often chosen to appraise estates.

<u>James boys</u>
<u>-Letters No. 1 & 7</u>

This reference is to the James brothers, Frank and Jesse, who rode with Quantrill and later established reputations as outlaws in their own right. The legends of Frank and Jesse

KATE IN FACT AND FICTION

James have eclipsed and out-lived that of Quantrill's in American lore.

Grace (Mrs. James T.) Kenney
-Letters No. 1 & 2

Grace Surface, daughter of Dr. John Milton and Fanny Surface, was with her parents as a two-year-old child in the 1880 census. Grace married James T. Kenney on 11 June 1906 in Jackson County, Missouri. Fred correctly identified the father-in-law of James T. Kenney as Dr. Surface (see below).

Grace was also the granddaughter of Robert King's neighbor William E. Surface, who owned a large amount of land directly east of the King family farm. Grace apparently inherited some of this land of her grandfather's that she had rented to Fred Ford. She and her husband bought the walnut bedroom furniture from Fred before Fred learned the infamous origin and true value of it.

James T. Kenney
-Letters No. 1 & 2

James T. Kenney had married Grace Surface (See immediately above). They purchased the King walnut bedroom furniture from Fred. James T. and Grace lived in Kansas City in Jackson County, Missouri, when the Federal census was taken on 15 April 1910, and 19 January 1920. He was a dentist.

*Anson King
-Letters No. 1, 2 & 3

Anson Marion King was Kate's nephew, the son of her brother Francis Marion King. Anson inherited the King family farm when his father died in 1916. Anson Marion died intestate (without a will) suddenly of a ruptured aortic aneurism on 29 May 1920. His neighbor, William Boman, was the informant on his death certificate.

Because he left no Will, the many relatives of Anson's mother, Eveline Lynch King, including those from both of her parents' previous marriages, stepped forth to claim a share of the estate.

Floyd King
-recipient of Letter No. 1
(Note: Floyd King is NOT related to Kate.)

Neither Floyd King nor his wife, Josie (Potts) King, (see below) has any known direct blood relationship to Kate, despite any assumptions or assertions of such relationships by Fred Ford or others. There were several King families in Jackson County, Missouri, before, during and after the Civil War. There is no known common lineage amongst or between the various family lines sharing the King surname in Jackson County.

Floyd Earl King was born 6 May 1901 in Blue Springs, Jackson County, Missouri. His parents were Thomas Riley King and Cora Belle Brown who both died in Blue Springs in 1962 and 1949, respectively. Thomas Riley King was born in Indiana, as was his father John King, who was the son of Sampson King and Priscilla Hoak. To date there has been no documentation of any genealogical connection between Sampson King and Robert L. King (and thus there is no known blood ties between Kate and her siblings and any of the many other King families in Jackson County, Missouri).

*Frank King
-Letter No. 1

Frank W. King, son of William Jasper King, was Kate's nephew who lived on an adjoining farm of 40 acres directly south of the original 80-acre King farm where Kate grew up. According to Fred, Kate lived with Frank for awhile in 1920.

Jasper King [*Robert King]
-Letters No. 2 & 3

Robert L. King was Kate's father. There is no record that he ever used the name "Jasper" as noted by Fred.

Jasper King [*William Jasper King] -Letter No. 2

William Jasper King was Kate's oldest brother. Fred referred to him as "Jasper" and said that he was his father's name sake. Perhaps William Jasper did use his middle name as many of the King family members did in later generations, and he was listed as Jasper in the 1860 census. However, there is no documentation that William Jasper was named after his father; it has been proposed that he, as the oldest son, was named after his paternal grandfather, William.

William Jasper King married America Jane Snodgrass who was from a large family of early Jackson County pioneers with roots in Virginia. William Jasper and America Jane were the parents of six nephews and four nieces of Kate; Fred identified only four of them by name although all except one -- other than Lucy A. King Young who Fred knew had died in 1911 and Earl R. Monroe King who had moved to South Dakota in 1912 -- lived in the Blue Springs/Independence area until their deaths.

Josie (Potts) (Mrs. Floyd) King -recipient of Letters No. 1 & 6, noted in Letter No. 2
(Note: Josie Potts King is NOT related to Kate by blood; she is distantly related to Kate by marriage only.)

Neither Josie Potts nor her husband Floyd Earl King (see above) has any known direct blood relationship to Kate. Josie Belle Potts King was a half-grandniece to America Snodgrass King, the wife of Kate's brother William Jasper King. America was Kate's sister-in-law. The only kinship Josie had to Kate was through this marriage of her half great aunt.

Josie Belle Potts was born 10 April 1901 in Jackson County, Missouri. Her parents, William Carroll Potts and Mary Ellen Steele, both came from well-established pioneer families of Jackson County, Missouri, that originated from Virginia roots. William Carroll Potts was the son of Levi Potts, who rode with Quantrill, and Sina Emily Slaughter, whose father Josiah Slaughter donated the land for the cemetery where many

King family members were buried. Mary Ellen Steele was the daughter of Samuel Jackson Steele and Mary Catherine Snodgrass, who was the half sister of America Jane Snodgrass. Mary Catherine Snodgrass was the daughter of Bartley Snodgrass and his first wife 'Betsy' Elizabeth St. Clair, while America Jane Snodgrass was the daughter of Bartley and his second wife Lucy Baker. America Jane Snodgrass married Kate's brother William Jasper King. Thus, Josie Belle Potts King was a half great niece of America Jane Snodgrass King, Kate's sister-in-law, which hardly qualifies Josie as a close relative of Kate.

While Josie's great great grandmother did carry the King surname (Josie>father William Carroll Potts>grandmother Sina Emily Slaughter Potts>great grandmother Elizabeth Koger>great great grandmother Mary King Koger), there is no connection between this King family and the lineage of Robert L. King.

Josie did a great deal of genealogical research and joined the D.A. R. (Daughters of the American Revolution) according to personal communication from her niece Carroll E. Moore of San Diego, California, in 1990. Thus, Josie was a good resource for Fred to consult regarding the complex and intertwined family relationships in Jackson County. However, it must be presumed that Fred Ford made the assumption that Josie was related to Kate and that Josie did not claim such a direct relationship to Kate herself.

Marion King [*Francis Marion King] -Letter No. 1 & 3

Francis Marion King was Kate's next older brother; he was about three years older than she was. He was listed as Marion in the 1860 census with his parents, but signed legal documents as either F. M. King or Francis M. King.

Francis Marion married Eveline Lynch who had complex familial connections; her parents each had offspring from previous marriages, plus children together. Francis Marion purchased the King farm from his father in 1880 and then willed it to his only son Anson Marion "for love and affection" in 1916. Eveline died 20 July 1912. Francis Marion died 7 May 1916.

According to Fred, Kate came back to Blue Springs to keep house for her brother Francis Marion and his son Anson Marion after Eveline died in 1912 and continued to live on the farm until 1920 when Anson Marion died. Kate may have returned to keep house for her brother, but she had left Jackson County before January of 1920. A maternal cousin was living with Anson in the 1920 census, while Kate was in Sapulpa in Creek County, Oklahoma with her daughter on 20 January 1920.

*Martha King Ragland -Letter No. 2

Martha Jane (King) Ragland was Kate's older sister. She married John Oath Ragland and they were the parents of 'Annie' Georeganna Ragland, who married Babe Hudspeth (Fred's "cousin").

*Samuel R. King -Letter No. 2

Samuel R. King was Kate's younger brother.

*Walter King -Letter No. 2

Walter R. King was Kate's nephew, a son of William Jasper King.

Edward D. Moore -Letter No. 1

Edward D. Moore was a reporter with the *Independence Examiner* whose article, "Family Lives in Home Once Quantrill's Sweetheart's," on 31 March 1962 prompted Fred's letter to Floyd and Josie King.

Appendix J

In this article, Mr. and Mrs. Leonard F. Davis who lived nine miles east and one mile south of Independence on East Truman Road, were featured as the current owners of the 40-acre (former) King family farm and the house that Kate had built. Fred Ford was mentioned as an expert on Quantrill who had made a handsome profit from selling the walnut bed once owned by Kate King.

Randy Morris [*Miranda Jane King Morris] -Letter No. 2

Miranda Jane King Morris was Kate's niece, a daughter of William Jasper King -- Kate's oldest brother, who lived in Independence. Apparently she wrote a history or a story about Kate that Fred discussed and offered both Donald R. Hale and Velma West Sykes the opportunity to read it. Unfortunately, this historical document cannot be located today (2014).

Annie Ragsdale [*'Annie' Georgeanna R. Ragland] -Letters No. 2 & 3

'Annie' Georgeanna R. Ragland was Kate's niece. Annie's parents were John Oath Ragland and Martha Jane King-Kate's older sister (as noted by Fred). Born 20 March 1864 in Jackson County, Missouri, Annie married relatively late in life at age 33 to 'Babe' William Napoleon Hudspeth. As noted in the discussion of Babe above, this was an unhappy pairing that ended in separation of the couple and estrangement between the two families. Annie Ragland Hudspeth died in 1929.

Mrs. Ragsdale -Letter No. 1 & 3

Fred referred to his mother-in-law as Mrs. Ragsdale who was a neighbor of the Kings and who knew Kate well enough to discuss Quantrill. There were several women known as Mrs. Ragsdale in Jackson County and it was impossible to determine whom Fred referred, or if he even meant 'Ragsdale' (versus 'Ragland). Fred's mother-in-law was neither Ragsdale nor Ragland.

Fred mistakenly used the name "Ragsdale" when he meant "Ragland" in two different letters. If it was Mrs. Ragland instead of Mrs. Ragsdale that he was discussing in this case, she was still not his mother-in-law. Perhaps Fred confused the actual relationship of mother-in-law when he mentioned Mrs. Ragsdale. After all, he repeatedly indicated Kate to be his Aunt.

Fred's mother-in-law was 'Susie' Susan M. Hupp, the daughter of Miner Hupp and Eliza Dorman, who, at age 18, married Fred A. Griswold, age 21, on 23 December 1899 in Dawson, Dallas County, Iowa. They lived in Spring Valley Township in Dallas County, Iowa on 1 June 1900. The family were not located in the 1910 census, but Fred died before 1917 when his widow Susie and daughter Pearl lived at 519 Park in Des Moines, Iowa. Susie remarried before January of 1920; on 8 January 1920 Susie was with her second husband Robert Turkington, a 45-year-old Iowa-born clerk in a drug store, living in Kansas City, Jackson County, Missouri. Pearl Griswold was with her mother and stepfather in 1920. However, Robert and Susie moved back to Iowa and lived in Des Moines in Polk County, Iowa on 11 April 1930; they were still there in 1940. It is obvious that Fred's mother-in-law, 'Susie' Susan M. Hupp Griswold Turkington, never lived near Kate. There has been no reason found as to why Fred might identify his mother-in-law as Mrs. Ragsdale.

Furthermore, in Letter No. 1, Fred contradicted the length of time Mrs. Ragland lived next to Kate, who was keeping house for her brother and his son, from first six years to then five years in the same sentence. Kate's brother Francis Marion King outlived his wife Eveline Lynch King by less than four years (she died 20 July 1912 and he died 7 May 1916). Fred's belief that Kate was still at that farm when Anson King died on 29 May 1920 was incorrect. Kate may have returned to Jackson County, Missouri, soon after Anson's death, but she was in Oklahoma in the 1920 census. In addition, Fred's ending to the sentence -- "and she had been gone for three years" -- adds more confusion. Does "she" refer to Kate or to

Mrs. Ragsdale? Does "gone" indicate she left the area or did she die? Three years from when?

Mrs. Ragsdale continues to remain a mystery.

Mrs. Nellie Strode
-Letter No. 2

The only Nellie Strode identified in Jackson County during this time period was not married. Nelle Omega Strode, born 15 November in 1866 and died in Independence on 18 February 1952, was the daughter of Bailey Strode and Victoria Twyman. Her death certificate indicated she was single and thus she would not normally be expected be addressed as "Mrs." However, the local custom or Fred's particular pattern of writing (note how he addressed Josie Potts King in Letter No. 6) may have "bestowed" the title of "Mrs." upon Nelle. She was another person whom Donald R. Hale had apparently contacted regarding Kate.

Dr. Surface
-Letters No. 1 & 3

Dr. Surface refers to John Milton Surface, the son of William E. Surface and Maria St. John, who died 23 August 1927 in Kansas City, Jackson County, Missouri. Dr. John Milton and his wife Fanny M. Allaire were in Blue Springs in Jackson County, Missouri, in 1880. His profession was listed as physician. Thus Fred was correct when he addressed him as Dr. Surface. In 1900, John Milton and his family were in Kansas City, Jackson County, Missouri and his profession was listed as druggist. John Milton and Fanny M. were the parents of Grace Surface Kenney (see above).

The father of John Milton, William E. Surface, was a neighbor to Robert King. In the 1877 Atlas of Jackson County, W. E. Surface owned the property directly west and immediately adjacent to the King family farm. He and his wife Maria St. John Surface were listed in Sni-a-Bar Township in the Blue Springs district of Jackson County, Missouri on 17 June in the 1880 census.

Velma West Sykes
-recipient of Letter No. 7

Velma West Sykes (1892-1976) was a Missouri poet who during her 60 year career wrote newspaper columns, hosted radio shows, reviewed books, edited a magazine and wrote plays and poetry. The collection of her papers in the Library of Congress encompasses 350 items.

It was Velma's article, entitled "Violence Stirs Kansans' Memories," about Quantrill and Kate King that appeared in the *Kansas City Star* on 19 May 1970, that prompted Fred Ford's letter to her.

Terrie [Edwin Terrell]
-Letter No. 7

Edwin Terrell was the Union mercenary guerrilla who hunted down Quantrill and his men near Taylorsville in Spencer County, Kentucky. On 10 May 1865 Terrell and his gang tracked Quantrill's group to the Wakefield farm where they wounded Quantrill and killed some of his men. John Langford shot Quantrill in the back, paralyzing him and then Edwin Terrell rode up and shot off Quantrill's trigger finger.

Terrell eventually turned Quantrill over to Federal authorities in Louisville in Jefferson County, Kentucky, who paid him his bounty money and sent him on his way.

Irvin Thompson (W. I. Thomason)
-Letter No. 1

W. I. Thomason was the court appointed administrator of the Anson King estate whose signature was appended to many documents relating to the settlement of the estate. The name W. I. Thomason also was on the sale bill advertising the auction of Anson's personal property.

Appendix J

Joe Vaughn
-Letter No. 2

'Joe' Joseph G. Vaughn was a Jackson County, Missouri resident who rode with Quantrill's band for about a year. Joe later married the disgraced Nancy Walker, Quantrill's former mistress. She left Vaughn after her father died. (Also see: 'Annie/Nannie' Nancy Walker)

Wakefield
-Letter No. 4

James H. Wakefield owned the farm five miles south of Taylorsville in Spencer County, Kentucky, where Quantrill was wounded and captured by Edwin Terrell on 10 May 1865. Quantrill was taken to Wakefield's house after he was shot and paralyzed. Three days later Quantrill was transported by Terrell to a Union prison in Louisville in Jefferson County, Kentucky.

James Heady Wakefield, son of Matthew Wakefield and Rebecca Heady, was born 30 August 1810 in Spencer County, Kentucky. He married Mary E. Taggart in Spencer County, Kentucky, on 10 December 1835. Mary E. was born 14 September 1813 in Ireland and died on 21 September 1882. James H. and Mary E. Wakefield were farming in Spencer County, Kentucky on the Federal census on 3 September 1850, 14 June 1860, 26 July 1870, and 1 June 1880. At least six children, all born in Kentucky between 1837 and 1855: Matthew, Mark or Marcus, John D., James M., Joseph W., Mary A., and Ann, were with their parents sometimes from 1850 through 1870. On 7 June 1900, James was living with his son John D. and family in Hokes, Jefferson County, Kentucky. James H. Wakefield died on 29 May 1909. He was buried next to his wife, Mary E. (Taggart) Wakefield, in Big Spring Cemetery, Bloomfield, Nelson County, Kentucky.

Annie/Nannie Walker
-Letter No. 2

"Annie/Nannie" Nancy Walker was the daughter of James Morgan Walker, born in Jackson County in 1841. She was reported to be the mistress of William Clarke Quantrill. She married first 'Riley' William Ryland Slaughter; after he divorced her she married 'Joe' Joseph G. Vaughn (see above). After she left Joe Vaughn, she reportedly went to Baxter Springs in Cherokee County, Kansas and operated a bawdy house. Fred simply stated she "did wrong" in Baxter Springs. Nancy eventually married David D. Wood. Confusion between Nancy and Kate lead to the long held belief that Kate had married a man named Wood. Nancy Walker Slaughter Vaughn Wood died in Weatherford, Parker County, Texas, in 1894.

Morgan Walker
-Letter No. 7

'Morgan' James Morgan Walker was a wealthy slave holder with large land holdings in the neighborhood near the King farm. It was here that William Clarke Quantrill first appeared in Jackson County, Missouri, and made a name for himself. Quantrill supposedly had an affair with Morgan's daughter 'Annie/Nannie' Nancy Walker.

Morgan's son 'Andy' Andrew Jackson Walker joined Quantrill's band of guerrillas. It is presumed that Kate knew the Walker family.

Lucy Young [*Lucy A. King Young]
-Letter No. 2

Lucy A. King was Kate's niece, the daughter of William Jasper. Lucy A. married Daniel W. Young and she died of tuberculosis on 21 February 1911 in Pleasant Hill in Cass County, Missouri. Thus it is surprising that Fred knew her since Lucy had left Jackson County with her husband before 1900.

Illustrations

Photographs

8. Sarah Catherine King, as a young woman, before she assumed the alias Kate Clarke. This image was procured in 1962 by W. Howard Adams, first President of the incorporated Jackson County (Mo.) Historical Society, Independence, Missouri, JCHS003808M. Also on the cover, top right, cropped and digitally enhanced.

10. Kate Clarke, as a madam, in St. Louis, Missouri. William Clarke Quantrill Society Records, originated and largely comprising of materials donated by Donald R. Hale, Jackson County (Mo.) Historical Society Archives, JCHS004160L. Hale received this original carte de viste from Fred Ford (Hale correspondence to Hoftiezer, 28 Aug. 1995).

    For the verso of this cabinet card, see Breihan, *The Killer Legions of Quantrill*, p. 12. Also, Virgil Hoftiezer Collection, from Mary Louis King Thompson Waldron Roberts Thompson, a great niece of Kate. A copy had come from Mrs. Herschel Strode (nee, Nellie Harris, who may have received it from Josie Potts King). Also on the cover, middle.

38. Towle "Old Colonial" dessert place spoon, gift from Kate to her niece. Virgil Hoftiezer Collection.

50. Kate's brother and sister-in-law, William Jasper King and America Jane Snodgrass King. Photo provided by their grand-daughter Halys Morris Wyrick Boman. Halys' mother, Miranda Jane King Morris, knew Kate well enough to write a personal history about her . . . although that history has never been seen by anyone except Fred Ford.

    William Jasper and America Jane were the parents of ten surviving children, Kate's nieces and nephews. Eight of these children lived and died in Jackson County, Missouri. All ten of them knew Kate and were known by Kate. Virgil Hoftiezer Collection, from Halys Morris Wyrick Boman.

KATE IN FACT AND FICTION

52. Kate's nieces and nephews, children of Kate's brother, William J. King. Virgil Hoftiezer Collection, from Halys Morris Wyrick Boman.

53. Earl R. Monroe King (1873-1963) at Watertown, South Dakota in 1938. Earl R. Monroe was the only child in this family to leave Missouri, which he did in 1912. He and his adult children did return to Missouri for visits with their relatives (including Kate) in Jackson County in later years. Virgil Hoftiezer Collection, from Halys Morris Wyrick Boman.

55. Walter R. King (1882-1971), twin of Oscar. Virgil Hoftiezer Collection, from Halys Morris Wyrick Boman.

55. Oscar King (1882-1939), twin of Walter, at Independence, Missouri. Oscar was crippled at birth and never married and he did not have offspring. All nine of Oscar's surviving siblings produced children and left heirs.

68. Sarah Catherine King, as an older woman, Sarah C. Batson. Virgil Hoftiezer Collection, from Audrey Lee Rauch Dick, Kate's great-grand niece. Also used on p. 175.

69. Barn on King family farm rebuilt by Kate in 1869. This barn was standing in 1992 when owned by the Davis family, and it remains today (2014). The house is not pictured/identified to respect the privacy of the current owners. Vicki Beck Collection.

73. William Clarke Quantrill, portrait in charcoal on paper, which was prominently displayed in a frame for years at Quantrill reunions. Jackson County (Mo.) Historical Society Archives, JCHS009241XX)

80-81. "Wedding Cabin" in Sni-a-Bar Township in Jackson County, Missouri, where Kate and Quantrill stayed after their clandestine marriage in 1863. When the cabin was around 100-years-old in the mid-1960's, the cabin was sold to the Jackson County Parks Department for $50, dismantled and the pieces used to repair other period buildings at Missouri Town 1855, an architectural preservation effort by the Jackson County Parks Department. Vicki Beck Collection, from Bill and Mary Dayton, owners in 1962.

89. Martial Law (or, Order No. 11) by George Caleb Bingham. From an original Sartain engraving signed by Bingham in the Jackson County (Mo.) Historical Society Archives, JCHS021291M.

Illustrations

94. Quantrill's Hideout in Howard County During the Summer and Fall of 1864. Supplied by William "Bill" D. Lay, Fayette, Missouri.

99. Quantrill's original gravesite. Three images courtesy of Max McCoy, http://maxmccoy.blogspot.com, as taken 24 March 2007.

106. Morgan Walker. Jackson County (Mo.) Historical Society Archives, JCHS021989XX.

126. Social Evil Hospital opened in 1872, in St. Louis, Missouri. "Women in Health Sciences," Bernard Becker Medical Library Digital Collection, Washington University, St. Louis, Missouri. (http://beckerexhibits.wustl.edu/mowihsp/win/Timeline/SocialEvil Hospital.htm).

133-136
and 138. Images from: Dacus, Joseph A., and James W. Buel. *A Tour of St. Louis: Or, The Inside Life of a Great City.* (St. Louis, Mo.: Western Publishing Co., 1878).
    Polytechnic Institute, p. 81
    Dozier, Weyl and Company Bakery, p. 290
    The Old Jail, p. 469
    Planters House, p. 40
    Court House, p. 36
    Tony Faust Cafe and Oyster, p. 297
    Gratiot Prison, p. 42

137. Southern Hotel, from: Scharf, J. Thomas. *A History of St. Louis City and County, From the Earliest Periods to the Present Day: including Biographical Sketches of Representative Men."* Volume II. (Philadelphia, Pa.: L. H. Everts & Co., 1883), as found online at (http://stlouis.genealogyvillage.com/hotels.htm).

147. Bertha Evans' birth registration, as digitized and available (though largely unreadable) on Ancestry.com.

153. Various online sources point to this historic structure, from which the images on this page derive: http://gohistoric.com/places/635577; http://www.zoopla.co.uk/property/9-randolph-road/london/w9-1an/25109274.

Edouard Mendes de Costa, from The Netherlands, lived at this house in 1905, according to *The London Gazette*, 1 Dec. 1905, p. 8659, which provided a list of naturalizations from the previous month.

By 1912, Arthur Dones lived at this house, according to John Parker's *Who's Who in the Theatre*. Volume 3. (Boston, Ma.: Small, Maynard and Co., 1912), 128.

Tragically, on December 6, 1941, five members of the Wils family were killed by a parachute mine during World War II. Four of them died at the home (http://www.cwgc.org/find-war-dead/casualty/3115474/ WILLS,%20VERA; http://www.doverwarmemorialproject.org.uk/Casualties/Civilians/ SurnamesUtoZ.htm). By 1958, Dr. P. R. Masek lived at this address (http://www.iafss.org/publications/frn/350/-1/view).

And, the owner as of 2014 is Paul Weiland, a member of Venrex II, LLP. (https://www.opencompany.co.uk/company/OC309270/ venrex-ii-llp)

154. Pliny Mannon Castanien (Bertha's husband, Kate's son-in-law) with his nephew and great-nephew in 1921. Pliny, on the right, is with his nephew, Ernest Oakley Castanien (1897-1948), holding his son, Lloyd (born 2 December 1920, in California). Ernest O. was the eldest son of Pliny's brother, Charles Ernest Castanien (1865-1942), who moved from Oklahoma to California between 1910 and 1920.

On the back of this photograph, from Jean Castanien Snyder,* written in ink: "Ernest, holding his son Lloyd (who was 50 yr on Dec 2 1970) Uncle Plin Do you know how old these pictures are -- I found the negatives in an old box of pictures & had some printed -- fun, eh. Taken in 1922;" and, written in pencil: "or probably 1921." The estimated age of the toddler in arms supports a photograph taken in 1921.

*=This family snapshot was sent to the author, Virgil Hoftiezer, from Jean, who had received it from, "Ethel Castanien, cousin of the younger Pliny, niece of older Plin. The baby was my husband Lloyd." Ethyl Castanien is the daughter of the brother of Pliny Mannon Castanien—Charles Ernest and his wife Musie (Small) Castenien. Virgil Hoftiezer Collection.

156. Sapulpa, 1901, from a brief history of the city, ca. 1981, supplied to the authors by the Genealogy Department of the Sapulpa Public Library, Sapulpa, Oklahoma.

159. Kate with her daughter, Bertha E. Evans Castanien, and grandson Pliny R. Castanien. Jackson County (Mo.) Historical Society

Illustrations

Archives, JCHS00159L. Also on the cover, bottom right, cropped and digitally enhanced.

161. Sapulpa, the Oil City of the Southwest, from a postcard in the Vicki P. Beck Collection.

170. 'Cas' Pliny Raymond Castanien (Kate's grandson; Bertha's son). This photograph from the "Biographical Note" in, *To Protect and Serve,* may have been taken much earlier than 1993, as Pliny looks younger than 84 years old. Compared to Kate's appearance in the 1912 photograph, there is a family resemblance between Pliny at this age, and his grandmother then.

175. Sarah Catherine King, as an older woman, Sarah C. Batson. Virgil Hoftiezer Collection, from Audrey Lee Rauch Dick, Kate's great-grand niece. Also used on p. 68.

180. Jackson County Home for the Aged and Infirm, formerly the Jackson County Poor Farm, as it looked when Kate lived there for nine years. *Results of County Planning, Jackson County, Missouri.*

181. John Marion "Jack" Ragland (20 May 1866-14 Jun 1939) was the second son and third child of Kate's sister, Martha Jane King Ragland. Jack Ragland was Kate's "guardian" in 1929, and should have been available for claiming Kate's body in 1930. Jackson County (Mo.) Historical Society Archives, JCHS025501X.

188-189. Kate's memorial marker, and King / Chism family plot in Slaughter Cemetery, Blue Springs, Jackson County, Missouri. Courtesy David W. Jackson, August 2014.

193. Kate's Tombstone in Maple Hill Cemetery in Wyandotte County, Kansas, courtesy findagrave.com submitted by campbell2u@aol.com. This tombstone was placed on Grave 6, Lot 63, Block 5 in Maple Hill Cemetery, Kansas City, Wyandotte County, Kansas in June 1997. Additional photographs taken by Donald R. Hale include a set of eight images (A-H) available at the Jackson County (Mo.) Historical Society Archives, William Clarke Quantrill Society Records, originated and largely comprising of materials donated by Donald R. Hale, JCHS022679S.

196. Donald R. Hale and Vicki P. Beck images of Robert and Malinda King's tombstones in Slaughter Cemetery. Vicki P. Beck Collection.

KATE IN FACT AND FICTION

197. Vicki P. Beck and Donald R. Hale at Kate King's grave, Maple Hill Cemetery, Kansas City, Kansas; digitally enhanced.

Documents

64. Robert King family in the 1880 Census, Blue Springs District, Jackson County, Missouri. National Archives and Records Administration, U.S. Decennial Census, Federal Population Schedules. Truncated columns to fit this view.

121. Kate's Statement before the Provost Marshal in St. Louis, Missouri, on 13 October 1863. National Archives and Records Administration, "Missouri Union Provost Marshal Records."

122. The name "Cate Clark" penciled on a supposed promissory note in Jackson County, Missouri, undated. This $100 note on a small piece of paperboard was claimed by the donor to have been passed down by a Rogers/Harris family member who had loaned "Cate Clark" the money. The names on the note are: Isom [Isham] Harris, Margaret Harris, Noel (sic.) Liddle and Joshua Land. Still, the researcher should know of its existence for further study. Jackson County (Mo.) Historical Society Archives, General Collections, Donation ID 72.038.001, Document ID 70F3.

123. Kate, as Kate Clark, in the 1870 Census, St. Louis County, Subdivision Number 10, St. Louis, Missouri. National Archives and Records Administration, U.S. Decennial Census, Federal Population Schedules. Microfilm Series: M593; Roll: 814; Page 155 (written) 845 (stamped).

142. Kate, as Kate Clark, in the 1880 Census, St. Louis County, St. Louis, Missouri. National Archives and Records Administration, U.S. Decennial Census, Federal Population Schedules. Truncated columns to fit this view.

151. Marriage Record of Bertha E. Evans Castanien (Kate's daughter). Oklahoma County Clerk's Office, Oklahoma City, Oklahoma.

158. Kate, as Sarah C. Batson, in the 1910 Census of Vian, Oklahoma. National Archives and Records Administration, U.S. Decennial Census, Federal Population Schedules.

162. Application for Social Security Account Number (Form SS-5) by Pliny R. Castanien (Kate's grandson). Indexed and located in the online through the Social Security Security Death Index (SSDI);

Illustrations

original application provided by the Social Security Administration, Office of Central Records Operations, 300 N. Green St., P.O. Box 33022, Baltimore, MD 21290-3022.

165. Death Certificate of Bertha E. Castanien (Kate's daughter). Kansas Department of Health and Environment, Office of Vital Statistics, Topeka, Kansas.

168. Marriage License of 'Cas' Pliny Raymond Castanien and Imogene Jones (Kate's grandson).

177. Anson King Estate "Public Sale" document. Probate File of Anson King, Jackson County, Missouri, Probate Court.

179. Receipt, 20 September 1921. Kate signed this receipt, "Mrs. Sarah C. Batson." Probate File of Anson King, Jackson County, Missouri, Probate Court.

179. Receipt (promissory note), 11 July 1921. Kate signed as, "Mrs. S. C. Batson." Probate File of Anson King, Jackson County, Missouri, Probate Court.

182. Header for the 1926 *Kansas City Star* article, "The Strange Romance of Quantrill's Bride: Kate King, Ending Her Days in an Alms House, Recalls Her Life with the Famous Guerilla Leader."

186. Death Certificate of Sarah Head (i.e., Sarah Catherine "Kate" (King) Quantrill-Evans-Batson-Head). Missouri State Archives, Missouri Death Certificate Collection.

187. Death Certificate of Walter Head (Kate's widower). Missouri State Archives, Missouri Death Certificate Collection.

190. 1976 letter from Donald R. Hale to Dorothy Butler at the Oak Grove Banner newspaper regarding Kate's burial site. In this letter Don briefly summarizes his quest to find the actual grave of Kate. The last paragraph emphasizes the need for persistence, documentation, and verification in seeking and finding the truth. Jackson County (Mo.) Historical Society Archives, William Clarke Quantrill Society Records, Document ID 25F15.

191. Maple Hill Cemetery map.

192. Burial record of Sarah T. Ready (whose marker was originally set upon Kate's grave), from Maple Hill Cemetery, Kansas City,

KATE IN FACT AND FICTION

Wyandotte County, Kansas. This document from Maple Hill Cemetery, Kansas City, Wyandotte County, Kansas, and the attached handwritten note indicate that a marker for Sarah T. Ready, who also died in January 1930, was mistakenly placed on the grave of Kate (Grave 6, Lot 63, Block 5) instead of on Grave 5, Lot 74, Block 5. This error was rectified by Donald R. Hale in 1992, and in 1997 a marker for Kate King was placed on Grave 6, Lot 63, Block 5). Virgil Hoftiezer Collection.

193. Message from Don (Donald R.) Hale in 1997 and the burial record of Sarah Head. The burial record from Maple Hill Cemetery, Kansas City, Wyandotte County, Kansas, verifies that Kate was buried in Grave 6, Lot 63, Block 5. This was the grave on which the marker was placed in June 1997. Virgil Hoftiezer Collection.

195. King and Chism Family Plot in Slaughter Cemetery, Blue Springs Jackson County, Missouri, by David W. Jackson, after an on-site investigation and dowsing process, August 2014.

Maps

44. Missouri in central United States. This map identifies the eight different states that surround Missouri. Shaded are counties with significance to this biographical work.

44. Western Missouri (including Jackson County, Missouri) and Eastern Kansas. Jackson County, Missouri, abuts along the state line of Kansas. Lawrence, Kansas, is still a considerable distance from Jackson County where guerrillas had refuge in the 'safety' of the hills and valleys.

47. Part of Sni-a-Bar Township (Township 49 North, Range 30 West of 5th Principal Meridian) in Jackson County, Missouri, from the *Illustrated Historical Atlas of Jackson Co, Missouri*, 1877].
The east half of the southeast quarter of Section 7 is the location of the Robert L. King family farm. The east-west section line dividing Robert L. King's property and that of W. J. [William Jasper] King to the south is present-day Argo Road in Blue Springs, Missouri. The north-south section line on the west side of their property is today Owen School Road. Two and a half miles west from this intersection (not visible in this historical view) is present-day 7-Highway.

129. Downtown St. Louis, Missouri, in 1870.
http://stlouis.genealogyvillage.com/

Illustrations

144. Modern day St. Louis, Missouri. Busch Stadium parking lot is now located on the site where Kate Clarke's establishment at 6th and Elm Streets was located in 1870.

150. Eastern Oklahoma. This map shows the three counties (Sequoyah, Muskogee, and Creek) and the three cities (Vian, Braggs, and Sapulpa) where Kate and Bertha were located on the 1910, 1920 and 1930 Federal census.

KATE IN FACT AND FICTION

Bibliography

Archival Resources

Beck, Vicki P. Research for *Kate: In Fact and Fiction*. Personal Correspondence. [Intended for eventual donation to Jackson County (Mo.) Historical Society Archives, Independence, Missouri.]

> Ballinger, Forrest, Blue Springs, Mo. Information about Slaughter Cemetery where Kate's memorial marker was placed, and where Kate was thought to have been buried.

> Blackman, Rusty. Blackman Funeral Home. Personal communication via telephone regarding Ketterlin Funeral Home who took care of Kate's funeral and burial.

> Carter, Barbara, and Cheryl Smith, Genealogy Librarians, Sapulpa Public Library, Genealogy Department, Sapulpa, Ok. Personal correspondence, April 2002.

> Curtis, Annette W., Independence, Mo. Personal communication regarding historical Jackson County, Mo., resources at the Midwest Genealogy Center and Jackson County (Mo.) Historical Society Archives.

> Dade County, Missouri, Recorder of Deeds Office, Greenfield, Mo. Personal correspondence, March 1996.

> Davis, Elvira "Mimo." *Abstract of Title* chaining the ownership of Robert L. King's property patented in 1857 in the southeast quarter of Section 7, Township 49, Range 30, Jackson County, Missouri; also, photographs of the Robert L. King family barn (pictured on page 69) and home that Kate paid to have re-built after Order No. 11 (not pictured/identified to respect the privacy of the current owners). Copyrighted images of the structures appear in Breihan's *Real West* article and in Margaret Olwine's *Kansas City Times* article.

> Dayton, Bill and Mary. Personal interview; photographs of Kate and Quantrill's reported 'wedding cabin.'

> Ford, Bill (Fred A. Ford's son), Glendale, Az. Personal communication via telephone interview.

Ford, Myrtle (Mrs. Robert P., brother of Fred A. Ford), Blue Springs, Mo. Personal communication via telephone interview.

Hubbard, Jim. Sapulpa, Ok. Personal correspondence.

Kirchner, Roy. Bolivar, Polk County, Mo., genealogist. Personal correspondence and communication via telephone in reference to the King family when they resided in Polk County, February and March 1996.

Kansas City, Wyandotte County, Ks., County Coroner.

Lafayette County, Missouri, Recorder of Deeds. Marriage record of William King and Eveline Lynch. Personal correspondence, May 1996.

Lay, William D., Fayette, Mo. Personal communication via telephone and correspondence about Quantrill and Kate in Howard County, Mo., January 2007.

Lentz, Betty Sue Ford, Springfield, Ma. (Fred A. Ford's sister). Personal correspondence, May, September and October, 1992.

Matney, Duane "Bud," and Michael Matney. Maple Hill Cemetery, Kansas City, Wyandotte, County, Kansas. Personal communication via telephone, in-personal interview, and correspondence about the burial there of Sarah Head (Kate King).

Meador, Victor P., Independence, Mo. Personal communication and correspondence regarding Kate's burial, April, 2008.

Morris, Peggy Brownfield. Personal interview regarding Fred A. Ford and his information.

Olwine, Margaret. Wrote Kansas City Times article, "True Story of Quantrill's Raiders Is Too Close to Home to be Revealed," 26 Oct. 1967. Personal communication via telephone.

Polk County, Missouri, Recorder of Deeds Office, Bolivar, Mo. Telephone interview and personal correspondence regarding King family when residents of Polk County, March 1996.

Zeiler, Pat. Vian, Ok. Research correspondence, April 2002.

Bibliography

Blue Springs Historical Society, Blue Springs, Missouri. Josie (King) Potts Papers. Personal letters from Fred A. Ford to Potts and Sykes.

Family History Center, Independence, Mo.

Hoftiezer, Virgil D., Ph.D. Research for *Kate: In Fact and Fiction*. Personal Correspondence. [Intended for eventual donation to Jackson County (Mo.) Historical Society Archives, Independence, Missouri.]

> Beckwith Funeral Home, Larned, Ks. Personal communication via telephone, 2012.
>
> Boman, Halys Morris. Personal communication, 1990-2000. Halys was the great-granddaughter of Robert L. King [Halys>MirandaJane>William Jasper>Robert L.], and lived in Independence, Missouri.
>
> Castanien, Donald G. Personal communication, 16 March 1996. Donald lives in Davis, California.
>
> Dick, Audrey Lee Rauch, compiler. *Earl M. King Family Record*, 1985. Audrey was the great-great-granddaughter of Robert L. King [Audrey Lee>'Marie' Lena Marie>Earl R. Monroe>William Jasper>Robert L.], and lived in Minneapolis, Minnesota.
>
> Eakin, Joanne Chiles. Personal communication, November 1995.
>
> Haberly, Mary Leona Beman. Personal communication, 1985-2007. Mary was the great-great-granddaughter of Robert L. King [Mary Leona>Leona Mae>Earl R. Monroe>William Jasper>Robert L.], and lived in Castlewood, South Dakota.
>
> Hale, Donald R. Personal communication, 1996-1997.
>
> Harper, Lee Ann Stone. Personal communication, 1996.
> Lee Ann is the great-great-granddaughter of Robert L. King [Lee Ann>Jessie Pearl Cummins>'Nan' Nannie (Nancy) Evelyn>William Jasper>Robert L.], and lives in Union Mills, North Carolina.
>
> Harris, Jon. Personal communication, 2000-2014.
> Jon is a descendant of the sister of America Jane Snodgrass King [Jon Harris>Russell Ernest Harris>Stella Russell>Alice Lynch>Elijah Lynch and Miranda Ann Snodgrass Lynch] and lives in Berkeley, California.

Hoftiezer, Lucy Mae Beman. Personal communication, 1985-2012.
Lucy is the great-great-granddaughter of Robert L. King [Lucy Mae>Leona Mae>Earl R. Monroe>William Jasper>Robert L.], and lived in Watertown, South Dakota.

Hostetter, Dorothy Bell King. Personal communication, 1995.
Dorothy was the great-granddaughter of Robert L. King [Dorothy>Robert Jasper> William Jasper>Robert L.], and lived in Independence, Missouri.

JaCoby, Alfred, Director, San Diego Union History Project (Copley Newspapers), 7776 Ivanhoe Avenue, LaJolla, Ca. Personal communication to Vicki Beck, 21 March 1996.

King, 'Peg" Lillie L. Lage. Personal communication, 2000.
Peg was a great-granddaughter-in-law to Robert L. King [Peg married to 'Clif' Earl Clifford>Earl R. Monroe>William Jasper>Robert L.], and lived in Watertown, South Dakota.

King, Douglas Earl. Personal communication, 1995-2012.
Douglas is a great-great-grandson of Robert L. King [Douglas Earl>Robert Vernon>Earl R. Monroe>William Jasper>Robert L.], and lives in Blasdell, New York.

King, Howard Lee. Personal communication, 2011.
Howard is a great-great-grandson of Robert L. King [Howard>Robert Monroe>Robert Jasper>William Jasper>Robert L.], and lives in Missouri.

Lahey (now Downey and Lahey) Funeral Home, Wichita, Ks. Personal communication, 2012.

McCarthy, Claudia. Personal communication, 2013-2014.
Claudia's great-great-grandmother [Elizabeth L. (Davenport) King Davidson] was a daughter-in-law [married to Samuel Robert King] of Robert L. King, and lives in Independence, Missouri.

Morell, Randal. Morell Funeral Home, Larned, Ks. Personal communication, 2012.

Petersen, Paul R. Personal communication, 28 November 2008.

Rabas, Charles. Personal communication, 2007.

Reed, Jeanne. Mid-Continent Public Library System, Excelsior Springs, Mo. Personal communication.

Bibliography

Royal, Bonnie King. Personal communication, September and October 2012. Bonnie is the great-great-granddaughter of Robert L. King [Bonnie>Clarence D.>Joseph Edward>Samuel Robert>Robert L.], and lives in Kansas City, Missouri.

Snyder, Jean L. Castanien. Personal communication, 22 April 1996. Jean lives in North Carolina and New Jersey. She also provided the photo of Pliny Mannon Castanien with his nephew.

Swinney, Ray F. Personal communication, 1995.
Ray F. was the great-grandson of Robert L. King [Ray F.>Julia Lee>William Jasper>Robert L. King], and lived in Wheatland, Missouri.

Thies, Randal M., "Quantrill's Three Graves and Other Reminders of the Lawrence Massacre," Markers XVIII. *Annual Journal of the Association for Gravestone Studies*, edited by Richard E. Meyer. (Greenfield, Ma.: Association for Gravestone Studies, 2001), 1-29.

Thompson, Mary Louise King Thompson Waldron Roberts. Personal communication, 1995. Mary is the great-granddaughter of Robert L. King [Mary Louise>Walter R. >William Jasper>Robert L.], and lives in Kansas City, Missouri.

Whites, LeeAnn. Personal communication, 1996-2014.

Wichita Park Cemetery, Wichita, Ks. Personal communication, 2012.

Jackson County (Mo.) Historical Society Archives, Independence, Missouri.

"Cate Clark" Promissory Note. General Collections, Donation ID 72.038.001, Document ID 70F3.

Donald R. Hale Papers, letter from Donald R. Hale to Dorothy Butler at the Oak Grove Banner, Oak, Grove, Missouri, 1976, Document ID 25F15.

J. Calvin and Fannie Iserman Family Letters, 1858-1863. Discussing the Civil War in Independence, Jackson County, Missouri. Mentions evacuations of the civilian population; the Morgan Walker farm raid by William Clarke Quantrill; slavery; scarcity of provisions; troops and troop movements; business and political conditions; border troubles; raid on the Liberty Arsenal; and, Christmas 1862, among other topics. Document ID 11F10.

> Josie (Potts) King Papers, Essay on Alley Family and Dealy Family Genealogy, Document ID 77.06F12; Essay on Potts Family, 77.06F13.
>
> William Clarke Quantrill Society Records, originated and largely comprising of materials donated by Donald R. Hale.

Jackson County, Missouri, 16th Judicial Circuit Court, Probate Court Records. Anson Marion King estate/probate case file, I4432, courtesy Bill Potter.

Kansas State Department of Health, Office of Vital Statistics, Topeka, Kansas.

Kansas State Historical Society, Topeka, Kansas.

> William Elsey Connelley Papers [Also found in the KSHS Connelley papers are William W. Scott materials (Scott's widow sold her husband's materials to Connelley). See also Connelley-related materials in the KSHS John Lutz Papers].
>
> Connelley's papers, correspondence, manuscripts, and research materials may be found in numerous manuscript collections around the U.S.; some are within collections of other historians' papers who corresponded with Connelley.
>
> Some of the Connelley and Quantrill-related collections include, but are not limited to: Kansas University, Kenneth Spencer Research Library, William Clarke Quantrill Collection; University of Oklahoma Libraries, Western History Collections; University of Southern Mississippi, McCain Libraries and Archives, Quantrill (William Clarke) Research Collection; Truman State University, Pickler Memorial Library; Jackson County (Mo.) Historical Society, William Clarke Quantrill Society Records; and Kansas City (Ks.) Public Library, William E. Connelley Collection (of and about Wyandot Indians).]

Louisville, Kentucky, city directories, 1865-1878.

Missouri Historical Society. Missouri History Museum Library and Research Center, St. Louis, Mo.

> Data on St. Louis madams provided by Dennis Northcott, Associate Archivist for Reference, September 2014.
>
> Newspaper coverage of J. R. Claiborne's death, provided April 1996.

Bibliography

National Archives and Records Administration. Missouri's Union Provost Marshal Papers. Online database at Missouri Digital Heritage points to a Series of this Record Group provided through the Missouri State Archives. (St. Louis County). Microfilm F1195, Missouri State Archives, Jefferson City, Mo.

St. Louis Public Library, St. Louis, Mo. St. Louis city directories and data on Cramer, Gross & Co., photographers.

State Historical Society of Missouri, Columbia, Mo. Newspaper Library. Also, Gregg, William H., "A Little Dab of History Without Embellishment," [1906], "is a memoir of his service under Confederate guerrilla William Clarke Quantrill from December 1861 to 1864, and includes a description of the sack of Lawrence, Ks."

United States Department of the Interior, Bureau of Land Management, Eastern States Office, Springfield, Va. Personal correspondence, May 1996. Robert L. King patent records for St. Clair and Johnson Counties, Mo.; and Elizabeth King patent records for Polk County, Mo.

Books and Periodicals

_____, "Tankersley v Castanien," 1916 OK 1051, 162P. 191, 63 Okla. 18, Case Number: 6800, Oklahoma Supreme Court Cases, Wyoming State Law Library.

Anderson, Galusha. *The Story of a Border City During the War*. (Boston, Ma.: Little, Brown and Company, 1908).

Ballou, M. E. *Jackson County, Missouri: Its Opportunities and Resources*. (Kansas City, Mo.: Rural Jackson County Chamber of Commerce, 1926).

Bank Commissioner of the State of Oklahoma. "The Bank of Braggs, Oklahoma" *Annual Report of the Bank Commissioner of the State of Oklahoma*. (Bank Commissioner of the State of Oklahoma,1908), 31.

Bartels, Carolyn M. *Bitter Tears: Missouri Women and Civil War: Their Stories*. "The Strange Romance of Quantrill's Bride." (Harrisonville, Mo.: Burnt District Press, 2002).

Barton, O.S. *Three Years with Quantrill: A True Story Told by His Scout John McCorkle*. (Norman, Ok.: University of Oklahoma Press, 1992).

Blackburn, Bob. L. *Heart of the Promised Land: An Illustrated History of Oklahoma County*. (1982).

KATE IN FACT AND FICTION

Breihan, Carl W. *Quantrill and his Civil War Guerillas.* (New York: Promontory Press, 1959).

Breihan, Carl W. *The Killer Legions of Quantrill.* (Seattle, Wa.: Superior Publishing Company, 1971).

Breihan, Carl W. "Kate King Quantrill." *Real West* (1977): 20: 153: 40-43.

Briggs, Edwin W., ed. *Directory of the Greater Oklahoma Agricultural and Mechanical College, 1926-1927.* Class of 1927. (n.p.: Y.M.C.A. and Y.W.C.A., 1927).

Brink, McDonough and Co. *Illustrated Historical Atlas of Jackson County, Missouri.* Originally published in 1877. Reprinted, with full-name and subject index, David W. Jackson, ed. (Independence, Mo: Jackson County Historical Society, 2008).

Brownlee, Richard S., and Carl W. Breihan. *Quantrill's Guerrillas*, Bushwhacker Museum, Nevada, MO, transcribed by Fred L. Harriman, edited by Patrick Brophy, 1990.

Castanien, Pliny. *To Protect and Serve: A History of the San Diego Police Department and Its Chiefs 1889-1989.* (San Diego, Ca.: San Diego Historical Society, 1993).

Castel, Albert. *William Clarke Quantrill: His Life and Times.* (Norman, Ok.: University of Oklahoma Press, 1962).

Christopher, Adrienne Tinker. "Kate King Clarke: Quantrill's Forgotten Girl Bride," *Westport Historical Quarterly.* (June 1968): 4:2: 21-22.

Connelley, William Elsey. *Quantrill and the Border Wars.* (Cedar Rapids, Ia: Torch Press, 1910).

Corbett, Katherine T. *In Her Place: A Guide to St. Louis Women's History.* (St. Louis, Mo.: Missouri Historical Society Press, 1999).

Cummins, James. *His Story Written by Himself: The Life Story of the James and Younger Gang and their Comrades, Including the Operations of Quantrell's Guerrillas, by One Who Rode With Them: A True but Terrible Tale of Outlawry.* (Denver, Co.: The Reed Publishing Company, 1903).

Dacus, Joseph A., and James W. Buel. *A Tour of St. Louis. Or, The Inside Life of a Great City.* (St. Louis, Mo.: Western Publishing Co., 1878).

Bibliography

Daughters of the American Revolution, Kansas City Chapter. *Vital Historical Records, Jackson County, Missouri, 1826-1876.* Reprinted and expanded with a full name- and subject-index by Suzanne Vinduska and David W. Jackson. (Independence, Mo.: Jackson County Historical Society, 2009).

Ditzel, Paul. *Quantrill:The Civil War's Wildest Killer And Other True Adventure Stories of the Civil War.* (New Albany, In.: FBH Publishers, 1991).

Donnelly, Gassette and Lloyd. *History of Greene County, Illinois.* (Chicago, Il.: Donnelly, Gassette and Lloyd, 1879). 724-725.

Dry, Camille, and Richard J. Compton. *Pictorial History of St. Louis, The Great Metropolis: A Topographical Survey Drawn in Perspective.* (St. Louis, Mo.: Compton & Company, 1875).

Dunaway, Maxine. *Some Early Families of Polk County, Missouri.* (1978).

Eakin, Joanne Chiles. *Recollections of Quantrill's Guerrillas as Told by A. J. Walker of Weatherford, Texas, to Victor Martin in 1910.* [Independence, Mo.: Two Trails Publishing, 1996]. [First printed in the *Daily Herald*, Weatherford, Texas, in 1910.]

Eakin, Joanne Chiles, and Donald R. Hale. *Branded as Rebels, A List of Bushwhackers, Guerrillas, Partisan Rangers, Confederates and Southern Sympathizers from Missouri during the War Years.* Volume 1. (Independence, Mo.: Wee Print, 1993).

Edwards, John N. *Noted Guerillas, or, the Warfare of the Border.* (St. Louis, Mo.: Bryan, Brand and Co.; Becktold and Company Binders, 1877).

Fellman, Michael. *Inside War: The Guerilla Conflict in Missouri During the American Civil War.* (New York: Oxford University Press, 1989).

Fido, Martin. *The Chronicle of Crime: The Infamous Villains of Modern History and Their Hideous Crimes.* (Carlton Books, 1993).

Ford, Anna Scrapbook. "When Quantrill's Mother Came to Blue Springs," *Westport Historical Quarterly.* (June 1968): 4:2: 16-20.

Gallup Map and Supply Co. *Atlas of Jackson County, Missouri.* (Gallup Map and Supply Co., 1931).

Geiger, Mark W. "Indebtedness and the Origins of Guerrilla Violence in Civil War Missouri." *The Journal of Southern History* (February 2009): LXXV: 1.

George, Beauford James. *Biography Of Captain William Henry Gregg, Confederate Officer, Quantrillian Officer, and Good Citizen.* (George, Beauford James, 1976.)

Gerteis, Louis S. *Civil War St. Louis.* (Lawrence, Ks.: University Press of Kansas, 2001).

Gilmore, Donald L. *Civil War on the Missouri-Kansas Border.* (Gretna, La.: Pelican Publishing Co., Inc., 2005).

Goodrich, Thomas. *Black Flag: Guerrilla warfare on the Western Border, 1861-1865.* (Bloomington, In: Indiana University Press, 1995).

Green, Nancy, Chapter, National Society Daughters of the American Revolution. *Creek County Burials.* (Sapulpa, Ok.: Nancy Green Chapter, National Society Daughters of the American Revolution, 1975).

Hale, Donald R., *We Rode with Quantrill: Quantrill and the Guerrilla War as Told by the Men and Women Who Were with Him, with a True Sketch of Quantrill's Life.* (Lee's Summit, Mo.: Donald R. Hale, 1992).

Harris, Charles F. "Catalyst for Terror: The Collapse of the Women's Prison in Kansas City," *Missouri Historical Review* (April 1995), 290-306.

Harris, Charles F. *Alias Charley Hart; William Clarke Quantrill in Lawrence, Kansas 1860.* (Independence, Mo.: Two Trails Publishing, 2001).

Hill, Luther B. *History of the State of Oklahoma.* (Chicago, Il.: Lewis Publishing Co., 1901), 475.

Hoftiezer, Virgil. *Beman/King Genealogy*, May 1997. A draft document generated for the author's first-cousin-once-removed, Mitchell S. "Mitch" Vander Vorst; excerpts of which were posted on various websites without author's prior knowledge. Much data has since been modified and corrected.

Hollon, Eugene. "Rushing for Land, Oklahoma, 1889." *The American West Magazine* (Fall 1966).

Holmes, Helen F., ed. *Logan County History, 1889-1977: Logan County, Oklahoma*, Volume 1: The Families. Cyrenus Castanien Family. (Guthrie,

Bibliography

Okla.: History Committee, Logan County Extension Homemakers Council, 1980).

Hubbard, James W. *History of Sapulpa.* Volume 1. (Sapulpa, Ok.: Sapulpa Historical Museum, 1981), 38-39.

Hyde, William, and Howard L. Conrad, eds. *Encyclopedia of the History of St. Louis.* Vols. I and II. (St. Louis, Mo.: The Southern History Company, 1899).

Jackson County Court. *Results of County Planning: Jackson County, Missouri.* (Kansas City, Mo.: Holland Engraving Company, 1933).

Jackson, David W. "Jackson County's Poor Farm Transformed into a Rich Healthcare Center." *Jackson County Historical Society Journal* (Spring 2004): 45: 1: 8-13.

Kansas State Historical Society. "Secretary's Annual Report." *Transactions of the Kansas State Historical Society* (1904): 8:124.

Leonard, John W. *Book of St. Louisans.* Biography of James Robert Claiborne. (St. Louis, Mo.: The St. Louis Republic, 1912).

Leslie, Edward E. "Quantrill's Bones," *American Heritage* (July-August 1995) as viewed online at http://wesclark.com/jw/quantril.html.

Leslie, Edward E. *The Devil Knows How to Ride.* (New York: Random House, 1996).

Levine, Philippa and Susan R. Grayzel, eds. "Race and the Regulation of Prostitution: Comparing Public Health in the U.S. and Greater Britain." Chapter 4. *Gender, Labour, War and Empire: Essays on Modern Britain.* (London: Palgrave Macmillan, 2009), 51-71.

Lindenbusch, John. "The Social Evil Ordinance: Legalized Vice (and Vice Versa)." *St. Louis* (June 1980): 12, 18-19.

Livingston, Joel Thomas. *History of Jasper County, Missouri, and Its People.* Biography of David D. Wood. (Chicago, Il.: Lewis Publishing Co., 1888).

Lutz, J. J. "Quantrell, the Guerilla Chief." *Midland Monthly Magazine.* (Jan.-Jun 1897): 7:509-520.

Monaco, Ralph A., II. *Scattered to the Four Winds: General Order No. 11 and Martial Law in Jackson County, Missouri, 1863.* (Independence, Mo.: Jackson County Historical Society, 2013), 194-200.

Monaghan, Jay. *Civil War on the Western Border 1854-1865*, (Boston, Ma.: Little, Brown and Co., 1955).

Montana, Sybil. *Quantrill's Scattered Bones Buried at Las*t. Revised, 1998. (Ozark, Mo: Sybil Montana, aka. DeKelley, 1994.

Morris, John, Charles Robert Goins, and Edwin C. McReynolds. *Historical Atlas of Oklahoma.* (University of Oklahoma Press, 1987).

Myers, Barton A. "Dissecting the Torture of Mrs. Owens: The Story of a Civil War Atrocity." *Weirding The War.* (Athens, Ga.: University of Georgia Press, 2011), 141-159.

Newsom, D. Earl. *The Cherokee Strip: Its History and Grand Opening.* (New Forums Press, 1992).

Oaks, Liz. "The Race to the Promised Land." *Kansas Heritage* (1993).

Payne, William Howard, ed. *Directory of the Oklahoma Agricultural and Mechanical College, 1929-30.* (n.p.: Y.M.C.A. and Y.W.C.A. and A. and M. Printing Department,1930), 27.

Petersen, Paul R. *Quantrill in Missouri: The Making of a Guerilla Warrior.* (Nashville, Tn.: Cumberland House, 2003).

Petersen, Paul R. *Quantrill in Texas: The Forgotten Campaign.* (Nashville, Tn.: Cumberland House, 2007).

Petersen, Paul R. *Quantrill at Lawrence: The Untold Story.* (Gretna, La.: Pelican Publishing Co., 2011).

Petersen, Paul R. and David W. Jackson. *Lost Souls of the Lost Township: Untold Life Stories of the People Buried in the Davis-Smith Cemetery, Kansas City, Jackson County, Missouri.* (Kansas City, Mo.: The Orderly Pack Rat, 2011).

Piercet, Barbara, and Brian Basore. *Oklahoma Cemeteries: A Bibliography of the Collections in the Oklahoma Historical Society.* (Oklahoma City, Ok.: Oklahoma Historical Society, 1993.)

Post, Truman A., Reporter. "State of Missouri, Respondent, vs Kate Clarke, Appellant." *Reports of Cases Argued and Determined in the Supreme Court of the State of Missouri.* (1874): LIV: 17-45. [The Judges: David Wagner, Wash Adams, H.M. Vories, T.A. Sherwood and W.B Napton.]

Quaife, M. M. *Absalom Grimes: Confederate Mail Runner, Edited from Captain Grimes' Own Story.* (New Haven: Yale University Press, 1926).

Romeo, Sharon. "The Sporting Woman: Vagrancy and Women's Rights in Reconstruction-Era St. Louis." *Gateway Heritage* (Fall 2004): 25: 2.

Sapulpa Daily Herald. *Sapulpa Centennial, 1898-1998.* (Sapulpa, Ok.: Sapulpa Daily Herald, 1998).

Scharf, J. Thomas. *A History of St. Louis City and County, From the Earliest Periods to the Present Day: including Biographical Sketches of Representative Men."* Volume II. "Southern Hotel." (Philadelphia, Pa.: L. H. Everts & Co., 1883), as found online at stlouis.genealogyvillage.com/hotels.htm

Schultz, Duane. *Quantrill's War: The Life and Times of William Clarke Quantrill: 1837-1865.* (New York: St. Martin's Press, 1996).

Sharp, Robert and Nadine. *Highlights of Blue Springs, Missouri.* (Little Blue Press, 1971).

Shepley, Carol Ferring. *Movers and Shakers, Scalawags and Suffragettes: Tales from Bellefontaine Cemetery.* (St. Louis, Mo.: Missouri History Museum, 2008), 153-155.

Sifakis, Stewart. *Who's Who in the Civil War.* (Facts on File, 1988).

Simmons, Henry E. *A Concise Encyclopedia of the Civil War.* (New York:: Fairfax Press, 1986).

Sneddeker, Duane R. "Regulating Vice: Prostitution and the St. Louis Social Evil Ordinance, 1870-1874." *Gateway Heritage* (Fall 1990): 11:2.

Stiles, T. J. *Jesse James: Last Rebel of the Civil War.* (New York: Alfred A. Knoff, 2002).

Tremeear, Janice. *Wicked St. Louis.* (Charleston, Sc.: The History Press, 2011).

Trow, Harrison. *Charles W. Quantrell: A True History of His Guerrilla warfare on the Missouri and Kansas Border During the Civil War of 1861 to 1865, as told by Captain Harrison Trow.* (Vega, Tx.: J. P. Burch, 1923).

Whites, LeeAnn. *Gender Matters: Civil War, Reconstruction, and the Making of the New South.* (New York: Palgrave Macmillan, 2005).

Whites, LeeAnn. "The Tale of Three Kates: Outlaw Women, Loyalty, and Missouri's Long Civil War." *Weirding the War,* Stephen Berry, ed. (Athens, Ga.: University of Georgia Press, 2011), 73-94. [Article is the outgrowth of Whites' lecture, "The Tale of Three Kates: Prostitution, Loyalty and Missouri's Long Guerilla War," presented multiple times and locations, 2007-2011.]

Winter, William C. *The Civil War in St. Louis: A Guided Tour.* (St. Louis, Mo.: Missouri Historical Society Press, 1994).

Wunsch, James. "The Social Evil Ordinance." *American Heritage Magazine.* (February/March 1982): 33: 2.

Yeatman, Ted P. *Frank and Jesse James: The Story Behind the Legend.* (Nashville, Tn.: Cumberland House, 2000).

Newspapers

Akron Beacon Journal, Akron, OH

O'Connor, Bill. "A burial of shame? The skull of Quantrill of the Civil War raider is interred in Dover, but the jury's still out on whether the man who terrorized Kansas was a hero or a scoundrel," 22 Nov. 1992, B1, 2.

Blue Springs Leader, Blue Springs, MO

"The Q-Men of Jackson County: The Men who Fought With Quantrill Often Met in a Reunion," 8 Oct. 1959, p. 7. [This article, found at the Blue Springs Historical Society, lists the names of the people who met with Mrs. Quantrill at the City Hotel in Blue Springs, Missouri, on 11 May 1888.]

Braggs Bugle, Braggs, OK

"Hotel Changes Hands," 20 Feb 1913.

"Personal and Local," 27 Feb. 1913.

"Braggs Briefly Reviewed," 6 Mar. 1913.

Bibliography

***Buffalo Daily Courier*, Buffalo, NY**

>"The Social Evil: An Elaborate Opinion Against the St. Louis Licensing System." Syndicated from a St. Louis newspaper, 23 Aug. 1873.

***Chicago Daily Tribune*, Chicago, IL**

>"Social Evil Ordinance Declared Invalid," 24 Aug. 1873, p. 2

***Daily Missouri Republican*, St. Louis, MO (see also *Missouri Republican* and *St. Louis Republican*)**

>"List of Letters Uncalled for in the Post Office at St. Louis, Missouri on Saturday, August 15 1863; Ladies List," 15 Aug. 1863, p. 1. [Kate Clark]

***Daily Ohio State Journal*, Columbus, OH**

>"St. Louis Social Evil Law to be Tested," 6 Aug. 1873.

***Deseret News*, Salt Lake City, UT**

>"St. Louis, 17—," 20 Aug. 1873.

***Dubuque Herald*, Dubuque, IA**

>"Deaths—The Bawdy House Case," 24 Aug. 1873, p. 1, c. 4.

***Emporia Gazette*, Emporia, KS**

>"He Had a History: The Man Who Killed Quantrill, the Guerilla, Died Peacefully in Missouri." 30 April 1910.

***Hutchison Kansas News*, Hutchinson, KS**

>"Deaths. Pliny Mannon Castanien," 14 Nov. 1938, p. 6.

>"Funerals. Pliny M. Castanien," 15 Nov. 19938, p. 10.

***Hutchinson News Herald*, Hutchinson, KS**

>"Widow of Noted Guerilla Dead," 5 Feb. 1930.

>[Untited], 24 Oct. 1937, p. 19.

KATE IN FACT AND FICTION

***Independence Examiner*, Independence, MO**

"Samuel R. King Dead," *20* June 1921.

"Legal Notice. List of Names of the Inmates of the Jackson County Home," 12 Aug. 1929.

[50th Golden Anniversary edition], 18 May 1948.

Moore, Edward D. "Family Lives in Home Once Quantrill's Sweetheart's." 31 Mar. 1962. [This article, including an image of the King home and barn, prompted the letter from Fred A. Ford to Mr. and Mrs. Floyd (Josie) Potts.]

Werts, Marcia. "Tidy Cemetery Becomes a Labor of Love," 29 May 1982. [This article, written after Arthur Dealy's death, mentioned that "Dealy maintained that Kate Quantrill, wife of William Quantrill, lies alongside her parents, Robert and Malinda King, who are buried there."]

***Indianapolis Sun*, Indianapolis, IN**

"Quantrill's Hard Heart Melted When He Thought of Mother: Sent Money to Her as Long as he Lived: She Enters Odd Fellows Home," 13 Dec. 1900.

***Iola Register*, Iola, KS**

[Quantrill's Mother Visits Blue Springs], 18 May 1888.

***Jackson Examiner*, Independence, MO**

"W. J. King Dead," 4 Apr. 1919.

***Kansas City Star,* Kansas City, MO**

"Giant of the Guerrillas," 11 Oct. 1903, p. 17.

"Ragland," 15 May 1918.

"Quantrill's Ride to Doom: Last Comrade [Allen Palmer] to See Him Alive Tells Story," *Kansas City* (Mo.) *Star*, 15 Sept. 1918.

Love, Robertus. "The Rise and Fall of Jesse James," 19 July 1925. Love was a member of the St. Louis Post-Dispatch editorial staff.

"The Strange Romance of Quantrill's Bride: Kate King, Ending Her Days in an Alms House, Recalls Her Life with the Famous Guerilla Leader," 23 May 1926. [Transcribed as an Appendix in this work.]

"Still No Funds for Burial: No Action by Relatives of Mrs. Sarah Head, Quantrill's Bride," 5 Feb. 1930.

"Quantrill's Bride is Buried: Only a Few Friends at Grave of Mrs. Sarah Head," 6 Feb. 1930.

Wellman, Paul I. "She remembers when Quantrill's Mother Came to Blue Springs," 30 Aug. 1942.

Hale, Donald R. "Historic Blue Springs Cemetery Restored," 18 May 1968.

Sykes, Velma West, "Violence Stirs Kansans' Memories," 19 May 1970.

Schofield, Matthew, "Obscure Cemetery Reminder of Jackson County Poor Farm," 13 June 1984.

Kansas City Times, Kansas City, MO

"A Visit To The Poor Farm: How Jackson County Cares For Her Helpless Wards," 29 July 1890.

"Quantrill's Bride Dead. End in Poorhouse here to widow of Famous Guerrilla," 5 and 7 Feb. 1930.

Hale, Donald R., "After Six Decades, a Claimant to Role of Quantrill's 13-Year-Old Bride," 6 Apr. 1963, p. 42.

Olwine, Margaret. "True Story of Quantrill's Raiders Is Too Close to Home to be Revealed," 26 Oct. 1967.

Lawrence Gazette, Lawrence, KS

Scott, William W. "W. C. Quantrill: The Name Recalls a Bloody History," 30 Aug. 1888, p. 4. [Also published in the *Atchinson* (Ks.) *Daily Globe*; Burlington Hawkeye; *Cedar Rapids* (Ia.) *Evening Gazette*; *LeMars Sentinel* (Lemars, Ia., on 7 Sept.); *Fort Wayne* (In.) *Gazette; Hamilton* (Oh.) *Daily Democrat; New Albany* (In.) *Ledger; New Philadelphia Ohio Democrat* (New Philadelphia, Oh.) newspapers, on or near the same day.]

***Leavenworth Weekly Times*, Leavenworth, KS**

"St. Louis, August 16—," 21 Aug. 1873, p. 4, c. 4.

***Ligonier Leader*, Ligonier, IN**

"Stories of Quantrill," 11 Dec. 1890.

***Memphis Daily Appeal*, Memphis, TN**

"St. Louis Social Evil Law to be Tested," 6 Aug.1873, p. 1.
"Important Decision," 24 Aug. 1873.

***Missouri Republican*, St. Louis, MO (see also *Daily Missouri Republican* and *St. Louis Republican*)**

"List of Letters Remaining Unclaimed in the Post Office at St. Louis, State of Missouri, July 10, 1869; Ladies and Gentleman's List," 17 July 1869, p. 4. [Miss Kate Clark]

***The Nevada Daily Mail*, Nevada, MO**

"Missouri and Missourians," 17 Nov. 1893, p. 2.

"She Shot at Her Husband," 26 June 1894, p. 2.

***New York Times*, New York, NY [via. online database]**

"The Social-Evil Law in St. Louis," 16 Feb.1873.

"The Social Evil in St. Louis: Opinion of Judge Calvin on the Constitutionality of the Ordinance," 24 Aug.1873. [Judge Colvin's name is misspelled in this article.]

"The 'Social Evil' Law in St. Louis," 2 Dec. 1873. [Judge Colvin's name is spelled correctly here.]

***Press Spectator*, Salisbury, Chariton County, MO**

"Gone to Rest." 13 Aug. 1897.

[Untitled], 13 May 1902.

"A Sad Incident," 16 May 1902.

[Untitled], 23 May 1902.

Bibliography

St. Louis Daily Globe, St. Louis, MO

"Court of Criminal Correction," 3 Jan. 1874. [Kate Clark and Lizzie Saville; keeping bawdy houses; dismissed at prosecutor's costs.]

"The Word 'Regulate,'" 18 Feb. 1874.

"Social Investigation: A Friendly Visit from the Sages of Jefferson: They Would See for Themselves the Advantages of the Social Evil Law: A Tour by Gas Light," 22 Feb. 1874. [Transcribed as an Appendix in this work.]

"The Great Disgrace: Some of the Glaring Iniquities of the Social Evil Law," 24 Feb. 1874.

"The Social Evil Investigators Full of Wisdom and Experience," 24 Feb. 1874.

St. Louis Democrat, St. Louis, MO

"The Constitutionality of the Law to be Tested: Kate Clark and Lizzie Saville brought before the Court of Criminal Correction," 6 Aug. 1873.

"The Social Evil War: Kate Clark's Landlord Brought Before the Court of Criminal Correction," 9 Aug. 1873.

"Kate Clark's Landlord: The Dameron Case In The Criminal Court: An attempt to Throw the Responsibility on Others: Interviews with Mr. Dameron, Kate Clark and Trustees of St. Luke's Hospital," 10 Aug. 1873.

"Public Opinion: The Social Evil:To the Editor of the Democrat," 10 Aug. 1873.

"The Landlady's Landlord. A Card from the Officers of the Board of Trustees of St. Luke's Hospital," 13 Aug. 1873.

"Kate Clark's Case: Testing the Validity of the Social Evil Law: The Evidence and Arguments: Judge Colvin Takes the Case Under Advisement," 17 Aug. 1873. [Transcribed as an appendix in this biography.]

KATE IN FACT AND FICTION

[Untitled, beginning with, "The testimony in regard to the houses of prostitution....,"] 19 Aug. 1873.

[For a 23 Aug. 1873 St. Louis article syndicated article about, "The Social Evil: An Elaborate Opinion Against the St. Louis Licensing System," see the *Buffalo Daily Courier*.]

"Court of Criminal Corrections," 24 Aug. 1873. [Kate Clark, keeping a common bawdy house; defendant found guilty, and fined $10.]

"Social Evil. Judge Colvin's Decision in the Case of Kate Clark and Lizzie Saville. Do We live under a Christian Dispensation: What "Lex" Thinks about It—Interviews with Kate Clark and Lizzie Saville," 24 Aug.1873.

"St. Luke's Hospital Matter. The Landlady's Landlord—Card from Logan D. Dameron," 29 Aug. 1873.

"The 'Social Evil' War," 6 Sept. 1873.

"The Social Evil War," 7 Sept. 1873.

"A Social Evil Fiend," 9 Sept. 1873.

"Board of Health: Mayor Brown Starts Out on a New Idea [includes The Social Evil Hospital]," 12 Sept. 1873.

"Local Short Stops [includes 'social evil collections]," 22 Oct. 1873.

"The Courts: Abstract of Yesterday's Proceedings," 5 Nov. 1873.

"The Social Evil Law Valid," 1 Dec. 1873.

"The Social Evil Law: The Supreme Court Declares the City Ordinance Valid," 2 Dec. 1873.

"The Courts," 16 Dec. 1873.

"Social Evil: Mayor Brown Visited by Prominent Ladies," 18 Dec. 1873.

[Mardi Gras ball in St. Louis; lists prominent citizens and names of "ladies of the evening" in attendance], 18 Feb. 1874.

[Interviews with St. Louis madams], 21 Feb. 1874.

Bibliography

St. Louis Dispatch, St. Louis, MO

"They Have Rights. Which Even Sergeants are Bound to Respect," 8 Sept. 1874.

"Under The Hammer. A Bagnio Sold Out By a Reforming Courtesan—A Grand Rally of the Toodles Family in Search of Bargains," 4 Feb. 1875.

"An Old Trouble Revived, In Which a Bawdy House Keeper Figures Prominently," 25 Jan. 1877.

St. Louis Post-Dispatch, St. Louis, MO

[Lizzie Saville fined for keeping houses for immoral purposes,] 6 Apr.1880.

"District Police Court," 10 Aug. 1880. [Lizze Saville fined for keeping a bawdy house.]

"Dark Side Of St. Louis. Hot-Beds of Crime in the Very Center of This City. A Reportorial Tour Though the Lowest Dens of Vice and Iniquity—Sad Pictures of the Criminal Poor," 24 Feb. 1882.

"Purifying the City. Keepers of Disreputable Houses Fined in Police Court To-Day," 28 Jun. 1887. [Lizzie Saville fined $50.]

"Logan D. Dameron," 31 May 1891. [Will filed for probate; publisher of St. Louis Christian Advocate.]

St. Louis Republican, St. Louis, MO (see also *Daily Missouri Republican* and *Missouri Republican*)

"In Brief," 4 May 1872. ["Esther Wise, was examined in the court of criminal corrections yesterday on the charge of having stolen a gold locket worth $35 and a gold watch worth $75, belonging to Kate Clark. The defendant was held to answer in the sum of $800."]

"Case of the State vs. KATE CARK [no heading]," 2 Dec. 1873, p. 4, col. 4. [In the case of the State vs. KATE CLARK, the supreme court yesterday decided in favor of the defendant. The case was an indictment under the general statutes for keeping a house of ill-repute, the decision in the court of criminal correction being adverse. The supreme court declares that the city charter of 1870, authorizing the city authorities of St. Louis to "regulate" such houses, being in the nature of a special act, supersedes the general statute which forbids them. Chief-Justice NAPTON and Judges ADAMS and WAGNER concur in this decision. Judges VORIES and SHERWOOD dissenting. Capitalization of names are used throughout this short announcement. A long article comprising of more than a full column about this ruling appears on page 8 in the same edition.)

"SOCIAL EVIL LAW. Dr. Eliot's Test Case Decided. STATE VS. KATE CLARK. Judgment of the Supreme Court. The Law Sustained by Judges Napton, Wagner and Adams. Adverse Opinion by Judges Vories and Sherwood," 2 Dec. 1873, p. 8, cols. 1-2. [This extensive article discusses the intricate legal details and ramifications of this case.]

"Nolle Prosequi," 16 Dec. 1873. ["A nolle prosequi was entered in the court of criminal correction yesterday, in the case against Logan D. Dameron for the renting of the house on the northwest corner of Sixth and Elm Streets to Kate Clark for the purposes of a bawdy house. This action was a consequence of the decision of the Supreme Court affirming the legality of the social evil ordinance."]

"Local Brevities," 1 Jan. 1874. ["The mandate of the Supreme Court, discharging Kate Clark, who had been fined for keeping a bawdy house, was received at the Court of Criminal Correction yesterday."]

"Very Social Evils. Christians on Christy Avenue. RECLAIMING THE LOST LAMBS. What Has and What May Be Done," 4 Feb. 1874, p. 8, cols. 1-2. [This long article about a revival meeting held yesterday at Madam Stillman's house by Rev. Hammond, included visits by the reporter to Madam Stillman's *maison de plaisir*, Mrs. Niederowters' place, and Mistress Kate Clarke's "distinguished S.E.", with an interview with a well-dressed, well-spoken Kate Clarke, whose timely arrival saved her "faithful attendant" "tyler" from crucification on the hat-rack by "the REPUBLICAN man".]

"Local Brevities," 1 Apr. 1874. ["Kate Clark yesterday procured the arrest of Fred Uschal, alias Schumacher, on the charge of malicious trespass, the specific act complained of, being the breaking in of her window with an axe. The accused was admitted to bail in the sum of $400."]

"Criminal Notes," 12 Sept. 1874. ["Leon Baldwin was committed to jail yesterday on a charge of grand larceny preferred by Kate Clark, who alleges that on August 15 he stole from her three pictures of the value of $21."]

"Queer," 11 Jan. 1875. ["On Saturday afternoon a negro went to a drug store at the corner of Sixth and Market Streets, and offered a ten-dollar counterfeit bill in payment for a few medicines. When told that the bill was counterfeit he said he had been sent for the goods by Kate Clark, who gave him the bill to pay for them. He then took the money and started, as he said, the exchange it for something that would pass. Shortly afterwards a small boy appeared at the same store with a written order for a list of goods, which he said had been given him by a man at the Southern Hotel. After the goods had been put up for him he presented in payment the same counterfeit bill which had been previously offered by the negro. The proprietor told the clerk to keep the bill and went out for an officer, but when he returned the clerk had allowed the boy to get away with the counterfeit."]

"Local Brevities," 1 May 1876. ["Kate Clark, residing at 308 South Eighth Street, appeared at the City Dispensary last evening with a split lip and some teeth knocked out. She told Dr. Robinson that her father did it with a hatchet."]

"Court Notes, 18 Nov. 1876. ["Hansen vs. Turner, et al., motion for a new trial by Kate Clark withdrawn."]

San Diego Union, **San Diego, CA**

"Police Beat Reporter Plans Travel," 1 Jan. 1974.

The San Diego Union-Tribune, **San Diego, CA**

Traitel, Dee Annne. "Pliny Raymond 'Cass' Castanien, 85; author and longtime police reporter," Obituaries, 8 Feb. 1994.

Sandusky Daily Register, **Sandusky, OH**

"St. Louis. Test Case," 6 Aug. 1873.

"Pioneer Dies," [obituary of James W. Wakefield], 31 May 1909, p. 7, c. 7.

KATE IN FACT AND FICTION

Sentinel, **Blue Springs, MO**

    "Complete restoration of Slaughter cemetery," 5 Mar. 1970.

Sentinel, **Oak Grove, MO**

    Donald R. Hale series, 1963.

Sni-a-Bar Voice, **Jackson County, MO**

    [Untitled Obituary], 2 May 1916.

Southwest World, **Guthrie, OK**

    "Prolific Oklahomans," 10 Dec. 1902. [Article syndicated from the *Sapulpa Democrat*, Sapulpa, OK.]

Star Gazette, **Sallisaw, OK**

    "Vian Notes (from Sequoyah County Democrat)," 18 March 1910.

    "Vian Notes (from Sequoyah County Democrat)," 24 June 1910.

Town and Country News, **Oak Grove, MO**

    Burke, Charles. *Untitled.* 2 Mar. 1993.

Wichita Eagle, **Wichita, KS**

    "Oil Salesman is Dead at 67," 14 Nov. 1938.

Online Resources

_____, "Braggs, OK Fire, Jul 1911," GenDisasters: Genealogy in Tragedy, Disasters, Fires, Floods. (www3.gendiasters.com/oklahoma/9608/braggs-ok-fire-jul-1911)

_____, "The House of Industry," Women in Health Sciences, Washington University, St. Louis (beckerexhibits.wustl.edu/mowihsp/win/ TimelineSocialEvilHospital.htm)

_____, "William Clarke Quantrill."
    (millersparanormalresearch.com/Pages/Quantrill.htm)

_____, St. Louis~Pages in Time. (members.tripod.com/~Vide_Poche/map.html)

Bibliography

_____, Registry of Births, City of St Louis, p. 209 (ancestry.com)

_____, Social Security Death Index (SSDI) (familysearch.org)

Arenson, Adam, "How St. Louis Was Won." DISUNION Blog on Opinionator-Exclusive Online Commentary from *The New York Times*, May 2011. (opinionator.blogs.nytimes.com/ category/disunion) [Adam Arenson, Assistant Professor of History, University of Texas at El Paso, is author of "The Great Heart of the Republic: St. Louis and the Cultural Civil War."]

Barnes, Harper, "The Madame Years: Our City's Brief Embrace of the "The Social Evil," St. Louis Magazine, February 2009. (stlmag.com/St-Louis-Magazine/February-209/The-Madame-Years/)

Crouch, Barry A., "*A 'Fiend in Human Shape'? William Clarke Quantrill and His Biographers*," Kansas History: A Journal of the Central Plains, published quarterly by Kansas Historical Foundation, summer 1992, p. 142-156. (kshs.org/p/kansas-history-summer-1999/12402) [Barry A. Crouch is professor of history at Gallaudet University, Washington, D.C.]

Eliot, Charlotte C., "William Greenleaf Eliot (1811-1887)." Vol. III. The Preachers. *Heralds of a Liberal Faith*, edited by Samuel A. Eliot, American Unitarian Association, Boston, MA, 1910, p. 90-98. (harvardsquarelibrary.org/Heralds/William-Greenleaf-Eliot.php)

McCoy, Max. "Catholic Cemetery, Louisville." (maxmccoy.blogspot.com/2007/07/st-johns-catholic- cemtery.html)

Missouri Marriage Project. Howard County. http://usgwarchives.net/marriages/missouri/howard.htm.

Missouri Secretary of State. Missouri State Archives. Missouri Death Certificates, 1910-1963. (sos.mo.gov/archives/resources/ deathcertificates/#searchdeat)

Petersen, Paul R. "Solved! The Mystery of Kate King's Two Graves." (quantrillsguerrillas.com/en/articles/108-sloved-the-mystery-of-kate-king-s-two-graves-article.html). [This website is self-proclaimed as the most comprehensive on-line resource related to Quantrill. Many errors regarding Kate King prevail.]

KATE IN FACT AND FICTION

Petersen, Paul R., "The Mysterious Life of Sarah Catherine "Kate" King Quantrill."
(quantrillsguerrillas.com/en/articles/149-the-mysterious-life-of-sarah-catherine-kate-king-quantrill-article.html) [This website is self-proclaimed as the most comprehensive on-line resource related to Quantrill. Many errors regarding Kate King prevail.]

Phillips, Christopher, "Missouri's War Within the War." DISUNION Blog on Opinionator-Exclusive Online Commentary from *The New York Times*, May 2011. (opinionator.blogs.nytimes.com/category/disunion)
[Christopher Phillips, Professor of History, University of Cincinnati, has authored six books on the Civil War, including: *Damned Yankee: The Life of Nathaniel Lyon*; and, *The Rivers Ran Backward: The Civil War on the Middle Border and the Making of American Regionalism*.]

Authors

Virgil D. Hoftiezer, Ph.D., Professor Emeritus of Indiana University School of Medicine (Department of Anatomy and Cell Biology) retired ten years ago after 35 years of teaching, research, service and administration. He is an avid genealogist who continues to research his many elusive relatives, including Sarah Catherine King Quantrill-Evans-Batson-Head, the sister of his great-great-grandfather.

He is a member of Jackson County (Mo.) Historical Society, as well as several county genealogical societies and family associations. Virgil was born and raised in northeastern South Dakota, the crossroads where four sets of great grandparents, including Earl R. Monroe King, from three different states, intersected long enough for their descendants to establish roots and families of their own.

Virgil and Jan, his wife of fifty years, have four children, all born in Minnesota but now living in four different states, and five grandchildren. They have fulfilled one of their many travel goals and have visited all seven continents. Virgil now lives at Kendal at Granville, Ohio—the furthermost terminus of a gradual eastern trek—the exact opposite of an innate desire to go west.

Vicki P. Beck is an avid newspaper collector who, with the help of late friend and Civil War enthusiast and Quantrill expert, Donald R. Hale, rescued and retrieved numerous old, out-of-print newspapers for the State Historical Society of Missouri (Columbia, Mo.) for their Missouri newspaper microfilm collection. She has conducted extensive cemetery research and been involved with local cemetery preservation efforts.

Vicki worked for the *Blue Springs* and *Independence Examiner* newspapers for 17 years. While employed there, she researched historical text and compiled two local history books: *A Pictorial History of Blue Springs, Missouri;* and, *Historic Images of Fort Osage Township.* She also assisted on the publication, "Examiner 100th Birthday: Queen City of the Trails." She retrieved hundreds of photographs and documents for various historical societies. Vicki is past editor of, "The No Quarterly," for the William Clarke Quantrill Society, of which she is a charter member. She also edited, "The Western Campaigner," for the Missouri Civil War Re-enactors Association.

Vicki is also a charter member of the Civil War Round Table of Western Missouri, and a member of Jackson County (Mo.) Historical Society. She was born and raised in Jackson County, Missouri, in the vicinity of the King family farm…where she still resides.

INDEX

Married women are indexed under their married name, with maiden name (in parenthesis). In cases of multiple marriages, their last known surname is used. The only exception is for Kate, who is listed under various identities, most which are also consolidated and subcategorized under "King, Kate."

Allen, Lee N. 182
Alton, Il. 20
Anderson, "Bloody" Bill ....
.... 20, 95, 96, 297
Anderson, Galusha 27
Andrews, Ben ....
 See Pliny Raymond "Cas" Castanien
Arcadia, Ne. 65
Arrington, Lottie 261, 266
Arthur, Chester A. (U.S. President)....................... 25
Auburn, Placer County, Ca.
 .... 22, 45, 60, 206, 209
Baird Manufacturing Company...... 161, 164, 165
Banner Electric Company 159
Barren County, Ky. 56
Barrett, Felicia 13
Bartels, Carolyn.................. 74
Batson, Sarah C. ..... 1, 2, 3, 5, 15, 27, 28, 29, 30, 35, 37, 38, 61, 80, 154, 157, 159, 166, 176, 177, 178, 179, 183, 197, 208, 211, 238, 239, 259, 263, See Kate King
Baxter Springs, Ks. ... 19, 109, 110, 221, 284, 310
Beck, Vicki P. 3, 13, 172, 238, 279, 297
Bingham, George Caleb.... 83, 87, 88

Blair, Frank 75
Blue Springs, Jackson County, Mo.. 19, 24, 26, 29, 46, 51, 52, 53, 54, 57, 61, 62, 64, 84, 90, 101, 116, 173, 177, 189, 200, 205, 206, 211, 219, 230, 243, 270, 271, 279, 280, 282, 284, 287, 288, 289, 290, 291, 295, 297, 299, 301, 302, 304, 307
Blunt, James G. (U.S. General) 19, 213, 216
Bolger, John 260, 265
Bolger, Margaritam........... 265
Bolger, Martin 265
Bolger, Peter 260, 265
Boman, David Cortland 294
Boman, Halys (Morris) 295
Boman, James M. 294
Boman, Joan Ruth 294
Boman, Mayme Edith (Toomay)...................... 294
Boman, Pearl Mae 294
Boman, Willa Belle 294
Boman, William N.... 293, 294, 299
Boonesboro, Mo. ....
 See Howard County, Mo.
Boonesville, Mo. 24
Border War .... See Civil War
Botetourt County, Va. 49
Bowman, Elizabeth Webb .. 77

Bowman, Hiram (Reverend) 36, 77
Bowman, Isabell N. (Hoblet) 77
Boyle County, Ky. 63
Braggs, Ok...27, 28, 157, 159, 160, 166, 232, 234
Brett, Florence (Davenport) 64
Brown, Egbert B. (General) 94
Buchanan County, Mo. 108, 205
Buchanan, James (U.S. President) 16
Buckner, Mo. 51, 182, 240, 241, 279
Burrus, Dora (Ragland) 58, 59, 259, 264
Burrus, Shad' William Louthan 59
Burrus, William 58
Bushwhackers .74, 79, 84, 87, 272
Camp Jackson, St. Louis, Mo. 17, 119, 221
Carpenter, Mary Ella (Waldo) 260, 265
Carr, William Henry 182
Carrigg, Ellen (Bolger) 260, 265
Carroll County, Mo. 294
Casey County, Ky. 42, 201, 202, 203
Cass County, Mo. 53, 310
Castanien, Alexander 152
Castanien, Barbara Ruth (Anderson) 170, 172
Castanien, Bertha E. (Evans) 5, 24, 25, 26, 27, 28, 29, 35, 36, 70, 145, 147, 148, 149, 150, 151, 152, 154, 155, 157, 159, 160, 161, 162, 163, 164, 165, 166, 173, 175, 176, 185, 230, 231, 232, 233, 235, 236, 238
Castanien, Cyrenus .. 152, 154
Castanien, Imogene L. (Jones) 162, 165, 168, 169, 170, 172
Castanien, Janice L. 169
Castanien, Marley Pliny Mannon...27, 152, 155, 157
Castanien, Pliny Mannon ... 26, 29, 151, 154, 155, 159, 161, 163, 164, 166, 176, 231, 235, 237
Castanien, Pliny Raymond "Cas" 11, 27, 154, 159, 164, 166, 167, 168, 169, 171, 172, 173, 230, 231
Cedar County, Mo. 68
Centralia, Mo. (Civil War massacre) 20
Centropolis, Jackson County, Mo. 51
Chariton County, Mo. 107, 108, 113, 115, 116
Cherokee County, Ks. 109, 110, 111, 221, 310
Chiles, Jim "Crow" 93
Chism, Alexander 43
Chism, Eliza 30, 43, 194, 203, 245
Chism, Gabriel 43
Chism, Nancy (King) 25, 43, 194, 203
Chism, William 43
Cholera 21, 225
Christopher, Adrienne T. 74
Churchill, Winston 26
Civil War..... 2, 11, 12, 15, 17, 25, 26, 27, 45, 46, 49, 57, 74, 75, 85, 88, 92, 109, 178, 180, 199, 201, 208, 212, 213, 214, 215, 220, 221, 226, 230, 232, 234, 237, 245, 269, 270, 281, 283, 284, 287, 297, 301, 334

Index

Claiborne, James Robert .. 16, 21, 24, 35, 36, 37, 80, 130, 144, 145, 227, 228, 246, 254, 276
Clarke, Kate .... See Kate King
Clarke, William (Captain) ....
See William Clarke Quantrill
Clayton, Cynthia Anna 152, 154
Clements, John W. 30, 179
Cleveland, Grover (U.S. President) 25, 26
Colvin (Judge) . 130, 228, 253, 254
Confederate boat burners . *19, 20*, 21, 92, 120, See Louden, Robert
Confederate spy *18, 19*
Confederate underground . 10, 92, 120, 145, 224
Connelley, William E. ... 27, 36, 74, 78, 106, 107, 108, 109, 110, 111, 200, 212, 213, 215, 216, 217, 220, 221, 270, 282, 283, 293, 295
Coolidge, Calvin (U.S. President) 30
Cooper County, Mo. 24, 37
Cooper, Olivia D. 97, 100, 101, 216
Copeland, Levi 82
Corby, George 114
Corby, Mary Jane 114
Cowley County, Ks. 155
Creek County, Ok.. 27, 28, 29, 61, 69, 155, 159, 160, 161, 166, 176, 234, 235, 304
~~Cromwell, Nellie M. (King) ... 67~~
~~Cromwell, Walter Leo, Sr. ... 67~~
Cumberland Presbyterian Church 62
Cummins, 'Gertie' Mary Gertrude (Snodgrass) 54
Cummins, Jesse Lewis 54
Cummins, 'Nan' Nannie/Nancy Evelyn

(King) Young ... 51, 54, 260, 264
Dameron, Logan D. ... 24, 127, 128, 129, 140, 141, 143, 227, 229
Daniel, Miranda E. (Warren) 260, 265
Davenport, Mary Ann (Aldon/Alder) 63
Davenport, Samuel 63
Davidson, Elizabeth L. (Davenport) King24, 46, 63, 66, 264
Davidson, Frank 65
Daviess County, Ky. 183
Davis, Jefferson (Confederate President) 17
Davis, Leonard F. 280, 293, 295, 305
Dealy, Arthur D.. 31, 189, 190, 244
Dillingham farm (Blue Springs, Mo.) 90
Donaldson, Lillie 261, 266
Dooley, John 265
Dooley, Kate 260, 265
Dooley, Rose 265
Dooley, Sarah Ann (Lynch) Bolger 194, 265
Douglas, Stephen A. 16
Douthit, Roger 194
Dover, Oh. 25, 31, 97, 220
Eads, James B. 17, 222
Eakin, Joanne Chiles 108, 110, 209, 220, 238, 297, 298
Edwards, John Newman ... 23, 24
Eliot, William Greenleaf (Reverend) 10, 23, 128, 129, 130, 131, 140, 144, 226, 227, 254
Encino, Ca. 59
Eskildsen, Paul R. 169
Evans, Bertha E. .. See Bertha E. (Evans) Castanien

351

Evans, Martin 36, 149, 152
Evans, Robert 36, 149, 152, 153
Ewing, Thomas, Jr. (Brigadier General) 82, 86, 88, 94, 250, 251
Ford, 'Ella' Cinderella Belle (Hudspeth) 296
Ford, Alvina Thomas (Cancellor) 296
Ford, Betty Sue 296
Ford, Edmund Dorrel 296
Ford, Fred A. 5, 19, 31, 69, 71, 79, 102, 110, 176, 177, 189, 190, 200, 211, 213, 220, 238, 244, 279, 281, 284, 286, 287, 288, 289, 291, 292, 293, 294, 296, 297, 300, 301, 303, 305, 308
Ford, Fred Allen, Jr. 296
Ford, John Calvin 296
Ford, Pearl Hazel (Griswold) 296
Ford, Rhea Jean 296
Ford, Robert Pearl 296
Ford, William Highbridge .. 297
Fort Leavenworth, Ks 169
Fuson, Lethie 261, 266
Gamble, Hamilton R. 17, *19*
Garfield, James (U.S. President) 25
Geiger, Mark W 41
George, Gabriel William 77
Georgetown, Tx. .... *See* Sherman, Texas
Glasgow, Howard County, Mo 20, 95, 102, 124
Grain Valley Baptist Church 51
Grain Valley, Mo. ... 51, 55, 77, 109, 238
Grant, Ulysses S. (U.S. General) 21
Gratiot Street Prison 17, 24, 138, 224

Grayson County, Tx. 92, 93, 214
Greene County, Il ... 24, 25, 42, 43, 48, 49, 51, 201, 202, 203, 204
Greenlawn Cemetery (Jackson County, Mo.) ... 67
Gregg, Sarah Jane (Lynch) 265
Gregg, William H 274
Grimes, Absalom ... *19, 21, 28*, 30
Griswold, Fred A. 296, 306
Griswold, Pearl 306
Griswold, Susie (Hupp) 296
Guerrilla warfare 9, 12, 17, 18, 19, 20, 21, 23, 27, 41, 73, 74, 75, 77, 81, 82, 83, 84, 85, 86, 87, 89, 90, 91, 92, 93, 94, 95, 100, 110, 200, 204, 207, 208, 215, 220, 224, 247, 249, 269, 270, 272, 273, 274, 275, 277, 295, 308, 310
Guthrie, Ok. 155, 157, 232
Hale, Donald R. "Don" ... 3, 12, 31, 71, 73, 108, 110, 190, 194, 197, 219, 220, 231, 243, 244, 245, 279, 282, 285, 287, 288, 293, 297, 305, 307
Hall, Herbert Lee 116
Hall, Viola Pearl (Lane) 113, 116
Halleck, Henry W. (Major General) 82, 247
Hammons, Hattie Elizabeth (McCart) Smith 115
Hammons, Jeff 115
Hannahs, H. 251
Harding, Warren G. (U.S. President) 29
Harlan, Andrew Oliver 114
Harlan, David M. 114
Harrah, Ok. .26, 148, 230, 232
Harris, James 'William' 109

Index

Harris, Nannie (Henry) 109
Harrison, Edward 68
Harrison, Opal E. Dora
 (Webb) Turvey King 68
Harrisonville, Mo. 31, 251
Hayes, Rutherford B. (U. S.
 President) 24
Head, Eliza Jane Beall 183
Head, Joseph Franklin 183
Head, Sarah .... See Kate King
Head, Walter ... 30, 31, 35, 37,
 183, 184, 187, 240, 241,
 242, 297
Henderson, J. T 57
Hickman's Mills, Mo. 251
Hill, Alta Gregg 265
Hill, R. (Reverend) 63
Hill, Schuyler G. 260, 265
Hoftiezer, Jan 13
Hoftiezer, Virgil D., Ph.D. 1, 2,
 3, 12, 13, 31, 172, 193,
 194, 199, 229, 230, 236,
 279, 297
Hoover, Herbert (U.S.
 President) 30
Hostetter, James W. 182, 186,
 187, 212, 241
Howard County, Mo. ... 19, 20,
 87, 95, 102, 124, 199, 200,
 214, 215, 275
Hoy, Perry 82
Hudspeth, "Babe" William
 Napoleon... 26, 57, 58, 211,
 238, 239, 240, 282, 283,
 286, 293, 294, 298, 304,
 305
Hudspeth, 'Annie'
 Georgeanna (Ragland) . 26,
 30, 57, 58, 259, 264, 293,
 294, 304, 305
Hudspeth, Amanda (Beall) .....
 298
Hudspeth, Joseph William
 .... 294, 298
Hudspeth, Robert Napoleon
 .... 293, 298
Hudspeth, Samuel Mumford
 .... 294, 296
Hudspeth, Sarah Elizabeth
 296
Huntington, Thomas. 127, 229
Hupp, Eliza (Dorman) 306
Hupp, Miner 306
Hutchings, Dora M. 299
Hutchings, James E. 299
Hutchings, Lola Maude 299
Hutchings, Lucy A. 299
Hutchings, Mary Ann
 (Hackett) 299
Hutchings, Porter 293, 298
Hutchings, Sarilda (Cummins)
 299
Hutchings, Thomas C 298
Hutchings, Thomas W 299
Hutchings, Walter Lee 299
Independence, Mo. 18, 20,
 29, 30, 46, 51, 53, 54, 55,
 56, 57, 58, 59, 63, 65, 66,
 67, 96, 179, 183, 205, 208,
 209, 210, 211, 215, 218,
 219, 239, 240, 241, 243,
 245, 251, 259, 271, 279,
 283, 285, 302, 305, 307
Independence, Mo. (First Civil
 War battle) *18*
Iske, Lavina (Lynch) . 259, 263
Jackson County Court 181
Jackson County Home for the
 Aged and Infirm 11, 29,
 30, 37, 71, 162, 163, 180,
 181, 182, 183, 184, 185,
 187, 188, 189, 190, 239,
 241, 242, 269, 297
Jackson County Legislature
 181
Jackson County Poor Farm
 See Jackson County Home
 for the Aged and Infirm
Jackson County, Missouri ......
 2, 7, 11, 12, 15, 16, 19, 24,
 25, 26, 27, 28, 29, 30, 33,
 36, 45, 46, 49, 51, 52, 53,

54, 55, 56, 57, 58, 59, 61, 62, 63, 64, 65, 66, 67, 69, 70, 73, 74, 75, 77, 80, 83, 84, 86, 89, 90, 93, 94, 96, 97, 101, 105, 107, 108, 109, 110, 116, 119, 148, 149, 162, 163, 176, 177, 178, 180, 182, 183, 184, 185, 186, 187, 188, 189, 192, 199, 200, 203, 204, 205, 206, 207, 208, 210, 212, 213, 214, 215, 216, 218, 219, 238, 239, 240, 241, 242, 243, 244, 245, 259, 261, 262, 264, 294, 295, 296, 297, 298, 299, 300, 301, 302, 303, 304, 305, 306, 307, 309, 310
Jackson, Claiborne Fox 16, 75
Jackson, David W. 13
James, Alexander Franklin "Frank"....25, 108, 293, 299
James, Jesse....... 23, 24, 25, 293, 299
Jasper County, Mo...110, 111, 221
Jayhawkers..... 74, 77, 79, 84, 85, 87, 208, 271, 272, 274, 277
Jefferson Barracks, St. Louis, Mo.................................. 17
Johnson County, Ks............. 63
Johnson County, Mo........ 109, 208, 296
Johnson, A. W. 115
Johnson, Andrew (U.S. President) 21
Jory, Victor 170
Kansas City Bolt and Nut Works 65
Kansas City Live Stock Exchange 181
Kansas City Prison collapse *18*, 48, 83, *199*, *330*
Kansas City, Mo.18, 183, 215, 242, 249, 251

Kansas State Historical Society...27, 200, 213, 219, 220, 295
Kaufman County, Tx. 112
Keck, 'Mamie' Mary Ann (King) 64, 66, 212
Keck, Newton Benton Nicolas 66
Kenney, James T..... 280, 293, 300
Kenney, James T. (Mrs. Grace (Surface))...293, 300
Ketterlin Funeral Home.... 184, 185, 187, 243, 245
King, America Jane (Snodgrass)..... 20, 27, 49, 50, 51, 52, 60, 77, 93, 207, 208, 209, 220, 264, 302, 303
King, Anna E. (Baines) 54
King, Anson (estate/probate) 11, 30, 48, 49, 61, 66, 178, 179, 180, 190, 200, 209, 210, 211, 239, 267, 294, 308
King, Anson Marion 5, 28, 29, 60, 62, 69, 177, 178, 194, 210, 238, 259, 263, 280, 293, 295, 300
King, Arthur Cleveland.65, 66, 67
King, Bertha Adela (Branch) 54
King, Bessie (Taylor) 68
King, Cora Belle (Brown)..301
King, Cora Belle (Warren)...67
King, Dean 51, 54, 259, 264
King, Earl R....28, 51, 53, 212, 238, 244, 259, 264, 302
King, Emma J. Gleason (Wade)............................67
King, Ethel (Shrout) 56
King, Eveline (Lynch)...20, 28, 60, 62, 176, 178, 208, 209, 210, 211, 245, 300, 303, 306

Index

King, Floyd 211, 280, 293, 301, 302
King, Francis Marion ... 20, 22, 24, 28, 45, 48, 60, 61, 62, 69, 76, 90, 176, 178, 194, 204, 205, 208, 239, 245, 263, 280, 293, 299, 300, 303, 306
King, Frank W. 51, 52, 69, 177, 212, 238, 259, 264, 280, 293, 296, 301
King, George Samuel .. 65, 66, 67
King, Jasper (Robert) 293
King, Jennie Elizabeth (Anderson) 52
King, John 301
King, John C. 26, 99, 217, 218
King, Joseph Edward .. 65, 71, 75, 163, 269
King, Josie (Potts) ... 189, 200, 279, 282, 289, 293, 301, 302, 303, 307
King, Kate
  (and Order No. 11) 90
  (and Quantrill) 7, 17, *19*, 20, 21, 34, 73, 75, 90, 94, 95, 98, 100, 105, 117, 119, 273
  (and sterling spoon) 26, 37, 71
  (and Texas) *19*
  (as a caretaker) 176
  (as a grandmother) 11, 160, 166
  (as a hotel keeper) 159, 176
  (as a madam) 9, 10, 11, 22, 23, 35, 80, 92, 94, 96, 103, 120, 124, 125, 127, 128, 130, 132, 138, 139, 140, 141, 142, 143, 145, 148, 222, 223, 224, 225, 229, 253, 254, 255
  (as a mother) 11, 147, 149, 152
  (as a youth) .. 15, 16, 41, 46
  (as family caretaker) 61, 304
  (as Kate Batson) 65
  (as Kate Clarke) .. 1, 2, 3, 5, 9, 13, 34, 35, 38, 70, 73, 78, 80, 90, 105, 119, 120, 129, 133, 140, 143, 175, 197, 215, 228, 244, 254, 269, 270, 275, 276, 293, 294
  (as Sarah C. "Kate" Batson) 51
  (as Sarah C. Batson) 35, 37, 61, 68, 154, 157, 159, 166, 176, 178, 183, 197, 259, 267, 293
  (as Sarah Catherine King) 34, 41, 63, 152, 154, 197, 294
  (as Sarah Head) 7, 30, 35, 59, 78, 183, 193, 197, 293, 297
  (as Sarah Katherine King) 62
  (birth) 15, 33, 43
  (burial) 30, 70, 184, 185
  (death) 30, 70, 162, 184
  (funeral) 162
  (grave marker) 297
  (honeymoon cabin) . 19, 81, 84, 213, 214
  (in city directories) ... 22, 25, 28, 61
  (in court) 23, 130, 131, 132, 140, 141, 145, 253
  (in newspapers) 22, 23
  (in Oklahoma) ... 11, 27, 28, 29, 35, 37, 61, 69, 145, 148, 150, 157, 159, 166, 173, 175, 176, 177, 182, 183, 200, 212, 214, 216, 230, 232, 233, 234, 235,

236, 238, 242, 283, 284, 304, 306
(in St. Louis) 20, 23, 25, 35, 91
(in Texas) 149
(in the Census) .. 15, 16, 22, 25, 27, 29, 33, 37, 41, 43, 45, 61, 63, 69, 90, 120, 149, 152, 157, 159, 176
(married) 19, 23, 35, 74, 76, 183, 273, 277
(memorial marker) . 12, 188, 190, 194
(rebuilt parent's home) .. 21, 69, 178, 211, 230, 277, 305
(unclaimed letters) *18*
King, Laura F. (Fugate) Barker 67
King, Lucy A. 53
King, Malinda (Stringer) 12, 15, 16, 22, 24, 29, 41, 42, 43, 45, 46, 48, 49, 56, 60, 63, 65, 68, 152, 180, 188, 194, 201, 202, 203, 204, 205, 206, 230, 246
King, Mary Anne (Caldwell) 43, 203
King, Mary Isabela (Heisinger) 53
King, Maud May (Rolen) 55
King, Nancy A. 16, 48
King, Nellie M. 67
King, Opal E. Dora (Webb) Turvey 68
King, Oscar 30, 51, 55, 178, 211, 212, 238, 259, 264
King, Parmer 56
King, Priscilla (Hoak) 301
King, Robert Jasper 51, 56, 260
King, Robert L. 12, 15, 16, 22, 24, 26, 41, 43, 45, 46, 48, 49, 56, 60, 63, 68, 75, 76, 84, 91, 149, 152, 154, 180, 202, 204, 206, 208, 213, 220, 245, 263, 264, 271, 296, 299, 300, 301, 303, 307
King, Sampson 301
King, Samuel R. 16, 22, 24, 29, 45, 46, 48, 51, 56, 62, 63, 64, 65, 66, 71, 76, 90, 149, 178, 205, 212, 213, 239, 259, 262, 263, 293, 304
King, Sarah Catherine .... *See* Kate King
King, Thomas Riley 301
King, Walter R. 51, 55, 212, 238, 259, 264, 283, 293, 304
King, William James .. 43, 202, 203
King, William Jasper 20, 22, 29, 48, 49, 50, 51, 52, 62, 70, 76, 77, 90, 177, 205, 206, 207, 209, 212, 220, 238, 244, 259, 264, 285, 293, 295, 301, 302, 303, 304, 305
Kinyoun, James William (doctor) 182
Kirk, Lula 261, 266
Koger, Elizabeth 303
Koger, John 77
Koger, Mary (King) 303
Lafayette County, Mo ... 20, 49, 50, 52, 60, 87, 90, 109, 209, 227
Lake City, Mo ... 16, 57, 61, 63, 228, 283, 286, 288
Lane, Alexander 114
Lane, James H. 84, 85, 86, 274
Lane, Julia Ann (Tucker) Corby 114
Lane, Lula 113
Lane, Samuel J. 110, 113
Lane, Sydney Susan (Slaughter) 107, 110, 113

Larned State Hospital....... 163
Lawrence, Ks. . *18, 19, 74, 84, 85*, 102, *117, 124, 211,* 274, *285*
Leavenworth, Ks. 296
Lee, Robert E. (Confederate General) 21
Leslie, Edward E. 74, 78
Liberty, Mo. (bank robbery) 21
Lincoln County, Ky. ... 42, 201, 232
Lincoln, Abraham (U.S. President)..... 16, 17, 20, 21
Little Blue Church............... 62
Little Blue, Missouri .... *See* Jackson County Home for the Aged and Infirm
London, England 36, 149, 152, 153, 203, 221, 230, 231, 234
Lone Jack, Mo. (Civil War battle) *18*
Louden, Robert *18, 19, 20, 21, 92, 120, 138, 223*
Louisville, Ky. ... 21, 25, 26, 97, 98, 100, 101, 152, 182, 216, 217, 218, 243, 276, 308, 309
Lowry City, Ne. 68
Lumbley, Kenneth 116
Lynch, Elijah............. 260, 264
Lynch, Henry N. 260, 265
Lynch, James L. 260, 265
Lynch, Rebecca (Ginans) Waldo..................... 60, 263
Lynch, William 60, 263, 264
Lynch, Willis 260, 265
Lyon, Nathaniel 75
Manhunt (T.V. series)...... 170, 171
Maple Hill Cemetery (Kansas City, Ks.) ... 12, 30, 31, 185, 186, 187, 192, 194, 245, 297
Marion County, Ia. 67

Martial Law 17, 21, 82, 87, 88, 219, 247
McClasky, Isaac 97
McClelland, Della 261, 266
McFarland, W. B. (Reverend) 60
McKinley, William (U.S. President)....................... 26
McLean, N. H. 247
McVey, Patrick 170
Methodist Episcopal Church, Lafayete County, Mo. 60
Missouri State Convention . 17
Monticello Hotel.......... 28, 159
Moore, A. A. (Reverend) 49
Moore, Carroll E. 303
Moore, Edward D. ... 280, 293, 295, 304
Moore, Fannie 37, 228
Morgan, 'Polly' Mary (Cox)..... 105
Morris, 'Jack' Richard Jackson.................. 55, 295
Morris, Miranda Jane (King) 37, 51, 55, 70, 71, 260, 264, 295, 305
Muskogee County, Ok........ 27
Newton County, Mo............ 67
Northern Hotel............ 27, 234
Northfield, Mn. 24
Oak Grove, Mo. 51, 77
Oakland Cemetery (Blue Springs, Mo.)................ 295
Oklahoma Agricultural and Mechanical College...... *See* Oklahoma State University
Oklahoma City, Ok. ... 26, 148, 151
Oklahoma County, Ok. 26
Oklahoma State University 167
Olathe, Ks..................... *18, 82*
Olwine, Margaret............. 297
Order No. 2   17, 82, 247
Order No. 10.... 5, *18, 84*, 249, *251*

Order No. 11 ..... 5, 11, 19, 45, 49, 57, 60, 69, 86, 87, 88, 89, 90, 91, 97, 100, 178, 206, 216, 219, 251
Owens, Bill (Mrs.) 78
Palmer, Lester "Terry" 13
Palo Pinto County, Tx. 112
Parker County, Tx. ... 112, 113, 310
Partisan Ranger Act............ 18
Payne, T. D. (Reverend) 51
Pea Ridge, Ar. (Civil War battle) 17
Perdee Chapel Cemetery (Jackson County, Mo.) .. 51, 77
Perdee farm (Jackson County, Mo.) 92
Petersen, Paul R. ... 35, 77, 91, 92, 194, 200, 207, 208, 213, 214, 215, 230, 240, 243, 244, 245
Petty, George W. (Reverend) 62
Phillips, Essie 262, 266
Phillips, Lillie 261, 266
Pickering, England 43
Pierce, Franklin (U.S. President) 16
Pink Hill Road 280
Placer County, Ca. .22, 45, 57, 60, 63, 87, 90, 206, 209
Pleasant Hill, Mo. 53, 251, 310
Plumb, P. B. 250
Polk County, Mo. ... 15, 34, 42, 43, 45, 49, 56, 58, 60, 63, 67, 203, 210
Polk, James K. (U.S. President) 15
Poor Farm .... See Jackson County Home for the Aged and Infirm
Potter, James Monroe 114
Potts, Levi 302
Potts, Mary Ellen (Steele) . 302

Potts, Sina Emily (Slaughter) 302
Potts, William Carroll 302
Power, Michael (Reverend) 21, 24, 97, 98, 101, 216, 219
Powers, 'Pat' Patrick 45, 64
Powers, Mary Ann (Davenport) 64
Price, Sterling (Confederate General) 20, 22, 75, 90, 95, 247, 270
Price, Sterling (General) 96
Prisoners of War 82, 224
Provost Marshal ... *19*, 91, 119, *138*, 199, 200, 214, 223, 224, *249*, *250*
Quantrill, Caroline C. ... 25, 26, 27, 98, 101, 102, 216, 217, 218, 220
Quantrill, Kate .. *See* Kate King
Quantrill, Mary A. 272
Quantrill, William Clarke 9, *18*, 19, 21, 25, 26, 27, 31, 33, 34, 35, 36, 38, 57, 73, 75, 77, 82, 84, 90, 93, 96, 98, 100, 101, 105, 106, 108, 110, 113, 116, 117, 119, 124, 147, 173, 182, 214, 229, 269, 270, 277, 295, 297, 299, 302, 308, 310
Quin, Huston 182
Ragland, Charles H. 58, 59, 259, 264
Ragland, David 56
Ragland, Edna (Carpenter) 59
Ragland, Elizabeth (Hendricks) 56
Ragland, Eugenia Marie (Louapre) 59
Ragland, John Marion 'Jack' 30, 58, 59, 181, 185, 212, 240, 259, 264

Index

Ragland, John Oath 16, 27, 45, 56, 57, 58, 206, 209, 240, 299, 304, 305
Ragland, John Rider 259, 264
Ragland, Martha Jane (King) 16, 22, 29, 45, 48, 56, 57, 58, 62, 69, 90, 212, 238, 239, 240, 259, 264, 293, 299, 304, 305
Ragland, Mary Eliza (Rider)... 58
Ragland, Mary H. (Carmody) 59
Ragland, Nell W. (Jones) ... 59
Ragland, Robert O. 45
Ragland, Rufus Hudspeth . 30, 58, 59, 259, 264
Ragland, Ruth Malinda.... 259, 264
Ragland, 'Susan' Susanna . 56
Ragland, Vady Guy 26, 59
Ragland, William Robert ... 26, 58, 240, 264
Ragsdale, (Mrs.) 293, 296, 305
Ralston, Samuel 201
Randolph County, Mo. 115, 116, 227
Ready, Sarah T. 192
Red Legs ... 77, 84, 85, 86, 87, 211, 271, 275, 283, 290, 291
Reed, Jeanne 13
Reno County, Ks. 163
Rigney, 'Betsey' Elizabeth (Scott) Stringer 42, 202
Rigney, Anderson 201
Rigney, Elizabeth "Betsey" (Scott) Stringer 24
Rigney, Jesse 42, 201
Roosevelt, Franklin D. (U.S. President) 31
Roosevelt, Theodore (U.S. President) 26
Ross Neville (Mrs.) 100

Royal, Bonnie 75
Russell, Alice 260
Russell, Alice (Lynch) 265
Saline County, Mo. 87
San Bernardino County, Ca. 59
San Diego Historical Society 171, 199
San Diego Police Department 11, 169, 171, 172, 199
Sapulpa, Ok 27, 28, 29, 51, 61, 69, 155, 157, 159, 160, 161, 162, 166, 167, 176, 177, 185, 234, 235, 238, 304
Savannah, Ga. 166
Saville, Lizzie (St. Louis madam)... 23, 24, 124, 129, 131, 132, 141, 143, 144, 145, 253, 254, 256
Scott, William W. ... 25, 27, 98, 149, 212, 213, 216, 217, 220
Sedgwick County, Ks. 162, 163, 164, 165, 168, 235
Selvey, Armenia (Crawford) 48, 83
Sequoyah County, Ok. 27, 157, 176, 233, 234
Shawnee, Ks. *18*
Shelly, Bridget 25, 98, 217
Shelly, Patrick 25, 98, 99, 217, 219
Sherman, Texas 93, 213
Sherman, William Tecumseh 82
Shiloh, Tn. (Civil War battle) 17
Silverton, Or. 53
Skaggs, Larkin 85
Slaughter Cemetery (Jackson County, Mo.) 12, 30, 31, 46, 62, 116, 188, 189, 190, 194, 203, 220, 244, 245, 246, 302

359

Slaughter, 'Riley' William Ryland 107, 116
Slaughter, Elizabeth (Koger) 107
Slaughter, Florence Elizabeth 108
Slaughter, Josiah 107, 111, 302
Slaughter, Mary Elizabeth (Rudisaile) Welker 107
Slaughter, Nancy .... *See* Nancy Elizabeth (Walker) Slaughter Vaughn Wood
Slaughter, Susan E. (Thomas) Winn 108
Slaughter, Sydney Susan . 113
Snodgrass, 'Betsy' Elizabeth (St. Clair) 303
Snodgrass, Bartley 49, 303
Snodgrass, Ephriam 93
Snodgrass, Lucy Ann (Baker) 49, 303
Snodgrass, Parmer 51
Social Evil Hospital 126
Social Evil Ordinance 5, 10, 22, 23, 119, 124, 125, 126, 127, 128, 131, 132, 139, 140, 141, 142, 143, 145, 199, 223, 224, 225, 226, 227, 229, 253, 254
South Dakota 28, 51, 53, 212, 238, 302
Spader, Kate 260
Spanish-American War 26
Spencer County, Ky .. 215, 309
Springfield, Oh. 27
St. John's Cemetery (Louisville, Ky.) 25, 216
St. Louis, Mo. 5, 9, 10, 11, 16, 17, 18, 19, 20, 21, 22, 23, 24, 25, 26, 27, 35, 37, 80, 90, 91, 92, 94, 95, 96, 100, 101, 102, 103, 119, 120, 124, 125, 126, 129, 130, 131, 132, 133, 137, 138, 140, 142, 143, 145, 147, 148, 149, 175, 199, 208, 212, 214, 219, 221, 222, 223, 224, 225, 226, 227, 228, 229, 230, 231, 234, 247, 253, 255, 256, 257, 258, 276, 277, 344
St. Luke's Hospital 21, 22, 24, 127, 140, 141, 143, 225, 226, 229
St. Mary's Cemetery (Louisville, Ky.) 98
Stanley farm (Blue Springs, Mo.) 90
Steele, Mary Catherine (Snodgrass) 303
Steele, Samuel Jackson ... 303
Stillwater, Ok. 167
Stratton, Dora 261, 266
Stringer, Ann 42, 201, 203
Stringer, Levi 42, 201, 202
Stringer, Limeledge 42, 201, 202
Stringer, Rachel 42, 201
Stringer, Sarah A. 42, 201
Stringer, William 202
Stringer, William M. 25, 42, 201
Strode, Bailey 307
Strode, Nellie 284, 293, 307
Sugar Creek, Mo. 65, 211
Supreme Court of the State of Missouri 11, 16, 23, 130, 142, 144, 145, 228, 235, 253, 254
Supreme Court of the State of Oklahoma 161
Surface, Fanny M. (Allaire) 300, 307
Surface, J. M. (doctor) 281, 293, 299, 300, 307
Surface, Maria (St. John) .. 307
Surface, William E. ... 300, 307
Swinney, Julia Lee (King) 51, 54, 212, 238, 260, 264, 285

Index

Swinney, Rolla Lewis, Jr. ... 54
Swinney, Rolla Lewis, Sr.... 54
Sykes, Velma (West)....... 102, 279, 290, 293, 305, 308
Taft, William Howard (U.S. President)...................... 27
Taylor, Charles Fletcher "Fletch"..... 74, 78, 109, 111
Taylor, Zachary (U.S. President)...................... 15
Taylorsville, Spencer County, Ky..... 21, 97, 101, 308, 309
Terrell, Edwin 293, 308
Terrill, Edwin 97, 112, 215
Thomason, W. I. 178, 179, 280, 293, 308
Thompson, Ella 157, 176, 233
Todd, George .. 20, 90, 95, 96, 108, 215, 273, 276
Torpey, Lucy C. (Hutchings) 299
Torpey, Thomas Henry 45, 299
Torpey, Thomas, Sr. 299
Truman Medical Center Corporation 188
Truman Medical Center-Lakewood..................... 188
Tunnel, Luther 43
Turkington, 'Susie' Susan M. (Hupp) Griswold 306
Turkington, Robert 306
Twyman, Victoria.............. 307
Union Hotel......................... 83
Vandever, Susan Jane (Crawford) Whitsett.. 48, 83
Vaughn, Albert 108
Vaughn, Elsie 109
Vaughn, Francis E.............. 74
Vaughn, Joe 110, 283, 293, 309, 310
Vaughn, Joseph 108
Vaughn, Joseph G. 108
Vaughn, Joseph L. 108
Vaughn, Josephine 109

Vaughn, Marie.................. 109
Vaughn, Minerva (Gibson) 108
Vaughn, Nancy......................
See Nancy Elizabeth (Walker) Slaughter Vaughn Wood
Vaughn, Samuel Gibson .. 109
Vaughn, Sarah Belle (Harris) 109
Vaughn, Stella Elizabeth .. 109
Vian, Ok....... 27, 28, 157, 159, 176, 233, 234
Wade, John Henry 67
Wakefield, Ann 309
Wakefield, James H. 97, 215, 287, 291, 292, 293, 308, 309
Wakefield, James M......... 309
Wakefield, John D. 309
Wakefield, Joseph W. 309
Wakefield, Marcus............ 309
Wakefield, Mary A. 309
Wakefield, Mary E. (Taggart) 309
Wakefield, Matthew.......... 309
Waldo, Albert............ 261, 266
Waldo, Anson........... 260, 265
Waldo, Anson H. 260, 265
Waldo, Anson S. 261, 266
Waldo, Charley......... 261, 266
Waldo, Chester......... 261, 266
Waldo, Edith 261, 266
Waldo, Esther............ 261, 266
Waldo, James........... 260, 266
Waldo, Jesse J. 261, 266
Waldo, John W. 261, 266
Waldo, Leroy N................. 261
Waldo, Mary 261, 266
Waldo, Minnie........... 261, 266
Waldo, Murrell 261, 266
Waldo, Ottie L........... 261, 266
Waldo, Richard......... 261, 266
Waldo, Robert 261, 266
Waldo, Royce........... 261, 266
Waldo, Rufus............ 261, 266
Waldo, W. H. 261, 266

361

Waldo, William B. 261, 266
Walker, Andrew Jackson 105, 310
Walker, Anna ....
See Nancy Elizabeth (Walker) Slaughter Vaughn Wood
Walker, Collins 107
Walker, James Morgan 105, 106, 107, 109, 293, 310
Walker, John Riley 105, 107
Walker, Nancy ....
See Nancy Elizabeth (Walker) Slaughter Vaughn Wood
Walker, Nannie ....
See Nancy Elizabeth (Walker) Slaughter Vaughn Wood
Walker, Sidney Clay 107
Walker, Zachariah Taylor . 105
Warren, James Normal 265
Warren, Lucy B. (Lynch) ... 265
Warren, Normal F. 260
Warren, William A. 260, 265
Washington County, Il. 56
Washington University 10, 128, 226, 227, 229
Weece, Elizabeth 261, 266
Westport, Mo. 251
Westport, Mo. (Civil War battle) ... 20, 63, 64, 96, 200, 215, 219
Whites, LeeAnn ... 12, 92, 145, 199, 214, 224, 225, 230
Wichita Park Cemetery (Wichita, Ks.) 165
Williams, Kate (Bolger) Spader 265
Wilson, Henry 63
Wilson, Woodrow (U. S. President) 28

Wise, Esther 125
Wodo, 'Dora' Eudora Frances Andrews 112
Wood, 'Dee/Doc/Dock' Dansler Ocho 112
Wood, 'Fannie' Frances Jones 112
Wood, 'Lon' Bess Lonzo W. 112
Wood, 'Monie' Mona Belle (Low) 112
Wood, Benjamin F. 112
Wood, Charles Alexander. 112
Wood, David D. 22, 35, 36, 111, 113, 221, 310
Wood, Lonzo 112
Wood, Nancy Elizabeth (Walker) Slaughter Vaughn 26, 36, 105, 111, 112, 117, 293, 309, 310
Woodlawn Cemetery (Jackson County, Mo.) .. 57, 58, 65, 66, 205, 211
World War I ... 28, 29, 112, 211
World War II 166, 169
Wyandot County, Oh. 154
Wyandotte County, Ks. 12, 30, 31, 162, 185
Young, Daniel E. 260, 261, 264
Young, Daniel W. 53, 261, 264, 310
Young, Homer J. 260, 261, 264
Young, James M. 54
Young, Jesse W. 260
Young, Lucy A. (King) .. 28, 53, 238, 264, 283, 293, 302, 310
Young, Willis L. 260, 264
Younger gang 23, 24

Westville Public Library
153 Main St. PO Box 789
Westville, IN 46391

Made in the USA
Charleston, SC
20 November 2014